Shaping Modern Shanghai

MW00358405

Shaping Modern Shanghai provides a new understanding of colonialism in China through a fresh examination of Shanghai's International Settlement. This was the site of key developments of the Republican period: economic growth, rising Chinese nationalism and Sino-Japanese conflict. Managed by the Shanghai Municipal Council (1854–1943), the International Settlement was beyond the control of the Chinese and foreign imperial governments. Jackson defines Shanghai's unique, hybrid form of colonial urban governance as transnational colonialism. The Council was both colonial in its structures and subject to colonial influence, especially from the British empire, yet autonomous in its activities and transnational in its personnel. This is the first in-depth study of how this unique body functioned on the local, national and international stages, revealing the Council's impact on the daily lives of the city's residents and its contribution to the conflicts of the period, with implications for the fields of modern Chinese and colonial history.

ISABELLA JACKSON is Assistant Professor in Chinese History at Trinity College Dublin, having previously held positions at the Universities of Oxford and Aberdeen. She has published her research in *Modern Asian Studies* and in edited collections on Chinese treaty ports, Britain and China, the Scottish experience in Asia and the 'habitable city' in China.

Shaping Modern Shanghai

Colonialism in China's Global City

Isabella Jackson

Trinity College Dublin

CAMBRIDGE
UNIVERSITY PRESS

University Printing House, Cambridge CB2 8BS, United Kingdom

One Liberty Plaza, 20th Floor, New York, NY 10006, USA

477 Williamstown Road, Port Melbourne, VIC 3207, Australia

314-321, 3rd Floor, Plot 3, Splendor Forum, Jasola District Centre, New Delhi - 110025, India

79 Anson Road, #06-04/06, Singapore 079906

Cambridge University Press is part of the University of Cambridge.

It furthers the University's mission by disseminating knowledge in the pursuit of education, learning and research at the highest international levels of excellence.

www.cambridge.org
Information on this title: www.cambridge.org/9781108411639
DOI: 10.1017/9781108303934

First published 2018
First paperback edition 2019

A catalogue record for this publication is available from the British Library

ISBN 978-1-108-41968-0 Hardback
ISBN 978-1-108-41163-9 Paperback

For my grandmother, E. P. M. M.

Contents

Figures

Maps

Tables

Acknowledgements

My research for and writing of this book were supported by numerous people and institutions. My first and deepest thanks go to Robert Bickers at the University of Bristol, who inspired my interest in Chinese history and encouraged me to take this interest ever further. He has always been generous with his time, personal collection of source materials and wealth of knowledge. Most of the research for this book was conducted during my PhD, supervised by Robert and funded by the Economic and Social Research Council through the British Inter-university China Centre. I am grateful to both organisations.

I have learnt a great amount from Rana Mitter at the University of Oxford. Rana helped me hone my skills as a historian and encouraged me to see the bigger picture of why my research matters. I am very grateful for all his guidance. I would like to thank my former colleagues at what was then the Institute for Chinese Studies at Oxford for their encouragement and support as I finished my dissertation alongside my first academic position, particularly Margaret Hillenbrand and Laura Newby. I am grateful to the members of the Leverhulme Trust-funded 'China's War with Japan' project in the History Faculty for helpful comments on Chapter 3, especially Helen Schneider and Karl Gerth. I would also like to thank Henrietta Harrison for helping me to undertake later research in Oxford.

I am grateful to my friends and former colleagues at the University of Aberdeen, particularly Andrew Dilley and Robert Frost who read and provided valuable advice on parts of the book. I would like to thank my colleagues at Trinity College Dublin, particularly Carole Holohan and Ciaran O'Neill in History and Lorna Carson in the Trinity Centre for Asian Studies, for their encouragement and friendship. My thanks also go to my students at both Aberdeen and Trinity for their insightful questions and ideas as we discussed Republican China.

I am indebted to the Shanghai Academy of Social Sciences for hosting me while I conducted the bulk of my research. Wang Min, Ma Jun and Xu Tao deserve particular thanks. I am very appreciative of the work done by the staff of the Shanghai Municipal Archives, who helped make it a pleasant place to conduct research, and I appreciated Yuan Zhe's friendship when we were both working there. My thanks also go to members of faculty at the University of Sydney for welcoming me and helping me clarify many of my ideas, especially Kirsten McKenzie and Alison Bashford. The Kluge Center at the Library of Congress was an inspiring place to work and I am very grateful to the people there for helping me expand my source base and the horizons of my intellectual enquiry. I would like to thank Tom Mann at the Library in particular for his enthusiastic help in finding diverse materials that enhanced my research. The librarians at Trinity, Aberdeen, Oxford and Bristol have all provided valuable materials, as have staff at the British Library, The National Archives in Kew, the US National Archives and the State Library of New South Wales in Sydney. I am grateful to Marcia Ristaino for her friendship and to Cecil Uyehara for his kind assistance with my research on his father. Christian Henriot and Simon Potter provided valuable suggestions for refining the project. Sincere thanks to Lucy Rhymer at Cambridge University Press for her efficiency, advice and enthusiasm at every stage of bringing the book to publication, and to the anonymous reviewers for the Press for their constructive feedback on the manuscript.

Taylor and Francis granted permission to use work originally published under their Routledge imprint. Material for Chapter 2 is drawn from 'Who Ran the Treaty Ports? A Study of the Shanghai Municipal Council', in Robert Bickers and Isabella Jackson (eds.), *Treaty Ports in Modern China: Law, Land and Power* (London: Routledge, 2016), pp. 43–60; and material for Chapter 3 is drawn from 'Expansion and Defence in the International Settlement at Shanghai', in Robert Bickers and Jonathan Howlett (eds.), *Britain and China, 1840–1970: Empire, Finance and War* (London: Routledge, 2015), pp. 187–204. I am grateful to the *Virtual Cities Project,* Institut d'Asie Orientale, Lyon and Historical Photographs of China, University of Bristol, for the use of their images.

My friends, particularly Felicitas von Droste zu Hülshoff and Nicola Leveringhaus, have been a constant source of support and inspiration. Some of the people I have met in the course of my research, including Hoito Wong and Sophie Loy-Wilson, have offered direct assistance in locating sources; Sophie also kindly commented on the manuscript, as did Catherine Phipps. For comments and questions when presenting parts of the research, I am grateful to Felix Boecking, Chris Courtney, Sarah Dauncey, Jon Howlett, Pamela Hunt, Hirata Koji, Toby Lincoln, Jo Smith Finley, Norman Stockman, Jeffrey Wasserstrom and many more. Erika Hanna generously shared her expertise on global cities with me.

I would like to extend warm thanks to all my family, particularly my mother, father and grandma, for encouraging me throughout this lengthy project. My most heartfelt thanks go to Adam, for supporting me tirelessly and for having so much faith in me.

Note on Chinese Usage

Chinese names of places and people are Romanised using the standard pinyin form in most cases except where the transliteration in contemporary use is the only form available or the preferred form, primarily for personal names such as for Chiang Kai-shek (Jiang Jieshi). Where appropriate and possible, Chinese characters are also provided in the main text and index for clarity.

Introduction: The Transnational Colonialism of the Shanghai Municipal Council

On Saturday 14 August 1937, five bombs fell on central Shanghai, killing over 1,200 people and injuring hundreds more. Three fell on the Bund, the western Huangpu riverfront, which was the symbolic and economic heart of the British colonial presence in China; its neo-classical banks and clubhouse would have looked very much in keeping on the streets of central London. The art deco hotels and newspaper office were more reminiscent of New York, however, reflecting the strong American influence in the city. A closer look reveals greater diversity: Japanese banking, insurance and shipping companies served the imperial subjects of East Asia's newest empire; a Russian bank designed by German architects betrayed earlier colonial interests; the French Banque d'Indochine hinted at the French-controlled part of the city just to the south of this stretch of river. Sassoon House – hit by one of the bombs – was the centre of the business empire of Sir Victor Sassoon, who divided his time and trading investments between China and India.[1] The first modern Chinese-owned bank in China was situated on the Bund. Behind this grand visage lay thousands of other Chinese and foreign firms, notably on Nanjing Road, the busiest shopping street in China; the first three bombs landed on the intersection where Nanjing Road met the Bund. Minutes later another two bombs fell at a busy intersection a mile west of the Bund. The aeroplanes that dropped them were Chinese, targeting a Japanese naval ship moored in the Huangpu, but the bombs fell tragically short.[2] The western community in Shanghai had always feared Chinese attack, but when Chinese bombs landed in their midst, it was accidental. The victims were Chinese and foreign (though there were but a dozen foreign dead) and the loss of life was reported around the world.[3] A global city was at war.

---

[1] The damage to Sassoon House is detailed in Shanghai Municipal Archives (SMA hereafter) U1-14-5965: Memorandum, 25 October 1937.

[2] Low cloud cover probably caused the pilots' error. Christian Henriot, 'August 1937: War and the Death *en masse* of Civilians', in Lü Fangshang (ed.), *War in History and Memory* (Taipei: Academia Historica, 2015), 76–87.

[3] 'Havoc in the Streets', *The Times*, 16 August 1937, 10.

The Bund is the most obvious physical legacy of the foreign influence on China's most prosperous city.[4] The buildings reflected the transnational colonial presence in Shanghai and China more widely: 'transnational' because it cut across and transcended national allegiances and was developed by non-state actors who moved between different parts of the world. The International Settlement that extended north and west from the Bund, encompassing 8.66 square miles at the centre of Shanghai, was a unique political entity that exemplified the peculiar form that colonialism took in China. It has rightly been recognised that the British were dominant economically and politically, but this has been assumed to mean that only British colonialism mattered. In fact, and increasingly, other colonial and transnational forces influenced how the Settlement developed, and Chinese business leaders were eventually included in its governing council. This book examines how this unusual form of colonialism functioned through the Shanghai Municipal Council (SMC), which governed the International Settlement. In doing so, it provides a new way of understanding both China's experience of colonialism and the diverse forms taken by colonial authority.

The SMC was a unique colonial institution, exerting extensive governmental authority but independent of imperial oversight. Through its policies, the SMC shaped the development of Shanghai in terms of the politics of its inhabitants, their everyday lives and the built environment that still survives today. Shanghai was the most important city in Republican China: Beijing was in decline and the new capital from 1927, Nanjing, never rivalled Shanghai economically or culturally. Chinese political and cultural life centred on the economic powerhouse of Shanghai, while the key developments of the period, particularly the growth of nationalism and anti-imperialism, grew out of Shanghai.

As with the incremental way in which colonial authority was achieved elsewhere, however, such influence would have been inconceivable when the SMC was first established. The SMC originated in the modest Committee of Roads and Jetties, which early British traders founded in Shanghai in 1845 to provide basic infrastructure in the newly established English Settlement. The perimeters of the original Settlement, an area of less than one square mile to the north of the walled city of Shanghai, were laid out in the same year by the local Chinese Daotai (道台, translated as 'circuit intendent': the sub-provincial level official who was the primary local representative of the Qing state). The Daotai had permitted Britons to rent land and property in Shanghai since 1843, but conflicts between the foreign merchants and local Chinese led him to delineate specific ground for the foreigners. The 1842 Treaty of Nanjing had opened Shanghai to British trade and settlement, among other terms demanded by the

---

[4] The term 'Bund' is itself Anglo-Indian, betraying a major source of influence on the city.

British following their defeat of China in the First Opium War (1839–1842). Alongside Shanghai were the other new treaty ports of Guangzhou (Canton, to which a Qing imperial edict had limited foreign traders until 1842), Xiamen (Amoy), Ningbo and Fuzhou, while Hong Kong was ceded to Britain as a colony. Subsequent wars and treaties with 14 different foreign powers opened up as many as 92 treaty ports in China by 1917, but Shanghai would dwarf them all politically and economically.

The city boasted an advantageous position on the Huangpu River, near the mouth of the great Yangtze River and with access to its fertile delta, long the most populous and wealthiest region of China. The delta region of 50,000 square miles supported, by 1930, a population of 180 million, and a foreign observer declared that 'In no other part of the world does a population of this volume and density depend for its commercial intercourse upon one main river and one distributing port.'[5] The wider watershed of the Yangtze extended over 750,000 square miles, all feeding into the trade at Shanghai. Shanghai was the eighth port of the world by tonnage: over 50 shipping companies were based there, representing between them 600 vessels with 5 million tons of cargo capacity. It was also the principal banking centre of China, with 20 branches of foreign banks (19 of them in the International Settlement), 39 modern Chinese banks (all in the International Settlement) and 77 traditional Chinese banks (70 in the International Settlement).[6]

Mid-nineteenth-century Shanghai was a walled city of some regional import with a population of 400,000, yet its English Settlement was but a small enclave for traders of the British East India Company and others primarily selling opium or buying tea or silk. The USA established a concession to the north of the English Settlement in 1848, and the French opened theirs to the south the following year. The three settlements were lightly governed by their consuls, who were each responsible for their own national subjects, and there was not yet any indication that a municipal authority would supersede their influence.

Chinese were not permitted to rent land in the foreign settlements and neither the consuls nor the Chinese authorities anticipated Chinese living in them. But the popular rebellions that swept China in the mid-nineteenth century, most famously the Taiping but also the Small Sword Uprising, prompted a rush of Chinese refugees to seek the shelter afforded by the foreign authorities in Shanghai. From the 1850s on, the Chinese population of the settlements was many times greater than the foreign, though it would be over 70 years before Chinese had a formal say in the municipal governance.

[5] Richard Feetham, *Report of the Hon. Mr. Justice Feetham, C.M.G. to the Shanghai Municipal Council* (Shanghai: North-China Daily News and Herald, 1931), I, 188.
[6] Feetham, *Report*, I, 301.

In the face of the threat of rebellion outside the settlements and disorder from the swelling population within, the foreign residents agreed in 1854 to elect a municipal council. The council would be responsible for not only the public works that had been provided by the Committee of Roads and Jetties, but also oversee a new municipal police force. The council was funded by rates paid by property-owners and answerable to them in annual meetings. This cooperative venture between the various foreign nationals in Shanghai was cemented in 1863 with the merging of the English and American Settlements to form the International Settlement; the French were prevented by Paris from joining in.[7] The timing of this Anglo-American venture was striking: the American Civil War was raging and yet United States diplomats were willing to endorse a joint venture with Britons in Shanghai despite British companies supplying ships and arms to the Confederate forces. Repeatedly, foreign shared interests in China trumped loyalties to home governments. The SMC was from its earliest days a transnational institution, answering not to the foreign consuls but to the ever-shifting foreign community, or at least those with the funds and long-term investment in Shanghai to own or rent sizeable property there.

Reflecting its Anglo-American pedigree, the governance of the International Settlement combined elements of English municipal councils with the New England tradition of town hall meetings: the former emphasising decisions deliberated on by committees informed by salaried officials; the latter promoting a form of democratic representation through speeches and voting on local business at public meetings. The SMC is readily comparable to the City Council of Birmingham in England, which oversaw a similar size of population (approaching 500,000 in the first decade of the twentieth century) and performed the same wide range of functions. Birmingham boasted in *The Municipal Year Book* in 1908 that:

The City Council has extended its control over almost every department of municipal life. It owns twelve parks and eight gardens and recreation-grounds; manages markets and slaughter-houses, tramways, electric lighting, baths and wash-houses, cemeteries, libraries, museum, art gallery, school of art, artisans' dwellings, sewage farms, hospitals, industrial schools, asylums, &c.[8]

These were all areas of municipal life that came under the SMC's purview (with the exception of the museum in Shanghai, towards which the SMC contributed funds but did not manage directly, and artistic ventures, which were not valued in Shanghai as in Birmingham). The SMC joined in the global developments in municipal governance, dubbed 'transnational municipalism'

---

[7] Feetham, *Report*, I, 28.
[8] Donald Robert (ed.), *The Municipal Year Book of the United Kingdom for 1908* (London: Municipal Journal, 1908), 8.

by Shane Ewen, and some of its functions would be familiar in cities from Manchester to Melbourne.[9] But the SMC was also responsible for an extensive and quasi-military police force and a volunteer army, combining as it did municipal with colonial state governmental roles.

The International Settlement had what was effectively a constitution in the form of the Land Regulations, first drawn up by the Chinese authorities in 1845, but modified by the foreign consuls as the Settlement boundaries expanded in 1854, 1869 and 1898 to grant greater powers to the SMC. The 1869 and 1898 Regulations were sanctioned by the foreign diplomats in Beijing and the latter also by the Qing government, but even when this ratification did not take place, the Regulations were held up as law, local authority trumping national or international rubber-stamping. The Regulations granted the SMC what the American missionary Francis Lister Hawks Pott described in his history of Shanghai as 'the highest powers in all government, those of taxing and policing the community'.[10] The Regulations also determined that this governing authority, though instituted by the consuls, was elected by and reported to those who paid the rates that funded its activities. The SMC was initially intended to merely administer the policies determined by the ratepayers, subject to the higher authority of the consuls. But over time it acquired the authority in practice to govern in its own right, determining and implementing policies, with occasional advice from the consuls, that were rubber-stamped by the ratepayers. In 1933, the secretary-general of the SMC wrote confidentially to the council chairman that 'due to force of circumstances the Council exercises power analogous to those possessed by an independent state' with the 'tacit assent' of the foreign powers, from whom the Council's authority ultimately derived.[11] Other foreign settlements in China were run quite differently, by individual consuls in their national interest as they saw fit, often with advice from local representative councils. But in its distance from imperial oversight, the SMC epitomises the peculiarity of colonialism in China.

The preoccupation of the early foreign settlers with business and trade ensured the Council also operated like a company board of directors, with a chairman elected from among its members to lead meetings and represent the SMC.[12] British merchants predominated among the SMC's elected councillors

[9] Shane Ewen, 'Transnational Municipalism in a Europe of Second Cities', in Pierre-Yves Saunier and Shane Ewen (eds.), *Another Global City: Historical Explorations into the Transnational Municipal Moment, 1850–2000* (Basingstoke: Palgrave, 2008), 103.

[10] Francis Lister Hawks Pott, *A Short History of Shanghai, Being an Account of the Growth and Development of the International Settlement* (Shanghai: Kelly and Walsh, 1928), 36.

[11] SMA U1-6–141: Secretary-general to chairman, 8 July 1933.

[12] 'Shanghai Municipal Council' was and is used to refer to both elected members of the Council specifically and the whole municipal organisation. In this book, 'Council' is used to mean the elected body of councillors and 'Shanghai Municipal Council' or 'SMC' to refer to the

throughout its existence, but they never operated alone. Americans and Germans (Japanese councillors replacing the Germans from the First World War on) were consistently elected to the Council by the ratepayers, alongside Britons.

As the International Settlement grew in population and as a centre of global finance, trade and investment, the SMC's role as the authority ensuring that the Settlement was conducive to business was increasingly important. By 1929, 77 per cent of British investment in China and 65 per cent of American investment went into Shanghai, the vast majority into the International Settlement.[13] These investors wanted to be sure that their capital was secure for the foreseeable future, that the infrastructure they needed would be maintained, that their legal rights would be protected by courts and a police force, that their staff in Shanghai would be protected from disease and that the labour required for their mills and factories would be reliable. The court system was overseen by the foreign consuls and Chinese authorities and enforced the law of any foreign nationals implicated in a case, in accordance with the extraterritorial privileges secured by treaty, as explained in Pär Cassel's comprehensive study.[14] But all other aspects of the business environment in Shanghai were the responsibility of the SMC.

The whole city's population passed 1 million in 1880 and 3.5 million by 1930, making it the world's fifth-largest city. Over the same period the population of the Settlement grew from 100,000 to over 1 million, including 970,000 Chinese, 18,000 Japanese, 6,000 Britons and 42 other nationalities in smaller numbers.[15] Taxing, policing and regulating this population was a large administrative task, and the SMC employed a staff of almost 10,000 to meet it, making it one of the city's largest employers. It was a transnational body of people, comprising 25 different nationalities who came to Shanghai with diverse international experience, but Britons dominated senior positions while 74 per cent of all staff were Chinese. Municipal employees' work brought them into contact with the residents of the Settlement in myriad ways and they provided the primary experience of foreign colonialism for hundreds of thousands of Chinese.

The transnational SMC was at the heart of what I identify as 'transnational colonialism' in China. By the early twentieth century, the form that foreign authority took and how it affected the lives of Chinese living in Shanghai was

---

governmental institution, including both councillors and salaried staff, although some ambiguity between these two names is unavoidable.

[13] C. F. Remer, *Foreign Investments in China* (New York: Howard Fertig, 1968), 282, 395.

[14] Pär Cassel, *Grounds of Judgment: Extraterritoriality and Imperial Power in Nineteenth-Century China and Japan* (Oxford University Press, 2012).

[15] Shanghai Municipal Council (hereafter SMC), *Report for the Year 1930 and Budget for the Year 1931* (Shanghai: Kelly and Walsh, 1930), 337.

Figure 0.1 Shanghai municipal flag, with a white space next to the American flag where the German flag had been up to the First World War.

determined on the ground by colonial, non-state actors – the Council members and staff – of many nationalities. While Britons dominated, no national group could act alone. The diversity of the International Settlement was celebrated by its Council as evidence of the desirably cosmopolitan community they claimed for themselves. The municipal seal, designed by the SMC's Chief Engineer and approved by the Council for use from 1869, incorporated the flags of twelve western nations with interests in Shanghai (Figure 0.1). By the interwar period, when cooperation between nations was heralded as the harbinger of a peaceful and prosperous future, the International Settlement was dubbed 'a miniature League of Nations'.[16]

The study of the League of Nations has been at the centre of recent scholarship on the concept of transnationalism, as Patricia Clavin, Susan Pedersen and others have emphasised networks of people transcending national boundaries and inter-state relations.[17] Similar connections governed relations between

[16] I. I. Kounin (ed.), *The Diamond Jubilee of the International Settlement of Shanghai* (Shanghai: Post Mercury Company, 1941), unpaginated foreword, cited in Jeffrey Wasserstrom, 'Questioning the Modernity of the Model Settlement: Citizenship and Exclusion in Old Shanghai', in Merle Goldman and Elizabeth J. Perry (eds.), *Changing Meanings of Citizenship in Modern China* (Cambridge, MA: Harvard University Press, 2002), 126.

[17] Contributions by Patricia Clavin, Jens-Wilhelm Wessels and Andrew Webster to the special issue on transnationalism of *Contemporary European History*, Vol. 14, No. 4 (2006); Susan Pedersen, *The Guardians: The League of Nations and the Crisis of Empire* (Oxford University Press, 2015).

groups of people in Shanghai, especially in the SMC: the members of the Council and the staff it employed were strongly aware of their national identities, but they cooperated at a personal, professional and institutional – not an international – level. The foreign councillors and staff were all transnational, having roots in other countries and experience of various colonial settings, and being engaged with trading or professional networks around the world. In Shanghai, representation of the British and other foreign states through the consuls was of much less import than the activities of the SMC. 'Transnational colonialism' thus captures the cooperation of individuals belonging to different nations and networks in this institution more accurately than 'internationalism', which implies state-to-state relations, and without the implied positivity of 'cosmopolitanism'.[18] 'Transnational' here does not imply equal influence of different national groups, as British influence clearly dominated. Not all nationals in Shanghai were equally able to access its cosmopolitanism: it was fundamentally a colonial city.

The concept of transnational colonialism and its impact in Shanghai's International Settlement has broad implications for our understanding of how imperialism worked in China. This is particularly relevant in cities like Tianjin with its numerous foreign settlements and in the broader negotiations of different imperial powers together claiming concessions from the Chinese government. While the 'cooperative financial imperialism' of banking and investments, led by British interests but involving many other nationalities, has been recognised,[19] the example of the SMC shows how cooperation between different nationalities went beyond finance to what was effectively colonial governance by non-state actors.

Understanding transnational colonialism also has implications far beyond China. Portrayals of colonial history often emphasise the rivalry between imperial powers; the SMC was but one example of cooperation between non-state representatives of such powers, cooperation that was rooted in local circumstances. Other examples of sites of colonial cooperation include Siam, which was subject to a late-nineteenth-century 'scramble for concessions' by the same foreign powers encircling China, and Egypt, where the Mixed Courts combined French Napoleonic law, English common law, Islamic law and local laws to try cases involving more than one nationality.[20] Cooperation between

[18] Robert Bickers, 'Incubator City: Shanghai and the Crises of Empires', *Journal of Urban History*, Vol. 38, No. 5 (2012), 863.
[19] Niels Petersson, 'Gentlemanly and Not-so-Gentlemanly Imperialism in China before the First World War', in Shigeru Akita (ed.), *Gentlemanly Capitalism, Imperialism and Global History* (Basingstoke: Palgrave, 2002), 103–22; Jürgen Osterhammel, 'Britain and China, 1842–1914', in Andrew Porter (ed.), *The Oxford History of the British Empire, Vol. III: The Nineteenth Century* (Oxford University Press, 1999), 165.
[20] Nigel Brailey, 'The Scramble for Concessions in 1880s Siam', *Modern Asian Studies*, Vol. 33, No. 3 (1999), 513–49; Mark S. W. Hoyle, *Mixed Courts of Egypt* (London: Graham and Trotman, 1991).

the foreign powers was accompanied in Egypt and Siam, as in Shanghai, by jostling and rivalry, but it served colonial interests. The concept of transnational colonialism is thus not only applicable to the peculiar circumstances of the SMC, but to a range of colonial settings around the world.

Shanghai's transnationality was closely related to its status as a global city. The concept of the 'global city' was coined by Saskia Sassen to describe cities hosting a critical mass of multinational corporations in the 1980s, rendering globalisation tangible and local and bringing with it great wealth and inequality.[21] As a sociologist, Sassen was concerned with contemporary society, but the concept can be readily adapted to the earlier twentieth century. Republican Shanghai similarly brought together multinational firms and shared the accompanying inequality of Sassen's global cities. Shanghai, moreover, was connected to all corners of the globe through trade, finance, immigration and, as the greatest port in Asia, transport and communications. While many cities were connected internationally as nodes of empires, Shanghai was unusual in bringing together so many overlapping imperial networks, and the result was a diverse and polyglot population. Like the global cities of the late twentieth and twenty-first centuries, in many ways Republican Shanghai resembled other global cities of the day – London, New York or Buenos Aires – more than it did the rest of China: physically in its great buildings on and around the Bund, but also culturally from its cosmopolitan art and literary scenes to the music enjoyed in its nightclubs.[22] These factors, constituting Shanghai's globalism, developed because of the transnational colonialism epitomised by the SMC.

Many scholars of Shanghai have emphasised the city's transnationalism, though few use the term. For Leo Ou-fan Lee and Meng Yue, Shanghai's 'cosmopolitanism' signalled its 'modernity'; Jeffrey Wasserstrom contests this claim while rightly championing Shanghai as a 'global' city.[23] What existing studies have overlooked is the way in which transnationalism bolstered the autonomy of the foreign community and its governing council, enabling it to determine its own policies and, at times, ignore the national interests of the foreign powers. British consuls could direct the activities of the smaller British concessions in other Chinese ports like Tianjin and Hankou, but in Shanghai the consul-general could only offer advice, with no guarantee it would be heeded by the autonomous SMC. The SMC could and did resist interference from the

---

[21] Saskia Sassen, *The Global City: London, New York, Tokyo* (Princeton University Press, 1991).

[22] James Farrer and Andrew Field, *Shanghai Nightscapes: A Nocturnal Biography of a Global City* (Chicago, IL: University of Chicago Press, 2015), 11.

[23] Leo Ou-fan Lee, *Shanghai Modern: The Flowering of a New Urban Culture in China 1930–1945* (Cambridge, MA: Harvard University Press, 1999); Meng Yue, *Shanghai and the Edges of Empires* (Minneapolis, MN: University of Minnesota Press, 2006); Wasserstrom, 'Questioning the Modernity of the Model Settlement', 110–32 and *Global Shanghai, 1850–2010: A History in Fragments* (New York: Routledge, 2009), 16–20.

British and American governments much more easily as a transnational institution than it could have had it consisted of representatives of only one of those nations or of state officials.

Imperial metropoles were comparatively insignificant in the exercise of colonial power in Shanghai, as the autonomy of the SMC resulted in a different form of colonial governance. The influence of the dominant imperial power, Britain, was checked by the input of different nationalities and the consequent independence from directives originating in London. Many contemporaries commented on how British the International Settlement looked and felt – an American visitor called it 'about as international as the Tower of London or Westminster Abbey' – and the American consul-general complained in 1927 that the international status of the Settlement served only as a smokescreen for British imperialism.[24] Yet at the same time, the British consul-general, diplomats and home government were regularly frustrated that they could not exercise control over the SMC. Members of the House of Commons frequently asked why the British government did not bring the SMC into line, whether over closing opium dens in 1908, ending the employment of child labour or introducing Chinese representatives in the 1920s, or responding to Japanese demands in 1937. But the answer was always the same: 'The Municipal Council are responsible to the ratepayers of the Settlement, and are not under the control of His Majesty's Government'; 'The Shanghai Municipal Council is an independent international body, over which His Majesty's Government have no control'.[25] The SMC shows the extent to which colonial authority could exist with little direct input from a metropolitan imperial power.

The local issues that gained international attention were some of the most contentious in modern Chinese history and the SMC's policies were critical to how they developed. British gunboats forcing China to allow the sale of opium is central to the narrative of the 'century of national humiliation' that still informs China's view of itself on the world stage.[26] For the SMC to permit the continuance of opium dens in China's largest city in the early twentieth century, when the Qing government and local Chinese authorities had banned them, makes the drug-pushing record of the British much more recent. The SMC bowed to public opinion following pressure from the International Opium Commission and Hague Convention on opium of 1911–12 (which had more effect than the British government) and temporarily closed the dens, but permitted some to reopen in

---

[24] George Digby, *Down Wind* (London: Collins, 1939), 11; US NARA, Consular Posts, Shanghai, RG 84, Vol. 1686, 810.1: letter from American Consul-General, Shanghai, to Secretary of State, Washington, DC, 5 May 1927.

[25] HC Deb 3 February 1908, Vol. 183, cols 518; HC Deb 14 August 1913, Vol. 56, cols 2624–8; HC Deb 18 June 1925, Vol. 185, cols 800–1; HC Deb 13 December 1937, Vol. 330, cols 836W.

[26] William A. Callahan, 'National Insecurities: Humiliation, Salvation, and Chinese Nationalism', *Alternatives: Global, Local, Political*, Vol. 29, No. 2 (2004), 199–218.

1913.[27] The legal consumption of opium in the International Settlement only ended in 1917, and the SMC's defiance of Chinese law contributed to the growing anti-imperialist anger over extraterritoriality.

The notorious shooting by the SMC's own Shanghai Municipal Police (SMP) of Chinese protestors on 30 May 1925 is recognised as one of the key turning points in the development of Chinese nationalism and the Chinese communist movement. The SMC subsequently agreed to admit Chinese to the Council, long after representation was gained by colonised people in British colonies elsewhere in Asia. At times the SMC's transnational colonial status weakened its position: the Council was unable to push through legislation against child labour in the Settlement's factories because it lacked the law-making authority of a colonial government. The ambiguous status of the International Settlement provided a cloak for growing Japanese imperialism in China. In 1932, the SMC's defence scheme ensured that the Chinese authorities were taken by surprise by Japanese troop movement, prompting the first shots of the Sino-Japanese hostilities that were a violent prelude to the full-scale war from 1937. War would have come anyway, but the SMC's role in such pivotal movements in China's recent past demands much greater recognition than has been afforded it up to now.

One of the most original contributions to our understanding of Shanghai has come from Hanchao Lu, whose work examining life in Shanghai 'beyond the neon lights' found that most ordinary Chinese residents did not experience the modernity for which the city was famed. The dense low-rise tenements of the International Settlement lacked electricity or running water, and traditional patterns of life persisted among the rural migrants who made up the majority of the urban population.[28] By extension, we might assume that the SMC's impact on people's everyday life was limited, in the same way as Eric Stokes and others argue that the lives of most Indians were shaped by structural forces such as class rather than anything the colonial government attempted.[29] Yet this book shows myriad ways in which the SMC had a clear impact on the lives of the Settlement's inhabitants, whether paying taxes or licence fees, encountering the police or municipal inspectors, being subject to anti-plague drives or vaccination programmes, or buying rice imported by the SMC during the shortage caused by the Sino-Japanese War. Chinese business elites engaged with the SMC politically, but Shanghai's ordinary residents were also affected by its activities, even if they were not to be found promenading along the Bund.

[27] Frederic Wakeman, Jr., *Policing Shanghai 1927–1937* (Berkeley, CA: University of California Press, 1995), 35–6.

[28] Hanchao Lu, *Beyond the Neon Lights: Everyday Shanghai in the Early Twentieth Century* (Berkeley, CA: University of California Press, 1999), 121.

[29] Eric Stokes, *The Peasant and the Raj: Studies in Agrarian Society and Peasant Rebellion in Colonial India* (Cambridge University Press, 1980).

The SMC existed to serve business interests, and the conditions that benefited foreign companies were also favourable to Chinese concerns. As most of the big firms were British, Britons exerted the most influence over the Council. Britain was China's largest trading partner throughout the century between the First Opium War and the Sino-Japanese War, with the USA a close second and Japan and Germany increasing their share in the 1930s. But as the Chinese bourgeoisie grew, their interests increasingly coincided with foreign concerns, particularly the desire for stability – the most pressing need of businesses everywhere. Jürgen Osterhammel has drawn attention to the many foreign companies – especially British but also German and other nationalities – that made alliances with Chinese businesses to further their penetration of Chinese markets.[30] Even without such arrangements, the low taxes and public order available in the International Settlement were just as attractive to Chinese capitalists as to their foreign counterparts. The SMC therefore always had Chinese allies, even though it represented colonial authority on Chinese soil.

The neglect of the SMC in the history of colonialism in China is peculiar. Extensive studies exist of the Imperial (latterly Chinese) Maritime Customs Service, which was established in Shanghai in 1854 by the British consul-general and served China's foreign debts.[31] British investment and the employment of Britons and later Americans in another branch of the Chinese state, the Salt Administration, have also been studied.[32] These were examples of what John King Fairbank called 'synarchy': joint Sino-foreign ventures that he claimed were critical to China's modernisation.[33] But to grasp the full complexity of colonialism in China, it is vital to understand how the treaty ports were governed, especially the largest treaty port, Shanghai. Foreign colonial influence was not only exerted on the Chinese state, but shaped the development of China's most important cities and affected the lives of those who moved to them for work from the rest of the country. And in China, that influence was not confined to individual foreign powers acting alone, and was not directed from an imperial metropole, but was transnational colonialism: non-state actors of many nationalities cooperating to further their mutual interests. Osterhammel acknowledges that 'imperialism in China was fundamentally a co-operative venture' and that the International Settlement was 'the linchpin of the foreign

---

[30] Jürgen Osterhammel, 'Imperialism in Transition: British Business and the Chinese Authorities, 1931–37', *China Quarterly*, No. 98 (1984), 282.

[31] Hans van de Ven, *Breaking with the Past: The Maritime Customs Service and the Global Origins of Modernity in China* (New York: Columbia University Press, 2014); Catherine Ladds, *Empire Careers: Working for the Chinese Customs Service, 1854–1949* (Manchester University Press, 2013).

[32] S. A. M. Adshead, *The Modernization of the Chinese Salt Administration, 1900–1920* (Cambridge, MA: Harvard University Press, 1970).

[33] John King Fairbank, *Trade and Diplomacy on the China Coast: the Opening of the Treaty Ports, 1842–1854* (Stanford University Press, 1969), 465.

establishment', yet even he makes no mention of the SMC and fails to explore its role.[34] This book addresses this major gap in the literature, exploiting the vast holdings of the Shanghai Municipal Archives, and offers the concept of transnational colonialism to explain the nature of colonialism in China.

It is vital to recognise the precise nature of colonialism in China if we are to understand the development of Chinese nationalism. Three decades of 'China-centred history' have provided a necessary corrective to the 'Harvard School', led by Fairbank, which was (sometimes unfairly) accused of depicting China's modern history as simply a response to the impact of western imperialism, where western implicitly stood for British. The intention of China-centred historians was to provide what Paul Cohen called 'a more interior approach' to China's past, which cast China as the active creator of its own history.[35] Many valuable studies resulted, particularly of China's regions, but the pendulum swung too far with an attempt to write Chinese history as though there had been no foreign influence on the country. In a backlash against this trend, William Kirby declared in 1997 that 'everything important had an international dimension', while Robert Bickers criticised writing Chinese history with only 'a caricatured foreign presence'.[36] Now there is wide recognition of the importance of colonialism in key developments in China, economically, culturally and politically, among the most important of which is in the strongly anti-imperial tenor of Chinese nationalism.[37] Bryna Goodman and David Goodman criticise the generalised way in which certain scholars, particularly those publishing in *positions*, write of a vague 'colonial modernity', without recognising the different manifestations of colonialism in China and the various ways they influenced the country.[38] This book corrects such a tendency by providing a detailed study of one of the most important colonial authorities in China.

Historians in China never shared the American aversion to examining the role played by colonialism in the nation's history, and many are quite comfortable with the 'western impact–Chinese response' paradigm. Zhang Zhongli

---

[34] Jürgen Osterhammel, 'Semi-colonialism and Informal Empire in Twentieth-Century China: Towards a Framework of Analysis' in Wolfgang J. Mommsen and Jürgen Osterhammel (eds.), *Imperialism and After: Continuities and Discontinuities* (London: Allen and Unwin, 1986), 300.

[35] Paul A. Cohen, *Discovering History in China: American Historical Writing on the Recent Chinese Past* (New York: Columbia University Press, 1984), 151–3.

[36] William C. Kirby, 'The Internationalization of China: Foreign Relations at Home and Abroad in the Republican Era', *China Quarterly*, No. 150, Special Issue: Reappraising Republican China (1997), 433; Robert Bickers, *Britain in China: Community, Culture and Colonialism 1900–1949* (Manchester University Press, 1999), 6.

[37] Isabella Jackson, 'Chinese Colonial History in Comparative Perspective', *Journal of Colonialism and Colonial History*, Vol. 15, No. 3 (2014), doi: 10.1353/cch.2014.0042.

[38] Bryna Goodman and David Goodman, 'Introduction: Colonialism and China', in Bryna Goodman and David Goodman (eds.), *Twentieth Century Colonialism and China: Localities, the Everyday, and the World* (London: Routledge, 2012), 6.

and Pan Yunxiong portrayed China as a passive receiver of modernisation from the west, primarily through the foreign presence in Shanghai.[39] There is considerable interest in China in the history of the SMC and its Settlement, and while the SMC is denigrated as an imperialist body, disenfranchising Chinese residents and excluding them from its public parks,[40] it is nevertheless portrayed as an unwitting benefactor of China as a whole by introducing the advantages of modern society. Ma Changlin (马长林) offers a more nuanced assessment, but is still frequently positive about the 'urban management methods' introduced by the SMC, noting that many remain in place today.[41] This book does not echo this view – my research has found more failings in the record of the SMC than successes – but there should be no doubting the importance of this institution in the development of China's only truly global city.

Among historians in China, and many in the west, there is a limited appreciation of the independence of the SMC from the formal diplomatic avenues of power through the consuls to the British imperial state in London. Bickers has rightly stressed the place of China and particularly Shanghai in the British empire.[42] Yet in contrast to the French Concession in Shanghai, where the French consul-general acted much like a colonial governor and the *Conseil municipal* played a merely advisory role, the British consul-general and other members of the consular body had no formal authority over the SMC and could only offer advice and a channel of communication to the diplomatic corps in Beijing and home governments. Although the foreign community appealed to the British and American governments for support in times of difficulty, it was proud of the autonomy of the International Settlement. Other foreign settlements in China were more like the French Concession in their administration, the only other international settlement being the small enclave at Gulangyu, an island off the coast from Xiamen (Amoy). But Shanghai was far and away the most prominent treaty port and as such the developments and administration there were observed, discussed and often implemented in the smaller settlements up and down the China coast. The International Settlement was not the

---

[39] Zhang Zhongli and Pan Yunxiang, 'The Influence of Shanghai's Modernization on the Economy of the Yangzi Valley', in Frederic Wakeman, Jr. and Wang Xi (eds.), *China's Quest for Modernization: A Historical Perspective* (Berkeley, CA: University of California Press, 1997), 284.

[40] For a discussion of the controversy over a mythical sign banning 'Dogs and Chinese' from the public gardens, which did indeed exclude Chinese until 1928, see Robert Bickers and Jeffrey N. Wasserstrom, 'Shanghai's "Dogs and Chinese Not Admitted" Sign: Legend, History and Contemporary Symbol', *China Quarterly,* No. 142 (1995), 423–43.

[41] Ma Changlin et al., *Shanghai gonggong zujie chengshi guanli yanjiu* (*Research on the Urban Management of the Shanghai International Settlement*) (Shanghai: Zhongxi shuju, 2011), ii.

[42] Bickers, *Britain in China*; *Empire Made Me: An Englishman Adrift in Shanghai* (London: Allen Lane, 2003); *The Scramble for China: Foreign Devils in the Qing Empire, 1832–1914* (London: Allen Lane, 2011).

'model settlement' the Shanghailanders (local British and, in smaller numbers, American settlers) proclaimed it to be, but it was influential throughout China and beyond.[43]

The International Settlement is usually translated as the 'public concession' (*gonggong zujie* 公共租界), or less commonly the 'British concession' (*Ying zujie* 英租界) or 'British-American concession' (*Ying-Mei zujie* 英美租界) – all terms employed by contemporaries of the SMC and still used today. The latter two names for the Settlement reflect the dominance of the British and, to a lesser extent, Americans. Describing it as a 'public concession', however, carries connotations of openness and public ownership: a far cry from the reality of a settlement under the management of the SMC, elected by a privileged few from among an even smaller number of men eligible to be councillors. The use of 'concession' (*zujie*) was also inaccurate: both the International and French quarters of the city were technically settlements (*juliudi* 居留地), indicating that rather than being 'land granted or leased directly by China to a foreign government in return for the payment of a nominal ground rent', they were merely 'place[s] set aside where foreigners might live and deal directly with individual Chinese owners in buying or leasing land'.[44] The Chinese name thus reveals a widespread perception of the International Settlement as both British and enjoying a greater degree of permanency than it in fact held in law.

Shanghai's International Settlement supposedly belonged to what is often called, particularly by British historians, Britain's informal empire. Insofar as this concept reflects Ronald Robinson and John Gallagher's emphasis on free trade ('free', that is, on British terms) as the primary motive for imperial expansion and the importance of peripheral over metropolitan influences on empire-building, it seems appropriate.[45] The unity of formal and informal empire in Robinson and Gallagher's view, differing only in degree, also applies well to Shanghai, which confounds the assumed dichotomy between the settler and dependent empires.[46] For Robinson and Gallagher, and those who have adopted their approach, informal empire was the preferred, lower-cost mode of imperialism. But there are problems with the concept. It applies

---

[43] Robert Bickers, 'Shanghailanders: The Formation and Identity of the British Settler Community in Shanghai, 1843–1937', *Past and Present*, No. 159 (1998), 165–6; Peter Ennals describes how Shanghai was a model for the Kobe foreign settlement and its administration in *Opening a Window to the West: the Foreign Concession at Kobe, Japan, 1868–1899* (Toronto: University of Toronto Press, 2014), 5, 30–2.

[44] Nicholas R. Clifford, *Spoilt Children of Empire: Westerners in Shanghai and the Chinese Revolution of the 1920s* (Hanover, NH: Middlebury College Press, 1991), 17.

[45] John Gallagher and Ronald Robinson, 'The Imperialism of Free Trade', *Economic History Review*, New Series, Vol. 6, No. 1 (1953), 1–15.

[46] Lorenzo Veracini claims that settler colonialism and colonialism are fundamentally distinct and mutually defining in *Settler Colonialism: A Theoretical Overview* (Basingstoke: Palgrave, 2010).

best to Latin America, where British imperial influence was extended primarily by investment and the creation of financial and trading dependency on Britain, but less well to China. John Darwin identifies two types of 'informal imperialism', allowing for the difference between the private enterprise model in Latin America and the more 'elaborate' structures of treaty and gunboat diplomacy in China.[47] Yet there was something qualitatively different about imperialism in Shanghai beyond the legal privileges secured by diplomats and the use and threat of force. It was colonial, in the sense that it was based on rule by foreign settlers, and it was governmental in the form of the SMC, run by settlers and expatriates. The degree of control that came to be exercised by the SMC did not feel very informal to the millions of Chinese who lived under its governance, even if the legal underpinnings of its authority were insecure. For this reason I also avoid the term 'semi-colonialism', coined by Lenin and favoured by American and Chinese scholars: the residents of the Settlement experienced a form of colonialism that was far greater in reach than the prefix 'semi' implies. Jeffrey Wasserstrom's 'quasi-colonial' implies Shanghai did not experience real colonialism but only something resembling it, which is even more problematic.[48] This book shows that colonialism in Shanghai was not a lighter-touch form of imperial control but locally directed autonomous governance by foreigners, which led to the development of a polity more akin to an independent city-state under foreign colonial control.

Another problem with applying the term 'informal empire' to China is the singular form of 'empire'. Studies of British imperialism have often all but ignored the fact that Britons operated in China alongside many other foreign powers. The International Settlement did not belong to Britain and British leaders increasingly shared authority with other nationals. Sun Yat-sen declared that China was a 'hypo-colony', its status lowered by being colonised by many nations, and Ruth Rogaski adapted this term to 'hyper-colony' to describe the multiple colonial powers operating side by side in Tianjin.[49] But in Shanghai's International Settlement, representatives of different colonial interests were not just coexisting but cooperating, whether as the elected members of the SMC, its staff, the elite ratepayers who funded and approved its budgets and operated their businesses under its regulations, or the consuls-general – collectively the consular body – who were formally

[47] John Darwin, 'Imperialism and the Victorians: The Dynamics of Territorial Expansion', *English Historical Review*, Vol. 112, No. 447 (1997), 617.

[48] Jeffrey Wasserstrom, 'The Second Coming of Global Shanghai', *World Policy Journal*, Vol. 20, No. 2 (2003), 56.

[49] Sun Yat-sen, *San Min Chu I: The Three Principles of the People*, ed. by L. T. Chen, trans. by Frank W. Price (Shanghai: Institute for Pacific Relations, 1927), 38–9; Ruth Rogaski, *Hygienic Modernity: Meanings of Health and Disease in Treaty-Port China* (Berkeley, CA: University of California Press, 2004), 11.

responsible for their own nationals in Shanghai. The French Concession remained separate, but in the International Settlement, Americans, Germans, Russians, Japanese and Chinese at various times sat on the Municipal Council and many more nationalities worked for or paid rates to it. For this reason, transnational colonialism is the most appropriate description of foreign authority in Shanghai.

The Chinese case shows that the implied dichotomy between informal and formal empire is unhelpful and misleading. The concessions held by individual powers – the French Concession in Shanghai and the dozens of foreign concessions in other treaty ports – should be categorised with colonies around the world. It is only if we fall into the trap of privileging the nation as a unit of analysis, only if we expect that the whole of China must be infiltrated by exploitative foreigners for it to qualify as subject to imperialism, that the concept of informal empire, or indeed semi-colonialism, makes sense. Decentring the nation (as advocated by both Prasenjit Duara and G. William Skinner in very different ways)[50] and focusing instead on people and localities shows that the treaty ports were as colonial as any other part of the European empires. What made the Shanghai International Settlement distinct was not informality but transnationalism: colonial authority in the hands of not one nation and its officials but many non-state actors from diverse backgrounds. This is the distinction that should be made in understanding the nature of colonialism in China.

The SMC is called literally the 'works bureau' (*gongbu ju* 工部局) in Chinese, a term coined by the SMC itself and taken from the similar bodies that existed in Victorian England for the provision of basic public works around the time of the establishment of the Council in 1854. This accurately represents the original function of the SMC, simply overseeing the maintenance of public roads, waterworks, cemeteries and other infrastructure, but gives no indication of the broad swathe of services that the SMC provided by the twentieth century as investigated in this book. The SMC's building and maintenance work was continued by its Public Works Department, but it also had a Finance Department and Secretariat to oversee its administration. The SMP and Fire Brigade, with the help of the Shanghai Volunteer Corps when it was called out, protected life and property in the Settlement. The SMK also had a Public Health Department and smaller Education, Legal, Orchestra, Library and Industrial sections. This book concentrates on the principal areas of municipal activity to examine how transnational

---

[50] Prasenjit Duara, *Rescuing History from the Nation: Questioning Narratives of Modern China* (Chicago, IL: University of Chicago Press, 1995); G. William Skinner, 'Regional Urbanization in Nineteenth-Century China', in G. William Skinner (ed.), *The City in Late Imperial China* (Stanford University Press, 1977), 215.

colonialism worked in practice in governing and shaping Shanghai, and how it affected the lives of the city's inhabitants.

The autonomy of the SMC depended on its ability to fund its own activities, so the first chapter examines how the SMC collected taxes, imposed licence fees and floated loans. Regular income came primarily from municipal rates on property and fees for licences to operate businesses. The SMC imposed fees on all forms of trade, from factories and theatres to butchers and ice-cream vendors, so it affected the everyday lives of the Settlement's traders and consumers. For the majority of its existence, the SMC faced no significant difficulties in collecting taxes from the Chinese population, indicating that it enjoyed a strong degree of legitimacy to govern the Settlement in their eyes, despite its weak legal position. Organised opposition to taxes in 1919 and 1927, however, galvanised the growing Chinese nationalist movement and pushed the SMC to respond to Chinese demands for a greater say in governing the Settlement. That Chinese protestors demanded representation on this colonial body shows its importance in the development of Chinese political consciousness. The transnational colonialism of the SMC is apparent in its direct connections to global capital through its borrowing for long-term investment in the International Settlement. Investors' confidence in the prospects of the SMC was predicated on its links to the British empire, though when a financial crisis brought on by war forced the Council to seek a loan from the British and American governments, both refused: the SMC was ultimately beyond the shelter of metropolitan imperial support.

The changing composition and increasing transnationalism of the SMC is a major theme in the second chapter, which examines the people who governed the International Settlement as members of the Council and those who implemented its policies on the ground as its employees. Landed rate-payers elected the councillors from among a small and wealthy pool of businessmen. Expatriates from the largest British firms dominated – men who moved between the various ports and countries where they did business – but over time more long-term settlers were elected and Japanese and then Chinese councillors were able to influence Council policy. The wealth and status they had in common, with exceptionally cosmopolitan backgrounds and valuable business and political networks, allowed them to overcome the racial prejudice of the period. These elected councillors, through municipal committees, oversaw the work of an international staff. Municipal employees were divided by a strict racial hierarchy, with Britons occupying senior posts, Chinese undertaking the vast majority of the work, and other nationals operating in between. This meant that, as elsewhere, colonial authority in Shanghai was experienced through local mediators, as Chinese tax collectors, inspectors, nurses and teachers interacted with the residents of the Settlement daily. Chinese gradually took on more senior roles and the SMC came to be more international in its staff, reflecting the International Settlement it governed.

The principal task of any government is the protection of life and property, and this function was performed by the SMC through its militarised police and large, transnational corps of volunteers. As examined in the third chapter, however, municipal policing was frequently in conflict with the Chinese authorities and population, who were seen as a threat. The bellicose nature of the Council is exposed as it sought to entrench and expand its territory, using the police and volunteers to seek formal extensions to the International Settlement, control areas beyond its limits, and crush protests and disorder. In doing so it acted like a colony or independent state, seeking ever more space for its expanding population and control over the Settlement's inhabitants. Protest movements in the Mixed Court riots of 1905 and the May Thirtieth Movement of 1925 exposed the brutality of its police and the vulnerability of its authority. In 1925, and again in the Sino-Japanese conflict of 1932, the SMC was at the centre of national and international developments that shaped not just Shanghai's but China's modern history. The most serious threat to the International Settlement ultimately came from the Sino-Japanese War, when the Council was in the unique position of including Chinese and Japanese, Allied and Axis nationals in one small governing body. The SMC insisted on its neutrality and aspired to self-reliance in defence, though it depended on British, American and Japanese military support in times of crisis, highlighting its anomalous position at the fringes of many empires.

The SMC sought primarily to sustain an environment conducive to business, for which a safe and hygienic public health system was essential. The fourth chapter shows how the Council gradually increased its activities in this area, from the bare minimum of ensuring a clean water supply and basic sewerage in the late nineteenth century, through opening municipal hospitals and regulating hygiene standards in the food industry in the early twentieth, to conducting extensive inoculation and health education programmes by the 1930s. Such an expansion in public health work was due to local, national and international pressures, as expectations changed of what governments – municipal, national and colonial – should provide in the field of public health. Imperial networks influenced the Council's public health staff, while transnational bodies such as the League of Nations and the Rockefeller Foundation were increasingly important. This facet of the SMC's work therefore illuminates a new aspect of transnational colonialism: the global forces shaping local activities, as medical workers shared their knowledge and practices. Public health was, however, also a great area of contention between different authorities. The International Settlement and French Concession differed in their approaches to such issues as the treatment of the insane and the prevention of venereal disease. Meanwhile the Chinese municipal authority sought to assert its claims to modern governance by competing with the SMC in this field. Municipal policies increasingly had to be negotiated, highlighting the complexities of transnational colonialism in practice. Public health measures had a direct impact on the Settlement's inhabitants, controlling diseases but also controlling aspects of daily life, so the importance of the SMC for the population of Shanghai is again apparent.

Perhaps the greatest change in the SMC's governmental role was in the area of labour conditions. Much of Shanghai's wealth rested on its well-developed light industry, and an increasing proportion of its inhabitants were employed in factories and workshops, generally in poor conditions. For most of its existence the SMC saw labour conditions as beyond its purview, sticking steadfastly to laissez-faire principles. But from the 1920s sustained pressure – locally from foreign and Chinese women, nationally in the form of new Chinese legislation on labour conditions, and internationally in the form of the League of Nations' International Labour Organisation – forced the SMC to take on greater responsibility for workers' welfare. Reluctant attempts to reduce the employment of child labour, following a sustained campaign by women in religious and philanthropic organisations, were run aground by Chinese nationalism following the May Thirtieth Incident of 1925. But the Council's desire to contain Guomindang (Nationalist Party) efforts to apply its new Factory Law in the International Settlement in the interests of the Settlement's long-cherished independence prompted the SMC to appoint its own staff to improve labour conditions. This staff developed into the last department added to the municipal organisation, the Industrial Division. It secured modest improvements in factory conditions through persuasion rather than legislation: the limited powers of the SMC forced a creative approach by the energetic Eleanor Hinder, the SMC's only female head of department. Chapter 5 therefore adds a gendered dimension to transnational colonialism, through the role of women in Shanghai who belonged to a transnational network of feminist social reformers. The Industrial Division's greatest contribution to the welfare of Shanghai's workers came during the Sino-Japanese War, when it compiled data on the rising cost of living that was widely used by employers to calculate the allowances sorely needed by their staff. It also provided a labour exchange to help refugees find work in the Settlement and helped pay for the unemployed to relocate to their native place. Through such measures, the SMC had a significant impact on the lives of thousands of the poorer inhabitants of the International Settlement.

The Sino-Japanese War heralded by the bombs of 1937 ushered in the end of the International Settlement, but the economy and society that the SMC oversaw, dominated by foreign and transnational business interests, persisted until the arrival of the Communists in 1949. Many of the policies of the SMC had far-reaching consequences, not least in contributing to the nationalism that characterises modern China. The Bund, which symbolised the prosperity of and international influences on the International Settlement, survived the turmoil of the following decades and remains one of the most recognisable riverfronts in the world, rivalled though it is today by the skyscrapers facing it on the eastern riverbank. Shanghai was shaped indelibly by transnational colonialism in the form of the SMC, as revealed on the following pages. Modern Chinese history cannot be fully understood without appreciating how colonialism operated in Shanghai.

1   Funding Transnational Colonialism

> The cost of defraying the expenses of the Government of the Settlement is borne exclusively by the residents within it, and by dues which are levied on goods which are landed or shipped within its limits – neither the national authorities of the Foreign Residents, nor the local authorities of the Chinese Residents, contributing one farthing towards the Budget of expenses.[1]

The Shanghai Municipal Council proudly and repeatedly declared its independence from the foreign powers in China and from Chinese control. It insisted on and energetically exercised its right to manage the affairs of the International Settlement without outside interference. Consuls and other foreign representatives were consulted or kept informed of the Council's decisions as it saw fit, but were unable to dictate municipal policy. Such autonomy derived from the international status of the Settlement, but depended in practical terms on the fact that the SMC was entirely self-funded. Its fiscal autonomy marked it out from Britain's dependent colonies: although imperial governments aspired to their colonies being self-funding, they were often a drain on the metropolitan budget. The quotation above, from a Council statement to ratepayers in support of revisions to the Land Regulations in 1866, shows how awareness of its need to fund itself informed the Council's efforts to formalise and extend its powers from its earliest days. By 1900, it benefited from a number of sources of revenue in addition to rates from the Settlement's inhabitants and customs duties – debenture loans from a transnational range of investors being the most significant. But it remained true that the Council had no outside sources of funding and had to meet the costs of managing the heart of China's most modern and populous city on its own.

The SMC therefore sought to keep spending as low as was deemed possible. It was strongly influenced by the nineteenth-century British belief that in good government 'administrative and fiscal efficiency were ends in themselves', an outlook that Zoë Laidlaw traces back to the years following the Napoleonic

---

[1] Memorandum submitted by a committee of the Shanghai Municipal Council with the revised Land Regulations to the Ratepayers' Meeting in March 1866, in Feetham, *Report*, II, 55–6.

22

Wars.[2] The areas in which large-scale spending was tolerated, defence and capital investment in infrastructure, reveal the priorities of the colonial presence in Shanghai. Investigating the costs of administering the International Settlement and how they were met is thus essential to understanding how colonial authority shaped the city. It also enables us to understand the priorities of a colonial body independent from imperial oversight.

Despite the treasurer's best efforts to keep expenditure to a minimum, all areas of municipal governance expanded over the decades as growing expectations of the Council's role prompted higher levels of spending and a greater reach into the lives of the Settlement's inhabitants. All the activities of the SMC as it shaped the city of Shanghai depended on its ability to fund them, and as the work of the Council expanded, so did its budget. The municipal staff grew, adding to the burden of paying salaries. The area of the Settlement expanded, requiring more defence, more roads, more bridges and more amenities. The number of residents grew faster still, meaning more public order issues and public health problems to address. The number of buildings and businesses in the Settlement needing inspection and regulation increased, while expectations of how much control the Council should exert over buildings and businesses to ensure the safety of the Settlement's residents rose. Meeting the costs of the municipal government required ever-greater revenues.

The coffers were filled by rates, paid by individuals and businesses with a certain amount of property or wealth, by customs dues and licence fees, and by loans, notably the annual municipal debentures. All these sources of revenue required strong governance. Councillors and members of the Shanghailander establishment often voiced the concern that local disturbances would damage the creditworthiness of the Council. The same sections of the community worried that property values would be affected by political uncertainty,[3] but as the early twentieth century was characterised by property booms, this fear was unfounded.[4] Similar concerns preoccupied colonial authorities in the Dominions, anxious for London investors not to be

---

[2] Zoë Laidlaw, *Colonial Connections, 1815–1845: Patronage, the Information Revolution and Colonial Government* (Manchester University Press, 2005), 7.

[3] The retrocession of Hankou in 1927, for example, was seen to have caused uncertainty about Shanghai's future status and therefore threatened the value of property investments in the Settlement. The assessed values of foreign and Chinese houses inside the Settlement and in the extra-Settlement area where the Special Rate was collected show, however, that values continued to rise steadily.

[4] Huge profits were made by the real estate companies that proliferated in Shanghai in the early years of the twentieth century, as the price of land in the Settlement increased from 12,000 taels of silver per *mu* in 1903 to 35,000 taels in 1907. Meng, *Shanghai*, 175–6; Chiara Betta, 'The Land System of the Shanghai International Settlement: the Rise and Fall of the Hardoon Family, 1874–1956', in Robert Bickers and Isabella Jackson (eds.), *Treaty Ports in Modern China: Law, Land and Power* (London: Routledge, 2016), 64.

put off by reports of instability.[5] Banks and investors alike gave credit to the SMC and to Shanghai businesses based on Settlement real estate, assuming it to be secure collateral.[6] The financial security of the SMC thus underpinned the wealth of the city.

An ability to secure loans at affordable rates of interest is dependent on the debtor's credit rating, and the Council had to ensure it maintained the trust of its creditors, locally and internationally, foreign and Chinese. Investment came from many different markets, but the majority of municipal bondholders were in Britain, reflecting British financial dominance in China. The vital role played by the overseas investment of London financiers in expanding British imperial reach in China, as elsewhere, has been demonstrated by Peter Cain and A. G. Hopkins, but they focus on banks and expatriate companies at the expense of investment in governmental institutions.[7] The SMC attracted investors partly because of its 'gilt-edged' status: the presumed backing of the British government for the Council gave the impression of absolute stability. Niall Ferguson and Moritz Schularick identified this as 'the empire effect', yet it is clear that even informal links to the British empire lowered interest rates.[8] This fits with the findings of Gary Magee and Andrew Thompson that information based on people's personal networks was another major influencing factor determining where metropolitan investors entrusted their capital.[9] Though Magee and Thompson apply this only to what they call 'the British world', Shanghai's international population ensured a transnational range of investors in the SMC.

A governing body's capacity to exact taxation from its populace (without resorting to coercion) rests on its legitimacy to do so, and thus to rule, in the eyes of the taxpayers. Challenges to the collection of rates and licences were therefore direct, anti-colonial attacks on the right of the SMC to govern the International Settlement. For much of its history, the SMC collected its low rate of taxation with relative ease, indicating that it enjoyed a degree of political legitimacy among both foreign and Chinese ratepayers. But in 1919, Chinese ratepayers refused to pay their rates, demanding a greater say in the running of the Council (consciously invoking the maxim 'no taxation without

---

[5] Andrew Dilley, *Finance, Politics, and Imperialism: Australia, Canada, and the City of London, c.1896–1914* (Basingstoke: Palgrave Macmillan, 2012), 74–8.

[6] Tomoko Shiroyama, *China During the Great Depression: Market, State, and the World Economy, 1929–1937* (Cambridge, MA: Harvard University Press, 2008), 71.

[7] Peter Cain and A. G. Hopkins, *British Imperialism, 1688–2000* (Harlow: Pearson, 2002), 360–80.

[8] Niall Ferguson and Moritz Schularick, 'The Empire Effect: The Determinants of Country Risk in the First Age of Globalization, 1880–1913', *Journal of Economic History*, Vol. 66, No. 2 (2006), 283–312.

[9] Gary B. Magee and Andrew S. Thompson, *Empire and Globalisation: Networks of People, Goods and Capital in the British World, c. 1850–1914* (Cambridge University Press, 2010), 170–1.

representation', just as Indian nationalists had been doing since the 1860s).[10] As a consequence, the influential Chinese Ratepayers' Association (CRA) was established the following year to campaign for the rights of these elite members of the Chinese community. When Chinese residents again refused to pay the rates in 1927, the Council finally reached an agreement with representatives of the local Chinese business community on how to achieve Chinese representation. Opposition to taxation was thus a major catalyst for political change in the Settlement. Standing up to the SMC in this way raised local political consciousness and contributed to broader nationalist developments at this pivotal time, showing the importance of colonialism and the SMC to modern Chinese history.

Organising the Municipal Finances

The finances of the Shanghai Municipal Council were organised in the same way as those of all modern states. Regular, 'ordinary' expenditure on services was paid for primarily from taxation in the form of rates and Land Tax ('ordinary income'), while the cost of long-term capital investment projects such as building works and land procurement was spread across many years by floating loans ('extraordinary income'). This is the 'fiscal state' model which developed in the eighteenth century in western Europe, most successfully in Great Britain, in place of the 'tax state' which relied solely on income from direct and indirect taxation.[11] It required a sophisticated bureaucratic structure.

The Finance Committee operated on the same lines as all the municipal committees of the Settlement, following practice borrowed from English local government.[12] It met monthly (latterly fortnightly) with a summer recess and deliberated on financial matters, drawing on information provided by relevant staff (the treasurer and later the commissioner of revenues attended meetings, along with the secretary who kept the minutes and on occasion the heads of other departments whose expenditure was under consideration). It then made recommendations to the full Council; only when approved by the Council proper was policy decided. Established in 1897 and initially consisting of three members, the Committee increased to four in 1915 with the

---

[10] Sabyasachi Bhattacharya, *The Financial Foundations of the British Raj: Ideas and Interests in the Reconstruction of Indian Public Finance 1858–1872* (Hyderabad: Orient Longman, 2005), 282.

[11] M. J. Daunton, *Trusting Leviathan: the Politics of Taxation in Britain, 1799–1914* (Cambridge University Press, 2001), 5; Richard Bonney, 'Introduction', in Richard Bonney (ed.), *The Rise of the Fiscal State in Europe, c. 1200–1815* (Oxford University Press, 1999), 3 and *passim*. Daunton and Bonney agree that the tax state in turn had broadly replaced the 'domain state' of medieval Europe, in which monarchs relied on the income from their landed domains.

[12] Herman Finer, *English Local Government* (London: Methuen, 1950; first published 1933), 232.

addition of a Japanese member, five in 1922, six in 1928, including for the first time two Chinese committee members, and finally seven members from 1930. Throughout the SMC, increases in international representation over time resulted in a growth in the size of the administration: transnational colonialism was necessarily bureaucratic.

A dedicated Finance Department was established in 1909, as the volume of work became too much for the Secretariat. The newly appointed treasurer, as head of the department, was responsible to the committee for the smooth running of the Council's finances and for balancing the budget each year. This was submitted to the ratepayers at their annual meeting for approval, and every penny (or, rather, copper cash) of municipal income and expenditure was accounted for. The treasurer recommended the rate at which municipal loans should be floated and other important aspects of municipal financial policy, which were almost always adopted by the committee and then the Council. The Taxation Office, under the Superintendent of Revenues (Overseer of Taxes from 1918) with responsibility for collecting the rates, was kept within the Secretariat (as its management called for 'little if any improvement') until 1914, when all financial business was brought under the purview of the treasurer.[13] The size of the bureaucracy thus expanded in line with the growing budgets necessitated by the Council's expanding activities.

The establishment of the Finance Department and the introduction of independent auditing from 1902 signalled a move towards a more professional footing for the municipal finances.[14] The Finance Committee justified the changes on the basis that they followed common practice in 'certain Colonial Government Services and other civil services', making the case that municipal practice should be modelled on colonial and home governments rather than the norms in business with which committee members were more familiar. Examples from British colonies were of great importance in many areas of municipal governance, even as the SMC's independence from imperial oversight was maintained. Auditing was also mandated in British town councils in 1902, so the SMC was keeping up with metropolitan trends in good municipal governance.[15]

As was common practice for foreign organisations in Shanghai, the Council had a Comprador through whom almost all municipal revenues passed into the municipal accounts, and who oversaw and guaranteed the shroffs who collected monies owed to the Council. He was also responsible for paying the salaries and wages of the Chinese municipal staff, for paying interest owed to

[13] SMA U1-1-65: Finance Committee Minutes, 18 November 1909.
[14] SMA U1-1-56: Finance Committee, 11 April 1904.
[15] Robert, *The Municipal Year Book 1908*, 8.

Chinese investors in municipal debentures, and for moving money between different municipal departments. Through the Comprador, payments to Chinese were kept separate from payments to all foreign employees and investors, demonstrating the limits to the internationalism of the International Settlement. The Comprador's high level of responsibility was rewarded with the highest salary paid to any Chinese in the municipal service: in 1936 the annual salary of Comprador Pon Ming Fan was increased to 21,000 dollars: more than the 15,500 dollars paid to the Chinese Deputy Commissioner of Police and comparable to the pay of senior British members of staff.[16] Pon was entrusted with responsibility for large sums of money, but only because he had provided valuable title deeds as security. The continuance of the post of municipal Comprador so late demonstrates how the Council, while adopting modern and metropolitan financial practices such as independent auditing and long-term borrowing, at the same time perpetuated arcane practices peculiar to the foreign colonial presence in China. By this point even colonial firms like Butterfield and Swire had found alternatives to the old-fashioned comprador,[17] so the SMC was more wedded than private foreign employers to such institutions.

Shroffs were another institution peculiar to the China coast. These debt collectors were sent in person to collect monies owed by individuals as best they could, though debtors were notorious for evading payment.[18] The life of a shroff could be dangerous as the large quantities of cash they carried made them targets for armed robbers, one being robbed of 848.56 dollars in municipal funds in 1927.[19] Alongside the Council's shroffs were the 'rates coolies', (renamed 'assistant shroffs' in 1925 when the Council finally abandoned the derogatory title 'coolie') who were responsible for collecting rates and fees from Chinese. These positions provided lucrative opportunities for personal gain. The SMC punished severely such cases that came to its attention in an effort to cut 'squeeze', a matter of pride for the Council, which considered itself an example of incorruptibility.[20] The rest of China, by contrast, was held by self-satisfied foreigners to suffer from endemic corruption. Many tax collectors were members of the Municipal Police on secondment or former constables, chosen for their perceived discipline, integrity and authority. Nevertheless,

---

[16] SMA U1-1-62: Finance Committee, 19 May 1936; SMC, *Report for 1935*, 388

[17] Bickers, *Britain in China*, 183–4.

[18] The term 'shroff' was borrowed from India, where it referred to an indigenous banker (Rajat Kanta Ray, 'Asian Capital in the Age of European Domination: The Rise of the Bazaar, 1800–1914', *Modern Asian Studies*, Vol. 29, No. 3 (1995), 494); in China 'shroffs' were simply Chinese go-betweens, mainly involved in the collection of debt.

[19] SMA U1-1-61: Finance Committee, 18 March 1927; see also armed robbery of a shroff when collecting rates in 1938, U1-6-143: Deputy Treasurer, Revenue, to secretary general, 13 September 1938.

[20] See, for example, *The North-China Herald, Supreme Court and Consular Gazette* (hereafter *NCH*), Vol. 88, 5 September 1908, 585.

cases of corruption were uncovered from time to time, such as the individual who absconded with 1,627.05 dollars,[21] hinting at more widespread graft that did not come to official notice. As the men who knocked on residents' doors demanding money, shroffs and their assistants brought the authority of the Council right into people's homes, where it was often unwelcome. These representatives of the municipal authority to charge rates and taxes from the Chinese and foreign residents of the city were themselves Chinese, as transnational colonial power was mediated through local employees.

Spending Priorities

The SMC sought at all times to keep spending to a minimum. When heads of departments presented their budgets each year, the treasurer invariably found ways of cutting their projected spending by removing items that were considered non-essential. Those areas where large amounts were spent are therefore telling. Figure 1.1[22] shows a breakdown of ordinary municipal expenditure on the main municipal departments. The SMP was the largest expense every year, followed by the Public Works Department's spending on maintaining roads and bridges, bunds and wharfs, and public buildings from hospitals and prisons to housing for nurses and the police. These two departments reflect the Council's *raison d'être*: to provide an environment suitable for conducting business, which meant the provision of a basic infrastructure and the defence of life and property.

The SMC developed from the Committee of Roads and Jetties of the original English Settlement, and the work of this committee was continued by the Public Works Department. This department was also responsible for purchasing land for municipal use, such as roads, and for municipal building work, although such capital investment was listed separately as extraordinary expenditure. As the cost of land rose, extraordinary expenditure rose to be greater than the sum spent on any one department, usually around one third to one quarter of total municipal expenditure, and in some years exceeded all ordinary expenditure combined, as the SMC confidently invested in the physical assets of the International Settlement.

Ordinary income from taxation and licences was divided among the everyday expenses of maintaining the Settlement. The largest portion was spent on policing and defence; from the days of the Taiping Rebellion (1850–1864),

---

[21] SMA U1-1-61: Finance Committee, 1 December 1927.
[22] Data up to 1930 is converted from taels to dollars at a rate of 0.72 dollars per tael, the official exchange rate. Arthur N. Young, *China's Nation-Building Effort, 1927–1937* (Stanford University Press, 1971), 474, using data from the Central Bank of China. Comparisons can therefore only be approximate. Original dollar totals are available from 1933 following the abolition of the tael that year.

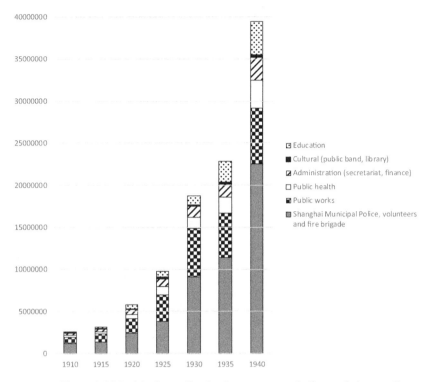

Figure 1.1 Municipal spending by department, excluding capital expenditure (Chinese dollars).
Source: SMC, *Reports for 1910–1940*.

the Council's driving concern was the protection of life and property. The Fire Brigade came under the same category, overseen by the Watch Committee. It was maintained on a cost-saving volunteer basis until it was found necessary in 1919 to move to a professional fire service because too many men volunteered for both the Shanghai Volunteer Corps (SVC) and the Fire Brigade, meaning there could be insufficient fire-fighters available in an emergency.[23] Staffing costs were high in the largest departments of Finance and the Secretariat, necessary to keep the municipality running smoothly.[24] Other departments were given low priority, although the proportion of municipal revenues spent on health and education grew. These areas had been considered non-essential, but as the Council bowed to internal and external pressure, and took more

[23] SMA U1-1-86: Watch Committee Minutes, 16 April 1919.
[24] Ma Changlin et al., *Shanghai gonggong zujie*, 313–30.

notice of the interests of the Settlement's Chinese residents, health and educa-tion, and later industrial welfare, took on greater significance.

Smaller amounts were spent on enhancing the cultural life of the Settlement, such as the Public Band, later rebranded as an orchestra, and the Public Library. The band, which came under municipal control in 1881 and cost 50,000 taels per year by 1915,[25] played in the public gardens and for dances and concerts in the town hall, attracting up to 1,000 primarily foreign listeners. It was in high demand among well-heeled Shanghainese for funerals and other occasions, who would 'pay almost anything to get the municipal band'.[26] SMC investment in the band could thus be partially recovered in charging fees for its performances. The SMC took over the library in 1912 when financial difficulties threatened to force it to close: where free trading principles failed, the SMC was there to ensure that the International Settlement maintained the key markers of a civilised western city.[27] The SMC also provided annual grants-in-aid to the Shanghai Museum from 1877, just three years after it was founded by the North-China Branch of the Royal Asiatic Society as the first public museum in China, including a grant of 2,000 taels in 1909 to fund a full renovation of the museum.[28] The French *Conseil municipal* contributed to the museum's finances, providing 20 per cent of the amount granted by the SMC, and it also helped fund the Public Band; it was not unusual for both municipalities to support the same charitable concerns. While the SMC was slow to dedicate resources to public welfare, therefore, it was willing from comparatively early to devote funds to the civic institutions one would have expected to find in a prosperous city in Europe, the USA or the settler colonies.

Expenditure on all areas of municipal activity increased over the years (though rampant inflation makes the figures for 1940 outliers). The same pattern was not discernible across the British empire: revenues did not rise sufficiently to fund increased expenditure in much of British Africa, while gov-ernment expenditure in India fell after peaking in 1921.[29] Colonial expenditure

---

[25] SMA U1-1–58: Finance Committee Minutes, 11 March 1915.

[26] SMA U1-130: Orchestra and Band Committee Minutes, 26 June 1919, cited in Robert Bickers, '"The Greatest Cultural Asset East of Suez": The History and Politics of the Shanghai Municipal Orchestra and Public Band, 1881–1946', in Chi-hsiung Chang (ed.), *China and the World in the Twentieth Century: Selected Essays*, II (Nankang: Academia Sinica, 2001), 850.

[27] Wu Jian Zhong and John Harris, '"An Absolute Necessity": The Evolution of the Public Library of the Shanghai Municipal Council, 1849–1943', *Journal of Librarianship and Information Science*, Vol. 25, No. 1 (1993), 7–14.

[28] Tracey Lie Dan Lu, *Museums in China: Power, Politics and Identities* (London: Routledge, 2014), 66; SMA U1-1–56: Finance Committee, 4 January 1909.

[29] Ewout Frankema, 'Colonial Taxation and Government Spending in British Africa, 1880–1940: Maximizing Revenue or Minimizing Effort?', *Explorations in Economic History*, Vol. 48, No. 1 (2011), 140; B. R. Tomlinson, *The Political Economy of the Raj, 1914–1947: The Economics of Decolonization in India* (London: Macmillan, 1979), 153.

increased in the 1940s with the growth of the developmental state,[30] while the SMC's finances conversely faced crisis in this late period. Though Shanghai was a municipality rather than a state, its extensive powers over all aspects of governmental life in the International Settlement were similar to those of state and colonial governments. Closer comparison is possible to Hong Kong, where spending per capita rose at a steadier rate than in Shanghai's International Settlement: Hong Kong per capita expenditure was double that in Shanghai in the early twentieth century, but did not increase as rapidly, so by 1930 the SMC was out-spending its southern colonial counterpart.[31] The pattern in the Straits Settlement, particularly Singapore, was a similar one of slower increases, while per capita expenditure in the settler colonies remained at still steadier (and higher) rates.[32] Greater increases in government expenditure were witnessed in Britain and Europe,[33] so the SMC's growing spending was more in line with metropolitan governments than colonial ones, albeit with much lower spending per capita. Its fiscal independence meant that spending in the International Settlement differed from the colonies, but the SMC was influenced by trends towards greater government taxation and spending emerging in Europe in the 1920s. Independence did not lessen metropolitan influence on economic policy; rather, metropolitan cities were taken as models more readily than colonies.

Sources of Revenue

Taxation

Taxation in the Settlement was low. The rates charged were controlled by the Land Regulations, which specified that taxes should not exceed one twentieth of one per cent of the gross value of land or one per cent of the annual rent of a house.[34] In fact, Land Tax was kept well below this one per cent maximum, rising very gradually over the years from 0.5 per cent in 1900 to 0.8 per cent from October 1939.[35] The greatest source of revenue for the SMC was the General Municipal Rate (GMR), which was set at a higher percentage and rose more rapidly: from 6 per cent on western-style houses and 8 per cent on

---

[30] Stephen Constantine has demonstrated how limited earlier efforts at colonial development were. Stephen Constantine, *The Making of British Colonial Development Policy 1914–1940* (London: Frank Cass, 1984), 271.

[31] *The Colonial Office List* (London: Harrison, 1910–1940).

[32] Ibid. Expenditure in New South Wales, for example, was consistently £10 per capita throughout this period.

[33] Martin Daunton, *Just Taxes: The Politics of Taxation in Britain, 1914–1979* (Cambridge University Press, 2007), 2.

[34] Feetham, *Report*, I, 74.

[35] SMC, *Report for 1939*, 241.

Chinese-style houses in 1869 to a flat rate of 18 per cent by 1939. From 1940 rates shot up and ever-higher surcharges were added to all forms of taxation in response to rampant inflation caused by the war and the fall in value of the Chinese dollar.[36] Council expenditure grew dramatically during the Sino-Japanese War at the same time as revenue sources dried up. But until this late juncture, the low rates made the Settlement something of a tax haven, free from the high and complex taxes of the Chinese-administered parts of the city (where there were 61 different taxes in 1927)[37] and elsewhere in China.

The GMR was just a quarter of the level of rates in a large British city: Manchester, Birmingham and Liverpool were taken as comparators.[38] Taxes in the International Settlement were also less burdensome than in British colonies, notwithstanding the latter's low levels of taxation compared to the imperial metropole. In its low taxation the Settlement was similar to Hong Kong, which did not impose income tax even after most other colonies had by the early twentieth century.[39] Yet Hong Kong's rates in urban areas were set between 13 and 17 per cent of property rental value in the interwar period, generally higher than the GMR in Shanghai, despite the fact that rates made up a smaller proportion of revenues in the colony.[40] Even by the standards of a low-taxed colony, the Settlement's rates were unusually low. The general trend in the formal empire, set by India, was to keep taxation low, as civil servants saw this as key to the successful government of a sound economy, although Indian tax levels rose from the last quarter of the nineteenth century as the demands of governance increased.[41] The SMC persisted in its low taxation and low expenditure longer than colonial governments, prioritising the preferences of big business (owing to the preponderance of expatriate influence on the Council) over the welfare needs of poorer residents. Municipal spending increased steadily, but by 1939 the secretary-general was still able to assert that 'Shanghai is one of the lowest rated cities in the world.'[42]

Until 1898, Chinese were charged a municipal rate two percentage points higher than that paid by foreigners. The SMC and foreign ratepayers justified the difference on the basis that Chinese who owned land within the Settlement

[36] SMC, *Report for 1940*, 255, 345.
[37] Christian Henriot, *Shanghai, 1927–1937: Municipal Power, Locality, and Modernization*, trans. Noël Castelino (Berkeley, CA: University of California Press, 1993), 47.
[38] F. C. Jones, *Shanghai and Tientsin* (London: Oxford University Press, 1940), 16; SMA U1-6–101: C. Harpur to S. H. Peek, 18 April 1936.
[39] Michael Littlewood, *Taxation without Representation: The History of Hong Kong's Troublingly Successful Tax System* (Hong Kong University Press, 2010), 25.
[40] *The Colonial Office Lists* (London: Harrison, 1910–1937).
[41] B. R. Tomlinson, *The Economy of Modern India, 1860–1970* (Cambridge University Press, 1993), 149–52.
[42] TNA T160/1142: Statement to Ambassador by Godfrey Phillips, enclosed in Keswick to Ambassador, 19 September 1939.

that was not registered with a consulate were not charged Land Tax, because they were continuing their land use in the same way as they or their forebears had done prior to the establishment of the Settlement. In 1898 foreign rate-payers consented to pay the same rate as their Chinese counterparts for the sake of equity, a move which the then chairman of the Council, F. Anderson, declared was 'highly appreciated by the native community' and 'increased their confidence in and respect for our local government'.[43] Anderson used this indication of strong and improving relations with Chinese ratepayers in support of his plea for foreign ratepayers' approval for the use of a small fraction of municipal funds for Chinese education, as was provided for the education of foreign children at the public school. Elite members of the Chinese community had approached the Council seeking funds for this purpose, in an early demand for fairer treatment. Despite an opposing resolution tabled at the ratepayers' meeting, the majority voted to pass the motion, showing some willingness among foreign residents to expand the Council's responsibilities to benefit Chinese inhabitants of the Settlement in the interest of cordial relations with the Chinese community.

The GMR was calculated on the value of houses occupied within the Settlement, as assessed by investigations every few years by professional surveyors. Appeals could be and were made against the assessed value of houses, as was the practice in the assessment for municipal rates in England. Appeals were heard by the Finance Committee and many were upheld, from both foreign and Chinese applicants, suggesting a degree of responsiveness to the public on the part of the Council. In some cases appeals sought higher rather than lower assessments, demonstrating the influence the Council's decision had on land values as well as the extent to which property speculators in Shanghai were willing to pay more in tax in order to maximise their investments.[44]

For properties on municipal roads outside the Settlement, which could not be subject to the GMR imposed within its limits, a Special Rate was charged from 1907, again adopting practice from English municipal authorities. The extra-Settlement roads area grew rapidly, so by 1928 it was almost 50 per cent larger than the Settlement proper at 7,923 acres.[45] The Council provided limited policing, fire-fighting and utilities services to these residents and in return demanded a reduced contribution, initially half the GMR but, from 1920, pegged at just two percentage points lower than the full rate. In this way, the Council extended its influence well beyond the limits of the Settlement itself.

---

[43] Speech given by Anderson at the annual meeting of ratepayers in 1900, quoted in Feetham, *Report*, I, 136.

[44] Appeals seeking higher valuations were not upheld, the Finance Committee declaring that the assessors' view was fair. SMA U1-1-59: Finance Committee, 23 November 1920.

[45] Feetham, *Report*, I, Plan of Shanghai insert at back of volume.

The practice was based not on agreement with the Chinese authorities, but on provisions made in the Waterworks and Telephone Agreements between the Council and the utilities providers.[46] Like so many of the Council's powers the basis was flimsy, but long-term precedent meant the SMC viewed it as an entitlement. Indeed, councillors anticipated that at some point these areas would be brought formally into an expanded International Settlement. There were Chinese public utilities providers, such as the Zhabei Water Company, but the SMC's support for the Shanghai Waterworks Company, including ensuring its monopoly within the Settlement, helped make alternative providers uncompetitive in the external roads areas. Utilities therefore furthered the Council's expansionist aims. Indeed, Xing Jianrong of the Shanghai Municipal Archives describes utilities as the 'sharpest weapon' in the SMC's arsenal.[47] The residents of these outside roads protested little at paying the Special Rate for many years, accepting the quid pro quo of rates for services, although it was not collected with as much success as the GMR. The Chinese authorities first raised objections to the policing of external roads in 1907,[48] but serious problems only emerged for the SMC in the late 1920s as the strengthening Chinese authorities sought to reclaim Chinese autonomy in Shanghai.

While attempting to collect taxes outside the Settlement limits, the Council opposed the collection of Chinese taxes within its boundaries as an infringement of its independence. It was the Settlement's extraterritorial status that enabled its residents to avoid paying Chinese taxes, although extraterritorial privileges did not originally apply to Chinese. The Land Regulations of 1845 assumed that the few Chinese residents of the Settlement would remain under Chinese jurisdiction, and even when their numbers swelled with the arrival of refugees from the Small Swords Uprising, the revised Regulations of 1854 in no way exempted them from Chinese jurisdiction. Yet many of these new arrivals were wealthy entrepreneurs who enriched the Settlement and drove up land values, so it was in the Council's interests to ensure their continued investment in the area. Even so, in 1862, amid a major influx of refugees from the Taiping Rebellion, the SMC offered no objection to assisting the Daotai in collecting a local tax on the transit of goods collected for defence that came to be known as *lijin* (釐金, also known as *likin* or *lekin*).[49] The British consul-general, W. H. Medhurst, sought approval from the British Minister in Beijing, Sir Frederick Bruce, as there was no precedent for

---

[46] SMA U1-1-59: Finance Committee, 19 March 1920.

[47] Xing Jianrong, '*Shui dian mei: jindai Shanghai gongyong shiye yanjiang ji huayang butong xintai*' ('Water, Electricity, Gas: The Different Mentalities of Chinese and Westerners Regarding Public Utilities in Modern Shanghai'), *Zhongguo jindaishi* (April 1994), 100–1.

[48] SMA U1-1-1247: A. M. Kotenev, 'Extra-Settlement Roads, 1853–1930', 1 December 1930, 35.

[49] Edwin George Beal, *The Origin of Likin, 1853–1864* (Cambridge, MA: Harvard University Press, 1958).

such taxation, and Bruce confirmed that 'The Tao-tai is entitled to levy taxes as he pleases.'[50] Yet Medhurst was uneasy about Chinese tax collectors operating within the Settlement, and the Council came to share his view, going against Bruce's wishes (which had been reinforced by the British Secretary of State for Foreign Affairs) and arresting Chinese tax collectors, bringing them before the consuls for fining or imprisonment. A compromise was reached whereby the Council would collect a higher tax from Chinese residents and pay the balance to the Daotai, and in 1864 the tax ceased with the capture of Nanjing by the Imperial Army, which brought the Taiping Rebellion to a close. Local Shanghai concerns trumped British metropolitan views on Chinese taxation.

Thus the principle that Chinese tax collectors could not operate within the Settlement was established, though without any solid legal basis, and the SMC continued to prosecute Chinese tax collectors, with varying success. It argued that Chinese residents were subject to imperial taxation set by Beijing but not local taxation, under which they classed *lijin*, but this view was rejected by the consular body. In 1904 a tax office was discovered within the Settlement that had been collecting *lijin* from Chinese traders. The SMC took swift action, prosecuting the staff of the office in the Mixed Court.[51] The problem resurfaced in 1910 and at regular intervals until the Nationalist government abolished *lijin* in 1927, by which time the SMC faced bigger issues of Chinese intervention in the Settlement. The Shanghai Chamber of Commerce was more concerned about new proposed duties from the Nationalist government on imports, as the Guomindang set about modernising the country's system of taxation.[52] The Council now had to come to terms with being powerless to influence legitimate Chinese taxation set by the newly assertive government, showing the limits of colonial authority.

Chinese contributions to municipal tax receipts were slightly higher than those of foreigners, as shown in Figure 1.2, though not in proportion to their great numerical dominance in the Settlement where over 90 per cent of residents were Chinese. In Tianjin, Chinese residents contributed a large majority of the income of the British Municipal Council through rates and fees;[53] in Shanghai Chinese and foreign contributions were closer in value but Chinese still paid more, especially when licence fees were taken into account. The Overseer of Taxes acknowledged in 1912 that the influx of Chinese, 'notably of the better class', seeking security following the 1911 Revolution had had a significant impact on GMR receipts, contributing to a 5.6 per cent rise in ordinary

[50] SMA U1-1-1246: A. M. Kotenev, 'Chinese taxation and government bureaux and officials in the International Settlement of Shanghai 1843–1930', compiled 16 May 1930, part II, quoting Sir Frederick Bruce to W. H. Medhurst, 5 November 1862.

[51] Ibid., 33–6.

[52] *Shanghai Mercury*, 13 August 1927, 6.

[53] Bickers, *Britain in China*, 137.

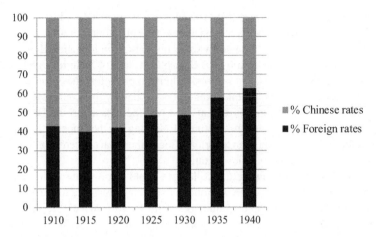

Figure 1.2 Percentage of SMC rates paid by Chinese and foreign ratepayers. Source: SMC, *Reports for 1910–1940*.

income over the previous year.[54] The Chinese population of the Settlement grew at a faster rate than the foreign population throughout the first half of the twentieth century, yet the Chinese contribution to tax revenues gradually decreased proportionately in the 1920s and 1930s. One factor was the shooting of Chinese protestors by the SMP on 30 May 1925 and the consequent surge in anti-foreign and specifically anti-SMC sentiment, which made rates harder to collect from Chinese residents and businesses.[55] The number of disadvantaged Chinese arrivals in the Settlement also increased, as refugees fled civil war in the 1920s and Sino-Japanese conflict in the 1930s, many of whom brought little with them and therefore scarcely contributed to municipal revenues. Yet broadly speaking, in the Republican period the SMC enjoyed roughly equal foreign and Chinese rates contributions. Chinese contributions to the costs of the municipal administration would be significant when calls were made for Chinese representation.

After the GMR, Land Tax was the next most important source of ordinary revenue, contributing at least a fifth of ordinary municipal income, as shown in Figure 1.3. This was paid by foreign landowners, largely the British, who owned the majority of municipal lots. Chinese were not permitted to register land ownership within the Settlement, so necessarily did not pay Land Tax to the SMC, though in practice many foreigners registered land at their consulates

---

[54] SMC, *Report for 1912*, 7c.
[55] On the May Thirtieth Incident and Movement, see Clifford, *Spoilt Children*, chapters 6–9 and Richard W. Rigby, *The May 30 Movement: Events and Themes* (Folkestone: Dawson, 1980).

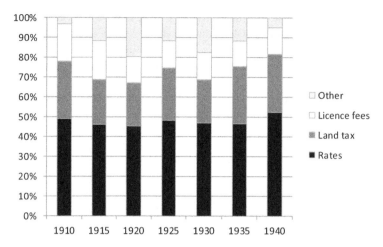

Figure 1.3 Sources of ordinary municipal income, i.e. excluding loans (per cent).
Source: SMC, *Reports for 1910–1940*.

for the sole use of Chinese in return for handsome payment. As in Hong Kong, the high value of the land made this area of taxation particularly lucrative, despite the Land Tax being set at less than 1 per cent of the value of the land (assessed periodically in the same way as house values). It was estimated at the beginning of 1900 that ordinary income for the year would reach 995,730 taels, exceeding that for 1899 by almost 80,000 taels due to the anticipated rates from the newly expanded area of the Settlement and to the re-assessment of land. (The Shanghai tael, weighing about 33.5 grams of pure silver, was the standard currency in the region.)[56] Of the total income for 1900, 216,640 taels

---

[56] The dominant currency of trade in China until around 1920 was the silver Mexican dollar, but the standard currency used for trade calculations and formal transactions was the tael, which could vary in value between different parts of China. The Shanghai tael, adopted by the foreign community in 1858, had a net weight of about 517 grains (33.5 grams) of pure silver, and it was in this form that local banks stored silver reserves. Other currencies were accepted, including European and American coins and notes, and in 1914 the Chinese government issued its own dollar, which contained about 369 grains (23.9 grams) of pure silver. These gradually overtook the Mexican dollar as the standard currency, until in 1933 the Nationalist government coined a new dollar, worth about 1.7 per cent less than the 1914 dollar. The tael was abolished the same year, so the new Chinese dollar became the standard currency for use in trade and formal transactions. Until 1933, therefore, the SMC recorded its finances in taels, with the exception of dealings with Chinese in dollars, and this is reflected throughout this book. On the Shanghai tael and the Chinese dollar, see Frank H. H. King, *Money and Monetary Policy in China, 1845–1895* (Cambridge, MA: Harvard University Press, 1965), 171–81; John Parke Young, 'The Shanghai Tael', *American Economic Review*, Vol. 21, No. 4 (1931), 682–4; and Dickson H. Leavens, 'The Silver Clause in China', *American Economic Review*, Vol. 26, No. 4 (1936), 650–9.

were anticipated from Land Tax, an increase of more than 50 per cent on the previous year.[57] However, almost half the increased revenue from Land Tax was due to the re-assessment of the value of land within the previous limits of the Settlement and to the registration of new lots by subdividing existing lots, a lucrative exercise for the SMC. The fact that Chinese did not pay Land Tax was used by foreigners resistant to Chinese representation to defend their political exclusion, despite the large fiscal contribution by Chinese ratepayers and licence fee payers.

Licence Fees and Dues

Licence fees, wharfage dues, rent from municipal properties, and income from municipal undertakings, from quarries to printing by prisoners in the municipal gaols, contributed the remainder of the SMC's ordinary income. These fees and dues were also a significant source of revenue for such colonies as Hong Kong. Licence fees were used by the SMC to regulate businesses and industries, from rickshaw-pulling to prostitution.[58] The majority of licence fees were paid by Chinese on their small businesses, demonstrating the Council's reach into the everyday lives of the Settlement's inhabitants. Licences were required for everything from dogs to motor cars and from firearms to nightclubs. Licensing premises entitled municipal police and inspectors to ensure some basic safety measures in buildings such as hotels, theatres and factories. Health inspectors similarly insisted on certain basic hygiene standards among dairies, restaurants and even ice cream sellers, which all needed to pass regular inspections to maintain their licences. Regulations governing licences were the main way the SMC was able to overcome its limited ability to legislate in the Settlement, so licences played a much greater regulatory role than in independent or colonial states.

The SMC licensed opium shops, opium houses – establishments for smoking the drug – and opium brothels, which combined drug-taking with prostitution. An imperial decree banned the selling of opium in 1906, after which opium houses in the Chinese-administered city in Shanghai were given notice to close and the Daotai requested the SMC to enforce a similar ban in the Settlement. The British consul-general and Minister both supported the ban, but the Council was reluctant. Licensing opium establishments was a lucrative source of revenue for the SMC, while councillors like E. I. Ezra made their fortunes in the opium trade and fought measures that would damage their

[57] SMC, *Report for 1899*, 368.
[58] Tim Wright has investigated the Council's failed efforts to reform the rickshaw industry. Tim Wright, 'Shanghai Imperialists versus Rickshaw Racketeers: The Defeat of the 1934 Rickshaw Reforms', *Modern China*, Vol. 17, No. 1 (1991), 76–111.

business.[59] Other members expressed concerns over the morphine-based substitutes to which opium addicts were turning. As an interim measure, new applications for opium houses and brothels were declined from 1907. A stronger response followed the first International Opium Commission, which was held in Shanghai in 1909, and the Hague Conference of 1911–1912, when the SMC revoked all opium house licences. Foreign opium traders successfully campaigned for a more gradual approach, however, and the Council compromised by permitting the sale of opium in the Settlement but gradually withdrawing the licences until they were phased out entirely in 1917, coinciding with the end to opium imports into China.[60] Licence fees were thus used to attempt to control opium consumption, though their primary purpose was revenue. In 1906, before the limits were introduced, over 20,000 opium houses were licensed, and over 1,000 opium shops, bringing in over 70,000 taels in licence fees: the largest single source of fee revenue after rickshaw licences.[61]

In other areas, licensing was primarily a stepping stone to closing premises down, as was the case for brothels. The licensing of brothels was not strictly enforced until the Moral Welfare Committee, representing foreign religious and philanthropic organisations and dominated by American and European women, raised a storm of moral outrage.[62] As a result of the Committee's campaign the ratepayers passed a resolution at their annual meeting in 1920 requiring the SMC to license all brothels and gradually withdraw the licences until none were left. The licence fee was set at one dollar every six months, so was a mere token rather than a serious source of revenue. But as the brothels were closed down, those who ran them either moved to the more tolerant French Concession or Chinese city or otherwise evaded the need to register for a licence.[63] Opposition to the licensing and closure policy came from different quarters, from the pragmatic, who noted these means to evade control, to the business-minded, who feared the consequences of closing higher-class houses of entertainment for their networking. "Sing-song girls" entertained their customers, almost exclusively Chinese and primarily wealthier businessmen, through music and conversation and did not consider themselves prostitutes, though prostitution could form part of the entertainment

[59] Chiara Betta, 'Marginal Westerners in Shanghai: the Baghdadi Jewish Community, 1845–1931', in Robert Bickers and Christian Henriot (eds.), *New Frontiers: Imperialism's New Communities in East Asia, 1842–1953* (Manchester University Press, 2000), 44–5.

[60] Wakeman, *Policing Shanghai*, 37; Zhang Qian (ed.), *The Minutes of the Shanghai Municipal Council*, Vol. 16, 17 July 1907, 28 August 1907, 482, 494.

[61] SMC, *Report for 1906*, 230.

[62] Cheng Hu, 'Venereal Disease Prevention, Moral Welfare and Civilized Image: The Shanghai Moral Welfare Committee and the Anti-Prostitution Campaign in the Shanghai International Settlement, 1918–24', *Frontiers of History in China*, Vol. 6, No. 2 (2011), 243–63.

[63] SMC, *Report for 1923*, 49; Gail Hershatter, *Dangerous Pleasures: Prostitution and Modernity in Twentieth-century Shanghai* (Berkeley, CA: University of California Press, 1997), 277–81.

on offer.[64] Withdrawing all licences removed the Council's main source of authority to regulate the activities of such establishments.

Charging duty on wharfage on Shanghai's waterways gave the SMC a degree of governmental control of local imports and exports. The Council secured the right to the fees by agreement with the Imperial Maritime Customs in 1899.[65] The Customs service collected the fees and passed them on to the SMC, just as it collected dues elsewhere and submitted them to the Qing government. This British-administered arm of the Chinese state was thus cementing the position of the British-dominated SMC, treating its authority over trade in the International Settlement as equivalent to the Qing's right to such revenues outside the Settlement. From 1929 the Chinese city government campaigned to receive income from fees from outside the foreign settlements, finally succeeding in 1931: a small curtailment of the SMC's governmental reach beyond the Settlement.[66]

Residents protested against new or rising fees, though the fees were generally low, from one to a few dollars at regular intervals, calculated to be affordable to those paying so as not to put people off applying for the licence. The Butchers' Association and ten other representative bodies of market stall holders wrote to the SMC in 1923 objecting to the introduction of a licence fee of two dollars per quarter on ground-floor stalls at the Hongkew (Hongkou) market.[67] The market had been newly re-built by the SMC's Public Works Department and the Council argued that the standard of the premises and the cost of inspecting food vendors justified the fee. The chairman, H. G. Simms, argued that claims 'that conditions of the licence are too onerous [were made] whenever a levy of any nature whatsoever is imposed, and invariably without cause or justification', dismissing the protestors out of hand.[68] The fees at the Hongkew market were duly collected, the benefits of the new market building apparently outweighing the costs for most stallholders. Despite support for the protest by the Chinese General Chamber of Commerce, the Chinese Advisory Committee and the Commissioner for Foreign Affairs, who all queried the cost of the licence, the SMC's authority to charge such fees, enshrined in the municipal byelaws which were passed by the ratepayers, was unchallenged. The SMC was occasionally taken to court by businesses challenging the right of the SMP to inspect their premises, but the consular court found in favour of the Council on the basis that

[64] Hershatter, *Dangerous Pleasures*, 278–9, 507 n. 41.
[65] SMC, *Report for 1900*, 160; *Report for 1901*, 501.
[66] *Shenbao*, 23 April 1931, 13; Henriot, *Shanghai 1927–1937*, 139.
[67] SMC, *Report for 1923*, 62–4. See SMA U1-6-97 for other examples of letters to the SMC from Chinese residents protesting against charges and fees.
[68] H. G. Simms to G. de Rossi, consul-general for Italy and senior consul, 23 June 1923, reprinted in SMC, *Report for 1923*, 64.

all licensed premises faced the same regulations and inspections.[69] The SMC could rely on consular support of its authority.

Fees and dues represented 12 to 18 per cent of ordinary revenues: a significant proportion of the municipal income. The income from licence fees more than covered the costs of the inspectors in the health and public works departments that enforced licensing conditions. Wharfage dues brought in less revenue: around a third to a half of the amount brought in by licence fees. Fees and dues were, however, most important for allowing the SMC to regulate the activities of the residents and businesses of the Settlement and those importing and exporting goods through its wharves, extending its governmental activities to those of a small state.

Loans

Access to affordable, consistent sources of investment is a sign of a strong and stable government. The ability to borrow large sums at affordable rates enabled the SMC to invest in the long-term future of the Settlement. It demonstrated the confidence of investors, both Chinese and foreign, that the status quo would continue and the SMC would remain sufficiently financially secure to honour its obligations. The treasurer estimated that public works projects lasted, on average, 43 years, and loans were issued with a life of between 10 and 30 years to spread the cost of this large-scale expenditure, giving debenture-holders a stable, long-term investment.[70] The significance of borrowing to the municipal revenues is shown in Figure 1.4. Broadly speaking, as the scale of extraordinary expenditure on municipal projects increased, loans came to provide a significantly higher proportion of municipal revenues. In 1920 extraordinary income exceeded taxation receipts for the first time, but the general pattern was for loans to provide around one-fifth to one-quarter of municipal revenues. Extraordinary income consisted almost entirely of revenue from loans, with the exception of the years following the sale of the Electricity Department in 1929 for 81,000,000 taels, to be paid over five years,[71] obviating the need to borrow any funds until 1934. (This explains the spike in extraordinary income in 1930, when municipalities elsewhere in the world were beginning to feel the effects of the Great Depression.) In all other years, loans were crucial to the SMC's ability to invest in the Settlement's infrastructure for the benefit of

---

[69] SMC, *Report for 1923*, 62.

[70] SMA U1-1-57: Finance Committee, 9 February 1911. The Council kept the option of early redemption open to itself, but normally allowed the loans to extend for the full life of the debt, which made them popular with investors seeking long-term security. W. A. Thomas, *Western Capitalism in China: A History of the Shanghai Stock Exchange* (Aldershot, Hants: Ashgate, 2001), 61.

[71] SMC, *Report for 1929*, 330.

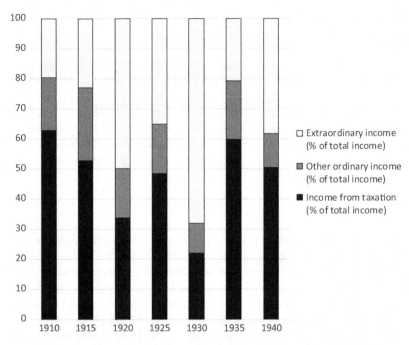

Figure 1.4 Percentage of municipal revenue from taxation, 1910–1940.
Source: SMC, *Reports for 1910–1940*.

local business and the wider community. Some worried that the SMC dominated the investment market to such an extent that local industrial and other
enterprises would be left short of capital.[72] The SMC countered that local firms
should invest in the municipal infrastructure, which enabled their businesses
to flourish.

As a supplier of stable investment opportunities, the SMC participated in
and contributed to the local financial markets that helped make Shanghai such
a wealthy city. The SMC made its first issue of fixed securities when it found
itself in debt in 1872. Modest borrowing of around 30,000 taels every few years
increased rapidly and by the 1890s the Council was borrowing hundreds of
thousands of taels each year. Large-scale government borrowing was the norm
in Britain's colonies and other countries; indeed, serving its sterling debts took
over half the total Indian government revenue by the 1930s.[73] Independence

---

[72] *NCH*, 28 October 1910, cited in Thomas, *Western Capitalism*, 60.
[73] Thomas, *Western Capitalism*, 60. On borrowing in the tropical colonies, see Michael Havinden
and David Meredith, *Colonialism and Development: Britain and its Tropical Colonies, 1850–
1960* (London: Routledge, 1993), 157, 174 and *passim*; on Indian Government debt, see
Tomlinson, *Economy of Modern India*, 153–4.

from imperial government did not prevent the SMC from embracing metropolitan and colonial financial practices. Municipal debentures in Shanghai were bought by local and international firms, banks, and wealthy individuals seeking a secure investment with a steady return: the Council was advised by a representative of the Hongkong and Shanghai Bank that most investors bought debentures 'for purposes of regular income'.[74] This, the bankroller of British enterprise in East Asia, was the Council's own bank. It advised the SMC on aspects of municipal financial policy and issued loans to and on behalf of the Council. The SMC supplied almost the entire local market for fixed interest securities, as shown by the table of local debentures printed in the *Weekly Share Supplement* which accompanied the *North-China Herald*.[75] The list was dominated by the Council's annual issues, followed by the utility companies (waterworks, gas, telephone, in all of which the SMC held significant shares), and then local firms (notably the Shanghai Land Investment Company) and establishments (such as the Shanghai Club and Race Club).[76] The SMC thus shaped Shanghai's financial market.

Investors in the SMC's loans hailed from many nations. Applications for municipal debentures were made either directly to the Council's offices or indirectly through a broker, in which case the SMC paid a small commission to the broker. Though foreign, especially British, investors dominated, a considerable number of Chinese individuals and firms chose to invest in municipal debentures, identifying their business interests and financial security with the success of the SMC. In 1919 there were 423 foreign investors, mainly based in Shanghai or Hong Kong and including many Japanese banks and firms, and 73 Chinese investors.[77] At least 14 of the investors of sums over 10,000 taels were Japanese, indicating the extent to which Japanese interests were tied to the SMC. The Council began to make a concerted effort to attract Chinese investors in 1919 to make up the shortfall in the municipal finances, as only one third of the year's debentures were subscribed. The SMC was struggling to compete with the attractive investment possibilities available abroad as Europe was rebuilt after the First World War.[78] Advertisements were taken out in the Chinese press and the Finance Committee appealed to Chinese bankers and others such as Song Hancheng of the Bank of China and Wu Yiqing, Deputy Postal Commissioner, as well as personal Chinese

---

[74] SMA U1-1-56: Finance Committee, 9 May 1910, quoting Mr Saunders of the Hongkong and Shanghai Bank. On the Bank, see Frank H. H. King, Catherine E. King and David J. S. King, *The History of the Hongkong and Shanghai Banking Corporation* (Cambridge University Press, 1987).

[75] The same information appeared in *Benjamin & Potts' Shanghai Weekly Share Circular*, a supplement to the *Shanghai Mercury* sponsored by a local brokers' firm.

[76] See, for example, *NCH, Weekly Share Supplement*, 5 July 1919, unnumbered: 2nd page.

[77] SMC, *Report for 1919*, 31c–32c.

[78] *NCH*, 13 September 1919.

friends of committee members, on how best to advertise municipal loans to attract Chinese investors.[79] The SMC was confident that the local Chinese establishment would support its investment in the Settlement alongside other nationalities.

Chinese investors responded to the SMC's appeal. The largest Chinese investor that year is listed as the Shanghai Benevolent Industrial Institution,[80] while the largest foreign investor was the Ewo Cotton Spinning and Weaving Company, owned by the British trading giant Jardine, Matheson and Company. Both invested 100,000 taels. Thus Chinese charitable concerns and British hongs alike chose to entrust their wealth to the SMC. In 1920 the largest investment, an unprecedented 201,000 taels, came from the Inspector General of the Chinese Maritime Customs, Sir Francis Aglen, among 469 foreign investors, while of 53 Chinese investors the largest, from the Tung Yih Cotton Mill, was a modest 13,000 taels.[81] The lion's share of investment in the SMC still came from outside China, primarily from Britain, reflecting the broader pattern of investment in China where British capital outweighed other sources up until the eve of the First World War, when it represented 38 per cent of foreign investment.[82] Thereafter, Japanese investment in China gradually outpaced British, but Japanese capital was directed more into heavy industry and the north of China. Shanghai attracted far more British capital than anywhere else in the country: £150 million of the total £200 million invested in China.[83] Most of this was going into the big trading houses, but the SMC was among the recipients as British firms continued to put their capital into its development of the Settlement. Chinese investors often chose to invest elsewhere. From 1927, Chinese contributed millions of dollars to the Nationalist Government in the form of debenture loans, so it may have been nationalism that limited investment in the SMC.[84] Nonetheless, there were always Chinese investors who, like their foreign counterparts, identified their interests with the stability of the International Settlement and trusted the SMC to give them a secure return on their investment.

[79] *Shenbao*, 1 July 1919. SMA U1-1-59: Finance Committee, 26 June 1919.
[80] The Shanghai Benevolent Industrial Institution was one of the largest Chinese free schools in Shanghai. It was a joint Sino-foreign concern, with M. Thomas Zhou, a Chinese man educated at the University of Glasgow, as its President and Arthur de Carle Sowerby, a British naturalist and pillar of the Shanghailander community, as its chairman. On Sowerby, see R. R. Sowerby, *Sowerby of China: Arthur de Carle Sowerby* (Kendal: Titus Wilson and Son, 1956), 38–41.
[81] SMC, *Report for 1920*, 37c–38c.
[82] Osterhammel, 'Britain in China', 159
[83] Wm. Roger Louis, *British Strategy in the Far East, 1919–1939* (Oxford: Clarendon Press, 1971), 163.
[84] However, more Chinese investors were attracted to the SMC's short-term loan issue in 1938 after the retreat of the Chinese national government to Chongqing. SMA U1-1-63: Finance Committee, 17 January 1938.

In 1927 the SMC published figures for the total investment in municipal debentures to that date: Chinese government concerns such as the Customs Service and the Post Office had invested 3,000,000 taels, other Chinese investors provided a further 2,600,000, while the balance of 39,400,000 taels had been invested by foreign residents and institutions.[85] The Council was seeking to illustrate that the wealth of the Settlement was not, as was being claimed by members of the Chinese community, the result of Chinese investment, but rather was built on foreign capital. In arguing this, the Council was claiming for itself and its public works projects the role of creating the environment in which Shanghai flourished, and in such a reading of history there was no room for credit to the city's Chinese entrepreneurs. 'Foreign' investment was recorded in one block, but in reality it was largely British capital, with significant contributions from Japanese investors and smaller amounts from other foreign groups. Nevertheless, in comparison with the dependent colonies of the British empire, which drew almost all their investment from Britain,[86] the SMC was drawing on a more international pool of investment.

Debentures were a global market. In addition to the regular annual silver loans, in 1906, 1920 and 1930 the SMC floated sterling loans in London to fund specific municipal liabilities in the British currency. While ordinary expenditure was made in taels or Chinese dollars, plant and equipment were often purchased in pounds sterling: in 1906 the main sterling liabilities were the Waterworks Company shares and the infrastructure for the new tramway system.[87] Currency fluctuations meant the cost of sterling against the tael could and did rise, so having income in both currencies helped spread the municipal risk. In 1925, local businessman Frederick Sutterle proposed that the SMC issue its own municipal currency, which was seriously considered by the Council before the May Thirtieth Incident put paid to such state-like ambitions.[88]

The SMC issued sterling debentures and compared its rates with those offered in Britain, as would a colonial government, but it also considered what terms were being offered by the governments of the United States, France and Russia, reflecting an international frame of reference. The Finance Committee expressed concern in 1916 that the prevailing exchange rate and availability of attractive rates of interest 'at home' would impact negatively the uptake of municipal loans. Yet local influences could be just as significant. The Chinese

[85] *The Municipal Gazette: Being the Official Organ of the Council for the Foreign Settlement of Shanghai*, 15 July 1927, 237. The Council pointed out that this meant more than 15 times more had been invested by foreigners than by Chinese, and to labour the point it even provided the average per capita investment for the residents of the Settlement: 1,313 taels per foreign resident compared to seven taels invested per Chinese resident.
[86] Havinden and Meredith, *Colonialism and Development*, 174.
[87] SMC, *Report for 1906*, 224.
[88] Zhang (ed.), *Minutes of the SMC*, Vol. 23, 18 March 1925, 30.

government was used as an example for financial practices, such as in 1911 when the Finance Committee decided to adopt an instalment method of loan issues, staggered through the year, as practised in Beijing.[89] In 1928, the collapse of a bubble in the rubber market drove investors to the security of municipal debentures, boosting the Council's borrowing capacity.[90] In this way, imperial, global, national and local factors all influenced the financing of long-term municipal investments to shape Shanghai.

Municipal debentures competed with a limited number of bonds issued by the Chinese government and fixed interest stocks in such local companies as were listed in the *Weekly Share Supplement*, but the rates of interest offered by the SMC were always among the lowest on the market as it was seen as a safe investment. Face value rates for municipal loans ranged from a low of 5 per cent in 1900 to a high of 8 per cent in 1921 and 1922, with a median of 6 per cent. In 1926 municipal debentures were trading near par, while the Chinese Reorganisation Loan issues had to trade at just 60 per cent of their face value due to the low credit rating of the national government.[91] The French *Conseil municipal* was able to offer loans at the same rates as those of the SMC, and thanks to their secure position, underwritten by the Council, municipal utilities companies also offered the same rate. These offerings could not, however, match the low rates offered by the municipal governments of the formal empire such as Calcutta or Bombay, and much less those of England where interest rates of just 3 per cent attracted investors at the turn of the century.[92] The members of the Finance Committee debated the interest rate to set in order to achieve sufficient investment at as attractive rates as possible for the Council, and also because they believed it sent a signal to the public about the security of municipal bonds. The fluctuating interest rates offered reflect both the changing financial security of the SMC and its response to the wider economic and lending climate.

Smaller-scale investment in the SMC was enabled by the Municipal Investment Bank, established in September 1919. The treasurer borrowed the idea from Britain, where the first municipal bank had recently been established in Birmingham.[93] The Bank allowed members of the public to deposit savings with the Council at the beginning of each month, which were converted into debentures twice yearly.[94] It also offered debenture holders the option of

[89] SMA U1-1-57: Finance Committee, 9 February 1911.
[90] Thomas, *Western Capitalism*, 202.
[91] *NCH*, 27 November 1926, referenced in Thomas, *Western Capitalism*, 63.
[92] Thomas, *Western Capitalism*, 59, 62.
[93] J. A. Chandler, *Explaining Local Government: Local Government in Britain since 1800* (Manchester University Press, 2007), 145.
[94] SMC, *Report for 1921*, 34c; *Municipal Gazette*, Vol. XII, No. 650, 6 September 1919, 303; Supplement No. 692, 15 May 1920.

reinvesting accrued interest on municipal loans in the bank. Two years later there were already 760 active depositors, putting a total of 1,729,766 taels at the Council's disposal.[95] As many as 81 per cent of new debenture holders were attracted to invest in municipal loans following initial interest in the Investment Bank, and the bank played an increasing role in the revenues of the SMC. With growing numbers of Shanghai residents and firms tying their capital to the Council, confidence in its fiscal security was high.

In addition to building projects – primarily roads – the SMC invested locally in land, industrial undertakings and local utilities companies. The latter enabled it to exert considerable influence to ensure customers received water, gas, telephone lines, and (after its privatisation) electricity at favourable terms. The low cost of energy ensured by the municipal ownership of the Electricity Department and then influence over the private Power Company after its sale helped fuel the industrial expansion of the city.[96] The Council also invested in local land investment companies, banks and such social establishments as the Country and Race Clubs, giving these institutions the municipal seal of approval and making a sound investment on behalf of ratepayers and Municipal Investment Bank customers. It held silver securities issued by the French *Conseil municipal*, while the latter held SMC debentures in return, tying the fortunes of the two settlements together. Furthermore, the SMC bought into the war loans of the British, French, Russian and American governments during the First World War, to advertise its credentials as standing with the Allies, even as the International Settlement remained neutral. Such investments on the world stage show the prominence of the SMC vis-à-vis other treaty port authorities, which did not have the available capital for anything like such diverse international investments. The SMC was an eminently confident municipal body, financially secure for the majority of its existence, until the disruption of its final decade.

Opposition and Protest

The collection of municipal taxes did not generally pose significant problems for the SMC, suggesting that it enjoyed a strong degree of legitimacy in the eyes of ratepayers, both foreign and Chinese. Prior to the 1911 revolution, the Council's right to charge taxes appears to have gone unchallenged, and it was only as Chinese nationalism grew and the expansion of the municipal government increased the tax burden that opposition emerged. At the turn of the century Chinese who lived in the area that was brought into the Settlement proper by the 1898 extension reportedly paid rates willingly because they saw them as directly linked to the

[95] SMC, *Report for 1921*, 35c.
[96] Ma Changlin et al., *Shanghai gonggong zujie*, 338–58.

provision of police protection, indeed calling the GMR the 'police tax'. As in any polity, however, increases in taxation in the Settlement were unpopular and residents demanded reductions on occasion, such as in 1913 as what had been billed as a temporary rise in GMR from 10 to 12 per cent in 1908 remained in place. The treasurer explained to the Finance Committee that the rise had resulted from the surplus in the ordinary municipal finances falling significantly below the agreed minimum of 200,000 taels, and until a substantial surplus had been maintained he could not sanction a reduction in rates.[97] The higher rate remained and opposition subsided.

From 1919 protests against taxes acquired broader political aims. That year the Council put up the General Municipal and Special Rates by a further two percentage points. The Finance Committee felt there was no other option as the budget for the year showed a deficit due to an increased projected expenditure for all departments on previous years, partly because of the expected return of foreign staff from war service: as for all employers, personnel was one of the Council's greatest expenses.[98] Chinese ratepayers responded with the first organised refusal to pay rates. The SMC believed that explaining the reasons for the increase in the Chinese press would overcome the initial opposition, but quickly discovered that the protesters had wider grievances.[99] For the first time, taxation was linked with calls for representation on the Council.[100] Chinese elite ratepayers were also angry at their exclusion from the growing number of parks and gardens acquired and managed by the SMC, starting with the public gardens on the Bund, but with the addition of the Hongkew (in 1901) and Jessfield (in 1920) parks. The injustice of spending an increasing proportion of municipal revenues, to which Chinese contributed through the rates on an equal basis as foreigners, on facilities from which Chinese were excluded was not lost on Chinese ratepayers. Simmering dissatisfaction with the status quo was given an outlet when Chinese residents were asked to increase their contributions to a municipal authority that disadvantaged them in its allocation of resources. Elite grievances about access to decision-making and public facilities struck a chord with middle-class and poorer ratepayers who felt increases in taxation keenly.

This coordinated refusal to pay rates came in the context of the May Fourth Movement in the wake of protests over China's treatment at the Paris Peace

---

[97] SMA U1-1-57: Finance Committee, 4 December 1913.

[98] SMA U1-1-59: Finance Committee, 28 February 1919.

[99] See, for example, *Shenbao*, 14 August 1919, 17. The newspaper explained the procedure of approval of the increase at the ratepayers' meeting and the rationale behind the decision. A reminder about the increase and an explanation of how it was approved at the ratepayers' meeting was also published the day it came into effect: *Shenbao*, 1 July 1919, 4.

[100] Zhang (ed.), *Minutes of the SMC*, Vol. 20, 16 July 1919, 121.

Conference.[101] Bryna Goodman has traced the process by which a new political consciousness emerged in the early Republican period, as members of local Chinese associations in Shanghai increasingly expected those associations to be representative and democratic.[102] This development pre-dated 1919, but provided the context in which ignoring Chinese interests at the Paris Peace Conference or in the Shanghai International Settlement was seen to be unacceptable. In response to the announced rates increase, Shanghai's new street associations of shopkeepers, formed during the May Fourth protests when shops closed in solidarity with the student's manifestations, met with the Chinese General Chamber of Commerce and insisted that the business community support their opposition to the SMC. Unofficial representatives of the Chamber then called on the chairman of the SMC, Edward Pearce, to seek a resolution to the problem. The Council negotiated, through its secretary, with the Chamber, which agreed, apparently quite readily and despite the position of the street associations, to encourage the payment of the increased rate. The Chamber asked simply that the special levy imposed at the same time as the rate increase to provide back-dated pay for municipal employees away on war service be collected quarterly to spread the financial burden on ratepayers. Meetings with the shopkeepers' associations were less successful, however, as they insisted that no increase should be paid, and the Council decided it had no option but to enforce the collection of the rate and levy. Only Chinese business elites who cooperated with the SMC could influence the Council through peaceful means. Rates collectors met fierce resistance, especially in the Nanking and Honan Road areas, as opposition to representatives of foreign imperialism took hold.[103]

The SMC was falling behind international trends in political representation. Not only were men and women gaining suffrage in the post-war settlements in many western countries, but colonies had begun to link the payment of taxes by indigenous people with the need for at least some political representation. In India, increased government spending was linked by more liberal British officials with the need to include Indians in the decisions over how funds should be spent. As Peter Robb explains, 'as government intervention grew, so too did the representative imperative'.[104] As early as 1882, Lord Ripon's Local Self-government Act gave Indians positions on municipal councils to

---

[101] On the May Fourth Movement and Shanghai, see Tiina Helena Airaksinen, *Love Your Country on Nanjing Road: the British and the May Fourth Movement in Shanghai* (Helsinki: Renvall Institute, 2005).

[102] Bryna Goodman, 'The Politics of Representation in 1918 Shanghai', *Harvard Journal of Asiatic Studies*, Vol. 60, No. 1 (2000), 45–88.

[103] Zhang (ed.), *Minutes of the SMC*, Vol. 20, 13 August 1919, 136.

[104] Peter Robb, *Empire, Identity, and India: Liberalism, Modernity, and the Nation* (New Delhi: Oxford University Press, 2007), 44.

influence spending on infrastructure, public health and education. The measure was intended to secure tolerance of British rule. Such changes were slow to reach the Chinese treaty ports, but from 1919 the British Municipal Council in Tianjin included a Chinese representative (with equal numbers of Chinese and Britons from 1927).[105] Yet there was no such recognition in the SMC of the need to link the growth of municipal spending with political representation for Chinese. By September 1919 the majority of the rates had been collected and the protest over the increase had died away for the time being. It would not, however, be the last time that a rise in taxation triggered calls for political change.

The next major protest the SMC faced over rates followed the May Thirtieth Movement, as the SMC became the primary target of Chinese nationalists following the callous shooting of protestors by its police force. This time, links between the payment of rates and representation arose with a refusal to pay the Special Rate by residents on extra-Settlement roads in 1926. Here the Council was on far shakier ground as it was acting beyond its own jurisdiction, a weakness the strengthening Chinese city authorities sought to exploit by encouraging Chinese residents on outside roads to refuse to pay the Special Rate. While the Council had the right under the waterworks contract to cut the supply of water to those houses which were not paying the rate, in practice it was not possible to isolate the supply for individual houses in large blocks. Initially only 412 houses were failing to pay the Special Rate, of a total 2,300 houses on external roads that were supposed to pay it.[106] With just one tenth of households not paying, the Council decided to take no action. The comparative contribution made by residents of the extra-Settlement roads is shown in Figure 1.5,[107] and it is clear that the income from outside the Settlement limits was insignificant in comparison with the revenues from the GMR.

The numbers refusing to pay grew, however, and the Council was forced to write off increasing amounts of revenue from the Special Rate.[108] With the establishment of the City Government of Greater Shanghai, the Commissioner of Foreign Affairs made repeated and strong protests against the collection of all municipal taxation beyond Settlement limits.[109] The

---

[105] British Municipal Council, Tientsin, *Report for the Year 1936* (Tianjin: Tientsin Press, Ltd, 1937), 25–6. A certain Tsai Shou Chi first represented the Chinese community on the Tianjin Council in 1899 and 1900, and a Chinese representative was included on the Tientsin British Municipal Extension Council from 1912, so the smaller municipality was far ahead of Shanghai. British Municipal Council, Tientsin, *Report for the Year 1938* (Tianjin: Tientsin Press, Ltd, 1939), 13.

[106] Zhang (ed.), *Minutes of the SMC*, Vol. 23, 21 June 1926, 281–2.

[107] Data up to 1930 is converted from taels to dollars at a rate of 0.72 dollars per tael.

[108] Zhang (ed.), *Minutes of the SMC*, Vol. 23, 9 February 1927, 31–2.

[109] Zhang (ed.), *Minutes of the SMC*, Vol. 23, 25 May 1927, 97; SMA U1-1–61: Finance Committee, 10 November 1927.

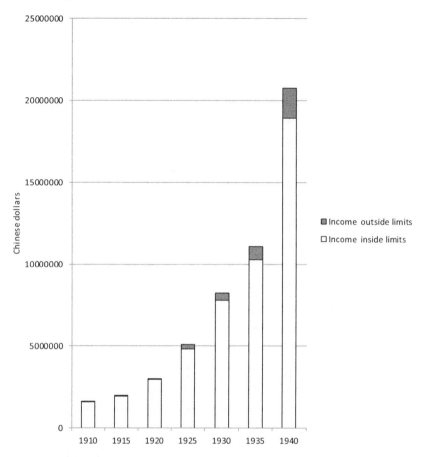

Figure 1.5 Municipal income from rates paid inside and outside the Settlement limits (Chinese dollars).
Source: SMC, *Reports for 1910–1940*.

Council responded by making it clear that residents were only charged the Special Rate on signing a written undertaking that they chose to do so in return for police protection, electric light and water supplies. Although the amount of revenue at stake was small, the SMC was not willing to concede the principle of its right to collect rates outside the Settlement in return for services. It decided that water supplies should be suspended after 15 days' notice to a non-paying resident, but deferred implementing this plan until it received the input of the new Chinese Council members in 1928.[110] The

[110] Zhang (ed.), *Minutes of the SMC*, Vol. 23, 8 June 1927, 450; Vol. 24, 15 February 1928, 20.

Council continued to defer action and the treasurer learned to expect little income from these areas.

The most significant refusal to pay the GMR within the Settlement itself came in 1927, a year of tension and conflict. The Nationalists established themselves as the government of a re-centralised China, from the nearby capital of Nanjing, and set about asserting greater influence throughout the country. The British concession at Hankou, 400 miles west of Shanghai on the Yangtze River, was seized by Nationalist forces in January 1927 and formally retroceded to Chinese control by the subsequent Chen-O'Malley Agreement. Meanwhile Tianjin's British Municipal Council saw the way the wind was blowing and sought to eliminate all discrimination against Chinese from 1927, successfully reforming the municipality sufficiently to ensure that Chinese nationalists shelved preparations for retrocession.[111] The SMC would be a harder nut to crack, but momentum was with the Nationalists.

The local Guomindang actively supported the protest of the Shanghainese against another increase in the rates. These protests took on a much stronger character than those of 1919. This time local associations, including the CRA and the Federation of Street Unions, coordinated a general refusal to pay all rates, rather than ratepayers refusing to pay only the increased amount as before. The 21 members of the CRA committee now took an oath 'to act in accordance with the directions of the Kuomintang', and a mass meeting in support of the protest concluded with shouts of 'Support the Nationalist Government! Long live the Kuomintang!', showing how closely the Nationalist Party was involved in opposition to the Council.[112] The city's Mayor, Huang Fu, praised the protesters, particularly shops that closed rather than pay the rate, for being willing to sacrifice their incomes for the greater good.[113] The CRA indicated that any efforts to employ force in the collection of rates would result in a general strike, the power of which had already been demonstrated during the May Thirtieth Movement in 1925. The SMC's ability to tax and therefore govern was under threat.

Rather than the residents of just a few streets protesting as in 1919, in 1927 the refusal to pay rates was almost universal. Only 40 Chinese households had paid the rates a week into July when the payment was due, compared to the 4,000 that would normally have paid by that point.[114] The Council took comfort from the few Chinese who paid in person at the Revenues Office and refused to take a receipt for fear of discovery by the street unions, seeing them as evidence that the majority of residents were not hostile to the SMC

[111] Bickers, *Britain in China*, 138–9.
[112] *Shanghai Mercury*, 2 July 1927, 6; 4 July 1927, 5.
[113] *Shanghai Mercury*, 25 July 1927, 6.
[114] Zhang (ed.), *Minutes of the SMC*, Vol. 23, 6 July 1927, 464–6.

but rather intimidated by the street unions. Given the attendance of 1,200 supporters of the protest at a mass meeting in the main hall of the Chamber of Commerce on 3 July, however, this was wishful thinking on the part of the Council.[115] The British in India were similarly complacent during the brief lull in political activism of the mid- to late 1920s.[116] Such sanguinity meant the Council refrained from using coercive measures to enforce collection of rates for fear of turning residents against it, despite urging from a Japanese member, Kimiji Fukushima, that the Council should use every means at its disposal to enforce collection so as not to show any sign of weakness. The Council was still ready to use force in cases of violent protest, as shown by the decision to postpone the planned disbandment of the Russian Unit of the SVC,[117] but would not this time be the first to strike. It had learned from its experiences in 1925.

The CRA had learned from the May Thirtieth Movement the power of mass action and galvanising local and international opinion. It took out advertisements in the press, urging residents not to pay their rates and providing the details of lawyers who offered legal advice free of charge should the Council take coercive measures to make them pay.[118] The Mayor reminded members of the CRA that 'The more aggressive the attitude adopted by the Shanghai Municipal Council in this matter, the easier it will be to facilitate the rendition of the Settlement in the future, especially when the whole affair will have been published to the world.'[119] The Council was therefore wise to refrain from the use of force. It, too, knew the value of appealing to international opinion, accepting an offer from the news agency Reuters to cable a memorandum explaining the necessity of the rates increase to America, Europe, Hong Kong, Beijing and Tianjin at a cost of 200 dollars.[120] It also established a committee in England 'for the purpose of counter-acting anti-Council propaganda', made up of former Councillors who returned to Britain. The Council thus showed both its global linkages and the primary importance of London in its worldview, as well as its readiness to use any means at its disposal to preserve its position.

The terms on which the SMC engaged in discussions with senior members of the Chinese community to find a solution to the protest had changed since 1919. This was particularly apparent at a specially convened meeting of the Union Club, where leading Chinese made the underlying causes of the protest

[115] *Shanghai Mercury*, 4 July 1927, 5.
[116] Andrew Muldoon, *Empire, Politics, and the Creation of the 1935 India Act: The Last Act of the Raj* (Farnham: Ashgate, 2009), 39ff.
[117] Zhang (ed.), *Minutes of the SMC*, Vol. 23, 28 June 1927, 457–9.
[118] *Shenbao*, 5 and 7 July 1927.
[119] *Shanghai Mercury*, 25 July 1927, 6.
[120] Zhang (ed.), *Minutes of the SMC*, Vol. 23, 16 July 1927, 471.

clear to the Council's chairman, Stirling Fessenden. They opposed the presence of the Defence Force and the erection of barricades, but primarily they demanded representation for Chinese on the Council in at least equal numbers as foreigners.[121] The SMC remained steadfast in its refusal to negotiate on these terms, however, and in insisting on the need for the increased rate to be paid. It prosecuted prominent businesses, such as the Sincere and Wing On department stores and the Chekiang Industrial Bank, to make an example of them. It also threatened to cut the electricity supply to Chinese newspapers unless they paid their taxes, to force them into an embarrassing position if they still wanted to advocate non-payment of the rates but paid them themselves in order to continue publishing.[122] It was negotiations with members of the Chinese business elite, however, that brought the protest to a close.

Yu Xiaqing (虞洽卿 Yu Ya-ching) was the leading figure in negotiations with the Council. He emphasised the financial hardship that the rate increase imposed on the poorest third of ratepayers, and asked that the SMC allow their shortfall to be made up by wealthier Shanghainese. Satisfied that the question of Chinese representation was being separated from the matter of payment of the rates, the Council agreed to address this matter again after the protest was concluded. The Commercial Federation duly issued an announcement that the increase was justified by the deficit in the municipal budget and should be paid, subject to the SMC addressing the question of greater Chinese representation before the end of the year and undertaking to make no more increases without reference to the Chinese ratepayers. Following the dissemination of this announcement, the SMC's collectors were able to obtain payment and the protest was effectively over.[123]

The nature of the demands made and the confidence with which the CRA manoeuvred opposition to the rate increase in 1927 contrasts sharply with the more respectful terms and modest means employed in 1919. This reflected the altered political landscape in Shanghai and China more broadly, both following the May Thirtieth Incident of 1925 and reflecting the newly confident position of the local Guomindang. In 1919, the Chinese General Chamber of Commerce had supported the SMC and sought to help persuade Chinese residents to pay their rates, but in 1927 the Chamber was one of the main backers of the protest, along with the CRA, which had been established in the wake of the 1919 protest. Nonetheless, the Council was still able to benefit from negotiating with members of the Chinese elite who had more to gain from the continuation of the status quo in Shanghai, where the existence of the

---

[121] Zhang (ed.), *Minutes of the SMC*, Vol. 23, 6 July 1927, 467–9.
[122] The *Shanghai Mercury* mocked the newspapers that paid the rates under this pressure, calling the protest a 'teapot tempest'. *Shanghai Mercury*, 26 July 1927, 5.
[123] Zhang (ed.), *Minutes of the SMC*, Vol. 23, 29 August 1927, 499.

stable municipality had helped them to amass great wealth.[124] The concessions demanded by Chinese businessmen were modifications to the municipal organisation to give them – rather than the mass of Chinese ratepayers – a greater say in the running of the Settlement.

Popular opposition to rates increases from 1919 shows the role played by the SMC in raising political consciousness among a large section of the Shanghai public. Yet the SMC's determination to negotiate only with elites, and the willingness of leading Chinese businessmen to be the sole beneficiaries of any concessions by the colonial authorities, ensured that the protest of ordinary people went unrewarded. The SMC still represented the interests of the wealthy only, but from 1928 this constituency included wealthy Chinese. For most of its existence, the SMC was able to collect rates facing little opposition, and even when it raised the level of taxation, controversial in any society, protests were short-lived and overcome with only small concessions from the Council. The link between municipal services and the payment of rates, as shown most clearly in the payment of the Special Rate beyond the Settlement limits, allowed a foreign-administered Council to tax the Chinese population on what remained Chinese territory. Despite its constitutional weakness, therefore, the SMC enjoyed a surprising degree of legitimacy in the eyes of the rate-paying public.

Financial Difficulties

The SMC had to be self-sufficient in funding its expenditure: all colonies were supposed to be, but the International Settlement could not call on metropolitan support when funds were insufficient. In this it conforms well to Ronald Robinson and John Gallagher's notion of informal empire providing advantageous trading opportunities on the cheap.[125] This meant that when income did not match expenditure, the SMC faced crisis. The treasurer promised in 1913 that when the municipality could afford it, the rates would be reduced, and eventually, after rises in the levels of taxation and consequent protests, the GMR was indeed lowered in 1930 from 16 to 14 per cent. This was possible due to the large surplus resulting from the sale of the Electricity Department, which had been intended for use for capital projects in lieu of borrowing, but the Council bowed to pressure from ratepayers for a reduction in rates. It proved extremely difficult to raise taxes again. Facing a potential budget deficit, the Finance Committee agreed that an increase was needed in December

---

[124] Josephine Fox notes criticism of the Chamber by protestors seeking more far-reaching reforms. Josephine Fox, 'Common Sense in Shanghai: The Shanghai General Chamber of Commerce and Political Legitimacy in Republican China', *History Workshop Journal*, No. 50 (2000), 39.

[125] Gallagher and Robinson, 'The Imperialism of Free Trade', 1–15.

1931. But after the outbreak of the Sino-Japanese conflict the following month the SMC decided against increasing 'the burdens on the community' in this way until the city had had time to recover.[126] The global depression damaged the municipal finances as the price of silver fell drastically (though Shanghai fared better in the 1930s than many colonies that depended on exports). Yet the local instability meant there was never a good time to restore the higher rate, and in 1936 a Staff Economy Committee was formed to identify areas where savings could be made, which included cutting salaries by 8 per cent, amalgamating departments and making staff redundant.[127] Over one million dollars was saved through these measures, but it was not enough.[128] Only in 1937 was the GMR finally returned to 16 per cent: not in time to return the Council to its former strong financial footing before the city was once again plunged into Sino-Japanese warfare.

Chinese opposition to higher rates, in the community and among the Chinese members of Council, was a major reason for the delay. But it was not only Chinese who refused to pay rates to the SMC. In 1928 Japanese residents too were refusing to pay the Special Rate on the grounds that their houses were outside the barbed-wire defences erected during the state of emergency in 1927. In 1934 issue was taken with a Spanish resident of the northern external roads area, Mr E. A. de Garcia, for refusal to pay the Special Rate.[129] The Council was losing the ability to demand taxation in return for services when it had no other justification for doing so, an indication of its generally weakening position in the face of Chinese nationalism and Japanese imperialism.

At the same time, the Chinese members were able to secure greater spending on their own community. In 1934, the year after the last of the five annual instalments of payments from the sale of the Electricity Department, which had compensated for the reduction in rates, municipal discussions centred on whether more could be spent on Chinese education without raising taxes. Chinese members of the Finance Committee like Xu Xinliu argued for retrenchment in other areas to keep within current revenue limits. On the opposite side of the debate, E. F. Harris stated that 'It is an accepted fact that a highly taxed city is more prosperous than one which is lightly taxed; for this reason he supports the proposal for an increase in taxation': an unusual view in a municipality that was generally a bastion of low-tax conservatism.[130] Nevertheless, an increase in spending on education was recommended without

---

[126] See the speech of the then chairman, Brigadier-General Macnaghten, to the annual meeting of ratepayers, as reported in *Municipal Gazette*, Vol. XXV, No. 1362, 14 April 1932, 170.
[127] SMA U1-6–100: Secretary to all departments, 17 December 1936; U1-14–966: SMC Annual Report 1936, 27.
[128] SMA U1-14–966: SMC, *Report for 1936*, 27.
[129] SMA U1-1–62: Finance Committee, 27 November 1934.
[130] SMA U1-1–62: Finance Committee, 4 January 1934.

the accompanying rise in taxation that the treasurer cautioned was required to fund it. The International Settlement was no longer quite such a liberal free-trade, low-government municipality.[131]

Increased municipal investment in Chinese education was a long-held demand of Shanghai's Chinese business community, on which the Council had made small concessions from 1898 on. In the 1930s the cause was primarily championed by the Federation of Street Unions, one of the Council's most vocal opponents and not a body from which it was in the habit of taking suggestions. Justice Richard Feetham, whom the SMC invited to investigate how to improve its relations with the Chinese community, endorsed the proposal, however, and it was one of the few aspects of his report that the Council implemented, thanks to sustained pressure from Chinese councillors.[132] From 1931 a section of the municipal income from Chinese rates was set aside for Chinese secondary education in the Settlement, both directly in Council schools and indirectly through grants-in-aid to existing Chinese schools. In 1934, the Chinese councillors lobbied for the grant to Chinese schools to be increased, and at the same time the Japanese members made a similar claim for Japanese schools.[133] The chairman, A. D. Bell, responded that, if anything, the spending on education should be curtailed due to the current economic difficulties, and H. E. Arnhold (as vice-chairman) added that as both Chinese and Japanese members had fought increases to the rates the previous year, they could not now demand higher expenditure. A compromise was nonetheless reached that increased the grant to both Chinese and Japanese schools, though by less than was demanded, which went a little way to assuage Chinese opposition to the Council. Judicious municipal spending in this way was an important tool in improving the Council's relationship with the Chinese community, while such funding decisions would have an impact on the lives of the Settlement's inhabitants. By 1940, over 4,000 pupils attended the SMC's nine Chinese municipal schools, while thousands more attended the 139 schools supported by municipal grants-in-aid, so many young lives were directly affected by the policy of funding Chinese education.[134]

---

[131] As a point of comparison, see Neil Englehart's discussion of the extent to which Burma can be considered to have been run on liberal principles. Neil A. Englehart, 'Liberal Leviathan or Imperial Outpost? J. S. Furnivall on Colonial Rule in Burma', *Modern Asian Studies*, Vol. 45, No. 4 (2011), 759–90.

[132] Feetham, *Report*, II, 9. On the Feetham Report, see Wang Min, '*Zhong-Ying guanxi biandong beijing xia "Feitang baogao" de chulong ji geqian*' ('In the Background of the Change in Sino-British Relations, the Publication and Running Aground of the "Feetham Report"'), *Lishi yanjiu*, No. 6 (2012), 83–96.

[133] SMA U1-1-62: Finance Committee minutes, 4 January 1934; U1-6-98: H. E. Arnhold to A. D. Bell, 4 January 1934.

[134] SMA U1-16-165: Draft of Economy Committee's interim report on Municipal Public Health Department (1940); SMC, *Report for 1940*, 179, 183.

Alongside the demands of Chinese councillors in such areas as education, the main driver of increased spending in the 1930s was the dramatic rise in the population of the Settlement, with the concomitant demands on resources. The population of the Settlement had grown rapidly throughout its existence, doubling from 500,000 in the 1911 census to one million in 1931. But by 1940, three years into the Sino-Japanese War which sent refugees flooding into the Settlement, the estimated population was 2.5 million, and municipal services struggled to meet the needs of an unsettled population. Although total municipal spending rose dramatically, per capita expenditure fell for the first time, from a peak of 37 taels per resident in 1930 to the equivalent of 22 taels in 1935 and 11 taels in 1940. The weakness of the SMC and its low taxation regime was finally laid bare. Spending on policing grew most markedly, reflecting the defence role of the force, but the proportion of municipal expenditure on most departments remained stable as all areas of municipal activity grew with the increased population (see Figure 1.1). The SMC was also grappling with high inflation, as prices reached ten times their pre-war levels.[135]

Facing insurmountable financial problems, and with its usual sources of loans exhausted, the Council turned for help to the foreign powers, swallowing its long-held pride in the municipality's financial independence. In 1939, the secretary-general, Charles Godfrey Phillips, asked the British and American consuls-general to approach their respective home governments with a request for a loan of one million pounds each, or half that sum if only that were possible. The American referred it to Washington, but warned that he saw 'no prospect whatsoever of any money being voted by Congress for this purpose'.[136] His British counterpart also forwarded the request to London, adding that if the British government could guarantee a bank loan to the SMC this would address its current predicament. The presumed gilt-edged status of the Council's bonds was now being put to the test. Godfrey Phillips described the impossibility of increasing receipts from taxation as the Japanese community now constituted a sufficiently large number of ratepayers to block any attempt to pass a resolution to raise the rates, which he said was now a greater problem than Chinese opposition to increased taxes. The plea for a government loan was not met: the American authorities had little sympathy for the Council's position, while the British government had just declared war on Germany and so had more pressing calls on its budget. The diplomats did negotiate a loan for the Council from the Hongkong and Shanghai Bank, but not enough to prevent it from sliding deeper into debt. In its moment of crisis, the SMC discovered that it could not after all rely on assistance from the imperial metropole.

---

[135] Eleanor Hinder, draft autobiography, Mitchell and Dixson Libraries Manuscripts Collection, Library of New South Wales, Sydney (MLMSS) 770/13/11, 12g.
[136] TNA T160/1142: Sir Archibald Clark Kerr, Ambassador, to Foreign Office, 3 October 1939.

All was not lost, or rather, not yet. The SMC appealed to leading business-men for a loan instead, and secured over $16 million: $8 million from British concerns including $2 million from the (usually philanthropic) Lester Trust, $4 million from Americans including $2 million from the National City Bank of New York in China, $4 million from Chinese investors, and $700,000 from local transport companies.[137] Most of these concerns offered their funds not for investment but to underwrite the SMC, and where public subscribers were found for the loan, the SMC took them and refunded the large investors. So in the final analysis, the SMC was as self-sufficient as the British govern-ment wanted it to be, but only thanks to the local and multinational businesses whose interests it had served for so long. The SMC also finally succeeded in obtaining the (unanimous) approval of the ratepayers to impose a 50 per cent surcharge on the GMR and licence fees.[138] Such was the tenacity of trade in the International Settlement that the economy recovered sufficiently to deliver higher than expected receipts in rates and fees for the SMC from 1940.[139] The higher density of population during the war naturally helped in this, as GMR revenues increased and the number of licences issued, each at a fee, doubled for eating houses and hotels and increased eight-fold for sing-song houses.[140] The Council had to dip into its Reserve Fund to balance the extraordinary budget, but the treasurer, J. W. Morcher, nonetheless reported that 'The year 1942 judged from the financial point of view will rank as one of the most suc-cessful in the long history of Shanghai.'[141] It was to be the Council's last full year, but municipal self-confidence (or at least bluster) was not lost amidst the turmoil brought by war.

Conclusion

The fiscal independence of the Shanghai Municipal Council was a source of municipal pride, ensuring it could ignore imperial injunctions and determine its own policies in shaping the city, but also a source of weakness when financial pressures became too great. As a transnational colonial authority, the Council could not turn to metropolitan governments for support as formal colonies could, as was proved when it finally attempted to seek British and American government support in 1939. The SMC was nonetheless influenced by metro-politan norms, following the organisation of English municipal budgets and increasing spending in line with European trends in the first half of the twen-tieth century, though at much lower levels per capita. Metropolitan influence

---

[137] TNA FO 371/ 24683: British Consul-General A. E. George to HM Ambassador, 29 April 1940.
[138] SMC, *Report for 1940*, 13.
[139] SMC, *Report for 1940*, 267.
[140] SMC, *Report for 1942*, 115–18.
[141] SMC, *Report for 1942*, 109.

was not confined to the formal structures of imperial power but was perhaps greater as a model for a municipality divorced from imperial control.

The secure finances of the SMC reflect its strength through most of its existence. It kept rates as low as possible, among the lowest in the world, and met only occasionally with major protest. Chinese and foreigners paid rates in roughly equal measure. The Council was able to float loans at affordable rates of interest, which were, in most years, oversubscribed and drew on a transnational range of investors, demonstrating their confidence in the long-term stability of the International Settlement. Spending this income on capital investment similarly showed the SMC's own conviction that it was there to stay. It guarded jealously its right to tax the population of the Settlement, protesting strongly at attempts by the Chinese authorities to collect taxes from which, by practice rather than by right, the residents of the Settlement were exempt. In return, there was a surprising degree of acceptance of municipal authority from the disenfranchised Chinese, taxation being linked in the minds of most residents not to representation but to the delivery of services, especially police protection and defence. Of course, the majority of foreign residents, owning or renting property of too little value to qualify for a vote, also had no say in the setting of rates or the allocation of resources. The Council had the legitimacy to govern the Settlement in the eyes of most residents, despite its unrepresentative nature, as it fulfilled its primary function of providing infrastructure for and defending the Settlement. These priorities were reflected in its allocation of funds, though other areas grew in importance.

The municipal finances were intimately bound up in the changing politics of the period. As Chinese nationalism and the strength of the Nationalist government grew in the late 1920s, the Council was forced to take more account of the residents who provided the majority of its revenues. The Council's cash-flow was affected by external factors such as fluctuations in currency exchange rates, war in China and overseas, and the weakness of the Chinese state. Financial challenges could act as catalysts for change, most notably when, in 1919 and especially in 1927, tax rises due to deficits in the municipal finances produced protest movements that resulted in political change in the Settlement. It was the pressure of a popular refusal to pay taxes that forced the SMC to bow to demands for Chinese representation. The SMC and its finances were thus important factors in the development of Chinese political consciousness.

It was only from 1928 that the Settlement's majority Chinese population was able to exert any influence over rates of taxation or how taxes were spent, when Chinese councillors were finally able to contribute to the municipal decision-making process. In doing so, they transformed the nature of transnational colonial governance, ensuring that a more diverse range of interests were represented and that funds were spent in ways that benefited the whole population. But the SMC's increasingly state-like aspirations as it took on a greater governmental role and increased its provision for the public welfare coincided with a time when raising taxes became more difficult, due to the stronger Chinese state, Japanese imperial ambitions, global economic challenges, and local Chinese and Japanese opposition. The transnational voices in the SMC demanded more from it and contributed to its difficulties in meeting those demands.

2 Electing and Serving: The Municipal Councillors and Staff

[The founders of the Shanghai Municipal Council] determined ... to establish an electorate limited to those persons who (according to their ideas) were to be classed as 'respectable' and confine the right to sit on the Council to the much smaller class of those who may perhaps be called 'people of importance'.[1]

The transnational nature of colonialism in Shanghai stemmed from the individuals who directed it. The men who led the Shanghai Municipal Council (SMC) were drawn from the worlds of global business and empire and employed an international staff, many of the most prominent of whom had cosmopolitan backgrounds and networks. They were never intended to be representative of the community they managed. As the Council's legal advisor explained in the quotation above, the franchise was designed to be limited to those deemed respectable, and the men charged with shaping the International Settlement from the Council's chambers were to be those perceived as important. For the Council, the way to establish respectability and importance was by wealth in the form of property. There was no thought that Chinese might qualify as either voters or councillors. A balance of different non-Chinese – 'foreign' – nationalities was maintained on the Council to roughly reflect the size of each nation's business interests in the city. This gave Britons the greatest representation, but ensured that British councillors had to cooperate with people of many other nationalities in determining municipal policy. The International Settlement was thus governed by some of its wealthiest foreign inhabitants: directors of multinational firms whose connections spread far beyond Shanghai and China.

Although imperial rivalry was constant throughout the existence of European empires, the management of the International Settlement at Shanghai depended on cooperation between the different foreign powers and individuals. The SMC

[1] Duncan McNeil, Legal Advisor to the SMC, commenting on Land Regulation XIX, concerning the qualifications to vote for and stand for election to the SMC, on 7 May 1909. McNeil went on, 'I do not know how these objects could have been carried out otherwise than by classification based on (a) ownership of property or (b) amount of income as shown by expenditure.' SMC, *Report for 1909*, 280.

ran the Settlement with limited oversight by the consular body, representing over a dozen signatories of unequal treaties with China. The men who served on the Council were individual Britons, Americans, Germans, Russians and, later, Japanese and, eventually, Chinese, representing not their states but the ratepayers who elected them. This was no 'synarchy', as John King Fairbank described what he perceived as 'a Manchu-Chinese-western rule' of the late Qing: the SMC did not represent joint rule between nations, but the incorporation of different nationalities into one governing institution.[2] It was transnational colonialism.

This executive council was synonymous with the whole organisation that it oversaw. Yet the vast majority of the people involved in the SMC's day-to-day activities were its employees. It was they who shaped the Settlement by policing its streets, implementing public health and hygiene measures, and regulating buildings and businesses. The SMC was one of the largest employers in Shanghai. Senior officers were foreign, the vast majority British, but the middle ranks were drawn from as many as 25 nationalities,[3] and the bulk of the staff was Chinese: as Lucian Pye asserts, the SMC was maintained 'by a civil service that was essentially Chinese'.[4] Over time, the British grip on the control of municipal affairs weakened, as Japanese influence grew and as Chinese nationalism won Chinese representation on the SMC and among the higher ranks of its staff. It was no coincidence that the great turning point of 1928, when Chinese were first admitted as members of the Council, was accompanied by a broadening of opportunity for advancement to senior positions for Chinese (what was called in Shanghai 'localisation', comparable to the 'Indianisation' of the Indian civil service from 1919) and other non-British nationals.

This chapter traces the changing profile of those who governed and shaped the International Settlement and their transnational backgrounds and connections. The Land Regulations, which provided the constitutional foundation of the SMC, established how its members would be chosen, whom it existed to serve – the ratepayers – and the extent and limits of its authority. The electoral process provided for a high turnover of councillors to reflect the expatriate foreign community's transitory nature. As increasing numbers of long-term settlers became involved in municipal affairs, the Council's priorities evolved to take account of their aspirations for the Settlement. The kinds of people on the Council and the clubs in which they mixed show who was shaping municipal policy and how they knew one another.

---

[2] Fairbank, *Trade and Diplomacy on the China Coast*, 465.
[3] Feetham, *Report*, II, 170.
[4] Lucian Pye, 'How China's Nationalism was Shanghaied', *Australian Journal of Chinese Affairs*, No. 29 (1993), 118.

The centre of power shifted in the years up to 1928, as Chinese nationalism – initially as a popular movement and then led by the Guomindang – forced concessions from the SMC. From 1928, the foreign Council members had to consider the views of their new Chinese colleagues, diversifying the influences on municipal policy-making, although Chinese councillors were drawn from similar business and international backgrounds to their foreign counterparts. Exploring their role in the Council writes Chinese back into the story of the governance of the Settlement, which has often been presumed in both the Chinese and the western literatures to have been a solely British or Anglo-American endeavour.[5] Recognising the Chinese contribution to the governance of the Settlement complicates the picture of Chinese nationalism and anti-imperialism, as many of the Chinese members of the Council also belonged to organisations that opposed its very existence.

Tracing the changing constitution of the SMC demonstrates a certain dynamism in this generally conservative governing body that was reflected in greater ambition for what it should achieve in the management of the Settlement. At a time when international organisations such as the League of Nations were urging states to take on a greater role in providing for public welfare, the SMC sought to burnish its reputation for good governance. As the policies of the Council became more ambitious, it required an ever greater staff to implement them. Foreign employees in management positions were typically recruited from Britain. They nonetheless belonged to the worlds of empire and the 'local China coast establishment',[6] benefiting from the opportunities afforded by Britain's imperial intervention in China to make their fortunes. The study of such individuals therefore engages with the body of work on 'colonial lives' and the 'imperial networks' in which officials moved and operated through their 'colonial connections'.[7] The Shanghai example shows that such movement was far from being confined only to the formal British empire and demonstrates the extent to which the treaty ports were linked to formal colonies. The different nationalities employed in Shanghai brought a wide range of experiences and influences to the SMC. The autonomy of the Settlement from Chinese or foreign imperial oversight depended on its international status, which became less a rhetorical claim and more a reality as Chinese ratepayers, councillors and employees increasingly influenced its work. Understanding who determined and implemented municipal governance in Shanghai's International Settlement

---

[5] Bickers, *Britain in China*; Clifford, *Spoilt Children of Empire*; Ma Changlin et al., *Shanghai gonggong zujie*.

[6] Bickers, *Scramble for China*, 366.

[7] David Lambert and Alan Lester (eds.), *Colonial Lives across the British Empire: Imperial Careering in the Long Nineteenth Century* (Cambridge University Press, 2006); Alan Lester, *Imperial Networks: Creating Identities in Nineteenth-Century South Africa and Britain* (London: Routledge, 2001); Laidlaw, *Colonial Connections*.

is therefore crucial to appreciating the history of this global city and the transnational nature of colonialism in China.

Election to the Council

The population of Shanghai doubled from 1.3 million in 1910 to 2.6 million in 1927, and almost half of the city's inhabitants lived in the International Settlement. As the population grew, so did the number of nationalities represented. In 1920, over 35 nationalities were recorded in the Settlement, from Armenians to Venezuelans, rising to 45 nationalities over the following decade, making Shanghai a truly global city.[8] The 'foreign' population numbered 23,000 in 1920. The most numerous group were Japanese at over 10,000 residents, followed by more than 5,000 British. There were 2,000 Americans; the Indian, Portuguese (including Macanese) and Russian communities were each 1,000 strong; and individuals from other countries numbered between one and a few hundred. Only New York and Buenos Aires had a comparably cosmopolitan mix of nationalities. The Chinese population within the Settlement dwarfed the foreign with 760,000 Chinese residents, though over 75 per cent of them were, like their foreign neighbours, comparatively recent arrivals.[9] People from neighbouring provinces and all over the country came to exploit the opportunities on offer in the burgeoning economy of the Settlement and the surrounding area.

The SMC, however, did not reflect the city's diversity for most of its existence. The Land Regulations, effectively the constitution for the International Settlement, determined that the Council would consist of between five and nine members, a maximum that did not increase from 1866 until 1928. Seats were unofficially reserved for certain nationalities, though the number of each rested on precedent not statute and evolved to reflect the dominant foreign powers in different periods. Between 1871 and 1914 there were usually seven Britons, one German, and one American. The *North-China Herald*, the weekly digest of the influential *North-China Daily News* favoured by the British community, claimed this was 'strictly representative of the ratepayers according to their numbers',[10] though in the second half of this period the proportion of Americans and Japanese in the city increased.

The established pattern of Council membership began to change in response to global developments: in the 1915 election, the first since the outbreak of the First World War, the German member came last due to the

---

[8] SMC, *Report for 1920*, 271a–272a; *Report for 1930*, 333.

[9] SMC, *Report for 1920*, 271a–272a; Marie-Claire Bergère, *The Golden Age of the Chinese Bourgeoisie* (Cambridge University Press, 1989), 100.

[10] *NCH*, 29 January 1902, 165.

strength of anti-German feeling among the ratepayers.[11] The British diplomats hoped the German would be replaced by a Japanese member, but a
Russian count was elected to the council instead. The Japanese Minister
to China, Eki Hioki, wrote to his British counterpart Sir John Jordan
to express his 'feeling of deep affliction' at the result: 'Our interest in
Shanghai is incomparably greater than that of Russia and the fact the
British voters had elected a Russian instead of a Japanese at this juncture
would be regarded as the extreme of ingratitude and unkindness on the
part of the subjects of our esteemed ally.'[12] Hioki predicted that it would
encourage sympathy for Germany against Britain in the war, and Jordan
took this threat seriously, but confided to Sir Everard Fraser, the British
consul-general in Shanghai, that 'we could not properly have gone further
than we did' to persuade the ratepayers to vote for the Japanese candidate
in British national interests and 'they have exercised their rights as free
voters to reject' the advice.[13] Fearing that Japan might exercise its right
under the Treaty of Shimonseki to open its own settlement at Shanghai,
the SMC agreed to co-opt the Japanese candidate onto the Council later
that year to replace a retiring British member, under British diplomatic
pressure and with the explicit intention of improving relations with the
Japanese community.[14]

The Russian left in 1918 in the wake of the Russian Revolution and from
1919 there were usually two Americans on the Council.[15] The Japanese membership was increased to two in 1927 and from the landmark year of 1928 three
and then, from 1930, five Chinese members were finally admitted, matched by
five Britons. (The Land Regulations were not updated to reflect the increased
size of the Council until 1936, showing that they could be ignored for several
years when politically expedient.[16]) British dominance of the Council membership thus declined slightly in the twentieth century until parity was reached by
Chinese members, numerically if not in actual influence.

The franchise was based on property: foreigners who had paid all taxes owed
and who owned land worth 500 taels or more or who paid rent of the same
value each year could vote. The qualifying threshold remained unchanged from
1866, so as land values rose, the numbers of eligible voters increased from a
few hundred to a couple of thousand, but still only 8 per cent of the foreign
population were eligible in 1919. The proportion rose to almost 20 per cent

[11] Robert Bickers, *Getting Stuck in for Shanghai: Putting the Kibosh on the Kaiser from the Bund* (Melbourne: Penguin, 2014), 54.
[12] TNA FO 800/31/227, 23 January 1915.
[13] TNA FO 800/31/227, 24 January 1915.
[14] Zhang (ed.), *Minutes of SMC*, Vol. 19, 28 July 1915, 285.
[15] Feetham, *Report*, II, 166; SMC, *Reports*, 1871–1927.
[16] SMA U1-14–966: SMC, *Report for 1936*, 26.

of Britons; more than half of the voters were British.[17] Many ratepayers held multiple votes by virtue of being representatives of property-owning firms as well as owning a qualifying amount of property in their own right.[18] The SMC therefore represented not the general views of the local community but those of a small number of wealthy foreign businessmen.

To stand for election to the Council, ratepayers had to own land requiring them to pay at least 50 taels per year in land tax or 1,200 taels in rent per year. Just 3 per cent of the foreign population met this requirement: only those with the income of company directors and the like could aspire to a seat on the Council. Similar property-based systems governed municipal franchises in Britain and its settler empire, so Shanghai was not unique. What was more unusual was the transient nature of many of those qualified to stand for election as individuals circulated through various ports and financial centres. In practice, if a firm owned or rented sufficient property in the Settlement, its director could stand for election, bending the rules further in favour of the largest companies.[19]

The Land Regulations set out the form to be taken by annual municipal elections: any two ratepayers qualifying to vote could nominate a candidate, and if more than nine were nominated, ratepayers would vote for their preferred candidates. Those with the most votes would be duly elected. If fewer than five candidates were nominated, a meeting would be held to elect further members.[20] Between 1900 and 1940, only 24 elections were contested; in 16 years the number of candidates was equal to or fewer than the number of seats, so members were nominated unopposed or co-opted to the Council. The *North-China Herald* instructed its readers how to vote: eligible ratepayers should go to the Council's Board Room and strike out the names of any candidate for whom they did not wish to vote, leaving nine names or fewer.[21] It was not a secret ballot – ratepayers signed their names – though only the poll clerks saw the ballot papers.

A cartoon in *The Rattle* in 1901 mocks the election process and especially a candidate who had the audacity to campaign, which was deemed gauche in turn-of-the-century Shanghai (Figure 2.1). The candidates are depicted

[17] Bickers, *Empire Made Me*, 51, 360, n. 26.
[18] TNA T 160/1142/16454/1: Stirling Fessenden, Chairman SMC, to G. de Rossi, Senior Consul, Shanghai, 4 September 1925.
[19] SMA U1-6-126: Fessenden to Charles Maguire, 29 December 1931.
[20] Land Regulations, Article XVIII, A. M. Kotenev, *Shanghai: Its Mixed Court and Council* (Shanghai: North-China Daily News and Herald, 1925), 563–4.
[21] *NCH*, 23 January 1901, 142. In later years polling stations, supervised by officers of the Revenue Office, were established at prominent properties in the Settlement: in 1920, for example, there were two, one at Sassoon House, part of the Cathay Hotel on the Bund, and one in the Hongkong and Shanghai Bank's Hongkew branch at 9 Broadway. SMC, *Report for 1920*, 44c.

Figure 2.1 *Rattle* cartoon of campaigning candidates for the municipal election of 1901. The caption reads, 'Never too proud to take a hint, our City Fathers propose in future to proclaim their "platforms" to the public before the general election.'
Source: *The Rattle*, 20 March 1901.

wearing sandwich boards promising free services according to the candidate's line of business, so Charles Ede of the Union Insurance Society of Canton offers 'free risks'; Silas Hardoon, one of the city's biggest property investors, advertises 'free rents'; and E. A. Hewitt of the Peninsular and Orient Shipping Company promises 'free transport'. It was these men's business connections that ensured their influence over municipal affairs, and all the main areas of business in Shanghai were represented. That year there were two more candidates than seats, one of whom was the 'pushful' candidate, judged inexperienced and ignorant of municipal process, while the other was an American who lost out to the incumbent of the unofficially American seat. In reality there was little contest.

In 1902 the candidates included seven Britons, one American and one German (all of whom were elected), as well as Swiss and Japanese candidates who failed to win election. The Swiss and Japanese had little chance of success given the established pattern of seven Britons, one American and one German, but their candidacy shows transnational engagement with the electoral process even though it favoured the traditional foreign powers. There was little difference in the number of votes cast for the nine successful candidates, each gaining between 202 and 259 votes apiece.[22] This pattern of limited contestation continued into the 1920s, each year the *Herald* providing its editorial view of who were the strongest candidates for election, which was generally a good predictor of electoral success.

The demands on Council members' time (estimated at four hours per day by 1931),[23] combined with general apathy, often meant that insufficient numbers of businessmen were willing to serve – unpaid – on the SMC. Elections were thus sometimes less a competition between candidates than a struggle to persuade enough candidates to stand. This reflected a wider apolitical atmosphere among the foreign community in Shanghai. Ratepayers' reluctance to turn out to the annual ratepayers' meeting meant that the meetings were not always quorate, stymieing efforts to pass new bylaws on more than one occasion. Even in 1927, when civil war threatened Shanghai and great constitutional changes were taking place, only 547 attended the foreign ratepayers' meeting out of a possible 2,368.[24]

From 1928, however, in the context of a Nationalist government of China and Chinese representation on the Council, municipal affairs took on new importance and more British candidates stood for election. Campaigning became acceptable as candidates competed in their claims to serve the interests of British ratepayers, and the issues debated reflected the preoccupations of ratepayers. Their concerns were largely local issues, ranging from good governance to the degree to which Chinese should influence the municipality. In 1930, for example, Harry Arnhold declared that he stood for 'efficiency, economy, and the maintenance of the authority of the SMC in the face of the continued attempts to undermine the same'.[25] Yet alongside this apparently uncompromising line, Arnhold also advocated 'a better understanding and ... closer cooperation between the Foreign and Chinese ratepayers'. Arnhold lost his seat, possibly due to insinuations by fellow councillor A. D. Bell that under Arnhold's chairmanship there was unprecedented 'acrimony' in SMC meetings as Arnhold acted alone rather than consulting the Council.[26] Bell called for less secrecy in municipal business, a popular promise that recurred in other election campaigns as the Council continued to refuse the entry of the press or public into its chambers.[27] Otherwise Bell's manifesto was practical, advocating more improvements in public works, particularly refuse disposal, and the immediate sale of the Telephone Company, to the profit of the SMC.[28] Bell won re-election, defeating, among others, P. W. Massey, who advocated the

[22] *NCH*, 29 January 1902, 160.
[23] Our Correspondent, 'Shanghai Municipal Elections', *The Times*, 9 March 1931, 11.
[24] Manley O. Hudson, 'International Problems at Shanghai', *Foreign Affairs*, October 1927.
[25] *Shanghai Times*, 28 February 1930, 4.
[26] *Shanghai Times*, 28 February 1930, 4.
[27] *Municipal Gazette*, 17 April 1930, 152.
[28] *North-China Daily News* (*NCDN*), 28 February 1930.

continued municipal control of the Telephone Company and the more extensive employment of Chinese on the municipal staff.[29] Norman Leslie similarly missed out on a seat, partly because of his statement favouring 'friendly
cooperation with our neighbours'.[30] Many Shanghailanders found even the
conservative SMC too liberal, especially following the admission of Chinese
councillors.

Ranald McDonald, a British lawyer who made an impassioned speech
against admitting more Chinese Council members at the subsequent ratepayers' meeting, wrote to the British-owned *Shanghai Times* listing his preferred
candidates based principally on their stance on this issue.[31] He claimed to speak
for the rest of the British community, and four of his five choices were indeed
elected. The SMC was thus beholden to a largely reactionary electorate.[32] As
was common, the American candidates in 1930, V. G. Lyman and Clifford
French, were elected without campaigning as they were the only two of their
countrymen standing for the two seats unofficially reserved for Americans.[33]
The debates in the press concerned only the British candidates, and it was they
who set the tone of the Council.

The Land Regulations provided checks on the SMC's authority from both
the foreign rate-paying community, to which the SMC was answerable through
the annual meetings, and the consular body. Each spring, ratepayers held their
elected representatives to account at the ratepayers' meeting, on occasion
quoting back to the councillors the promises they had made during the election. S. H. Peek, Municipal Land Commissioner, proposed an amendment in
1936 requiring the Council to improve housing in the Settlement, noting that
three councillors had promised to tackle overcrowding.[34] He suggested that
the Council only acted with 'a little jogging from the outside', but the chairman insisted that the councillors were seeking to deliver their pledges and the
amendment was watered down to require investigation of the problem only,

---

[29] *Shanghai Times*, 28 February 1930, 4. Massey was successful in standing for office in 1923–
1926, in 1929, and again 1932–1934.

[30] *Shanghai Times*, 28 February 1930, 4. Leslie was elected the following year.

[31] *Shanghai Times*, 4 March 1930, 7.

[32] Two years later, Arthur de Sowerby, the editor of the *China Journal* and leading member of
the Shanghai Fascisti and British Residents' Association, stood (unsuccessfully) for election
in 1932 on a platform of representing Shanghailander rights against the SMC and lobbying
against the reform of extraterritoriality. *NCH*, 15 March 1932, 403; 28 December 1932, 498,
referenced in Bickers, 'Shanghailanders', 199.

[33] Lyman was an expatriate who worked for Standard Oil, while French was Vice-President of
Andersen, Meyer and Company, a firm established by the Dane Vilhelm Meyer and incorpo-
rated in New York, representing General Electric in China. Christopher Bo Bramsen, *Open
Doors: Vilhelm Meyer and the Establishment of General Electric in China* (Richmond: Curzon
Press, 2001), 183.

[34] SMA U1-14–966: SMC, *Report for 1936*, 20–4.

which was already under way. Individual ratepayers often spoke at length at these meetings in opposition to or defence of policy proposals and amendments, but the Council usually got its way.

The foreign consuls were responsible for setting the date of the annual and special ratepayers' meetings and both the consuls and qualifying ratepayers had to approve bylaws before they could be enforced. In the nineteenth century, the ratepayers' meetings were usually held in the British consulate with the consul in the chair. Yet the SMC was generally free from consular interference: consuls were kept informed of municipal decisions and wrote to the Council chairman highlighting issues or offering recommendations, but policies were decided and implemented by the Council. From 1896 ratepayers' meetings were held in the town hall (Figure 2.2) and later in the administration building (Figure 2.3), signalling greater independence from the British consul. Indeed, ratepayers' meetings were compared to town hall meetings in New England, demonstrating that influence came from both sides of the Atlantic.[35]

The Foreign Office in London intervened in 1922 to attempt to ensure that a British candidate was elected to the chair. Word reached Whitehall that the then chairman, H. G. Simms, did not intend to stand for re-election. Believing that Simms's employer, Charles Ede – himself a former member of the SMC but now a property developer in Hong Kong and member of the colony's Legislative Council – was responsible for Simms stepping down, the Foreign Office demanded that Ede be asked to reconsider 'in British interests'.[36] In fact, Simms's decision to leave Shanghai was his own, so the Foreign Office cast around for other British candidates and even asked the British Minister in Beijing to travel to Shanghai and use his influence to persuade a suitable man to stand.[37] Finally, in the absence of other appropriate and willing candidates, the American Stirling Fessenden was approved as the next best thing to a British chairman. Such instances of interference from London were rare, and they demonstrate both the importance placed on ensuring British interests predominated in municipal affairs but also the limited effect of imperial influence.[38] In 1932, the chairman criticised the indiscretion of whichever Council member or officer had allowed the British

[35] *China Weekly Review*, 4 December 1926, 8; Wasserstrom, 'Questioning the Modernity of the Model Settlement', 128.

[36] TNA FO 228/3176: Foreign Office to Hong Kong, 13 February 1922.

[37] TNA FO 228/3176: Garstin, Shanghai, to British Minister, Beijing, 30 March 1922. Garstin also attempted to persuade alternative candidates to the incumbent British council members not to stand in 1929 and 1930 so as not to split the British vote and risk the informal quota of five Britons failing to be met. Bickers, 'Changing Shanghai's "Mind": Publicity, Reform and the British in Shanghai, 1928–1931', China Society lecture, 20 March 1991, 14.

[38] Anxiety over the increasing Chinese nationalism aroused by the May Fourth Movement may have been behind the Foreign Office's interference in 1922.

Figure 2.2 The Town Hall from 1896 to 1922, Nanjing Road.
Source: *Shanghai by Night and Day* (Shanghai: Shanghai Mercury, 1902),
image courtesy of the *Virtual Cities Project*, Institut d'Asie Orientale, Lyon.

Figure 2.3 The administration building, 209 Kiangse (Jiangxi) Road, erected
in 1921.
Source: *Shanghai of To-day. A Souvenir Album of Thirty-Eight Vandyke
Prints of the 'Model Settlement'* (Shanghai: Kelly and Walsh, 1927), cover,
image courtesy of the *Virtual Cities Project*, Institut d'Asie Orientale, Lyon.

consul-general to hear of a decision taken by the Council, emphasising the
need for confidentiality.[39] It transpired that Fessenden had told the American
consul-general, but the chairman believed that loyalty to the transnational
Council should trump national ties.

[39] Zhang (ed.), *Minutes of SMC*, Vol. 22, 19 February 1932, 221.

Chinese Representation

Chinese representation had been mooted from the earliest days of the International Settlement. In 1863, the foreign ministers in Beijing agreed that 'there shall be a Chinese element in the municipal system to whom reference shall be made and assent obtained to any measure affecting the Chinese residents.'[40] They recognised that the character of the Settlement had changed from that initially envisaged for the first foreign settlements in Shanghai, in which it was not expected many Chinese would live. Yet consultation with the Daotai over decisions concerning the Chinese residents, particularly taxation, was the only concession to the principle of Chinese representation. By contrast, the French Land Regulations allowed for Chinese representation on the *Conseil municipal* in Shanghai; Hong Kong's first Chinese member of the Legislative Council was appointed in 1880; while the Legislative Council in Singapore included Chinese representatives from 1869.[41] Similarly, no racial bar existed in Indian municipalities: only ratepayers qualified by property or income could vote in Delhi's municipal elections, but Indians were not excluded.[42] These bodies lacked the autonomy of the SMC, however, being subordinate to the authority of the French consul-general, the Governor, or the colonial Indian government. In the International Settlement, real administrative control was at stake and the battle for Chinese representation would be hard-won.

The first Chinese calls for representation in the Settlement came in December 1905 during the Mixed Court riots. The protestors, numbering in their thousands and led by Guangdong merchants, demanded a Chinese councillor be installed on the SMC. The mistreatment of a woman from Guangdong by the Shanghai Municipal Police (SMP) was the catalyst for expressing a new anti-imperial nationalism, targeting the SMC. The British consul intervened to have the widow released by the SMP, but the protests continued until a wave of violence was met with a fierce police crackdown. In the wake of the riots, the

---

[40] Feetham, *Report*, I, 113. The account of the history of Chinese representation in the Settlement is drawn largely from this chapter (VI) of Feetham's report. The South African judge made a detailed study of the subject, and while he was broadly sympathetic to the Council, he was critical of the failure to give representation to the Settlement's Chinese and implied, with justification, that the problems with the Settlement that he had been invited to investigate stemmed in part from this failure.

[41] The first Chinese member of Hong Kong's Executive Council, however, did not take his seat until 1926. G. B. Endacott, *Government and People in Hong Kong, 1841–1962: A Constitutional History* (Hong Kong University Press, 1964), 89–96; Liu Shuyong, 'Hong Kong: A Survey of Its Political and Economic Development over the Past 150 Years', *China Quarterly*, No. 151 (1997), 584–5; C. M. Turnbull, *A History of Modern Singapore, 1819–2005* (Singapore University Press, 2009), 114.

[42] Narayani Gupta, *Delhi Between Two Empires 1802–1931: Society, Government and Urban Growth* (Delhi: Oxford University Press, 1981), 119.

Chinese guilds suggested that similar problems could be averted in future if they were given the opportunity of putting the views of the Chinese community to the Council before its actions produced such outrage. Yu Xiaqing, a comprador in the Ningbo Guild who would become the most influential Chinese businessman in the city, led the approach to the SMC.[43] Yu informed Frederick Anderson, Council chairman, that the guilds had decided to elect seven men to form an Executive Committee of the 40-strong Consulting Committee of Chinese Merchants, to represent their interests to the SMC. Five of the members of the Executive Committee were to be from Zhejiang (Yu's native province), one from Guangdong and one from Jiangsu, thus representing the most important native place associations in Shanghai. The proposal fell short of actual Chinese representation on the Council, but it was a compromise that would have given a platform to Chinese in the governance of the Settlement.

Anderson defended the proposal against the doubts expressed by other Council members and replied to Yu welcoming the initiative. He was assured that the Consulting Committee was free of Chinese officials and would not interfere with the running of the Settlement. Yet the foreign ratepayers rejected the proposal, fearing 'undue influence and intervention in the affairs of the Foreign Settlement'.[44] The foreign community was determined that the Settlement was fundamentally foreign, with no place for Chinese. Transnational colonialism meant authority shared among foreign sojourners but not with Chinese.

The question of Chinese representation re-emerged in the context of bargaining for further extensions to the Settlement boundaries in 1909.[45] The following year the SMC recognised 14 guilds as representing Chinese opinion, and consulted some or all of them when it wanted input on decisions affecting Chinese residents directly.[46] In 1915 a more formal Chinese Advisory Board representing the guilds and local Chinese authorities was approved by the foreign ratepayers in return for an extension to the Settlement, but failed to materialise when no extension was agreed.[47] The French Concession had agreed such a deal with the Chinese authorities the previous year, gaining a large extension to the concession in return for welcoming Chinese members to the *Conseil municipal*. The Chinese rarely actually attended its meetings, however, and the power of the French consul-general over the concession made Chinese representation largely symbolic.

A Chinese Advisory Committee was finally established in the International Settlement in 1919 with the unanimous approval of the ratepayers, who

[43] Bergère, *Golden Age*, 142–4, 194–5.
[44] SMC, *Report for 1906*, 392–5.
[45] Zhang (ed.), *Minutes of SMC*, Vol. 17, 24 March 1909, 230.
[46] Bryna Goodman, *Native Place, City and Nation: Regional Networks and Identities in Shanghai, 1853–1937* (Berkeley, CA: University of California Press, 1995), 153.
[47] Feetham, *Report*, I, 124.

recognised the need to make some concessions to Chinese public opinion in the wake of the surge of nationalism in the May Fourth Movement.[48] (The proposal by Edward S. Little, a British former missionary and ex-Council member of unusually liberal bent, that three Chinese members be admitted to the Council was, however, roundly defeated. One reason given was that admitting Chinese would bring 'squeeze' – corruption – into the supposedly clean SMC.)[49] The creation of the Advisory Committee was cautiously welcomed by the major newspaper *Shenbao*, which covered the meetings of the Chinese Advisory Committee in detail, suggesting strong interest in the participation in municipal affairs among its readers.[50] At the same time, discussions of the need for genuine Chinese representation appeared regularly in *Shenbao* from 1919 and some guilds objected to the idea that the Chamber of Commerce could represent the whole community.[51] The Chinese Ratepayers' Association (CRA), which led the campaign for Chinese representation on the Council, was established in part to select the five members of the Committee, who met the Council for the first time in May 1921. Yet the Committee had little impact, the SMC failing to refer questions to it, and it subsequently resigned in 1925 over the Council's failure to respond adequately to the May Thirtieth Incident.

The May Thirtieth Incident, when the SMP fired fatally on Chinese protestors (described in the next chapter), sparked the largest nationalist movement yet seen in China. The Council's response was stubborn and inadequate, failing to admit that its police officers had acted wrongly and attempting to curb the protest movement. As a result, calls for true Chinese representation on the Council grew to an unavoidable clamour, which reached the ears of the Foreign Office and the floor of the House of Commons.[52] In the face of imperial and local pressure, the foreign community finally resolved to admit Chinese members at the annual meeting of ratepayers in 1926. It took two more years for the details to be worked out between the Council and the CRA and the negotiations were reported avidly in *Shenbao*, as Chinese ratepayers awaited their first opportunity to contribute to the running of the Settlement.[53]

---

[48] On the events that led to the establishment of the Chinese Advisory Committee, see Bryna Goodman, 'Being Public: The Politics of Representation in 1918 Shanghai', *Harvard Journal of Asiatic Studies*, Vol. 60, No. 1 (2000), 45–88.

[49] SMA U1-16-10: 'Chinese representation on the Shanghai Municipal Council', 11.

[50] *Shenbao*, 3 April 1921, 10; 2 May 1920, 10; 9, 12 and 19 February 1921, 10 of each issue; 14 May 1921, 11.

[51] 'Hua shang yaoqiu shiminquan ji' ('An Account of the Demand of Chinese Merchants for Municipal Democratic Rights'), *Shenbao*, 2 December 1919, 10. See also 3 April 1921, 10; 2, 23 and 28 May 1923, 13 of each issue. On the guilds' stance, see Goodman, *Native Place*, 50.

[52] Clifford, *Spoilt Children of Empire*, 151 and *passim*; HC Deb 22 June 1925, 23 February 1927, 21 March 1927.

[53] *Shenbao*, 7 July 1927, 14; 27 August 1927, 14; 23 November 1927, 13 and 10 November 1927, 1 of supplement.

The CRA discussed who should represent the community, to what extent the Chinese government should be represented, and how to ensure Chinese interests were appropriately represented in municipal committees as well as the full Council meetings, demonstrating a sincere desire to make the new arrangement work for the interests that the association represented.[54] On the other hand, an opinion piece put the advent of Chinese councillors in the context of the May Fourth Movement, arguing that it could not satisfy Chinese calls to control the Settlement.[55]

A protest over the municipal rates in 1927 (see previous chapter) over the slowness of progress on the issue of Chinese representation finally forced the SMC to concede greater influence for Chinese within the municipal apparatus. In the context of the retrocession of the British concession at Hankou to Chinese control in February, the SMC belatedly recognised the need to compromise. Warning the Chinese negotiators that a proposal to elect more Chinese councillors than the three already approved would not be accepted by the foreign ratepayers at their annual meeting, which was necessary for such constitutional change to be made, the Council instead proposed that a further six Chinese representatives should join municipal committees. Crucially, committee members could be appointed without reference to the foreign ratepayers. Yu Xiaqing agreed to the plan, undertaking to ensure that the three Council members and six committee members were nominated and took their seats, on the condition that the SMC would increase the number of Chinese councillors further should the experiment prove successful. It was on these terms that the first Chinese finally joined the Council in 1928.

This was a sea-change in the governance of the Settlement and represented a major victory for those Chinese who would now influence municipal affairs: the business elite. As Jeffrey Wasserstrom notes, this was 'activist citizenship' in the parlance of political science: Chinese were actively participating in the democratic process as citizens.[56] Wasserstrom stresses the limits of this citizenship, confined as it was to a wealthy few, to demonstrate that the Settlement cannot be seen as modern. The SMC was certainly no paragon of enlightened governance, but Chinese ratepayers now had representatives on the Council like other nationalities. The fact that Chinese could only select three, later five, members was comparable to the defined numbers of American, British and Japanese councillors, reflecting not the size of the various national populations in the Settlement but their propertied wealth. It was an inequality based now almost entirely on class and not race.

[54] Shenbao, 9 February 1927.
[55] Shenbao, 10 November 1927, 1 of supplement. See also a similar opinion expressed on 13 January 1928, 13.
[56] Wasserstrom, 'Questioning the Modernity of the Model Settlement', 123.

In 1930 the SMC resolved to keep its word to increase the number of Chinese Council members from three to five.[57] First, the foreign ratepayers had to be convinced, so Chairman Ernest Macnaghten made a plea at the annual meeting, quoting Fessenden's uncharacteristically tactful praise the year before:

> Our Chinese colleagues have shown themselves to be men of character, ability, breadth of view and energy, who have sincerely endeavoured to promote harmony and good will in the solution of many difficult and perplexing problems regarding which the Chinese and Foreign communities do not always see eye to eye.

Macnaghten added his own qualified support:

> The cooperation of the Chinese members during the past year has been as full and complete as is possible in this international community, where national interests and points of view in the natural course of things must at times appear almost irreconcilable.[58]

This was the reality of transnational colonialism: cooperation in the face of intractable differences.

Macnaghten argued optimistically that keeping to the planned increase of Chinese members voluntarily would promote 'amicable Sino-foreign relations' for the benefit of the Settlement. Others disagreed: Ranald McDonald spoke for over half an hour on the folly of admitting more 'Chinese sphinxes' whose political views were unknown to the Council. Calling the proposal a 'dangerous and insidious change' he argued that the Settlement was and always had been foreign; to pass the resolution 'would appear to be an act of fawning sycophancy' with repercussions throughout China and 'all over the world'; and it would inevitably lead to more Chinese councillors within a year or two 'and you will thus have irretrievably sold the past and betrayed not merely those now in Shanghai but posterity'.[59] McDonald contrasted the standard of governance in the Chinese city unfavourably with the Settlement's administration as evidence that Chinese were unable to contribute positively to the Council. He also stirred up the defensive feelings of the proudly independent Shanghailanders against alleged interference from the Foreign Office, Consular Body and Diplomatic Body, which Macnaghten denied. McDonald evoked all the reasons for which Shanghai's British community had so long opposed Chinese representation. They were still persuasive in 1930: the resolution was rejected and the Council was forced to hold a special meeting to try

---

[57] '[I]n accord with a tacit understanding between the foreign and Chinese communities at the time the three Chinese members first took their seats upon the Council that with the full cooperation of the Chinese the number of Chinese members, in the ordinary course of events, would be increased.' SMC, *Report for 1930*, 39.

[58] *Municipal Gazette*, 147, 17 April 1930. The foreign members of council publically praised their Chinese colleagues while complaining about them in private. Bickers, 'Changing Shanghai's "Mind"', 11.

[59] *Municipal Gazette*, 150, 17 April 1930.

again, lobbying intensely and even laying on special buses to bring ratepayers to the meeting during a strike.[60] With 1,668 votes represented by 1,226 ratepayers at the special meeting (compared with only 252 ratepayers at the previous meeting), the motion to admit the additional two Chinese members was carried after two hours of impassioned speeches.

A large Japanese turnout helped carry the Council's motion: Japanese broadly favoured greater Asian representation to balance the power of westerners in the Settlement, in accordance with the imperial ideology of pan-Asianism.[61] Japanese councillor Kimiji Fukushima was among those who spoke at the meeting in favour of admitting more Chinese members, stressing that 'the foundation of foreign control' of the Settlement remained unchanged, but recognising the justice of allowing the majority Chinese residents meaningful representation and emphasising that winning Chinese favour would be good for foreign business.[62] Fukushima did not believe that Chinese were capable of self-government but claimed that Japanese were 'sympathetic' to Chinese aspirations, remembering their own experience of unequal treaties: he carefully showed support for both British and Chinese positions.

A major argument in favour of augmenting the Chinese membership of the SMC was that it was Chinese business people who were represented: 'the bankers, merchants, property owners and other Chinese residents in this Settlement whose interests are identical with our own', in the words of British property-investor Arnhold.[63] Chinese members were elected annually by the 81 members of the CRA election committee, one third of which was chosen by the association itself, one third by the Nantao and Chapei Chambers of Commerce, and one third by the guilds and street unions of the Settlement.[64] It was an arrangement that suited these bodies and the SMC, which would not countenance a system of direct election of Chinese councillors as operated for the foreign councillors. One objection was that 'Chinese candidates of the best type' would be unwilling to stand for political election on the western model, but the SMC would never have risked expanding representation beyond the business community.[65] Chinese ratepayers were not invited to attend the annual ratepayers' meetings, as they were in the British municipality in Tianjin, with

---

[60] Bickers, 'Changing Shanghai's "Mind"', 12. 1930 also saw the publication of the annual report and *Municipal Gazette* in Chinese (in condensed form) for the first time, with the cooperation of the CRA. Chinese were finally being genuinely involved in the municipal administration. SMC, *Report for 1930*, 328.

[61] Cemil Aydin, *The Politics of Anti-Westernism in Asia: Visions of World Order in Pan-Islamic and Pan-Asian Thought* (New York: Columbia University Press, 2007), 162–5.

[62] SMC, *Report for 1930*, 44.

[63] SMC, *Report for 1930*, 43.

[64] SMC, *Report for 1930*, 39.

[65] Feetham, *Report*, II, 188.

the convenient excuse that there were simply too many ratepayers in Shanghai for it to be practicable.[66]

The CRA was one of the Council's most vocal critics, so its members had to reconcile their opposition to the municipal system with their active participation in it. Bryna Goodman is dismissive of the CRA as inadaptable, 'overly exclusive' and lacking real political power, but it consistently represented Chinese interests in negotiations with the SMC.[67] *Shenbao* reported the results of the CRA's competitive elections to the committee, complete with the percentage of votes cast for each candidate.[68] All members of the CRA were eligible to vote, and the qualifications for membership were modelled on those that entitled foreign ratepayers to vote in municipal elections: the ownership of real estate worth not less than 500 taels in value in the International Settlement, the payment of rates of at least 10 taels on property in the Settlement, or the payment of rates on an annual rental of 500 taels or more.[69] Marie-Claire Bergère suggests that Chinese institutions such as guilds and the General Chamber of Commerce (and latterly the CRA) adopted democratic procedures due to the influence of the SMC and other foreign organs, echoing claims made by the SMC's foreign champions that it was a beacon of democratic process in China.[70] Goodman makes the more persuasive case that the CRA consciously adopted the form of the foreign Ratepayers' Association in order to assert parity with the foreign community and so achieve the aim of representation.[71] The result was that business interests dominated the Chinese selection process, as they did the foreign vote. As Chinese businessmen tended to be conservative, favouring the stability of the status quo in the Settlement, those selected were somewhat more sympathetic to the SMC than some other sections of the local Chinese community. In the end, class was a more fundamental barrier to representation on the SMC than race.

The SMC maintained the structure of five Britons, two Americans, five Chinese and two Japanese until 1941, resisting Japanese pressure that year to increase the number of Japanese councillors to four by removing one Briton and one American. Clarence Gauss, the American consul-general, reported that his Japanese counterpart threatened military force to achieve greater Japanese representation, but Gauss 'told him bluntly' that he could not agree, and even if he did concede to reduce the American municipal representation 'the American

---

[66] Feetham, *Report*, II, 159.

[67] Bryna Goodman, 'Democratic Calisthenics: The Culture of Urban Associations in the New Republic' in Goldman and Perry (eds.), *Changing Meanings of Citizenship*, 89, 80–90.

[68] *Shenbao*, 23 November 1927.

[69] Hsü Shuhsi, *Japan and Shanghai*, No. 4, Political and Economic Studies (Shanghai: Kelly and Walsh, 1928), 7; Feetham, *Report*, II, Appendix XXI, 12–13, and Land Regulations in II, Appendix IV, 80.

[70] Bergère, *Golden Age*, 54.

[71] Goodman, 'Democratic Calisthenics', 89.

ratepayers would not do so, so that it was quite useless to consider the matter'.[72] Gauss explained that the franchise was based on the payment of rates, and he had found that Japanese paid only 7 per cent of municipal rates, so their representation would only increase if they paid their taxes. The autonomy of the SMC and its property-based franchise helped him avoid conceding ground to Japanese pressure. But the pressure increased and in advance of the usual election due to be held in 1941, the British councillors, consul-general and SMC secretary-general worked out between them a Provisional Council Agreement to prevent Japanese dominating the Council as a result of their greatly increased number of ratepayers. The rest of Shanghai had fallen to Japan in 1937 as the invading force swept the east coast of China. But the International Settlement persisted, even after Pearl Harbor shattered the illusion that the Sino-Japanese War was separate from the conflict between Allied and Axis powers in Europe. The Provisional Council Agreement suspended the Land Regulations and the electoral process in order to introduce a consular-appointed Council. It diluted British dominance with a Dutch and a Swiss councillor whilst maintaining a strong British presence and a balance between Axis and Allied nationals, as Shanghai remained neutral.

On the morning following the bombing of Pearl Harbor on 7 December 1941, the Japanese consul-general invited the SMC's Chairman and most senior American and Dutch members to meet him and asked them to carry on in their current roles. He promised that although Japanese were occupying British and American enterprises, they had 'no intention of disturbing the international make-up of the Council'.[73] The chairman agreed, in the interests of the residents of the Settlement, on the understanding that he and his colleagues would do nothing that compromised their loyalty to their own countries. Yet three weeks later, all the Allied members resigned from the Council on Japanese demand, although they continued to serve on committees for several more months and the British and other Allied municipal staff continued to perform their duties. Good relations between British and Japanese staff, argues Bickers, indicate 'the ongoing strength of the rhetoric of internationalism'.[74] But it was more than rhetoric: the International Settlement could only be run by an international council, despite the radically altered circumstances in Shanghai. Transnational colonialism lasted as long as the Settlement.

---

[72] Gauss to the Secretary of State, 5 February 1938, in Matilda F. Axton, Rogers P. Churchill, N. O. Sappington et al. (eds.), *Foreign Relations of the United States, 1938: The Far East, Vol. IV* (Washington, DC: United States Government Printing Office, 1969), document 144.

[73] MLMSS 770/13/14: E. M. Hinder, address to The Australian Institute of International Affairs, Melbourne, 18 April 1945: 'Shanghai 1942, Philadelphia 1944, Sydney 1945'.

[74] Robert Bickers, 'Settlers and Diplomats: The End of British Hegemony in the International Settlement, 1937–1945', in Christian Henriot and Wen-hsin Yeh (eds.), *In the Shadow of the Rising Sun: Shanghai under Japanese Occupation, 1937–45* (Cambridge University Press, 2004), 248.

Council Members

Holding elections annually allowed a high turnover in the Council membership, reflecting the transitory nature of the Settlement's population when the
Land Regulations were devised. Through the twentieth century, however,
increasing numbers of Council members held their seats for several years as
the number of long-term settlers in Shanghai increased. A total of 156 different
men were members of the SMC between 1900 and 1943, holding their position
for anything from one to eleven years. Between them they represented more
than 65 foreign companies, banks and other concerns, both locally based and
multinational. Members of the SMC were elected by qualified ratepayers, who
included both settlers who had made their permanent homes in Shanghai and
expatriates who typically worked for trading houses based in London or Hong
Kong. The first man born in Shanghai to sit on the Council was E. I. Ezra, who
was first elected in 1912. Settlers owned and controlled much of the property
in Shanghai, but while their interests were well represented, for a long time
political influence in the SMC rested primarily in the hands of the expatriates
with global business links.

The most important trading companies in Shanghai, representing the interests of big business, dominated, and most of these companies were British.
The Hong Kong Legislative and Executive Councils were similarly dominated
by big business until reforms in 1991.[75] The largest firm in China, Jardine
Matheson, a British company trading primarily in opium, cotton, tea and silk
from its Hong Kong headquarters, had the closest links to the SMC, providing a total of 12 councillors spanning 33 years between 1900 and 1941. Four
of them acted as chairmen, between them occupying the post for eight years.
Jardine's' rival, Butterfield and Swire, headquartered in Shanghai, was represented for 15 years in the twentieth century, as was another British concern, the
Hongkong and Shanghai Bank – the SMC's own bankers. The Bank dominated
more in the 1920s, supplying at least one councillor every year from 1920
to 1928, while the heyday for influence by Swire's came in the later 1920s
and 1930s. Between the 1870s and 1910s the British Peninsula and Orient
Steamship Navigation Company was well represented, but its last Council
member was elected in 1918.

Councillors were supposed to act as representatives of the rate-paying electorate and not of their employers, stepping out of discussions that directly
involved their firms' interest, but this principle was not always followed. In
1929 G. W. Sheppard told his employers, Jardine's, of confidential discussions among the British councillors about the future of Shanghai's governance,

[75] Ming K. Chan, 'The Legacy of the British Administration of Hong Kong: A View from Hong
Kong', *China Quarterly*, No. 151 (1997), 575–6.

which the company's directors passed on to the Foreign Office in London. The chairman, Arnhold, rebuked him as the discussions had not even been communicated to the rest of the Council and insisted that communications with the British government had to go through proper channels to protect the SMC's relationship with it.[76] Sheppard's loyalty was to his employer and to Britain, but Arnhold maintained that the Council's deliberations had to be kept confidential and local. Through foreign expatriates, the SMC did not simply represent the vocal Shanghailander community, as may be assumed, but was a more internationally minded group of men, many of whom, while spending many years in Shanghai, continued to identify their interests largely with Britain, the USA, Germany or Japan.

The chairmen exerted the greatest influence on the Council. Table 2.1 shows the business interests of the 18 chairmen of the twentieth century (three of whom can be seen in Figure 2.4). In this period 13 chairmen were expatriates (working for companies based or operating overseas), holding the position for 27 years between them and connecting the Council to transnational business networks. Just five chairmen were settlers (employed in local firms), occupying the chair for a total of 16 years. An almost unbroken line of expatriates held the chair until 1923, whereafter settlers were much more likely to be given the position, reflecting the increased localisation of municipal authority.

Chairmen were British, American, or once in 1876, German. Seven Americans occupied the chair for 16 years between them, ranging from 1868 to 1939. But otherwise Britons held the position until the brief tenure of the only Japanese chairman in 1942–1943. Edward Pearce and Stirling Fessenden were the longest-serving chairmen with seven-year terms and were both settlers in Shanghai. Pearce was the epitome of the British Shanghai establishment: he moved to China in 1884 at the age of 22, having been educated at the prestigious English school Charterhouse (where he in turn sent his son), and earned both wealth and status in the city.[77] His firm, Ilbert's, was an innovator in importing to China and ran a spinning and weaving company.[78] Pearce not only chaired the SMC but also the Shanghai Chamber of Commerce and later the China Association. He was knighted in 1922 and was awarded the Chinese Order of the Excellent Crop. Other Council members and senior staff were similarly decorated by the Chinese government, confirming their prestige among not only British but also Chinese authorities.[79]

---

[76] SMA U1-6–126: H. E. Arnhold to G. W. Sheppard, 13 November 1929.

[77] 'Sir E. C. Pearce', *The Times*, 10 September 1928, 17.

[78] Albert Feuerwerker, 'The Foreign Presence in China', in John King Fairbank (ed.), *Cambridge History of China*, Vol. 12, Republican China, 1912–1949, Part I (Cambridge University Press, 1983), 194.

[79] Six other men connected to the SMC were awarded the Order of the Excellent Crop with Pearce in 1925. *Edinburgh Gazette*, 5 May 1925.

Table 2.1 *SMC chairmen and their business interests, 1900–1942.*

Name	Period on SMC (years as chairman in brackets)	Nationality	Settler/ expatriate	Business
E. A. Hewitt	1897–1901 (1900–1901)	British	Expatriate	Peninsula and Orient Shipping Co.
William G. Bayne	1901–1903 (1902–1903)	British	Settler	North China Insurance Co.
H. De Gray	1903–1907, 1909–1912 (1911–1912)	American	Expatriate	China and Japan Trading Co.
Frederick Anderson	1904–1905 (1904–1905)	British	Expatriate	Ilbert and Co. (imports; textile manufacturing)
H. Keswick	1905–1907 (1907)	British	Expatriate	Jardine, Matheson and Co.
C. Holliday	1906 (1906)	British	Expatriate	Holliday and Co. (traders)
David Landale	1907–1910 (1908–1910)	British	Expatriate	Jardine, Matheson and Co.
E. C. Pearce	1911–1919 (1913–1919)	British	Expatriate	Ilbert and Co. (imports; textile manufacturing)
A. Brooke Smith	1919–1921 (1920–1921)	British	Expatriate	Jardine, Matheson and Co.
H. G. Simms	1920–1923 (1922–1923)	British	Expatriate	Property, insurance
Stirling Fessenden	1923–1928 (1923–1928)	American	Settler	Law
Alexander Dunlop Bell	1924–1933 (1932–1933)	British	Expatriate	Barlow and Co. (tea and rubber traders)
Ernest Macnaghten	1926–1927, 1929–1931, 1935, 1936, 1938 (1930–1931)	British	Expatriate	British American Tobacco
Harry Edward Arnhold	1928–1929, 1932–1936 (1929, 1934–1936)	British	Settler	Arnhold and Co. (property)
Cornell Sidney Franklin	1933–1939 (1937–1939)	American	Settler	Law
William J. Keswick	1936, 1938–1940 (1940)	British	Expatriate	Jardine, Matheson and Co.
John Hellyer Liddell	1934–1935, 1939, 1941 (1941)	British	Settler	Liddell Bros. and Co. (traders)

Figure 2.4 The Council of 1936–1937. On the front row, Chairman H. E. Arnhold is centre left, Vice-Chairman C. S. Franklin is to his right, and Yu Xiaqing is third from the right. William J. Keswick is third from the right on the back row.
Image courtesy of Historical Photographs of China, University of Bristol. HPC ref: Bi-s085.

Stirling Fessenden was one of the most prominent figures of the 1920s and 30s. He joined the Council in 1920 and held the chair from 1923 to 1929, when he refused to continue in the unpaid role and was made Director (later Secretary) General. The post allowed Fessenden to continue to direct municipal activities until his retirement in 1939.[80] Described as 'one of the best known Americans in the Far East', many contemporaries nevertheless considered Fessenden to be 'more British than the British'.[81] Indeed, while popular with the local foreign community (references to his long service and friendship to the Council, made when his retirement was announced at the annual meeting of ratepayers in 1938, were effusive and accompanied

---

[80] SMC, *Report for 1939*, 9.
[81] George F. Nellist (ed.), *Men of Shanghai and North China: A Standard Biographical Reference Work* (Shanghai: Oriental Press, 1933), 129; Clifford, *Spoilt Children of Empire*, 22.

by 'loud applause')[82] he was unpopular with the American authorities. In 1927 the US consul-general, Clarence Gauss, sought to use his influence to remove Fessenden from his powerful position. Gauss directed the American Minister in Beijing to tell his British counterpart that the re-election of Fessenden 'would not be acceptable to the American authorities', but the Minister thought such intervention inadvisable.[83] This illustrates the independence of the Council, even as it caused considerable problems to the consular and diplomatic authorities, as well as the significance of Fessenden's role as chairman of the SMC, drawing the attention of such senior figures. Following Fessenden's re-election, Gauss wrote angrily to the Secretary of State in Washington that

The truculent attitude of this American citizen, who, through no fault or favor of the American Government, or its authorities in China, has been hoisted by his colleagues on the Shanghai Municipal Council to the position of its Chairman ... – constantly emphasized in foreign houses of parliament to show the 'international' character of the Shanghai municipal administration – by his attitude of faithful obedience to the will of the reactionary majority of the Council and their supporters, is in my opinion distinctly unbecoming and distasteful.[84]

The US consul-general believed that his community was sidelined in the Settlement where British interests held sway, and the presence of Fessenden, rather than boosting the position of Americans in Shanghai, in fact enabled the status quo to continue under a cloak of internationalism. The impression of internationalism was, however, crucial to the SMC.

Fessenden had practised as a solicitor in Shanghai from 1905 and he used his legal expertise in the service of the SMC as it negotiated the tricky waters of growing Chinese nationalism and accelerating Sino-Japanese tensions. He negotiated with the Green Gang's Du Yuesheng (杜月笙) in February 1927, agreeing to allow Du to bring his gangsters through the International Settlement in order to assist Chiang Kai-shek's purge of the Communist Party.[85] He also oversaw the Council's reluctant agreement to admit Chinese members.

The councillors and senior staff of the SMC circulated with the Shanghai business elite in the city's many clubs and associations. As befitted a man of his local social and political standing, Fessenden was a member of a number of societies including the exclusive (British) Shanghai Club on the Bund, the

[82] SMC, *Report for 1939*, 9.
[83] US NARA, Consular Posts, Shanghai, RG 84, Vol. 1686, 810.1: telegram from US Consulate to US Legation, 12 April, and reply, 13 April 1927.
[84] NARA, Consular Posts, Shanghai, RG 84, Vol. 1686, 810.1: letter from American consul-general, Shanghai, to Secretary of State, Washington, DC, 5 May 1927.
[85] Brian G. Martin, *The Shanghai Green Gang: Politics and Organized Crime, 1919–1937* (Berkeley: University of California Press, 1996), 104–6; Robert M. Farnsworth, *From Vagabond to Journalist: Edgar Snow in Asia, 1928–1941* (Columbia, MO: University of Missouri Press, 1996), 27.

American Club, and the Rotary, a Sino-foreign organisation that encompassed many of the city's elite.[86] The latter was established in 1919 with the explicit aim of being 'international' (which is to say, to include Chinese as well as westerners in its membership), but three years later just four of its almost 70 members were Chinese,[87] demonstrating the difficulties involved in forming transnational organisations at this early juncture. Fessenden also belonged to the more genuinely cosmopolitan *Cercle Sportif Français*, the main French Club, which was highly popular and, unusually, admitted Chinese and even women.[88] Wasserstrom emphasises the significance of the connections forged in Sino-foreign organisations, and Fessenden certainly mixed with people of senior standing from all nationalities, but his social connections did not extend beyond the Anglo-American elite. The circles in which the members of the Council moved both reflected their elevated social position and shaped the interactions they were able to have with different sections of Shanghai society. The Settlement elite was small and incestuous and the SMC reflected this.

Many SMC members and staff, Chinese and foreign, were members of the North China Branch of the Royal Asiatic Society (RAS), affiliated to branches of the Society throughout East Asia and in London. The RAS boasted its own library, museum and journal, and held regular lectures. Council members in the RAS included Frank Raven, A. D. Bell and Xu Xinliu. Dozens of SMC employees also belonged to the RAS including Chief of the Industrial Section Eleanor Hinder and her Chinese assistant Zhu Yubao; Secretary W. E. Leveson and Chinese Deputy Secretary He Dekui; and Commissioner of Public Health J. H. Jordan and Dr Miao Weiguang, who also worked in the Public Health Department. The RAS was aided financially by the SMC and other sponsors, such as Dr Wu Liande, head of the Chinese government's quarantine service, who donated one fifth of the cost of the new RAS building in 1930, the largest individual donation the Society received.[89] The SMC's support for the RAS, including an annual grant of 1,000 taels, was a rare example of municipal spending on non-essential services, reflecting the status it had in Shanghai but also the Council's willingness to patronise a British institution: none of the other associations discussed benefited from direct municipal donations. The RAS strengthened imperial ties to

---

[86] On Sino-foreign organisations, see Jeffrey Wasserstrom, 'Cosmopolitan Connections and Transnational Networks', in Nara Dillon and Jean C. Oi (eds.), *At the Crossroads of Empires: Middlemen, Social Networks, and State-Building in Republican Shanghai* (Stanford University Press, 2007), 208.

[87] Connie Fan and April Ma, 'A Brief Look at the Rotary Club of Shanghai from 1919 to 1949' (Rotary Club of Shanghai, 2006), www.rotaryshanghai.org/index.php?id=6&lang=en.

[88] Clifford, *Spoilt Children of Empire*, 72.

[89] SMA U1-1-56: Finance Committee, 4 January 1909; U1-1-61: Finance Committee, 29 October 1932.

Britain and Britons around the world through imperial networks, but also contributed to the 'cosmopolitan intimacy' of Shanghai society in which Council members and employees interacted.[90]

British members of the Council and staff were drawn from the whole British Isles, as in other treaty port organisations such as the Maritime Customs service,[91] and brought transnational experience of different parts of Britain's imperial world. British employees hailed from everywhere from Aberdeenshire to Bournemouth.[92] Councillors included Brigadier-General Ernest Brander Macnaghten who had roots in County Antrim in Northern Ireland, but was born in India and served in Africa. As Director of British American Tobacco in China, the largest company in the country, he negotiated with the Nanjing government to secure tax deals in return for huge advances to the government. The Council's foreign members were well connected with Chinese authorities.[93] Among the Scottish councillors were Alexander Dunlop Bell and William J. Keswick, who held the chair in 1932–1933 and 1941 respectively. Bell belonged to the British tea and rubber trading firm Barlow and Company, which operated throughout Asia; Keswick was a Director at Jardine's, as had been his father Henry and grandfather William, who had both also chaired the Council, and all three moved regularly between London, Hong Kong and Shanghai. Benjamin Beith, another Scottish Council member in the 1930s, was also a Jardine's Director. Beith had previously been an unofficial member of the Hong Kong Legislative Council, further strengthening the ties between the Settlement and the colony.[94] Glaswegian N. S. Brown, deputy Chairman of the Hongkong and Shanghai Bank, was made manager of Butterfield and Swire specifically to deploy his networking skills to be elected to the SMC.[95] The domination of the Council by big British businesses remained clear throughout its existence, and it was often the transnational directors of the firms who stood for election: certainly the 'people of importance' intended by the Land Regulations.

While the SMC had included a Japanese member since 1916, Japanese began to have real influence within the Council from 1927 when the number of Japanese councillors increased to two and they were invited to join the Council's

---

[90] Robert Bickers, 'Shanghailanders and Others: British Communities in China, 1843–1957' in Bickers (ed.), *Settlers and Expatriates: Britons Over the Seas* (Oxford University Press, 2010), 277.

[91] On the Irish emphasis within the Customs, see Catherine Ladds, ' "Youthful, Likely Men, Able to Read, Write and Count": Joining the Foreign Staff of the Chinese Customs Service, 1854–1927,' *Journal of Imperial and Commonwealth History*, Vol. 36, No. 2 (2008), 233.

[92] FO 371/43540.

[93] Osterhammel, 'Imperialism in Transition', 282–3.

[94] Nellist (ed.), *Men of Shanghai*, 23.

[95] Bickers, *Britain in China*, 178.

committees, where specific policy decisions were deliberated.[96] Jordan Sand's characterisation of Japanese as 'subaltern imperialists', the latecomers to imperialism who both participated in and were kept outside its forums, is amply illustrated in the SMC.[97] Japanese were imperial powers in China from their victory in 1895, and gradually came to be accepted as partners by the other foreign powers represented in Shanghai, but were never seen as equals by the Britons and Americans who dominated the Settlement. Transnational colonialism operated with a clearly understood hierarchy; Japanese were increasingly significant, but remained low in status in the eyes of other foreigners.

Japanese members of the SMC were elected by the large Japanese ratepayers bloc, which turned out to vote more consistently than other national groups. They were nominated by the Japanese Residents' Association (membership of which was compulsory for all Japanese residents of Shanghai under Japanese law),[98] which usually chose the Japanese candidates by consensus in advance of the vote to avoid splitting the constituent community.[99] Mark Peattie claims there was a 'surprising degree of unanimity and cohesiveness' within Shanghai's Japanese community, suggesting that, uniquely among the Council members, the Japanese councillors might have represented the broad interests of their constituent ratepayers as a whole.[100] Yet Christian Henriot argues that there was a deep cleavage within the community between the expatriate minority and the vast majority of lower and middle class residents,[101] akin to that between British expatriates and Shanghailanders. Japanese Council members were drawn from the expatriate class so represented its interests above those of the resident majority, similarly to most of the British councillors.

Those nominated and elected were still chosen to best fit in with the British-dominated SMC, such as Otoichi Okamoto, a member of the English bar. The banker Kimiji Fukushima was a member from 1927 to 1932 and served on the Finance and Watch Committees. He repeatedly sought an increase in the Japanese branch of the SMP, favoured exclusively Japanese policing of Hongkou where the Japanese community was concentrated, and advocated the promotion of senior Japanese police officers to senior positions.[102] These

---

[96] Mark R. Peattie, 'Japanese Treaty Port Settlements in China, 1895–1937', in Peter Duus, Ramon H. Meyers and Mark R. Peattie (eds.), *The Japanese Informal Empire in China, 1895–1937* (Princeton University Press, 1989), 190–1.

[97] Jordan Sand, 'Subaltern Imperialists: The New Historiography of the Japanese Empire', *Past and Present*, No. 225 (2014), 275.

[98] Feetham, *Report*, II, 201.

[99] On the Japanese Residents' Association, see Joshua A. Fogel, ' "Shanghai-Japan": The Japanese Residents' Association of Shanghai', *Journal of Asian Studies*, Vol. 59, No. 4 (2000), 927–50. The first Japanese Councillor was a branch chief of the Association.

[100] Peattie, 'Japanese Treaty Port Settlements', 207–8.

[101] Henriot, ' "Little Japan" in Shanghai: An Insulated Community, 1875–1945', in Bickers and Henriot (eds.), *New Frontiers*, 154.

[102] SMA U1-1-89: SMC Watch Committee minutes, 21 June 1928.

were all key demands of the Japanese community which Fukushima explicitly saw as his duty to represent, referring to 'his constituents' in meetings.[103] He argued his case persuasively but stopped short of demanding full equality in pay and terms between Japanese and British officers, focusing on achievable goals. Japanese councillors thus cooperated with their colleagues and sought to maximise Japanese interests in a less militant way than local Japanese groups such as the Japanese Ratepayers' Association.[104]

Japanese representation on the SMC became more contentious from 1937 when Japan occupied the rest of the city. As the Japanese population and thus the number of Japanese ratepayers in the Settlement increased far more rapidly than the rest of the foreign population, there was serious concern in the SMC, in Shanghai's wider western community and in London about the possibility that the Japanese ratepaying bloc would elect more Japanese councillors at the expense of British and American members. Exploiting the rules that allowed residents to hold more than one vote if they qualified as ratepayers or property owners for firms and as individuals, Japanese companies split their holdings to allow more Japanese votes to be exercised. Concern about this reached Whitehall: Ashley Clarke of the Foreign Office reported worriedly to the Secretary of the Treasury that the number of Japanese votes had increased from 873 of a total of 3,763 (23 per cent) in 1936 to 1,930 of 3,841 votes (50 per cent) in March 1939.[105] British votes, meanwhile, fell from 1,403 (37 per cent) to 1,309 (34 per cent) in the same period, and as the number of Japanese votes continued to rise rapidly they looked to be in a position to out-vote British interests at the 1940 ratepayers' meeting and select their own choice of councillors. Special dispensation was therefore granted by the Treasury for the consul-general to waive the fee for British companies wishing to re-register their land in the name of more ratepayers, to split and thus increase British votes just as the Japanese community had done.

The tactic worked: British votes increased by over 1,000, the usual five British and two American candidates were elected with around 8,000 votes each, while two of the five Japanese candidates were elected with around 5,000 votes apiece, maintaining the status quo.[106] Britons and Americans worked together to negate the impact of the Japanese bloc: an American recalled that his father voted seven times in the election, once for each company that his underwriters' firm represented, in a process that took all day and 'was perfectly proper and correct – more or less'.[107] The episode shows how flawed

[103] SMA U1-1-88: Watch Committee minutes, 27 May 1927.
[104] Henriot, '"Little Japan"', 154.
[105] TNA T 160/1142/16454/1: Ashley Clarke, Foreign Office, to the Secretary of the Treasury, 2 November 1939.
[106] TNA T 160/1142/16454/1: Greenway, Shanghai, 3 and 12 April 1940.
[107] F. Richards, *Expatriate Adventures* (Bloomington, IN: Trafford, 2012), 137.

the democratic processes of the Settlement were, open to manipulation at the expense of the Japanese majority when Anglo-American domination was eventually threatened. For most of its existence, however, the balance of power was unquestionably with the British, and other members were selected in part for their ability to get along with the British and support their policies due to shared transnational business backgrounds.

Chinese Councillors were influential figures, drawn from the Chinese bourgeoisie that emerged in the early republican period, as detailed by Bergère.[108] None was more influential than Yu Xiaqing. 'The leading shipowner in China',[109] Yu chaired the Chinese Ratepayers' Association before and during his years on the SMC and was president of the Chinese General Chamber of Commerce. Yu also sat on the council of the Shanghai Municipal Government, which ran the Chinese municipality, from its formation in 1927.[110] Indeed, Yu was one of only five of the original 13 members who were re-selected to this council in 1932, identifying him as a faithful supporter of the Nationalist regime and a close ally of Chiang Kai-shek.[111] His links to Chiang dated to at least 1919 when he contributed funds to the future Guomindang leader.[112]

Yu moved from vocal critic of the SMC to chief negotiator with Fessenden over the terms by which Chinese would be admitted to the Council, and then to constructive Council member from 1929. Yu helped facilitate relations between the SMC and the Chinese Municipal Government by having a foot in each camp. In honour of Yu's 70th birthday and the 55th anniversary of his residence in Shanghai, the SMC renamed Thibet Road Yu Ya-ching Road in 1936 – a move that was enthusiastically welcomed by shopkeepers on the street, according to a letter they sent to the SMC secretary.[113] Just as the foreign members of the Council were pillars of the Shanghai establishment, so too were their Chinese counterparts. Their status made their arrival on the Council more palatable to foreigners who little over a decade earlier would have had few if any opportunities for social intercourse with Chinese and, moreover,

[108] Bergère, *Golden Age*.

[109] Nellist, *Men of Shanghai*, 470.

[110] On Yu Xiaqing, see Fang Teng, '*Yu Xiaqing lun*' ('On Yu Xiaqing'), *Zazhi yuekan*, Vol. 12, No. 2 (November 1943), 46–51; Vol. 12, No. 3 (December 1943), 62–7; Vol. 12, No. 4 (January 1944), 59–64; Ding Richu and Du Xuncheng, '*Yu Xiaqing jianlun*' ('On Yu Xiaqing'), *Lishi yanjiu*, No. 3 (1981), 145–66.

[111] Henriot, *Shanghai 1927–1937*, 53, 60. According to Feng Xiaocai, he also had links to the Chinese Communist Party as a 'bourgeois leftist'. Feng Xiaocai, "*Zuo*" "*you*" *zhijian: beifa qianhou Yu Xiaqing yu Zhonggong de hezuo yu fenbie* ('Between the "Left" and "Right": Cooperation and Division between Yu Xiaqing and the Chinese Communist Party around the Time of the Northern Expedition'), *Jindaishi yanjiu* (*Modern History Studies*) (May 2010), 31–48.

[112] Martin, *Shanghai Green Gang*, 81.

[113] SMA U1-6-101: Joint letter from shopkeepers of Thibet Road to Secretary, SMC, 10 July 1936.

would not have desired such opportunities.[114] Ruth Rogaski traces this process of interaction and guarded cooperation between foreign and Chinese elites in Tianjin,[115] and Shanghai was no different.

Other Chinese members of SMC were cosmopolitan business leaders, of the class identified by Bergère as the emergent bourgeoisie, which experienced a 'political awakening' in the years after the 1911 revolution.[116] Table 2.2 shows the transnational connections of key Chinese Council members, as well as their political affiliations and business concerns. One of the first two Chinese councillors, Yuan Lüdeng, had served on the Chinese and Foreign Famine Relief Committee, a self-evidently cooperative venture. He was educated at a Ningbo missionary college and became a Methodist pastor from 1904 until 1912. Yuan had been Deputy Chief Commissioner of Foreign Affairs and Communications in the Ningbo Military Government during the 1911 revolution.[117] Like his colleagues on the Council, he was a prominent businessman, working as Manager for Chinese tobacco and shipping firms and the American Trading Company.[118] Yuan's fellow Chinese pioneer on the Council, Shanghai native Zhao Jinqing, had a similar set of affiliations, as a deacon of the First Baptist Church in Shanghai, former president of the Shanghai Young Men's Christian Association (YMCA), and member of the central executive committee of the Chinese General Chamber of Commerce.[119] Zhao had strong ties to Nanjing, directing or helping direct a number of government departments including the Shanghai branch of the Ministry of Industry, Commerce and Labour.[120] Yuan and Zhao were typical of a section of the Shanghainese elite in their prominence in business and politics. Their Christianity demonstrates a degree of exposure to western culture that would have aided their interactions with other Council members.

These first Chinese councillors faced an uphill struggle to influence Council activities, but they maximised their influence by acting together on issues of importance to the Chinese municipal government, with some success. They criticised the Council's refusal to allow the Commissioner of Foreign Affairs to establish stamp tax collecting bureaux in the Settlement in September

---

[114] For prevailing British attitudes to Chinese in this period, see Bickers, *Britain in China*, 23–6, 43–8 and *passim*. Yu was also involved in Shanghai's criminal underworld, being 'sworn brothers' with Green Gang leader Huang Jinrong (黄金荣). Martin, *Shanghai Green Gang*, 21.

[115] Rogaski, *Hygienic Modernity*, 226–33.

[116] Bergère, *Golden Age*, 189.

[117] *Who's Who in China* (Shanghai: China Weekly Review, 1931), 487.

[118] Nellist, *Men of Shanghai*, 475.

[119] Shirley S. Garrett, 'The Chambers of Commerce and the YMCA', in Mark Elvin and G. William Skinner (eds.), *The Chinese City Between Two Worlds* (Stanford University Press, 1974), 234.

[120] Nellist, *Men of Shanghai*, 476.

Table 2.2 *Prominent Chinese SMC members and their affiliations.*

Name	Dates on SMC	Native place	Business	Political connections	International connections
Yuan Lüdeng 袁履登 (Yuan Li-tun)	1928–1941	Ningbo	Manager, Chinese tobacco and shipping firms among others; American Trading Company	Deputy Chief Commissioner of Foreign Affairs and Communications in the Ningbo Military Government during the 1911 revolution	Member, Chinese and Foreign Famine Relief Committee; missionary education and work as Methodist pastor
Zhao Jinqing 趙晉卿 (S. U. Zau)	1928	Shanghai	Member, central executive committee, Chinese General Chamber of Commerce	Director, Shanghai branch of Ministry of Industry, Commerce and Labour and other government bureaux	Deacon of First Baptist Church, Shanghai; former president, Shanghai YMCA
Xu Xinliu 徐新六 (Singloh Hsu)	1929–1938	Hangzhou	Director, National Commercial Bank, Shanghai, and other financial and insurance companies	Technical delegate to Paris Peace Conference	Studied in Birmingham, Manchester and Paris
Chen Tingrui 陳霆銳 (Chen Ding-sai)	Watch and Traffic Committees 1928–1932	Suzhou	Law; special editor of *Shenbao*	Member of 1924 delegation on the rendition of the Shanghai Mixed Court	Studied in Michigan
Yu Xiaqing 虞洽卿 (Yu Ya-ching)	1929–1940	Ningbo	Shipping; President, Chinese General Chamber of Commerce	Chair, Chinese Ratepayers' Association; council member, Shanghai Municipal Government; financially supported Chiang Kai-shek; 'sworn brother' of Green Gang leader Huang Jinrong	Worked for foreign as well as Chinese shipping companies
Liu Hongsheng 劉鴻生 (O. S. Lieu)	1930–1932	Dinghai, Zhejiang (born in Shanghai)	Industry, property, insurance	General Manager, government-controlled China Merchants' Steam Navigation Co.	Sons studied in USA, England and Japan; member, Rotary Club and Union Club (President 1932)
Hu Mengjia 胡孟嘉 (T. D. Woo)	1931–1933	Ningbo	Banker	Manager of the Treasury Department of the Central Bank of China	Studied in Birmingham and Manchester

1928, insisting on their opposition being recorded in the minutes in an astute use of municipal procedure.[121] As a result, the Council postponed the closing of the bureaux, despite the reservations of the foreign members that they signalled an infringement of the principle of excluding Chinese government bodies from the Settlement: the first Chinese members were affecting policy.

Yuan and Zhao were followed onto the SMC in 1930 by similarly cosmopolitan men. Prominent among them was Xu Xinliu, Director of the National Commercial Bank in Shanghai and other financial and insurance companies. Xu had an international education: a B.Sc. from Birmingham University, training in commerce at Manchester and in finance in Paris. He travelled to Europe again in 1918 and served as a technical delegate to the Paris Peace Conference.[122] Xu's transnational experience helped him to interact with the foreigners with whom he came into contact in the elite circles of Shanghai, which in turn facilitated his accession to the Council once Chinese were finally admitted. With his diplomatic work, Xu also illustrates the political prominence of the Chinese Council members.

Councillor Chen Tingrui also received his higher education overseas. He won a scholarship at the University of Michigan graduate law school: in admitting Chinese, the Council was able to benefit from a highly educated and intelligent skill-base. At Michigan, Chen completed a thesis entitled 'The Principles of State Succession as Revealed by the Versailles Treaty', demonstrating an extensive understanding of contemporary political issues.[123] He practised and lectured in law on his return to China and went to Beijing in 1924 as part of the delegation sent to help settle the contentious issue of the rendition of the Shanghai Mixed Court to Chinese control.[124] This prior involvement in the politics of the municipality paved the way for him to join the Council's Watch and Traffic Committees from 1928. He was a special editor of *Shenbao*, so may have given the newspaper the municipal line on contemporary issues.[125] Chen and Xu served side by side on the Watch Committee and actively raised the concerns of the Chinese community. In July 1928, in the first months of their membership, they suggested changes to improve security in the Settlement, including steps to restrict the trade in bullet-proof vests, which aided violent criminals.[126] Immediate action was taken, the Committee directing the Commissioner of Police to have the vests licensed in both foreign settlements, which suggests that the views of Chen and Xu were respected

---

[121] SMA: Kotenev, 'Chinese taxation', 81.
[122] *Who's Who*, 158–9.
[123] *Who's Who*, 64–5.
[124] Manley O. Hudson, 'The Rendition of the International Mixed Court at Shanghai', *American Journal of International Law*, Vol. 21, No. 3 (1927), 451–71.
[125] Nellist, *Men of Shanghai*, 60.
[126] SMA U1-1-89: Watch Committee Minutes, 20 July 1928.

by their foreign counterparts. On other occasions Xu's opinion was specifically sought, such as on the appropriate charges for hospital admission.[127] The chairman was making the most of having access to a Chinese perspective on municipal matters.

Chinese members of the Council were collaborators in the sense that they facilitated the continuation of a colonial authority. The SMC would have found relations with the Chinese community and Nanjing government untenable had it not granted representation to Chinese and the retrocession of the International Settlement might have been hastened. But it is clear that the Chinese councillors did not passively accept foreign authority and fought for the interests of the Chinese community. Ronald Robinson argued that the British could not find administrative collaborators in China as they had in India, holding back their colonial ambitions.[128] But collaborators were always vital to foreign business in China, whether as compradors or partners, paving the way for Chinese to collaborate in the administration of the International Settlement, where business and governance went together. All businessmen, Chinese or foreign, sought stability above all else, so it is no surprise that Chinese businesses were willing to cooperate with the SMC to preserve the Settlement and seek advantages for the Chinese community at the same time.

Both Chinese and Japanese Council members acted at times as national blocs to support the interests of their respective communities, primarily seeking greater Chinese or Japanese representation at senior levels of the municipal staff, increased municipal spending on education, and the maintenance of low taxes. The Chinese councillors and committee members insisted on the SMC following the rule established in 1933 that, before engaging a foreign employee, it had to ensure that the appointment could not be filled by a Chinese, resulting in more Chinese shaping and implementing Council policy.[129]

The Chinese councillors achieved a reversal in municipal policy on Chinese education. Since 1890 the SMC had contributed towards the education of the Settlement's foreign children, but expected Chinese to provide for their own offspring. The Thomas Hanbury Public Schools for (mainly Eurasian) boys and girls employed British teachers who taught in English from a curriculum suited to Britain rather than Asia, down to setting mathematics problems in pounds, shillings and pence. An international range of children attended, but Chinese children were excluded. By the late 1920s, the Federation of Street Unions, a vocal champion of Chinese residents, was demanding that more should be spent on schools for Chinese, and the five Chinese councillors took

---

[127] SMA U1-1–62: SMC Finance Committee Minutes, 22 September 1933.
[128] Ronald Robinson, 'Non-European Foundations of European Imperialism: Sketch for a Theory of Collaboration', in Roger Owen and Bob Sutcliffe (eds.), *Studies in the Theory of Imperialism* (London: Longman, 1972), 120.
[129] SMA U1-6–97: Chinese members of Council to Chairman, 6 June 1933.

up the issue.[130] The Chinese representatives were successful, despite opposition from other members,[131] and from 1931 a portion of the municipal income from Chinese rates was set aside for Chinese secondary education in the Settlement. Under further pressure from the Chinese councillors, the Council increased municipal funding for Chinese and Japanese schools in 1934, again in the face of determined opposition from the British and American members, including the chairman and vice-chairman, who cited budgetary pressures.[132] The budget was tight because Chinese and Japanese members of the Finance Committee had opposed raising rates the previous year, arguing that it would face significant popular opposition. They successfully held off a rise in taxation until 1936. Chinese and Japanese councillors were thus able to achieve victories in areas of importance to their communities, particularly where the two groups aligned in their aims.

In an effort to retain hold over key decisions, the British and American councillors met together privately to agree their approach to problems ahead of meetings of the full council. Such meetings were initially held at the office of the chairman, which under Arnhold meant taking Council business out of the administration building on Jiujiang Road and into Sassoon House on the Bund, with senior British municipal employees attending on invitation.[133] But after the outbreak of the Sino-Japanese War in 1937, Chinese and Japanese members were content for any Council business in relation to the conflict to be undertaken by the neutral powers alone, coming to full meetings only to discuss regular business, almost as if there were no hostilities.[134] The divide along national lines was, however, due to the context of war rather than racial animosity.

The minutes of Council and committee meetings reveal that the Chinese members contributed to municipal proceedings in a similar way to their British, American and Japanese counterparts, giving their opinions and pursuing areas of personal interest. As Bryna Goodman found in the Chinese General Chamber of Commerce and Chinese Ratepayers' Association, and Ruth Rogaski found in Tianjin, Chinese elites made use of western structures that served their interests. Chinese members influenced municipal policy by providing constructive solutions to controversial problems or simply by ensuring that Chinese interests were voiced at the appropriate moment. By the 1930s therefore, policy-making in the SMC was genuinely transnational.

[130] Feetham, *Report*, II, 9.
[131] Zhang (ed.), *Minutes of SMC*, Vol. 25, 3 June 1931, 59; 17 June 1931, 252–3.
[132] SMA U1-1–62: Finance Committee minutes, 4 January 1934.
[133] SMA U1-6–100: Secretary to secretary-general, SMC, 20 November 1936.
[134] SMA U1-6–142: Secretary to commissioner-general and chairman, 25 September 1937.

Municipal Staff

The Council was the executive body intended to put the wishes of the ratepayers into practice, but the day-to-day running of the Settlement was undertaken by the SMC's salaried staff. Municipal employees provided long-term administrative stability in contrast to the inherent instability in the annually elected Council membership. The staff was organised into departments under the direction of committees of Council members and local experts from among the ratepayers. Nicholas Clifford argued that the Council by and large simply approved the actions taken by its senior employees, which, though an exaggeration that overlooks the determination of policy at the level of committees, was true of much routine work.[135] Some senior figures exercised great authority. Heads of departments met regularly with councillors and ratepayers with relevant expertise in committee meetings, and committee recommendations were generally approved by the Council.

The SMC was among the largest employers in Shanghai and affected the lives of a significant number of people simply by employing them. By 1930, it employed 9,443 employees on contract, 6,856 of them Chinese.[136] This was comparable to the staff of the largest mills in Shanghai, and far greater than the 600 working in the Shanghai branch of the Hongkong and Shanghai Bank.[137] The SMC employed a further 3,000 Chinese on average each day as daily or weekly paid labourers on public works projects.[138] The police and public works were the two largest departments, employing 2,295 and 4,879 people respectively. The 2,587 foreign municipal employees were drawn from 24 different nations, including 964 Indians, the largest national group, all but two of whom belonged to the police or gaol services, 934 Britons, 371 Russians, 219 Japanese, 29 Americans, 16 Filipinos and 11 Italians.[139] Apart from five Koreans, the remaining foreign employees were all Europeans. All but two heads of department (of the Industrial Section and the Orchestra), however, were British, and Britons dominated the senior posts. A similar pattern pertained in the Chinese Maritime Customs Service.[140] The divide between a largely Chinese staff and foreign, largely British, senior officers, ensured that authority in the Customs and the SMC alike was British.

Prior to the First World War, far more Germans had been employed in the SMC, but after the sinking of the Lusitania in 1915 anti-German feeling supplanted earlier Anglo-German friendship.[141] The Council instructed

[135] Clifford, *Spoilt Children of Empire*, 22.
[136] Feetham, *Report*, I, 153.
[137] Jean Chesneaux, *The Chinese Labor Movement, 1919–1927* (Stanford University Press, 1968), 34; King, *Hongkong Bank*, 138.
[138] SMA U1-1-73: Works Committee, 17 May 1920.
[139] Feetham, *Report*, II, 170.
[140] Ladds, '"Youthful, Likely Men"', 237.
[141] Bickers, *Getting Stuck in for Shanghai*, 64.

departments to consider whether to terminate the terms of agreement of all German employees when they came up for renewal. If senior officers made a strong case for keeping individual German employees, however, their agreements were renewed despite their nationality. Local interests were balanced with national loyalties: Germans were not dismissed automatically. Two Germans were retained throughout the war as inspectors in the Public Works Department due to long and satisfactory service (Schultz since 1884 and Diercking since 1899). However, anti-German feeling was strong enough in 1919 for Charles Godfrey, Commissioner of Public Works, to recommend Schultz's dismissal 'partly because he is German' and partly because of his poor management of coolies, and to recommend Diercking's dismissal as 'the man is a cankerworm in his office'.[142] The Public Works Committee rejected the recommendation, noting that dismissing men of such long service would require 'unassailable grounds', but Godfrey's views reflect the tensions that arose between different nationals within the municipal staff in the context of international conflict.

The war also produced a major challenge in maintaining the municipal staff as recruitment from Europe ceased. The SMC usually preferred to recruit foreign staff directly from Britain as far as possible, though it also recruited locally and from the British empire, especially Hong Kong, the nearest colony. The primary recruiter of foreign staff was the Council's agent in London, John Pook and Company, which advertised and coordinated interviews for candidates recruited in London. Pook's placed advertisements in newspapers and magazines (where they appeared alongside similar advertisements for employees required throughout the British empire).[143] The agents interviewed candidates, with the help of retired senior municipal employees where possible. But the war prevented recruitment in Britain by the SMC as it did for imperial employers elsewhere. Local recruitment of foreigners in Shanghai therefore increased and a Japanese branch of the SMP was established.

All employees were subject to the management of the Secretariat, the nerve centre of the municipal administration. The secretary was the most influential and highest paid municipal employee.[144] J. O. P. Bland held the position from 1897 (after joining the SMC from the Customs service the previous year) to 1906. A Malta-born Ulsterman, married to an American, Bland had worked in various Chinese treaty ports and in Beijing during his career at the Customs service. He typified a particular brand of the British presence in China, moving between the spheres of British influence and seeking to build a new 'Raj'

[142] SMA U1-1–73: Works Committee, 27 October 1919.
[143] Bickers, *Empire Made Me*, 32.
[144] SMA U1-1–56: Finance Committee, 9 October 1908.

in China.[145] Bland stretched and re-moulded the position of secretary, from a largely administrative role to one that defined the Council and its stance on key issues of the day. He was instrumental in negotiating the dramatic extension of the Settlement in 1899, and even after he moved on from Shanghai Bland wrote to his successor, W. E. Leveson, in 1911 urging him to grasp opportunities for further expansion.[146] A number of Britons then held the post, re-designated Secretary and Commissioner-General, with increased pay, in 1921 in recognition of the scale and importance of the work, which often meant working until 10 or 11 pm.[147] Then in 1929 Stirling Fessenden became secretary-general and held the post for the next decade, directing municipal activities and policies much like Bland. Fessenden was succeeded by another lawyer, Charles Godfrey Phillips, who restored the British near-monopoly of the position. Educated at Harrow (where he was head boy) and Cambridge (where he earned a double first class degree in law and was president of the Cambridge Union), Godfrey Phillips was a high-achieving establishment figure.[148] He survived an assassination attempt on 6 January 1940 when gunmen 'poured bullets into [his car] at point-blank range'.[149] SMP investigations concluded that the Wang Jingwei puppet regime and the Japanese Military Police planned to derail an agreement on municipal policing of the extra-Settlement roads by blaming the assassination on the Chongqing government and thus damage foreign support for it.[150] It was the prominence of the secretary's position that made him an assassination target.

These secretaries were typical SMC employees in many ways, in terms of their background (British or Anglophile and middle class) and also, significantly, in the force of their personalities. They occupied commanding positions for unelected officers and used them to exert their influence over the direction of the SMC and how it angled for maximum advantage in Shanghai vis-à-vis the consular body and Chinese authorities. As secretaries, Bland, Fessenden and Godfrey Phillips were more powerful than the chairmen of the Council, who rotated more frequently and combined their roles with paid positions so had not the same undivided time devoted to the SMC. In correspondence with Justice Feetham in 1931, Fessenden dismissed the chairman's position favouring the immediate implementation of Feetham's report and was confident of winning the argument. He was open about his

---

145 Robert Bickers, 'Bland, John Otway Percy (1863–1945)', *Oxford Dictionary of National Biography* (Oxford University Press, 2004), www.oxforddnb.com/view/article/31920.

146 Bickers, *Scramble for China*, 362.

147 Zhang (ed.), *Minutes of SMC*, Vol. 21, 21 December 1921, 521.

148 British Library National Sound Archive, C409/105: Henry Pickthorn, http://sounds.bl.uk/related-content/TRANSCRIPTS/021T-C0409X0105XX-0000A0.pdf; Bernard Wasserstein, *Secret War in Shanghai* (New York: Houghton, 1998), 5.

149 'Mr. Godfrey Phillips', *The Times*, 25 October 1965, 14.

150 Wasserstein, *Secret War*, 59–60.

tactics: 'when the psychological moment arrives I shall do my best to persuade the Council'.[151] The secretaries also extended influence outside the Council: Godfrey Phillips met with the British consul-general over tiffin to present his views informally. He helped persuade the consul-general in 1937 that Chinese demands for the allocation of education funds according to the relative contributions of different national groups in taxation would set a dangerous precedent, a position he had successfully persuaded the British and American councillors to adopt.[152] There was no love lost between Godfrey Phillips and the Chinese councillors, who offended him by asking that he leave a committee meeting in 1937: he was not accustomed to being treated as a mere employee.[153] Present in all municipal meetings and author of almost all important Council correspondence, the secretary occupied a unique position of almost omniscient power.

The Treasurer (Treasurer and Comptroller from 1920) was also a highly significant position from its creation in 1909. Attending all committee meetings at which budgetary considerations were tabled, the treasurer exerted considerable influence reining in municipal expenditure. Edward Franklin Goodale (recruited from London, the son of an English coffee merchant) held the post from 1909 until his death in 1928.[154] Goodale worked tirelessly for the SMC, driving himself to illness in his later years. His doctor warned in 1924 that Goodale was 'suffering from neurasthenia and nervous debility from overwork and I think he is very liable to have a breakdown if he waits another year before going on leave'.[155] The leave was granted, but in 1928 Goodale died at sea on his way to England on further sick leave, leaving behind a wife and two children.[156] His commissioner of revenue was E. L. Allen, who was born locally in Shanghai in 1873 and dedicated his whole working life from 1889 until 1932 to the SMC. To commemorate his long service Allen was presented with a gift at the ratepayers' meeting in 1922, his heartfelt appreciation of which indicates that he was a contented employee: 'I need hardly say that the gift will always be one of my most treasured possessions'.[157] In 1929 the Staff Committee recommended that Allen be granted an increase in pay, noting that in his long years of 'excellent' and 'faithful' service, he had never raised the question of pay, despite receiving what was considered to be a low salary (1,000 taels in

[151] SMA U1-6–85: Fessenden to Feetham, 29 July 1931.
[152] SMA U1-6–102: Godfrey Phillips to Sir John Brenan, 27 September 1937.
[153] SMA U1-6–102: Godfrey Phillips to Singloh Hsu, 11 November 1937.
[154] SMA U1-3–312: Personnel file on Edward Franklin Goodale: baptismal certificate dated 5 September 1878.
[155] SMA U1-3–312: Dr Gauntlett to secretary, 23 April 1925.
[156] SMA U1-3–312: telegram from W. H. Trenchard Davis of the SS Mongolia, Peninsula and Oriental Steam Navigation Company, at Suez, 4 May 1928.
[157] SMA U1-3–66: Personnel file on E. L. Allen: Allen to A. Brooke Smith, Chairman, 24 April 1922.

1929).[158] The SMC benefited from a dedicated body of British employees who served far from home, like the many others in colonial outposts throughout the empire.

Heads of department were present at committee meetings and could answer questions, but had no formal authority to decide policy. It was increasingly the case, however, as committees grew in importance, that a strong character could persuade his or her committee to approve the actions he or she intended to take. While other senior officers did not enjoy the same degree of authority as the secretary or treasurer, heads of departments exercised considerable power in their respective fields and occupied positions of moderately high status in the Settlement community. Heads of department were almost all British, as were their deputies for most of the existence of the SMC. But following the arrival of Chinese councillors there was a degree of diversification of senior municipal staff, especially deputy heads of department, which was significant in view of the status and influence of these posts.

Commissioners of Police employed a large staff and were responsible for a budget to match. They brought transnational experience to Shanghai and were often highly respected in the foreign community due to military titles and reputations. Captain Alan Boisragon was an imperial hero, having been one of just two British survivors of the 'Benin Massacre' of 1897. Boisragon served as Captain Superintendent, as the post was then known, from 1901 to 1906, when he was replaced by British Army Colonel C. D. Bruce. Bruce was recruited from the Weihaiwei Regiment, which he led after service in the Indian Army in the 1890s. Those with experience of leading men in India were particularly valued by the SMC and often applied policing methods from Britain's most populous colony in their work in Shanghai, from crowd-control techniques to concern over indigenous political movements. After leaving the SMP (under a cloud) in 1913, Bruce became Advisor on Police Affairs to Yuan Shikai's government, showing that working for a colonial authority did not preclude service to the Chinese government.[159] Bruce's successor, Kenneth John McEuen, did not share such a military pedigree and did not earn the same public esteem enjoyed by military Commissioners. Captain E. I. Barrett replaced him in 1925 and pursued a politicisation of the SMP, using the force to target Chinese political activism deemed unfavourable to the SMP, despite the opposition of the Chairman of the SMC.[160] The SMC did not tolerate unpopular leadership of the police, combined with soaring crime figures, for long: Barratt was sacked in 1928 in favour of Major Frederick Wernham Gerrard, appointed from the

---

[158] SMA U1-3-66: Staff Committee, 28 February 1929.
[159] Lo Hui-min (ed.), *The Correspondence of G. E. Morrison*, Vol. 1, 1895–1912 (Cambridge University Press, 1976), 503, n. 1.
[160] Bickers, *Empire Made Me*, 68, 175.

Bombay police force with the assistance of the British Minister in China.[161] Gerrard was initially seconded solely to reorganise the SMP,[162] but stayed in post until 1938. Gerrard's appointment represents a closer relationship with British imperial authority that the SMC only sought as a result of crisis in the mid-1920s, but he and the SMC were nonetheless still operating independently from imperial control: influence could be accepted without fundamentally weakening autonomy in Shanghai.

The Chinese branch of the SMP was by far the largest and potentially the most difficult in which to ensure loyalty, so running it was vitally important to the security of the Settlement. Bruce appointed a fellow veteran of the Weihaiwei Regiment, Major Alan Hilton-Johnson, to lead the branch in 1908. Hilton-Johnson arrived in China during the Boxer War (after service in Egypt, Sudan and India) and gained proficiency as an interpreter of Chinese and Japanese.[163] It was his combination of language skills and military leadership that appealed to Bruce and the SMC, and esteem for him was such that he was appointed Commissioner-General of the Council in 1925. Chinese business leaders, including all Chinese members of the SMC and its committees, gathered to honour Hilton-Johnson at the Chinese bankers' club when he retired in 1928.[164] Yu Xiaqing presented him with an engraved silver tripod incense burner and gave a speech praising his contribution to good order, noting that 'In this city where people from over 40 nationalities come to do business, it is only natural that unfortunate incidents do sometimes occur'. The *China Press* report of the occasion even concluded with a poem of farewell by local businessman and philanthropist Feng Pingnan, which included the lines:

> Safeguard our welfare still,
> Strive for us yet!
> We here have need of thee,
> Do not forget.
>
> Graven upon my heart,
> These words I find,
> 'We are of diverse race
> Yet of one mind!'[165]

Such a lavish send-off shows that Hilton-Johnson had the support of the Chinese elite, who by 1928 shared a stake in the SMC. It is surprising that they should profess publically a need for his continued support after his return to Britain. The poem suggests a sanguine view of the Settlement's relationship

---

[161] SMA U1-1-89: Watch Committee, 6 August and 6 November 1930.
[162] SMA U1-1-89: Watch Committee, 6 August and 6 November 1930.
[163] Hilton-Johnson papers, with thanks to Patricia Hilton-Johnson.
[164] *China Press*, 29 May 1928, 1, 12.
[165] *China Press*, 29 May 1928, 12.

with British imperialism, indicating that the degree of autonomy that the SMC enjoyed was sufficient to satisfy Chinese when their interests were served. The poem ends with pragmatic adherence to the rhetoric of international endeavour that underpinned the municipality.

In charge of the Japanese branch was another notable Deputy Commissioner of Police, Shigeru Uyehara, who represents the shift away from exclusively British authority in the SMP in the 1930s. Originally from rural Gifu, 150 miles west of Tokyo, and a well-to-do family that could trace its roots to sixteenth-century *samurai*, Uyehara studied at Keio University and then joined the Ministry of Foreign Affairs.[166] He worked in Singapore, South Africa and London, and finally joined the Council's staff in 1930 as the nominee of the Japanese authorities for the position of Superintendant of Police, Japanese Branch (promoted to Deputy Commissioner of Police in 1937). He was the ideal man for the job, having broad experience of the British empire and fluency in English, the language of municipal business. Uyehara had a Master's degree from the London School of Economics, where he had met, fallen in love with, and married an Englishwoman.[167] Arriving in Shanghai with his wife and their young son, he was well placed to negotiate the increasingly conflicting interests of the Council and its police force with the Japanese community and authorities.

Men like Uyehara occupied pioneering positions in what remained a largely British world and his experience highlights the malleability of national loyalties in changing political circumstances. Uyehara got on well with Gerrard, whom he saw as a gentleman soldier, trained at Sandhurst, but found the other British officers and men irritatingly arrogant, having, in his view, little to justify their arrogance. It chafed when the lower ranks failed to salute him, as racial prejudice persisted in the Settlement.[168] His wife, Vera, also had difficulty finding her social position as a middle class British woman married to a Japanese, who felt herself to be of superior standing to the wives of many of the British police officers. Neither of them would have countenanced socialising with Chinese, so their social circle centred on the Japanese diplomatic elite and Uyehara increasingly allied himself with the Japanese position as the 1930s wore on.[169]

Uyehara was nevertheless accused by the Japanese community and authorities of failing to put his nation's interests first, and his memoirs

---

[166] Uyehara's university studies included French and he undertook dissertation research on the labour movement, when he 'began to think about the irrational differences between the rich and the poor'. Cecil Uyehara, 'The Uyehara Story: The Tale of Two People: Shigeru Uyehara and Vera Eugenie Foxwell Uyehara' (unpublished manuscript, 2009), 1, 8, 15, 18, 29–30, 33–6.

[167] Ibid., 59–67.

[168] Ibid., 86.

[169] Ibid., 188.

recall a sense that his first loyalty was to his municipal employers rather than the Japanese authorities who had nominated him for the position.[170] When the Japanese Residents' Association presented three candidates for election to the SMC in 1934 as a way to increase Japanese representation, Uyehara criticised their naivety in believing that the westerners would allow this infringement of their dominant position without a fight. Uyehara could see both sides of the increasingly tense relationship between the Japanese and Anglo-American communities, and although he became more nationalistic, he remained a life-long Anglophile.[171] While the Council's departments such as the police force became more diverse in the people they promoted to senior positions, sympathy to its fundamentally British roots was an asset.

Like the Commissioners of Police, Commissioners of Public Works were responsible for a large staff and budget, but their positions were far less prominent in Shanghai society and their holders were able to retain them for far longer. They were Englishmen such as Charles Mayne, who joined the municipal staff in 1889 and served as Engineer and Surveyor, as the post was then called, until forced to resign due to his wife's ill health 20 years later.[172] He was succeeded by Charles Henry Godfrey, who had moved to Shanghai from England in 1895 to become Assistant Engineer and Surveyor and led the department until he was invalided from the service in 1922. Charles Harpur took over, having belonged to the Public Works Department since 1902, and stayed until his retirement at the age of 55 in 1936. Harpur was also an active member of the Shanghai Volunteer Corps and earned an OBE in 1929 for services to the Shanghai Defence Force.[173] On his retirement, his achievements (which included overseeing the construction of concrete bridges, remodelling the Ward Road Gaol, a new abattoir and meat market, new district markets, the new Central and other police stations, a modern sewage treatment works, incinerators, schools, fire stations and wharves) and long service were praised at the annual ratepayers' meeting, to loud applause, and the council held a dinner in his honour.[174] Loyalty to the municipal service was valued and the physical legacy of Commissioners of Public Works on the city landscape was apparent to the ratepayers.

The next largest department, Public Health (the PHD), was headed by Arthur Stanley from 1898 to 1922, during which time he built it up to have a strong impact on the Settlement (see Chapter 4). This work was continued by C. Noel Davis and then passed into the capable hands of Ulsterman John Herbert Jordan

---

[170] Ibid., 90, 103–4.
[171] Cecil Uyehara, personal interview, 4 May 2011.
[172] Zhang (ed.), *Minutes of SMC*, Vol. 17, 10 November 1909, 136.
[173] *The London Gazette*, 26 February 1929, 1443.
[174] SMA U1-14–966: SMC, *Report for 1936*, 12, 30.

in 1930.[175] Jordan, recruited to be Assistant Health Officer in 1922, quickly proved himself an able manager. His starting salary of 700 taels was high in an attempt by the SMC to attract more qualified candidates, following disappointment in the recently hired Dr McKinstry on 545 taels.[176] Noel Davis told the Health Committee that McKinstry did 'not appear to be the type of man suitable for promotion to the senior positions in the department' due to 'a certain crudeness, immaturity or lack of educational refinement'.[177] Men who occupied senior positions in the SMC were representatives of the Council as much as its members, and there was an expectation that they should belong to the higher ranks of society.[178] McKinstry fell short and was destined to remain a mere technician.[179] Jordan, on the other hand, was the son of Sir John Jordan, one-time British Minister to Beijing, had studied at Cambridge and had been a Major in the Royal Army Medical Corps.[180] This was the kind of man the SMC wanted.

Jordan, like his fellow British heads of department, was resistant to efforts to promote Chinese in the municipal service, but foreign firms in China were following a 'localisation' strategy to assuage nationalist demands and pressure was growing on the SMC to follow suit. A representative of the League of Nations Health Organisation told Jordan that the SMC should meet the minimum demand made by Chinese associations in Shanghai of appointing a Chinese Deputy Commissioner to the PHD, arguing that there were many local Chinese doctors who were fit for such a post. Jordan replied pointedly that the local view differed from the international view, that he was not willing to tell his staff who had moved to Shanghai 'in good faith' that their chances of promotion had been closed, and nor could he remove the current deputy commissioner from his post to suit 'political emergencies'.[181] Jordan added that all staff should be able to move up in the service regardless of nationality. This belied the reality that foreign, particularly British, staff were much favoured for higher positions, and illustrates the slowness of the SMC to respond to the changed political environment, where Chinese were demanding a greater role in the running of administrations on Chinese soil.

---

[175] Davis was prominent in Shanghailander life, being a keen participant in the regular paper hunt (and master of the hunt 1925–1928) which several members of council also joined or led. C. Noel Davis, *A History of the Shanghai Paper Hunt Club, 1863–1930* (Shanghai: Kelly and Walsh, 1930), 29, 40, 166.

[176] SMA U1-1-123: Health Committee, 13 July 1922.

[177] Ibid.

[178] The provision of motorcars was similarly intended in part to maintain the prestige of the senior council staff.

[179] McKinstry's social position would have been something akin to that of the fictional Hong Kong bacteriologist Walter Fane in W. Somerset Maugham's *The Painted Veil* (London: Vintage, 2007, first published 1925).

[180] Information kindly provided by Adam Jordan, 12 April 2010.

[181] SMA U1-16-9-199: Jordan's notes on interview between himself and Rajchman, 19 January 1931.

The last municipal department to be established, the Industrial Section in 1930, was also the most international. Its Australian chief, Eleanor Hinder, was the only female head of department and her section was only the second, after the municipal orchestra's Spanish, German and Italian conductors,[182] to be led by a non-Briton. Hinder offered her services to the SMC to help it carry out its new policy of factory inspection, in response to the promulgation of a Factory Law by the Chinese government.[183] Ideally placed for this work as she had advised the Chinese government on the practical implementation of the new law, Hinder was employed by the Council as Director of the new Industrial and Social Section, a post she held until 1942. In this capacity she successfully held her own in the patriarchal SMC, where women were conspicuous by their absence from municipal governance.

At a time when women were entering the British parliament and beginning to claim their place in the public sphere around the world, no women were ever admitted to the Council (although the principle was reluctantly admitted in 1923).[184] In subsequent years women joined committees on which the Council felt they could make a contribution: the Education, Health, Film Censorship, Library and Orchestra Committees.[185] (There was deemed 'no point' in admitting women to the Rate Assessment Committee even though there were female ratepayers who voted in municipal elections.) Women were employed as nurses, teachers and typists, including such senior positions as matrons in municipal hospitals, the headmistresses of municipal girls' schools and the secretary to the municipal Secretary, but Hinder was the most senior female employee. She achieved her senior position due to her unique qualifications and offering her services at the right time (see Chapter 5). She won significant concessions towards gender equality in the SMC, such as successfully demanding equal pay for men and women employed in her department, even though this conflicted with standard practice across the SMC and among contemporary employers in Shanghai and overseas.[186]

Under Hinder's influence, the British dominance of senior posts seen in other departments was absent: Austrian, Chinese, Danish, Japanese and New Zealander staff worked together in the Industrial Section.[187] One such employee was Rewi Alley, a New Zealander (industrial reform was a

---

[182] Bickers, 'Greatest Cultural Asset', 843, 848, 853.
[183] SMA U1-6-111: Eleanor Hinder to E. B. Macnaghten, Chairman of the SMC, 13 December 1931.
[184] Zhang (ed.), *Minutes of SMC*, Vol. 22, 14 March 1923, 309.
[185] Zhang (ed.), *Minutes of SMC*, Vol. 25, 1 July 1931, 78.
[186] Eleanor M. Hinder, *Life and Labour in Shanghai: a Decade of Labour and Social Administration in the International Settlement* (New York: Institute of Pacific Relations, 1944), 24.
[187] Hinder, *Life and Labour*, 25.

somewhat Antipodean business in the SMC). Alley was politically opposed to the very existence of the International Settlement, later describing it in his memoirs as a place for 'get-rich-quick foreign imperialist adventurers and opium traders ... to carry on their nefarious business',[188] yet he nevertheless began his career in Shanghai working for the SMC, first in the Fire Department and then in the Industrial Section. Anne-Marie Brady writes that Alley's 'personal mission in the 1930s was to ameliorate the suffering of China's poor',[189] and for the time being he found Hinder's department the best place to pursue this goal. He had connections with the underground Communist Party in Shanghai in the 1930s, which may have extended to harbouring party members in his flat and allowing its use for Communist radio broadcasts. No such communist activity by him was known to the SMP, however, enabling him to serve the SMC as Chief of Factory Inspection while engaging with political circles that were antithetical to the SMC's free-trading principles. Alley thus demonstrates the broad mix of people who were represented among the municipal personnel in later years.

The vast majority of the municipal staff was Chinese, but they were confined to the lower ranks. This was common in foreign concerns throughout China and was justified by Sinophobic beliefs in the poorer economic performance of Chinese workers: 'It has been calculated that the nervous energy of the educated Chinese is 0.24 of the white man', opined an American in Shanghai as late as 1925, 'and that of the laborer 0.18... In an office it thus takes four Chinese to do the work of one foreigner and in manual work five men.'[190] But from 1928 the Council agreed to a policy of promoting more Chinese to senior positions, in response to pressure from Chinese councillors and the CRA. British senior officers found the transition difficult, however, and the top posts remained beyond reach for Chinese. By 1933 the localisation policy was bearing fruit, with increasing promotion of Chinese to posts defined as 'under letters of appointment', which had previously been a euphemism for foreign employee.[191] A Chinese auditor was appointed and heads of departments had to become used to working with a Chinese deputy. These changes made little difference to the experience of most Shanghainese with municipal personnel. The many members of staff who represented the SMC in an everyday capacity – tax collectors, police, teachers, nurses, public health assistants, public works employees and so on – had always been Chinese. While the Council

---

[188] Rewi Alley, *Travels in China, 1966–71* (Beijing: New World Press, 1973), 61.

[189] Anne-Marie Brady, *Friend of China: The Myth of Rewi Alley* (London: Routledge, 2003), 27.

[190] Putman Weale (Bertram Lenox Simpson), *Why China Sees Red* (New York, 1925), 282, quoted in N. Clifford, 'A Revolution is not a Tea Party: The "Shanghai Mind(s)" Reconsidered', *Pacific Historical Review*, Vol. 59, No. 4 (1990), 509.

[191] SMA U1-1-62: Finance Committee, 22 September 1933.

was dominated by the British, therefore, its authority was experienced through Chinese mediators.

The most senior Chinese member of staff for most of the SMC's history was the comprador, a post that was monopolised by one Shanghai family, as was common among the compradors of foreign companies.[192] In 1936, Arnhold as Chairman presented Comprador Pon Ming Fan with an engraved clock to mark the 50th anniversary of his employment with the SMC. His two sons worked in his office, and he had succeeded Pon Kuck Hien, who had retired aged 71 in 1930, having inherited the post from his father when the latter died in 1886. Arnhold stated that the Pon family had provided compradors to the SMC for its entire existence and listed seven members of the family who worked or had worked in the comprador's office. It was hardly a modern or meritocratic approach to employment, but the Pons' loyalty to the SMC was highly valued.

Under the localisation policy, the deputy secretary became the most senior Chinese official on the municipal staff. He Dekui (何德奎 T. K. Ho), former secretary of the CRA, joined the SMC in 1928, was made assistant secretary in 1931 and was promoted to deputy secretary two years later, a post he held until 1942. Like the Chinese councillors, He had an elite, international background, having attended Harvard, graduating with an MBA in 1921.[193] He worked closely with Fessenden and provided a key point of contact for the SMC with Chinese organisations and officials. As the most senior Chinese representative of the Council's staff, he was put in charge of such contentious issues as attempting to clear away communities dwelling in huts and reforming the rickshaw industry.[194] He Dekui's influence on these issues shows that significant authority was now in Chinese hands: his recommendation for the huts not to be summarily demolished was adopted by the Council.

Chinese petitioners hoped to find in He a more sympathetic representative of the SMC to hear their complaints, many coming to the Council's offices and demanding to see him in person to present their case: 700 hut-dwellers gathered outside the administration building in 1937 to appeal for their rights.[195] Janet Chen found that refugees appealed to He in very different language to that used when they wrote to foreign officers of the Council, invoking the tradition of imperial officials holding moral responsibility for the welfare of the people.[196] Yet their appeals were ultimately unsuccessful, He being unable to secure more

[192] Bickers, *Scramble for China*, 290.
[193] Janet Y. Chen, *Guilty of Indigence: the Urban Poor in China, 1900–1953* (Princeton University Press, 2012), 121.
[194] Christian Henriot, 'Slums, Squats, or Hutments? Constructing and Deconstructing an In-Between Space in Modern Shanghai (1926–65)', *Frontiers of History in China*, Vol. 7, No. 4 (2012), 513; SMC, *Report for 1940*, 29.
[195] SMA U1-6–102: 27 April 1937.
[196] Chen, *Guilty of Indigence*, 121.

funds for refugee relief from the financially straitened Council: while he exercised real authority, he was constrained by the norms of the Council. As a senior Chinese official, He Dekui was valuable to the SMC as it sought to portray itself as more sympathetic to the Chinese community.

Other senior Chinese employees were also highly qualified. Dr Wu Jingxiong (吳經熊 John C. H. Wu) was the Council's Legal Advisor for eight years from 1929, during which time he was the principal author of the new national constitution.[197] He advised the Council on delicate questions from the policing of the extra-Settlement roads to factory inspection, bringing both expertise in Chinese law and understanding of the Nanjing Government's position to bear on municipal negotiations. Jian Beiyou (Chien Pei-yu) was Chinese Press Officer, after being an editor at *Shenbao* and graduating from the University of Missouri School of Journalism.[198] His duties included translating Chinese press articles to keep the SMC abreast of how issues were being reported to the Chinese public and preparing statements favourable to the SMC in a form readily accepted by Chinese editors:[199] propaganda work that was deemed vitally important in reducing friction between the SMC and the Chinese population and authorities. *Shenbao* published all SMC departmental reports, suggesting public interest in its activities. Employing more Chinese at higher levels helped the SMC negotiate the political environment of the 1930s.

Scant sources are available on more junior Chinese municipal employees, but one remarkable transnational woman was interviewed in an oral history project in 1990s Beijing and part of her story recounted her years working for the SMC. Chen Yongsheng came from a progressive family in Changsha, Hunan: her father and other male relatives had studied abroad and were, she said, 'inclined to western ideas'.[200] Her feet were not bound, and she was sent to school in Changsha and in Beijing when the family moved there. Very much a child of the modernising imperative of her generation, in 1916 at the age of 16 she decided not to marry, determined instead to live independently and work in women's physical education in order to help build a 'strong nation'.[201] With this end in mind, in 1918 she joined the physical education school run by the Young Women's Christian Association (YWCA) in Shanghai, where she participated in the May Fourth Movement. Later, she won a scholarship to become the first Chinese student at the Baptist Baylor College of Women in Texas,

[197] SMA U1-6–102: Wu to Fessenden, 7 December 1937.
[198] Yong Zhang Volz, 'Transplanting Modernity: Cross-Cultural Networks and the Rise of Modern Journalism in China, 1890s–1930s' (Unpublished PhD dissertation, University of Minnesota, 2006), 175.
[199] SMA U1-6–87: 'Notes on Press Information Office', 12 October 1936.
[200] Wang Zheng, *Women in the Chinese Enlightenment: Oral and Textual Histories* (Berkeley, CA: University of California Press, 1999), 260.
[201] Ibid., 264.

graduating in 1927 with a BA in English. After teaching in Burma, becoming the first female school principal in Shandong and then the chief executive of the YWCA in Hangzhou, Chen returned to Shanghai to teach physical education in the University of Shanghai. When the university was forced to move to a smaller site with no room for physical education due to the Japanese occupation of the area from 1932, Chen joined the staff of the SMC girls' school, benefiting from the expansion of municipal spending on Chinese education won by her compatriots on the Council.

Chen described her ten years working at the school as her 'golden age' when she enjoyed 'a comfortable life' with good working conditions and a higher salary than her previous roles or other teaching posts. She could afford to rent a large apartment alone, employ a housekeeper and take taxis with friends to watch movies and eat in restaurants.[202] Benefiting from the SMC's laissez-faire approach to governance, Chen enjoyed being given 'a free hand' in her teaching, allowing her to initiate physical education programmes comparable to those in schools in the USA or Britain, which were forbidden in Chinese-run girls' schools.[203]

Several of Chen's colleagues at the school had studied overseas and all were college graduates, demonstrating the quality of employee the Council was able to attract to its schools with its generous salaries and the internationalism of its staff. The SMC's Chinese teachers wrote to the new Superintendent of Education, Leonard Charles Healey, when he was promoted to the position in 1929, welcoming his appointment and praising his courtesy 'which knows neither creed nor colour', and he continued to be popular as he managed the expansion of the Department of Education.[204] Not all municipal employees were perhaps as content as Chen, but her experience suggests that despite the inequality systemic in the Council's staff, with higher salaries and greater promotion opportunities for foreign employees, Chinese who worked for the Council were broadly better off than they might have been in comparable work elsewhere in the city.

Salaries were generous by local and international standards for Chinese and foreign staff alike, notwithstanding a great differential in the pay of foreigners and Chinese. The French Concession paid its top officials, who were employees of the French consul-general rather than the *Conseil* per se, less than

---

[202] Ibid., 260–71.
[203] After the conclusion of the Sino-Japanese War, Chen worked in a western school in Shanghai, then paid her own way through a Master's degree in special education at Columbia University. In 1949 she opened China's first school for disabled children, but was dismissed in 1951, beginning the trials that dogged her through the Mao years as her western experience made her a political target, particularly during the Cultural Revolution. Ibid., 271–6.
[204] Chinese members of the teaching staff to Healey, 20 December 1929, from the private collection of Andrew Healey.

two-thirds of the salaries received by their counterparts in the International Settlement: 11,100 taels for the chief of the *Garde municipale* in 1927, for example, as opposed to 18,000 taels for the Commissioner of the Shanghai Municipal Police.[205] SMC committees kept an eye on how competitive the salaries offered in Shanghai were compared with similar positions in Britain and raised them if needed.[206] High salaries generally ensured a steady supply of good applicants: typically eight per place for the SMP, though senior posts could attract dozens of applications: Boisraigon beat 264 others for his position.[207]

Foreign employees were paid an allowance in addition to the basic salary, ostensibly to compensate them for living abroad but in reality to ensure a standard of living considerably higher than that available to Chinese, in order to preserve the perceived status of foreigners in Shanghai. Foreign employees also received family bonuses (for a wife and up to two children), locomotion allowances to heads of department and other staff of sufficient importance to justify the ownership of a municipal motorcar, and other allowances typical of the paternalistic employers of the day.[208] Terms of service for foreign employees were similar to British colonial contracts (and the French Concession adopted the same for its staff): three- or more commonly five-year periods of employment each concluded with nine months' home leave, with shorter periods of annual leave to be taken within China.[209] The SMC had a sanatorium in the mountain resort town of Moganshan for employees (and their families) to take respite from the heat of the city for periods of up to 20 days during the summer months.[210]

War brought new tensions for councillors and staff. From the late 1930s, salaries were frozen as the SMC implemented a policy of retrenchment. Retention of foreign staff became difficult in the Second World War, as it had in the First, with men leaving to fight for their countries, and unattractive salaries in comparison with earlier levels of pay did not help. The rising cost of living (due to both rapid inflation and the falling exchange rate) became a serious source of discontent for all employees, and a threatened strike by the Chinese branch of the SMP in December 1940 forced the Council to address the issue of pay. Deciding that the long-delayed salary increase should be applied to all staff, the Council went to the ratepayers to seek their approval for an increase in rates to fund it.

---

[205] Clifford, *Spoilt Children of Empire*, 24.
[206] SMA U1-1-60: Finance Committee, 6 February 1922.
[207] Bickers, *Empire Made Me*, 33, 68.
[208] SMA U1-6-99: Terms of Service, amended 1 September 1935.
[209] Christine Cornet, 'The Bumpy End of the French Concession and French Influence in Shanghai, 1937–1946', in Henriot and Yeh (eds.), *In the Shadow of the Rising Sun*, 266.
[210] SMA U1-16-9: General Order, 17 April 1935.

The Japanese community was keen to flex its muscles as the long domination of the Settlement by the British seemed about to give way. The Chairman of the Japanese Ratepayers' Association, Yukichi Hayashi, tabled an amendment at the meeting opposing the resolution for increased rates. When the resolution was defeated, Japanese ratepayers approached the platform and Hayashi fired at the chairman, William J. Keswick, with his revolver, wounding Keswick and Japanese councillor Okamoto.[211] Christian Henriot suggests that Japanese anger at the increase in rates may have stemmed in part from the double burden this community was under as its residents' association also taxed its members.[212] The popular opposition to the rise had put the Japanese councillors in a difficult position: while representing the views of Japanese residents, they recognised the need to prevent a strike in the SMP that could have threatened the security of the Settlement. Indeed it was a Japanese member who proposed the controversial measure in the first place. The Japanese councillors were sympathetic to the consensus among the other foreign members of the Council.

The Council got its way: the meeting was rescheduled, the Japanese ratepayers abstained, and the motion was passed, enabling an approximately 40 per cent increase in salaries to municipal employees.[213] Municipal staffing and pay could be highly contentious issues in the charged political atmosphere of Shanghai, increasingly so as the balance of influence shifted from the British to the Japanese on the Council and among the staff. Transnational colonialism created new potential areas of conflict in addition to those common to sites of more conventional colonialism.

Conclusion

The SMC was far from representative of the International Settlement's population as a whole, rather reflecting the attitudes of those whose interests it existed to serve: the foreign business community. Many of the 'people of importance' on the Council were directors of multinational companies and the Chinese councillors from 1928 were all prominent businessmen. All were transnational in their background, often working for multinational companies or having lived

---

[211] TNA FO 371/27631: British consul-general, Shanghai to Foreign Office, London, 23 January 1941. Hayashi was sent to Nagasaki for trial where he was given a suspended sentence of two years' hard labour. For Hayashi's long-standing connections with Japanese nationalism in Shanghai, see Fogel, ' "Shanghai-Japan" ', 927–50.

[212] Henriot, ' "Little Japan" ', 162.

[213] The cost of living continued to rise, leading to resignations and petitions from the Chinese staff, and the SMC eventually took the unprecedented step of procuring essential foods to try to ensure the basic needs of staff were met. SMA U1-6–197: Staff sub-committee minutes, 6 July 1943; U1-16-12-266: I. Nagai to T. Fukuda, 19 March 1943.

in different parts of the world. The peculiar form that colonialism assumed in Shanghai is underlined by the varied input of the Foreign Office, at times able to influence the Council's membership, at others exasperated by the recalcitrance of the autonomous SMC.

The municipal staff who undertook the SMC's day-to-day activities, especially key individuals such as the secretary and heads of departments, had a greater role in shaping Shanghai than most councillors. Britons dominated the Council, but it included and employed an international range of people, including a large Chinese staff. The life stories of prominent individuals contributed to the Council's distinct nature, as the foreigners who shaped it identified at once with 'Home', the British empire, Shanghai and China. Like the governors and officials who moved around the formal empire, studied by Zoë Laidlaw and by David Lambert and Alan Lester, these individuals brought with them practices and attitudes developed in their previous positions, often in India, and applied them in Shanghai.

The SMC's nature evolved over time, changing most markedly from 1927 to 1928 when the first Chinese councillors finally took their seats and the number of Japanese councillors increased. Always international in its police and defence forces, the Council gradually and reluctantly allowed a more diverse range of people into its offices and chambers to influence and implement policy. Influence policy they did, especially in keeping down the rates of taxation and in securing increased funds for Chinese education. This was partly because they had an atypically cosmopolitan background: they were well-travelled, often western-educated, Christian or otherwise thoroughly exposed to western ideas, and mixed in the elite circles of Shanghai's more cosmopolitan clubs and societies. With the right cultural and business connections, all nationalities could eventually participate in transnational colonialism. Chinese and Japanese were promoted to positions of higher authority, such as He Dekui in the Secretariat and Uyehara in the SMP, and more diverse nationalities were represented among other branches of the staff, as in the Industrial Section. The old British grip on the SMC was loosening, as the body that ran the International Settlement finally became international itself.

3   Policing and Conflict in Shanghai

> [The Shanghai Municipal Council] has not only the moral but also the unquestionable legal right to defend, by force if necessary, the political and territorial integrity of the Settlement against military or mob aggression on the part of any political or military party or faction.
>
> The source of this legal right lies in the unique political status of Shanghai as a municipality, which has no exact counterpart in the whole world.[1]

The Shanghai Municipal Council's role in defending the International Settlement was intricately bound, in the minds of its advocates, with its political autonomy. The chairman's statement quoted above asserts the Council's moral and legal imperative to ensure the independent status of the Settlement was preserved against external or internal threats. The Settlement was not merely part of an informal empire existing solely for the conduct of free trade,[2] but something more akin to an independent city-state, with some of the protection of a colony, run by a council that sought to further entrench and expand its territory. This repeatedly brought the SMC into conflict with Chinese authorities, while it sought to manage conflict within the Settlement and protect it from conflicts taking place outside it. The anticipation of and response to conflict between the SMC and Chinese opponents fundamentally shaped the way in which the Settlement developed and operated.

The SMC was formed at a time of external threat and resulting internal disorder. In 1854, prompted by the seizure of the Chinese walled city by Small Sword Society rebels the previous year, the residents of the English and American Settlements came together to organise mutual self-protection in the form of a police force and a volunteer defence corps under the auspices of the Council. Overseeing the defence of what would become the International Settlement was one of the Council's primary functions, and the area it defended grew dramatically during the nineteenth century. From a small area established

---

[1] Chairman's speech to the Annual Meeting of Ratepayers, 14 April 1927, SMC, *Report for 1927*, 80.

[2] Gallagher and Robinson, 'Imperialism of Free Trade', 1–15.

in 1845, where it was anticipated that British traders would settle on a temporary basis to conduct trade, the Settlement expanded several times until the final expansion in 1899, when it extended over 5,583 acres: almost 40 times its original area. Still not satisfied with this territory, however, the SMC sought further expansions unsuccessfully for decades. Meanwhile, it quietly increased the area under its informal control by building municipal roads outside the Settlement and providing police protection to their residents in return for the payment of rates. In seeking to expand the Settlement, the SMC followed the logic of what John Darwin calls 'bridgeheads': local bases for the expansion of British imperial control.[3] Unlike other bridgeheads, however, the Settlement's international status – and therefore autonomy from British imperial oversight – meant the SMC was reliant on its own forces for expansion.

The SMC behaved like an aggressive and militarised city-state, despite its lack of formal authority in law, in trying to expand and protect its borders. The foreign settlers suggested as early as 1862 that the Settlement should be formally declared a 'free city', governed by its own officers under the joint protection of the Treaty Powers and China.[4] Although the foreign ministers never countenanced such a bold move, the persistent popularity of the notion underlines the state-like ambition of the foreign community. The Settlement was protected by two defence bodies, a quasi-military police force, like those that defended Britain's colonies, and a local volunteer militia. A wide range of nationalities belonged to both forces.

The police controlled the population through more violent means than would have been tolerated in British cities, following the same racist logic operating in Africa and India that force was required to prevent crime among colonial populations. Defence of property was a primary role for any authority, and all the more so in the trade port of Shanghai. As Frederic Wakeman demonstrated, the tendency to autocratic authority was common throughout modern China in the late Qing and through the twentieth century, so municipal police methods were not unusual.[5] The police and volunteers alike were called upon to defend the Settlement militarily when it was threatened from within, by protestors, or from without, by rebellions and civil warfare – all anticipated threats were Chinese. For the defence of the Settlement, the Council could also call on foreign military forces, notably the British, demonstrating Shanghai's position within the British imperial web. It was for this reason that Nicholas Clifford dubbed Shanghai's foreign settlers the 'spoilt children of empire': protesting their independence when it suited them but running for imperial cover when threatened.[6]

[3] Darwin, 'Imperialism and the Victorians', 629.
[4] SMA: Kotenev, 'Extra-Settlement Roads', 15.
[5] Wakeman, *Policing Shanghai*.
[6] Clifford, *Spoilt Children of Empire*.

But the diplomatic wrangling that concerned Clifford was less important for the Settlement's residents than the SMC's police and volunteers, which prompted, contained and engaged in conflict.

Conflict was inherent in the International Settlement's position, surrounded as it was by increasingly hostile Chinese administrations. Moreover, the Council played a significant role in conflicts during the tumultuous early decades of the twentieth century, influencing events far more than has been recognised. This chapter begins by explaining the transnational constitution and the roles of the Shanghai Municipal Police (SMP) and the Shanghai Volunteer Corps (SVC). Next, it traces the ways in which the SMC first expanded the territory directly under its control in the nineteenth century and then expanded its governmental functions beyond the Settlement proper. The rest of the chapter focuses on key flashpoints in the twentieth-century history of Shanghai: the Mixed Court riot of 1905, the SMC's attempt to seize Zhabei in 1913, the defence of the Settlement from civil war and the May Thirtieth Movement protests in the 1920s, and finally the Sino-Japanese conflicts of 1932 and from 1937. These events demonstrate the SMC's central role of governing conflict in the International Settlement, illuminating the bellicose nature of the transnational colonial presence in China. The pivotal years from 1925 to 1928, with the explosion of nationalism prompted by the May Thirtieth Movement, the Council's loss of judicial control in the Mixed Court, and the Guomindang takeover of local Chinese government, marked the end of expansionism and the shift to a defensive position by the SMC. The SMC saw itself as fulfilling a state's defensive role, but ultimately its autonomy was compromised in times of war when foreign forces were needed, revealing the British, American and Japanese backing that enabled transnational colonialism.

Policing Conflict

The Shanghai Municipal Council had two of its own organisations to call on for purposes of defence, the SMP and the SVC. When under serious threat, it also turned to the armed forces of the foreign powers (primarily the Royal Navy): the gunboat diplomacy that underpinned the European position in China from the nineteenth century. The SMC Watch Committee, which oversaw both forces, stated explicitly that 'the Shanghai Municipal Police forms the first line of defence and is quasi-military in nature'.[7] The SMP was the largest municipal department and often appeared to Shanghai's inhabitants to operate independently of the SMC, even though its actions were overseen by the Watch Committee, its employees were subject to the deliberations of

---

[7] SMA U1-1-86: Watch Committee, 4 July 1918.

the Staff Committee and it was answerable to the full Council. By 1930 the strength of the SMP was 4,879.[8] This was an international force, with four branches for the four categories of policemen: 'foreign' (essentially British), Chinese, Indian and Japanese.[9]

The first recruits were Britons obtained from Hong Kong in 1854, for defence rather than traditional policing. In the twentieth century foreign recruits were obtained directly from Britain and by 1930 the foreign branch numbered 511. Many senior posts were occupied by men with a background in the Royal Irish Constabulary, a militarised gendarmerie with significant influence in colonial policing. K. J. McEuan arrived from Ireland as an officer cadet in 1900 and rose to the rank of Commissioner of Police. Others were drawn from other colonial forces, such as E. I. M. Barrett, seconded and then appointed permanently from the Malay States Guides.[10] Many had a military background, such as Alan Hilton-Johnson, who joined in 1907 on the recommendation of the Captain Superintendent, C. D. Bruce, who had seen his capabilities in the Weihaiwei Regiment, and later became Commissioner-General of the force.[11] As in other colonial police forces, the men were housed in barracks and organised by military rank. Foreign members of the SMP were trained in musketry and the use of revolvers, and by 1916 the whole force was armed – a clear deviation from the Metropolitan Police model to the colonial approach of exercising control through force.[12]

The Chinese branch was by far the largest, up to ten times the size of the foreign branch and numbering 3,477 in 1930. Chinese constables were tasked primarily with patrolling duties and everyday policing. They were not well trusted; the foreign branch was intended to supervise the other branches. In 1905 the Watch Committee was so dissatisfied with the Chinese branch that it considered dismissing it entirely, its duties to be performed by a much enlarged Indian branch.[13] The Chinese branch nevertheless continued to provide the bulk of the policing of the Settlement.

Most members of the Indian Section were Sikhs, prized throughout the British imperial world for their imposing stature, military prowess and bravery in battle.[14] Sikhs were first brought to Shanghai from India in 1884 in response to fears from foreign residents on Council-built roads outside the Settlement about the dangers of the Sino-French war. They could be paid considerably

---

[8] SMC, *Report for 1930*, 101.
[9] On the SMP, see Wakeman, *Policing Shanghai* and Bickers, *Empire Made Me*, 64–94.
[10] SMA U1-1-82: Watch Committee, 5 February 1907.
[11] SMA U1-1-82: Watch Committee, 19 September 1907.
[12] SMA U1-1-85: Watch Committee, 31 May and 12 July 1915; 17 October 1916.
[13] SMA U1-1-82: Watch Committee, 5 December 1905.
[14] Isabella Jackson, 'The Raj on Nanjing Road: Sikh Policemen in Treaty-Port Shanghai', *Modern Asian Studies*, Vol. 46, No. 6 (2012), 1683.

less than European police officers and helped oversee the Chinese branch. The Sikhs in their striking red turbans became a great source of prestige for the British community, displaying the exotic splendour and power of the British Raj to the western and Chinese residents of Shanghai. Yet they increased Chinese resentment of the SMP: in 1913 the American consul-general warned E. C. Pearce, SMC chairman, that young Chinese in the YMCA, 'really excellent fellows, say that they will endure Chinese or foreigners to safeguard the [Northern] district but they will resist the "Black slaves" '.[15] Despite such Chinese animosity towards the Sikhs, the Council sought to increase their number from 200 to 1,000 for mobilisation against unruly crowds following the Mixed Court riot of 1905, but was prevented by concerns from the British consul-general and minister that this would constitute a standing army. British authorities thus constrained the SMC in areas where it relied on British imperial support. The Sikh branch nonetheless grew steadily and by 1930 there were 691 Indian policemen.

The small Japanese branch was established in 1916, due to pressure from the Japanese community and an acute shortage of European recruits during the First World War. Impressed by the discipline of the branch and the economy achieved by their lower salaries and shorter passage from home compared with their British counterparts, the SMC expanded the branch to 200 by 1930. In later years, under pressure from the Japanese consul-general and Council members, the Council promoted Japanese officers to senior positions. The different nationalities of the SMP did not cooperate as well as the Council would have hoped and tensions between the Chinese and Japanese communities affected the SMP. A clash between the two branches in 1918 resulted in a Chinese constable fatally shooting a Japanese colleague.[16] The Watch Committee nonetheless considered an expansion of the Japanese branch from 30 to 50 helpful to control 'the rowdy Japanese element' and counter Japanese attempts to 'usurp' the SMP's exclusive right to police the Settlement through the use of Japanese consular police in Hongkou. The committee believed that 'a section of the Japanese community' did not understand the status of the Settlement and were 'apparently under the impression that the municipality is to all intents and purposes a separate country' upon which they were 'entitled to make demands, ignorant of the fact that they are in fact themselves members of the municipality'.[17] The Japanese branch of the SMP was thus both a response to and an attempt to limit Japanese demands on the SMC as the Council negotiated the challenges of transnational colonial rule.

[15] SMA U1-2-437/1840: American consul to Pearce, 29 July 1913.
[16] SMA U1-1-86: Watch Committee, 7 October 1918.
[17] SMA U1-1-86: Watch Committee, 7 October 1918.

During normal times, the SMP provided general police protection to life and property. Fighting crime was a gargantuan task in Shanghai: the co-existence of great wealth and abject poverty, a high concentration of recent immigrants, and the legal loopholes afforded by extraterritoriality together provided ample opportunities for criminals. Crime was much higher than in other treaty ports: the chief of police for the British Municipality at Tianjin reported just three murders in 1936 and no armed robberies, while the SMP reported 25 murders and 379 armed robberies or attempted armed robberies in the International Settlement in the same year. Approximately half of the reported armed robberies resulted in a conviction, a fairly typical success rate for the SMP.

Criminals benefited from the divided jurisdictions of the city: the jurisdiction of police pursuing a criminal ended at the border of whichever of the three parts of the city (International Settlement, French Concession or Chinese City) to which they belonged. Criminals often claimed the nationality of one of the treaty powers and thus were tried in the Mixed Court, which was considered more lenient than the Chinese courts. Du Yuesheng, the notorious Green Gang leader, claimed French nationality to evade Chinese justice.[18] Cooperation between the different police forces was almost non-existent; it was only in 1925 that a direct telephone line was installed to connect the SMP and the French municipal police.[19] The French police were known to be deeply infiltrated by the Green Gang, and the Public Security Bureau of the Chinese city was also implicated in the narcotics trade. But the SMP itself was not immune from corruption.[20] Bribery was a particular problem, despite the SMC's hope that paying good salaries would obviate the attraction of 'squeeze'. Half of the Chinese police were suspected of taking a 'protection fee' from opium traders and a foreign inspector allegedly accepted 20,000 dollars from the Green Gang for classing murder cases as 'non-proven'.[21] The satisfied tone of municipal annual reports and off-hand reporting of kidnapping in the *North-China Herald* suggest that the foreign community and therefore the Council were content to allow a high prevalence of crime so long as it affected ordinary Chinese rather than the foreign or Chinese elites.

The majority of crimes that came to the SMP's attention involved Chinese as both victims and perpetrators, unsurprisingly given that the overwhelming majority of residents were Chinese, so the SMP did not only serve foreign interests. In 1900, of 70,069 recorded offenders, 69,331 were Chinese and

---

[18] Cassel, *Grounds of Judgment*, 39.
[19] Feetham, *Report*, 2, 159.
[20] Wakeman, *Policing Shanghai*, 127, 131.
[21] Bickers, *Empire Made Me*, 114; Rewi Alley, *Yo Banfa!* (Shanghai: China Monthly Review, 1952), 26–7, quoted in Wright, 'Shanghai Imperialists', 106.

738 were foreign. The crimes recorded ranged from arson (8 cases) to utter-
ing (an offence related to fraud: 23 cases). The most common offences were
obstruction (5,559 cases), larceny (3,008), misdemeanour (1,185), assault
(682), fighting or creating a disturbance (564) and 'squeezing' (bribery: 284
cases).[22] Crime increased with the growth of the Settlement and at times of
political upheaval, notably during the 1911 revolution and in the 1920s and
1930s. 1927 witnessed a surge in violent crime to its highest levels in the
history of the SMP, with 123 murders, 27 cases of armed abduction, and
1,458 armed robberies (over three times the previous record high set the year
before).[23] Things had calmed down by 1930, when there were 40 murders, 36
cases of armed abduction, and 702 cases of armed robbery.[24] Illegal gambling
had become a major target for the municipal police, with 840 individuals,
almost all Chinese, arrested for gambling offences in 1930. A special Opium
Preventive Section successfully raided 151 opium dens that year, seizing the
opium and smoking paraphernalia and arresting smokers and proprietors,
although the Commissioner of Police admitted that 'It is difficult to judge
whether there is any actual decrease in the number of smokers'.[25] The vast
majority of offenders were Chinese, but Japanese, Americans, Koreans and
Russians were also arrested for narcotics crimes.[26]

Much police work, however, involved the far more mundane work of enforcing byelaws and directing traffic. These efforts ensured the smooth running
of the Settlement for its residents and were taken seriously: the Commissioner
of Police took the opportunity afforded by his long leave in 1936 to study
traffic in London, New York and other large cities around the world, reporting
that their traffic problems were much worse than Shanghai's.[27] He even seconded an SMP officer to New Scotland Yard to study traffic control in London,
showing the close links maintained with metropolitan policing. Even everyday
policing could be contentious, particularly as the police were prone to heavy-
handed tactics. Indian constables had a particular reputation for violence, but
all the policemen were liable to strike a poor Chinese perceived as recalcitrant.
Resistance to violent policing grew in pace with Chinese nationalism and at
least 80 hawkers gathered at the SMC administration building in 1935 to protest
an assault of a hawker by a foreign constable.[28] The assistant secretary satisfied their demands by writing to the Louza Police Station requesting sympathy

---

[22] SMC, *Report for 1900*, 56–7.
[23] SMC, *Report for 1927*, 46–8.
[24] SMC, *Report for 1930*, 90–1.
[25] SMC, *Report for 1930*, 93. On the failing battle against narcotics, see Wakeman, *Policing Shanghai*, 116–31.
[26] SMA U1-14–966: SMC, *Report for 1936*, 28.
[27] SMA U1-14–966: SMC, *Report for 1936*, 6.
[28] SMA U1-6–99: Assistant secretary to secretary, SMC, 18 January 1935.

for hawkers. Poorer Chinese were now asserting their rights to fair treatment, but the SMP continued to see them as a source of disorder requiring control.

Convicted criminals were incarcerated in the SMC's notorious Ward Road Gaol, the largest prison in the world. By 1934 it had 6,500 inmates, equal to half the total prison population of England.[29] Controlling such a large number of convicted criminals could be interpreted as indicative of a Foucauldian 'disciplinary power' embodied in the SMC,[30] but the SMC's authority over the Settlement was too incomplete for this to be persuasive. Rather, the high prison population should be attributed to the high levels of crime in Shanghai combined with the municipal desire for greater control over the Chinese population, never fully realised. The gaol was always overcrowded. In 1933 British prison reformer Margery Fry inspected the gaol and complained to the Foreign Office about the conditions, particularly for juvenile offenders. The Watch Committee therefore sent two members, John Wu and O. Okamoto, both trained in law, to investigate in person.[31] They reported that they were 'much impressed' by what they found, to the satisfaction of the rest of the Council. The SMC felt the need to respond to metropolitan criticism, but dismissed it as unfounded. Local criticism instead focused on concern among foreign ratepayers about the cost of incarcerating so many Chinese, while Chinese authorities were content to reduce their own judicial costs by leaving the large number of criminals convicted in the Settlement to be paid for by the SMC.[32] Fighting crime was expensive.

In addition to regular policing, the SMC used the police to defend its autonomy and interests against the Chinese authorities. The SMP arrested eight Chinese soldiers who entered the Settlement without a permit in 1901, and regularly enforced the exclusion of Chinese police and military authorities.[33] This became more difficult following the establishment of the Chinese municipal government in 1927, and the SMP was on the front line of defending the Settlement against encroachment from Chinese authorities. In 1928 the Commissioner of Police drew Council attention to the presence of Chinese Stamp Tax collection bureaux in the Settlement, which he was ordered to close down.[34]

---

[29] Frank Dikötter, *Crime, Punishment and the Prison in Modern China* (London: Hurst, 2002), 311.

[30] Michel Foucault, *Discipline and Punish: The Birth of the Prison* (London: Allen Lane, 1977).

[31] SMA U1-4-2788: 'The Foreign Office and Miss Fry's criticisms', 246–56.

[32] Dikötter, *Crime*, 312–13.

[33] SMA U1-1–82: Watch Committee, 10 April 1901. The senior consul queried the arrests, concerned about the offence caused to the Chinese authorities, but the Watch Committee declared that the SMP's action 'was wholly in accordance with the Council's arrangements as notified to the consular body in August 1899.'

[34] SMA: Kotenev, 'Chinese Taxation', 60.

The SMP also gathered intelligence, making use of its transnational connections. It paid a network of informants to report to Chinese inspectors in the Criminal Investigation Department Intelligence Office (later renamed the Special Branch), who then translated their findings. Additionally, as Wakeman showed, the SMP cooperated with the intelligence organs of the Nationalist Public Security Bureau of the city government and the foreign powers, primarily the British and, to a lesser extent, Americans, who were united in their fear of communism.[35] Such transnational collaboration in intelligence gathering strengthened ties between the SMC and other political authorities and ensured its status alongside national governments in the fight against security threats. The *China Weekly Review*, targeting a primarily American expatriate readership in Shanghai, considered the Criminal Investigation Department to be effectively 'an unofficial branch of the British political intelligence and propaganda service', serving imperial interests, but paid for by local taxes.[36] Such criticism of the SMC as being in hock to Britain was a common American complaint, as the Settlement appeared much like a British colony. Fear of anti-imperial 'sedition' was common throughout the British empire, and in enthusiastically combating it, the SMP was demonstrating Shanghai's place within the colonial world.

The SMP's Reserve Unit, mainly comprising Sikhs, was modelled partly on anti-riot units in the Indian police – underlining the SMC's linkages to the formal empire. It was a small, disciplined armed force that could provide a rapid response to fires, labour unrest or riots, established in the wake of the May Thirtieth Movement. It also provided back-up for police operations against armed robbers and criminal gangs.[37] Described as 'the world's first SWAT team', the unit trained in confined spaces and developed innovative techniques for containing violence.[38] Lessons were learned from the events of 1925 and by the 1930s 'mobs were quelled and dispersed without bloodshed'.[39] That the SMP established the Reserve Unit demonstrates the kind of police work it believed it should perform: defending the Settlement against an internal threat of violence from the Chinese community. Fear of the Chinese majority was also the reason for the continued growth of the SMP: Commissioner of Police Captain Barrett stated in 1929 that his main aim in proposing another increase in the strength of the force was 'to perfect an organization which shall make it as difficult as possible for the Chinese community to regain possession of the

---

[35] Wakeman, *Policing Shanghai*, 142–4.
[36] *China Weekly Review*, 9 December 1928, 188–9, cited in Wakeman, *Policing Shanghai*, 145.
[37] E. W. Peters, *Shanghai Policeman*, ed. by Hugh Barnes (London: Rich and Cowan, 1937), 70.
[38] Leroy Thompson, *The World's First SWAT Team: W. E. Fairbairn and the Shanghai Municipal Police Reserve Unit* (Barnsley: Frontline Books, 2012).
[39] SMA U1-14–966: SMC, *Report for 1936*, 6.

Settlement.'[40] The prospect of losing the Settlement grew with the strength of Chinese nationalism through the 1920s, especially following the establishment of the Nationalist government in 1927. The SMP existed largely to protect foreign residents of the Settlement from a Chinese enemy.

In this way, the international but British-dominated SMP guarded the Settlement on behalf of the Council against physical and political threats alike. Chinese opposition to increases in the strength of the force in 1927 was based on both a conviction that the SMP served foreign rather than Chinese interests and resistance to the necessary increase in rates.[41] Certainly foreign concerns were placed well above Chinese needs in policing, while popular criticism of the outlay on policing was justified. Due primarily to the large numbers of foreign personnel, the SMP was an expensive force, monopolising between a third and a half of the Council's ordinary expenditure, or three million taels per year by the late 1920s.[42] The SVC, on the other hand, provided defence on the cheap as the single largest expense, salaries, was not required for volunteers.

Volunteering and Conflict

The Shanghai Volunteer Corps was formed in 1853, one year prior to the establishment of the SMC, when the rebel Small Sword Society seized the Chinese walled city. The British Minister sanctioned the creation of the armed force and the British, American, French, Prussian and Dutch consuls met with residents to coordinate their efforts.[43] The Corps was thus from the outset a transnational concern with the British predominating. The Volunteers' fighting at the Battle of the Muddy Flat the following year – defending the Settlement from the Qing forces camped on its edge rather than the rebels whom the Qing were fighting – unfortunately showed the difficulty of using an international force: the few casualties among the British and American volunteers were suffered at each other's hands rather than inflicted by the Qing soldiers. The short two-hour battle provided a founding myth for the foreign community in Shanghai, though pride that a 300-strong foreign force had seen off 10,000 Qing soldiers was tempered by recognition that the 'unexpected assistance' of the rebels was critical.[44] The foreigners' readiness to fight showed that the inviolability of the

[40] *China Weekly Review*, 30 March 1929, cited in Wakeman, *Policing Shanghai*, 70.
[41] *Shenbao*, 28 June 1927, 12; 3 July 1927, 13; 7 July 1927, 14; 11 July 1927 13; 27 August 1927, 14.
[42] Wakeman, *Policing Shanghai*, 70.
[43] *The Battle of 'Muddy Flat', 1854: being an historical sketch of that famous occurrence, written specially for the jubilee commemoration thereof at Shanghai* (Shanghai: North-China Herald, 1904), 1.
[44] Ibid., 6.

Settlement from encroachment by Chinese authorities was already a corner-stone of its self-image.

The SVC thus predated the vogue for volunteer forces that arose throughout the British empire following the Crimean War (1853–1856) and India's First War of Independence (Mutiny) in 1857. The volunteer forces of both Hong Kong and Singapore were founded in 1854 to provide local protection while the British Army was occupied in Crimea,[45] so unusually Shanghai was ahead of its influential colonial cousins. Citizen armies were established throughout the British world, from Ulster to Australia. The SVC was reconstituted under the authority of the SMC in 1870 and was greatly expanded in 1900 in response to the Boxer Uprising.

The SVC companies were organised by nationality: the British were joined by American, German, Austrian and Japanese companies.[46] There were also at various times Italian, Portuguese and even Chinese companies. In total 27 nationalities were represented.[47] This internationalism is reflected in the Chinese name for the Corps, *Wanguo shangtuan* (万国商团, 'the Militia of the Merchants of Many Nations'); indeed Zhuang Zhiling compares it to the Eight Nation Alliance that formed to fight the Boxer War in 1900.[48] There was, however, a strict racial hierarchy at work: 'A' Company was exclusively white while 'B' Company was reserved for Eurasians.

Volunteering was seen as a civic duty and the SMC asked all major firms to encourage their men to volunteer. Most did (the Chinese Maritime Customs Service provided a whole company), though they often begrudged the days it demanded their employees to be absent from the office. One third of eligible British residents belonged to the SVC in 1928, which, though a high proportion, was seen as inadequate at a time of high anxiety over the security of the Settlement.[49] The volunteers wore uniforms to reflect the armies of their home countries, from the cavalry-style uniform of the American Company to the kilts of the Scottish Highlanders.[50] From 1907, the Japanese Residents'

[45] T. M. Winsley, *A History of the Singapore Volunteer Corps, 1854–1937: Being also an Historical Outline of Volunteering in Malaya* (Singapore: Government Printing Office, 1938).

[46] I. I. Kounin (comp.), *Eighty Five Years of the Shanghai Volunteer Corps* (Shanghai: Cosmopolitan Press, 1938); SMC, *Report for 1900*, 27.

[47] Marcia Ristaino, *Port of Last Resort: The Diaspora Communities of Shanghai* (Stanford University Press, 2002), 56.

[48] Zhuang Zhiling, 'Shanghai gonggong zujie zhong de "duoguo budui" – wanguo shangtuan' ('The Multinational Militia of the Shanghai International Settlement – the Shanghai Volunteer Corps'), *Dang'an yu shi xue* (April 1997), 72–4.

[49] *North-China Herald*, 16 June 1928, 467, cited in Bickers, 'Death of a Young Shanghailander: The Thorburn Case and the Defence of the British Treaty Ports in China in 1931', *Modern Asian Studies*, Vol. 30, No. 2 (1996), 284.

[50] Isabella Jackson, 'The Shanghai Scottish: Volunteers with Scottish, Imperial and Local Identities, 1914–41', in T. M. Devine and Angela McCarthy (eds.), *The Scottish Experience in Asia, c. 1700 to the Present* (London: Palgrave Macmillan, 2017), 235–57.

Association assumed oversight of the Japanese Company.[51] Like other arms of the municipal organisation, the SVC was international yet dominated by the British. Britons made up the majority of the volunteers and the force as a whole was commanded by an officer seconded from the British Army, armed with British Army weapons, and supplied with ammunition from the British colony of Hong Kong. British concessions in Chinese treaty ports organised similar, though much smaller forces, including those at Tianjin and Hankou. There were small *Compagnies française de voluntaires* in French Concessions and local Japanese also briefly organised a volunteer force in Tianjin,[52] so volunteer forces were not unique to the British. The British-influenced SVC was, however, certainly the largest and most significant volunteer force in China.

The SVC expanded greatly over the decades, as each successive moment of tension justified recruiting more volunteers. In 1900 the Corps stood guard in case of disturbances in connection with the Boxer Uprising. The Major commanding the Corps attended a meeting of the SMC's Watch Committee to outline the defence scheme, which included specified centres for assembling the volunteers, a system of patrols and a method for sounding the alarm.[53] The foreign community was nervous, the *North-China Herald* claiming later that 'the settlement was in actual danger of annihilation', though fighting never came near the city.[54] At such times the SMP was at the disposal of the SVC commandant due to his senior military rank, and he recommended that the reserves of ammunition at each police station be increased. Officers of the Corps were issued with secret orders to open fire on rioters and looters, the chairman of the SMC advocating the words 'shoot to kill' be included, though these exact words were deleted on the insistence of the wider Council.[55] The SMC was claiming unity with foreigners in Beijing and Tianjin, who were genuinely subject to violent attack, to justify an increased militarisation of the Settlement.

In 1905, following riots over a dispute at the Mixed Court, leading members of the Chinese business community, including the influential Yu Xiaqing, organised a new Chinese volunteer force. Initially independent of the SVC, the Chinese volunteers formed one company of cavalry and four companies of light infantry under the Chinese Physical Recreation Association, but the number of volunteers declined until the SMC agreed to form a Chinese Company

[51] Fogel, '"Shanghai-Japan"', 930.
[52] Arnold Wright and H. A. Cartwright, *Twentieth-century Impressions of Hongkong, Shanghai and other Treaty Ports of China* (London: Lloyd's Greater Britain Publishing Company, 1908), 425; Fogel, '"Shanghai-Japan"', 943.
[53] SMA U1-1-82: Watch Committee, 15 June 1900.
[54] *NCH*, 23 January 1901, 142. The main practical problem for the SMC during the Boxer War was in fact that Chinese fled the Settlement fearing similar clashes as those witnessed in treaty ports further north. SMC, *Report for 1900*, 44.
[55] SMA U1-1-721: SVC sealed orders, 11 July 1900, cited in Bickers, *Scramble for China*, 346.

of the SVC from 1907.[56] The SMC took some persuading that the Chinese Company had a part to play in the defence of the Settlement (it had rejected a similar suggestion in 1900),[57] and insisted that foreign officers command the company. The Qing government was also concerned about Chinese volunteering for the SVC, but this was laid to rest by 1909 when Prince Zaixun visited the Company to present an ornamental banner.[58] From 1915 the company included Chinese officers, one of whom rose to the rank of major, commanding the Chinese Company and briefly serving as commandant of the SVC in 1934 between the departure of one British colonel and the arrival of the next.[59] The SMC exercised the authority to grant commissions to officers in the SVC, including to Chinese volunteers, acting much like a state or colonial government in doing so.

It is striking that Chinese residents wanted to defend the Settlement under the authority of British officers and the SMC. Business leaders like Yu Xiaqing had much to gain from the stability and protection afforded by the Settlement, but many less prominent Chinese men saw fit to volunteer to protect it. The Chinese Company grew rapidly from 83 members to over 160 to become one of the largest units. Competition for membership was fierce, in contrast to other companies; it was claimed that 'if any one man slacks, there are dozens who will not, and who will be pining to take his place'.[60] From 1913 Chinese volunteers were permitted to bear arms on the same basis as the rest of the Corps. The company held its own annual meetings, where it decided its priorities within the parameters set by the commandant, and it had a reputation for efficiency and accuracy in shooting.[61] Members of the company were awarded certificates for attaining a certain level of military training and medals for participation in every mobilisation of the SVC.[62] A significant number of Chinese thus committed their time and energy to unpaid service of the International Settlement.

All the SVC companies drilled and practised at the rifle range in Hongkou, honing skills that were used in open battle. The SVC Armoury, erected in 1903, was in the centre of the Settlement, near the Central Police Station and opposite the Health Department, so if the Settlement were attacked the weapons

---

[56] Kounin, *Eighty Five Years of the Shanghai Volunteer Corps*, 184; Xu Tao, 'The Chinese Corpsmen in the Shanghai Volunteer Corps', in Toby Lincoln and Xu Tao (eds.), *The Habitable City in China: Urban History in the Twentieth Century* (New York: Palgrave Macmillan, 2017), 28.

[57] SMC, *Report for 1900*, 3–7.

[58] SMC, *Report for 1909*, 5.

[59] Kounin, *Eighty Five Years of the Shanghai Volunteer Corps*, 185–6.

[60] Ibid., 184.

[61] '*Shangtuan huadui nianhuiji*' ('Account of the Annual Meeting of the Chinese Company of the Shanghai Volunteer Corps), *Shenbao*, 5 November 1924, 14.

[62] *Shenbao*, 20 March 1924, 13; Kounin, *Eighty Five Years of the Shanghai Volunteer Corps*, 188.

would be safely at the heart of the defended area and easily accessible to both volunteers and police.[63] Different companies of volunteers had different specialisms, from the prestigious all-British Light Horse Company to the Light Gun Battery of Dutch, Swiss and Scandinavian volunteers. The latter company was formed in 1924, following the threat posed to the Settlement by civil war and further diversifying the Corps. It manned artillery imported from India and, despite its international membership, was attached to the British forces in 1927 and sent for training in Hong Kong in 1933.[64] The Scandinavians' reported excitement at the trip suggests that they were content for their service to Shanghai to come under a British imperial banner. The all-British Machine Gun Company used armoured cars based on the standard British Rolls-Royce armoured car but built higher 'to enable the gunner to see and shoot over the local bamboo fences'.[65] In having special equipment built to suit local needs, the SMC was behaving like a state with its own armed forces to equip. But the SVC also had to improvise, using freighters requisitioned from the Public Works Department to tow the Light Artillery Battery and barriers that in times of peace were erected around public works projects: this was low-cost defence.

Following the outbreak of the First World War, the German and Austrian Companies continued to drill until 1917 when China entered the war on the Allied side, as local loyalties trumped national divisions. The Corps was substantially reorganised in 1932 in the wake of the Sino-Japanese conflict, when among others a Philippine Company was established under American command, demonstrating the influence of American imperialism. An Interpreters Company was formed of Chinese recruits to assist foreign companies of the SVC and, primarily, foreign troops in Shanghai without the language skills necessary to operate. A Jewish Company was established in 1933 in the last addition to the Corps before its disbandment in 1942.[66]

In a departure from the volunteer model, the SMC established a salaried Russian Unit in 1927. A force of 150 highly-trained Cossacks contributed to the defence of the Settlement from civil war, and within five years there were four Russian companies with over 400 men. Marcia Ristaino notes that this was one area of life in Shanghai where these previously elite refugees could gain the respect of an otherwise disdainful western population.[67] A Russian unit was first proposed in 1922 by officers of the former Russian Imperial Army who settled in Shanghai. The SVC commandant suggested that a Russian platoon might be attached to 'B' Company (the Eurasian Company) as the presence of

---

[63] SMA U1-1–82: Watch Committee, 27 January 1903.
[64] Kounin, *Eighty Five Years of the Shanghai Volunteer Corps*, 175–6.
[65] *Royal Tank Corps Journal* (1927), 182.
[66] Ristaino, *Port of Last Resort*, 62, 65–6.
[67] Ibid., 59–60.

an efficient platoon 'would probably stimulate keenness in the lower ranks ... or make them so ashamed that they would resign'.[68] He thought the platoon might help in the event of trouble with 'undesirable Russians', but the Watch Committee was unconvinced and decided to defer the decision 'until there is a stable Russian Government'.

Instead, it was the imperatives of defence that dictated the formation of the Russian Unit. With Chinese armies clashing around Shanghai, London threatened to remove the British Defence Force because it was undermining Sino-British relations.[69] Despite this vulnerability, a recruitment drive to increase the number of volunteers was deemed to have failed, as public confidence in the SMC plummeted. A paid Russian Unit seemed the only way to ensure adequate defence of the Settlement, and it meant that the business of Shanghai need not be interrupted by mobilising the volunteers 'except in cases of very widespread civil disturbance or external aggression'.[70] The paid unit essentially provided the Council with the standing army that it had been denied when the large expansion to the Sikh police branch was blocked 20 years earlier. It was even called the 'Russian Regiment' in 1932 when the Russian volunteers were incorporated with the salaried men.[71] It was supervised by a British major as an 'advisor', but its members celebrated their identity proudly with a regimental museum displaying military memorabilia from Russia.[72] Members of the Unit were deployed with or recruited to the police force, especially the Reserve Unit, reinforcing cooperation between the SVC and SMP.

Russians remained, however, low in the SVC hierarchy, reflecting wider prejudice against them in the foreign community. The SMC defrayed the costs of accommodation in the General Hospital for members of the Corps at first class rates for officers of all companies and second class for the men, with the exception of the Russian Unit whose officers and men were entitled only to second and third class rates respectively.[73] Yet the Russians proved their importance in the defence of the Settlement, particularly in 1937, when the unit guarded gates and blockhouses to try to keep the Sino-Japanese hostilities beyond the Settlement's limits, and was mobilised 16 times to crush riots.[74] Against these internal and external threats the SMC now had at its disposal a paid force of over 100 permanently employed soldiers, supplemented by almost 300 Russian volunteers at the core of a force of over 2,000 fighting men.

---

[68] Bickers, *Britain in China*, 71–2. In the commandant's view 'B' Company should ' "get on" or "get out" ', reflecting the prevalent prejudice against Eurasians.
[69] SMA U1-1-89: Watch Committee, 21 June 1928.
[70] Kounin, *Eighty Five Years of the Shanghai Volunteer Corps*, 132.
[71] Ibid., 129–32.
[72] Ristaino, *Port of Last Resort*, 59.
[73] SMA U1-1-88: Watch Committee, 22 April 1927.
[74] Kounin, *Eighty Five Years of the Shanghai Volunteer Corps*, 133.

By arming itself with a force that increasingly resembled an army, the SMC was behaving like a government with a state to protect. Between the SMP and SVC, the Council aspired to be able to defend its territory.

Expansion

The SMC achieved its earlier territorial gains as the local foreign population expanded with little opposition. The first extension to the English Settlement came in 1848, the same year as the establishment of the American Settlement and the signing of the agreement between the French consul and the Shanghai Daotai for the French Concession, which was founded the following year. The extension was achieved through a simple agreement between the British consul and the Daotai to extend the western boundary of the Settlement.[75] In 1863 the English Settlement combined with its American neighbour to form the International Settlement, as the foreign community sought to better defend itself from external disorder during the Taiping Rebellion. The local French community advocated joining the International Settlement, but Paris refused to concede control of the concession. The SMC secured a further extension in 1893, the golden jubilee year of the founding of the Settlement, which was celebrated with great fanfare in November. The greatest expansion was to be the last, agreed in 1898 and enacted the following year, tripling the size of the Settlement and bringing 10,000 more houses and over 50,000 more Chinese residents under the direct authority of the SMC.[76] The SMC pushed for these expansions, citing the numbers of foreigners living on the territory brought into the Settlement, but the negotiations were led by the British consul-general in Shanghai and the British legation in Beijing, reflecting British dominance among the foreign powers in the nineteenth century. Though the foreign powers were unable to annex China as a whole, their bridgeheads were growing.

The colony of Hong Kong expanded similarly in 1860, when the Convention of Beijing that concluded the Second Opium War granted Kowloon Peninsular to the British to add to Hong Kong Island, and in 1898 when the New Territories were leased to the British for 99 years.[77] The British concession at Tianjin also expanded in 1897. It is no coincidence that these colonial outposts won their greatest territorial expansions when China was weak following defeat by Japan in 1895. The foreign powers' appetites for territory were whetted anew and many believed that China would be carved up between them in much the

---

[75] Feetham, *Report*, 1, 29.
[76] Bickers, *Scramble for China*, 330.
[77] John M. Carroll, *A Concise History of Hong Kong* (Lanham, MD: Rowman and Littlefield, 2007), 1.

same way as Africa had been over the previous two decades. In what Robert Bickers calls the 'scramble for China', Britain claimed the Yangtze valley around and inland from Shanghai as a sphere of influence, while Germany laid similar claim to Shandong, Russia to Manchuria, and France to the south-west of China. The concentration of diverse imperial interests in Shanghai was writ large across China. The foreign expectation of ever-increasing imperial influence in China extended into the twentieth century, but with the growth of Chinese nationalism and the global shift away from colonial acquisition, there would be no carving up of China and no further additions to the International Settlement. The French Concession acquired a large extension in 1914, follow-ing protracted negotiations and in return for including Chinese on the *Conseil municipal*. But this council was advisory only, power lying with the French consul-general, and the members rarely met. The French expansion gave the SMC false hope for a similar enlargement of the Settlement; but in the absence of formal territorial expansion, the Council found other ways to extend its con-trol beyond the Settlement.

The SMC built many miles of roads external to the Settlement borders in anticipation of acquiring the areas they covered in subsequent extensions. As soon as the largest expansion was formalised in 1898, the Council embarked on further land purchase and road-building schemes (Map 3.1).[78] The 'extra-Settlement roads' were rendered in Chinese as 越界築路, *yuejie zhulu*, which carries a greater sense of overstepping a boundary. But the SMC did not believe its road-building activities overstepped any line, pointing to the pro-vision in the Land Regulations for the purchase of 'land leading or being out of the Settlement' for roads and public amenities.[79] Municipal investment in amenities also extended beyond the Settlement, from the municipal granite quarry at Pingqiao to the promised cool relief of 'the hills' owned by Jesuits ten miles from the city. In north-west Shanghai lay the district of Hongkou, the southern part of which was included in the Settlement while the northern area lay beyond. This did not stop the Council from purchasing 39 acres in northern Hongkou in 1896 for a rifle range for the SVC and the foreign armed forces. A decade later tennis courts, a swimming pool, a bowling green and a golf course had been added to what was to become known as the Hongkew Recreation Ground. The SMC intended to include this area in a later extension to the Settlement, but in the meantime the simple purchase of land enabled it to exercise foreign domination over the landscape.[80] This kind of expansion was not justified by the usual treaty-port narrative of the need to create and main-tain an environment conducive to foreign business. Rather, it indicates that

[78] SMA: Kotenev, 'Extra-Settlement Roads'.
[79] *China Year Book 1938*, 296.
[80] SMA U1-1–56: Finance Committee, 9 October 1908.

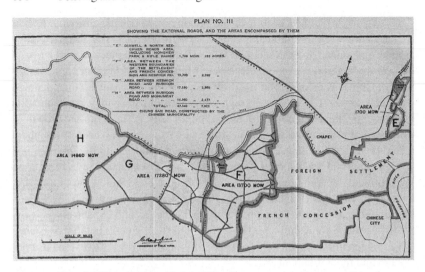

Map 3.1 Plan showing External Roads areas.
Source: Feetham, *Report*, III, facing p. viii, image courtesy of the *Virtual Cities Project*, Institut d'Asie Orientale, Lyon.

the SMC saw the Settlement like an independent state, with its own internal imperative to expand for the sake of future generations of residents in what was expected to be perpetuity.

The Council claimed its extraterritorial rights extended to the external roads because they were foreign property. As foreigners populated the extra-Settlement roads alongside Chinese, the SMC saw a need to protect them and their property, as well as its own investments in amenities, so included these roads in the beats of the SMP. Police functions extended beyond the simple preservation of law and order. Members of the SMP were responsible, for example, for the enforcement of byelaws and licensing regulations, which were imposed beyond the Settlement from 1909. The SMC argued that residents on the external roads were entitled to the security that licences offered of basic standards in safety and hygiene. Extending the area in which the SMP functioned thus entailed extending municipal authority over many aspects of residents' lives.

As a corollary to policing external roads, the SMC believed that the police forces of the Chinese authorities should be excluded from the external roads areas. It challenged the patrolling of Cemetery Road by the Daotai's police in 1898 and responded to a 'case of ruffianism' by police in Pudong in 1900 with a call to exercise municipal police control of the area 'with a view to furthering the future extension of the Settlement in this direction'.[81] The Council argued

---

[81] SMA U1-1-82: Watch Committee, 20 June 1898 and 27 March 1900.

that the Chinese authorities were not policing these areas effectively, so in the interests of law and order it had no choice but to act. This stance was supported by property developers such as the Shanghai Land Investment Company, which wrote to the Council in 1906 drawing its attention to the large number of new Chinese houses in the part of Hongkou that lay beyond the Settlement and pointing out the inadequacy of local policing.[82] In this way the Council's expansionist ambitions neatly intersected with those of Shanghai's capitalist elites and the Chinese middle classes who sought protection from the SMP.

Frustrated Expansionism

The SMC was slow to learn that the extensions to the Settlement won easily in the nineteenth century would not be repeated in the twentieth. One coveted area was the district of Zhabei, on the northern boundary. The SMC had sought to include Zhabei within the borders agreed in 1898, but the effort was resisted by the Chinese authorities. The SMC seized on small incidents as excuses for expanding the Settlement to the north, such as the assault in May 1908 on Police Constable Sinclair by Chinese police in Zhabei. For the Council, the fact that Sinclair was beyond the Settlement limits in no way restricted his right to operate there freely. This incident led the SMC to appeal to the consular authorities to seek to bring the area as far as the Shanghai-Nanjing railway line under formal municipal control.[83] They proposed two expansions, one needed 'as an urgent matter' and a second, much more extensive boundary that would satisfy the Council's ambitions 'for many years'.[84] The assumption was that the Settlement would continue to expand for the foreseeable future.

The extension considered immediately necessary was by no means modest, including Zhabei, the Hongkew Recreation Ground and surrounding area, a large extension to the west to include the SMC-built Edinburgh and Jessfield Roads, and 'so much of Pootung [Pudong] as will bring under taxation the wharves and godowns which at present unfairly compete with similar undertakings within Settlement limits'.[85] Here the imperative to tax is inflected with the justification of fair competition between businesses for the economic benefit of foreign firms. The larger, long-term proposed extension included a much greater area to the west and the French Concession, the hope being that negotiations in London and Paris might incorporate the latter into the International Settlement as originally hoped in the 1860s. The Council's expansionism was

---

[82] SMA U1-1-82: Watch Committee, 13 November 1906.

[83] Zhang (ed.), *Minutes of the SMC*, Vol. 17, 27 May 1908, 90.

[84] SMA U1-1-56: Finance Committee, 9 October 1908. The plans were not realised, but were clearly considered achievable in 1908.

[85] SMA U1-1-56: Finance Committee, 9 October 1908.

not confined to Chinese areas. The senior consul asked the Daotai to remove 'native' police from Zhabei pending the resolution of the boundary question, assuming that it would be settled in the SMC's favour. Consular support for the SMC was not universal, but they favoured the formal expansion of the Settlement.

Negotiations rumbled on but the consular and diplomatic bodies made no headway in convincing the Chinese government to grant the Settlement extension. Then, in July 1913, an opportunity arose to seize Zhabei by military occupation instead of diplomacy. A revolt led by the Guomindang against President Yuan Shikai erupted in Shanghai, surrounding the Settlement with gunfire.[86] The Council, dominated by expatriates and thus ever anxious to preserve peace and stability in the interests of good business, wanted the government forces to win a swift victory while maintaining a neutral buffer-zone between the open hostilities and the Settlement. The neutral zone was overly ambitious: even the *North-China Herald*, that die-hard advocate of foreign imperialism in China, recognised that it would not be practical.[87] But when the revolutionaries took control of Zhabei in order to launch an attack on the Chinese government arsenal, the SMC secretary, W. E. Leveson, urged that this was the moment to seize the district. Leveson, like his predecessor, J. O. P. Bland, was at the forefront of calls to expand the Settlement. The moment had been anticipated: the municipal finance committee had allowed for the expansion of the SMP in March 1913 in order to meet potential need in Zhabei.[88] But the councillors were thinking primarily in terms of defence: it was staff like Leveson and the heads of the police and volunteers who saw disorder as an opportunity to expand in Zhabei, though the Council members who ultimately bore responsibility for the decision were readily persuadable. This bullish stance chimed with popular Shanghailander opinion. According to the *Herald*, the presence of rebels north of Shanghai meant it was only a matter of time before the fighting entered Zhabei, 'a district so closely interwoven with the Settlement.'[89] It was therefore necessary for the Council, with its responsibility 'for the safety of thousands of innocent lives,' to order the occupation of the district: the newspaper cast the military expansion into Zhabei as the SMC's duty.

Captain Superintendent of Police C. D. Bruce marched the Police and Volunteers into northern Zhabei on the morning of Sunday 27 July.[90] The SVC was subordinate to the SMP in this operation, due to Colonel Bruce's superior

[86] Bickers, *Scramble for China*, 365–6.
[87] *NCH*, 2 August 1913, 313.
[88] SMA U1-1–57: Finance Committee, 21 March 1913.
[89] *NCH*, 2 August 1913, 313.
[90] SMA U1-2–673: Captain Superintendent to secretary, 30 July 1920.

rank to SVC Commandant Lieutenant Colonel Barnes.[91] Barnes reported that all volunteer companies contributed equally to the operation, highlighting the roles played by the Light Horse, Japanese and Portuguese companies, before the duty of occupying the district was handed over to the Chinese Company, presumably to reduce friction with Chinese residents and authorities. Bruce thanked both the SVC and the SMP's Criminal Investigation Department:[92] the latter's work thus extended far beyond traditional policing. The expansionist ambitions of the SMC were served by an international cross-section of men from both the SMP and SVC, with Chinese providing a crucial role in expanding the foreign colonial presence. The Chinese members of the SVC apparently identified their interests with the expansion of the Settlement at the expense of local Chinese authority. Their support was instrumental in the endurance of transnational colonialism in Shanghai.

The *North-China Herald* claimed that the occupation was successful, but Bruce's triumphal march of the SVC faltered somewhat when it was not met by the Chinese deputation that he anticipated would hand control of the policing of the district to him.[93] Nevertheless, the SMP policed the area and the SVC's Chinese Company stood guard. The Superintendent of Chinese Police in Zhabei complained primarily about the presence of Sikhs and the use of force to seize the weapons of his own police.[94] He and others argued that the SMC had overstepped its rights in employing force to disarm the rebels and Chinese police outside the Settlement, but the *Herald* argued that this action was 'as inevitable as if they had been found within the borders of the Settlement'.[95] The SMC had established the principle that the Settlement was neutral territory, to be free from any conflict that may affect surrounding China, and now this neutrality was being extended to areas on its border. The next logical step was the permanent inclusion of Zhabei in the protected zone of the Settlement.

It was not to be. Two days after the occupation was initiated, a counter-attack initially targeting the Sikh police forced the SVC 'to withdraw to the Settlement boundary', followed by the municipal police stationed in Zhabei. Barnes was at pains to emphasise that the rebels opened fire first and the SVC exercised 'patience and forbearance' in not retaliating for some time before

---

[91] Barnes, formerly of the Weihaiwei Regiment, was a Major in the British Army but received a promotion to the rank of Lieutenant Colonel by the War Office at the Council's request. When his successor, Major Trueman, asked for a similar promotion in 1915, however, the SMC decided that to ask the War Office would do 'little more than draw attention to the unofficial and unrecognised character of the Council's commission', showing the tenuous nature of the Corps' military status. SMA U1-1–82: Watch Committee, 12 July 1915.

[92] SMA U1-2–673/2555: Barnes to Bruce, 28 July 1913.

[93] Bickers, *Scramble for China*, 366.

[94] SMA U1-2–427/1863: Superintendent Mou, Chinese Police, to the Red Cross Society, 30 July 1913.

[95] *NCH*, 2 August 1913, 316.

returning fire.[96] Bruce reported that he was following the orders of the Japanese Admiral 'to enter Chapei, to rescue any foreign lives or persons then in danger and to retire'.[97] Any mention of Japanese involvement was omitted from the public records as inconsistent with the Council's claimed autonomy, but the foreign naval protection enjoyed by the Settlement came with an expectation that the SMC's own forces would cooperate with their aims. The Zhabei police resumed their duties: the SMC had failed to expand its boundaries. A combination of local Chinese outrage on the part of officials and residents and consular criticism had shown that the Council's position in Zhabei was untenable.

The SMC continued to expect the expansion of the Settlement boundaries in the near future. In the meantime, Yuan Shikai's government was highly respectful of foreign sensibilities in Shanghai, in return for the SMC support that helped crush the Guomindang rebellion. Military forces loyal to Yuan sought the permission of the Diplomatic Corps in Beijing to take troops through both Zhabei and the Settlement, indicating acceptance of the Council's claim that the level of foreign interests in Zhabei and its proximity to the Settlement allowed some foreign control over the district.[98] The diplomats, on the other hand, allowed the passage of troops through Zhabei but not through the Settlement, demonstrating their stricter adherence to the boundaries as the outer edges of foreign-controlled Shanghai.

Despite its failure in 1913, the Council's ambitions for expanding the Settlement remained undaunted and it resorted to its earlier tactics, building up its presence on extra-Settlement roads. The SMC exerted pressure on the consular body to negotiate a major new extension, citing public health concerns after an outbreak of plague in Shanghai. Plague as a pretext for greater control of a colonised population or territory was common imperial policy.[99] This time the SMC directed that the negotiations should be led not by the British but by the senior consul, who happened to be the Dane Theodor Raaschou by dint of his long service in Shanghai, on behalf of the whole consular body: British domination of Shanghai increasingly hid behind an international smokescreen.[100]

Against the backdrop of the First World War, the Council entered into direct negotiations with Beijing in 1914, floating the possibility of Chinese representation on the Council or the rendition of the Mixed Court to Chinese control in return for the desired extension of the Settlement limits.[101] In 1917 the Captain

[96] Barnes to Bruce, 31 July 1913.
[97] Bruce to Chairman, SMC, 2 August 1913.
[98] *NCH*, 16 August 1913, 507.
[99] Prachant Kidambi, *The Making of an Indian Metropolis: Colonial Governance and Public Culture in Bombay, 1890–1920* (Aldershot: Ashgate, 2007), 49–70.
[100] SMA U1-6–144: Chairman E. C. Pearce to Consul General and Senior Consul Theodor Raaschou, 28 July 1914.
[101] Feetham, *Report*, I, 124; Hudson, 'Rendition of the International Mixed Court', 459.

Superintendent of Police suggested that recent agitation in Pudong offered an opportunity to obtain municipal police control over all foreign property on the east of the river.[102] Again, staff rather than councillors advocated aggressive expansionism. The Watch Committee decided to defer (though not dismiss) the idea due to an impasse with the local Chinese authorities over China's measures against Germans and Austrians. The preservation of the Settlement's neutrality trumped wartime allegiances, so Chinese authorities could not be permitted to take action against the Central Powers. A compromise was reached whereby these nationals would be required to obtain permits and men would have to report weekly to SMP stations, but Chinese authorities would not be permitted to enforce the measures.[103] Transnational colonialism survived such concessions to wartime exigencies.

The Council continued to anticipate extensions to the Settlement right into the 1920s, without success. As late as 1925 the Council was hopeful that an extension could be achieved through land purchases from Jiangsu, where civil war made any means of gaining revenue attractive to local Chinese authorities, but nothing came of it.[104] In the end the SMC quietly abandoned its expansionist ambitions with the arrival on the scene of the Chinese Shanghai Municipal Government to administer the city surrounding the foreign settlements at the end of 1927, following its capture by Guomindang forces. Thereafter, the SMC concentrated on defence rather than expansion.

By 1932, following the Japanese invasion of Manchuria and assault on Shanghai, the western members of the SMC hoped merely for the continuation of the status quo as long as possible. The Japanese members, however, were now the expansionists, so when the Council discussed writing a telegram to the League of Nations seeking assurance that the League would support the continuation of the Settlement in future, whatever the outcome of the Sino-Japanese conflict, Kimiji Fukushima protested that 'any proposal dealing with the status of the Settlement should provide for its extension and not be confined to its existing limits'.[105] The Chinese members also objected to the proposed cable because they could not be seen to go explicitly against the stated national government policy that the Settlement should return to Chinese control. In the absence of unanimous agreement, the cable was not sent, but the discussion shows the extent to which British and American expansionist ambitions for the Settlement had been curtailed, to be overtaken by their Japanese counterparts. The leading forces in Shanghai's transnational colonialism were shifting.

[102] SMA U1-1-86: Watch Committee, 14 September 1917.
[103] SMA U1-1-86: Watch Committee, 8 October 1917.
[104] Zhang (ed.), *Minutes of the SMC*, Vol. 23, 4 February 1925, 21.
[105] Zhang (ed.), *Minutes of the SMC*, Vol. 25, 19 February 1932, 222.

Conflict over Jurisdiction

Conflict over control of the Settlement frequently focused on jurisdiction, due to the ambiguities inherent in the application of extraterritorial privilege to the foreign powers. From the SMC's perspective, jurisdictional authority necessarily followed the power to police, as criminals arrested by the SMP required prosecution and conviction. The SMC and foreign consuls increasingly exerted their influence over the Mixed Court, where cases involving Chinese in the Settlement were heard between 1864 and 1927.[106] The Court included both Chinese and foreign magistrates, so cases involving citizens of more than one nation could be heard by assessors of the two nationalities involved. By its last year the Mixed Court was highly international with seven Chinese, two British, two American, two Japanese and one Italian magistrate.[107] The foreign assessors, appointed by the consuls, were subject to pressure from the consular body and the SMC.[108] The Mixed Court increasingly tried not only cases concerning both Chinese and foreign interests, but also those involving Chinese only, even though these were beyond its jurisdiction. Members of the SMP, usually Sikhs, stood in trials, representing municipal authority. Prisoners were sent to the municipal rather than a Chinese gaol.[109] In matters of justice, the Settlement functioned very much as though it were a city-state separate from the rest of China.

A crisis of foreign jurisdiction over the Settlement's Chinese population resulted in the first major public disturbance of the twentieth century in Shanghai and 'the most violent antiforeign protest since the opening of the treaty port': the Mixed Court riot of 1905.[110] Smouldering resentment over Council interference in Chinese cases erupted when a widow, returning to her native place of Guangdong with her late husband's coffin and 15 servant girls, was arrested by the SMP on suspicion of kidnapping and transporting girls for sale. The Chinese Magistrate ruled that she should be placed in the Mixed Court gaol, but the Foreign Assessor ordered the municipal police to incarcerate her in the newly built municipal gaol, though he had no legal right to do so.[111] The SMP followed his orders, its members fighting with the Magistrate's runners to do so, injuring several of them and a Chinese official in the process.

---

[106] Cassel, *Grounds of Judgment*, 67.

[107] William C. Johnstone, *The Shanghai Problem* (Stanford University Press, 1937), 153.

[108] Thomas B. Stephens, *Order and Discipline in China: the Shanghai Mixed Court 1911–27* (Seattle, WA: University of Washington Press, 2002), 110–11.

[109] Goodman, *Native Place*, 187, n. 25.

[110] Bryna Goodman, 'The Locality as Microcosm of the Nation? Native Place Networks and Early Urban Nationalism in China', *Modern China*, Vol. 21, No. 4 (1995), 399.

[111] Goodman, *Native Place*, 188; Chu Xiaoqi, '*Yuan Shuxun yu danao huishen gongtang an*' ('Yuan Shuxun, the Tao-tai of Shanghai, and the 1905 Case of Madam Li Huang'), *Shilin* (2006), 6, 31–9.

Incensed by this overstepping of foreign jurisdiction, leading Guangdong merchants sent telegrams to the Ministry of Foreign Affairs and the Commercial Bureau, requesting support 'to calm people's hearts and assert China's sovereignty' against the SMC.[112]

Over 1,000 Shanghai notables gathered at the Chinese General Chamber of Commerce and asserted, for the first time, the need for Chinese representation on the SMC. Public anger at the police brutality was expressed at further open meetings of hundreds and, in one case, thousands of people.[113] The Chinese Ministry of Foreign Affairs and the foreign diplomatic body responded with pressure on the consuls in Shanghai to release the widow, dismiss the Mixed Court Assessor responsible and punish the police, and henceforth use the Mixed Court prison for female prisoners. The British consul-general followed the orders from Beijing, releasing Li to the Guangdong native place association, but this did not satisfy the wider demands of the now firmly nationalistic protestors, particularly the call for Chinese municipal representation.[114]

When the SMC refused to negotiate, thousands of protestors attacked the town hall and police stations around the Settlement. Inspector Wilson in charge of Louza (Laozha) station, near Nanjing Road, disarmed his men on the orders of the Captain Superintendent, but the crowd looted the station's bayonets and carbines before burning it down. The SMC called on the full force of the municipal police and volunteers, as well as the Royal Navy and Marines from men-of-war in the harbour, to restore order. Surprisingly, 100 Chinese sailors were offered by Rear Admiral Sah for municipal use and were detailed by the Watch Committee to bolster the River Police in the defence of Pudong, beyond the Settlement limits.[115] The right of the SMC to enforce order both within the Settlement and in the surrounding area was accepted by the Chinese military authorities to the extent that they were willing to contribute forces under foreign direction.

After peace had been restored, an inquiry by the Watch Committee concluded that police inspectors should have been given wider discretion in defending their stations and that the order to disarm had been mistaken (setting out the line that would contribute to the violent response to the protestors of 30 May 1925). Captain Superintendent Alan Boisragon was forced to resign. Nevertheless, the committee believed that the regrettable loss of property was more than compensated by 'the avoidance of sacrifice of innocent lives of

---

[112] *Shenbao*, 11 December 1905, translated and quoted in Goodman, *Native Place*, 189.

[113] Goodman, *Native Place*, 189–90.

[114] Kotenev attributed the nationalist turn of the protest to a combination of the influence of returned overseas Chinese students, anger over the recent Chinese Exclusion Act in the USA and the impact of the recent Japanese victory over Russia. Kotenev, *Shanghai: Its Mixed Court and Council*, 128.

[115] SMA U1-1-82: Watch Committee, 18 December 1905.

residents in the immediate vicinity' and the restraint shown by the police under attack '[could not] fail to produce a generally good effect on native feeling'.[116] In fact, the violence of the crackdown elsewhere, particularly at the town hall – the defence forces killed at least 15 protestors and injured many more – did nothing to improve relations between the SMC and Chinese residents or local authorities.[117] It merely demonstrated the Council's willingness to resort to force to defend its buildings and authority, and the readiness of foreign armed forces to come to its aid in a conflict with Chinese protestors.

Exclusive policing by the SMP was followed in 1911 with the securing of municipal control of the Mixed Court. During the 1911 revolution municipal police marched into the court, took possession of its buildings and records and dismissed the court runners and other 'hangers-on'.[118] From then until 1926, the court was run by the SMC on behalf of the consular body, in an expansion of municipal control over the justice system. The fees charged for hearing cases went to the Council to contribute to the upkeep of the SMP.[119] Thomas Stephens argued that the 'prompt, summary, and decisive' hearings of the Mixed Court, closely following jurisdictional procedures in western nations, allowed the Council to maintain much higher standards of public order than was found outside the Settlement.[120] Yet Pär Cassel, Eileen Scully and others have highlighted the inequality of the court and the 'pre-trial preemption and post-verdict maneuverings' in which the SMC engaged behind the scenes.[121] Dissatisfaction over the handling of cases contributed to Chinese opposition to the SMC. On 1 January 1927, at the turning point from the older British and western colonial dominance to Chinese nationalist ascendancy, the Mixed Court was succeeded by a Provisional Court in accordance with a compromise agreed between the Jiangsu provincial authorities and the consular body. Jurisdiction over Chinese was returned to Chinese control, and foreign judicial representatives had a merely advisory role, confined to cases involving foreigners.[122] It signalled a dramatic erosion of the Council's authority in the Settlement.[123]

---

[116] SMA U1-1–82: Watch Committee, 21 December 1905.

[117] Goodman, *Native Place*, 192.

[118] Stephens, *Order and Discipline in China*, 50.

[119] SMA U1-1–60: Finance Committee, 14 March 1921.

[120] Stephens, *Order and Discipline in China*, 103; also Wang Limin, '*Zhongguo de zujie yu fazhi xiandaihua – yi Shanghai, Tianjin he Hankou wei li*' ('China's Concessions and the Modernisation of the Legal System – using the examples of the concessions at Shanghai, Tianjin and Hankou'), *Zhongguo faxue* (March 2008), 167–77.

[121] Eileen P. Scully, *Bargaining with the State from Afar: American Citizenship in Treaty Port China, 1844–1942* (New York: Columbia University Press, 2001), 17.

[122] Wakeman, *Policing Shanghai*, 70–1.

[123] A. M. Kotenev, *Shanghai: Its Municipality and the Chinese* (Shanghai: North-China Daily News and Herald, 1927), 171–88; Gu Xiaoshui, '*1926 nian Shanghai gonggong zujie huishen*

The *Shishi xinbao* (時事新報, *China Times*) argued in 1930 that the establishment of an independent Chinese court in the Settlement and the disbanding of the SMP were two immediately necessary precursors to the dismantling of the International Settlement, which, the paper said, should be a priority for the Ministry of Foreign Affairs.[124] The police and the court, two key elements of the judiciary, were emblematic of foreign authority in the Settlement, and the Chinese recovery of legal jurisdiction in the Settlement curtailed the SMC's freedom to exert control over its territory.

Defence in Difficult Times

From September to October 1924 the Jiangsu-Zhejiang war raged between rival 'warlords' in the area surrounding Shanghai.[125] This was part of the civil war between the forces allied to the Zhili warlord Wu Peifu (the 'Jade Marshall') and the Fengtian warlord Zhang Zuolin. Arthur Waldron describes it as China's first modern war, with the same technologies and weapons as the First World War,[126] so the sense of fear in Shanghai as it came closer is understandable. The Chinese and foreign authorities – chambers of commerce, guilds, diplomats and the SMC – combined in 1923 to negotiate a guarantee respecting Shanghai's neutrality from the two local commanders, Qi Xieyuan, governor of Jiangsu and loyal to the Zhili forces, and Lu Longxiang, governor of Zhejiang.[127] It was not only the International Settlement that claimed neutrality in conflict, but the SMC was far more successful than the Chinese city in defending it. The Chinese authorities had little hope of keeping the rival armies away from the economic prize of controlling Shanghai and its valuable arsenal. When the Settlement's neutrality was first threatened in January 1924, the SVC expanded the Chinese Company of volunteers and issued a public notice warning of its intention to fire artillery from Suzhou Creek if provoked.[128]

Fighting erupted on 3 September and the Council declared a state of emergency on 9 September (as did the French Concession authorities), a necessary step for the landing of naval forces.[129] In fact, the SMC had no legal right under the Land Regulations or other agreement to declare a state of emergency like a colonial

---

gongxie shouhui jiaoshe shuping' ('Commentary on the Negotiations for the Rendition of the Shanghai International Settlement Mixed Court in 1926'), *Lishi dang'an* (February 2007), 97–109.

[124] *Shishi xinbao*, 21 May 1930.

[125] Arthur Waldron, *From War to Nationalism: China's Turning Point, 1924–1925* (Cambridge University Press, 1995), 73–90.

[126] Ibid., 4.

[127] Ibid., 41.

[128] *Shenbao*, 18 January 1924, 4 March 1924, 14.

[129] Clifford, *Spoilt Children of Empire*, 84–5.

or state government, but its authority to do so was never challenged.[130] At a cost of £645,000, a whole division of British forces from Britain and Malta – 10,000 men – were sent to China: the largest peacetime movement of troops in British history.[131] A further 1,500 American marines and smaller numbers of Dutch, Spanish and French marines, combined with 2,000 volunteers and 2,500 police, brought the total forces defending the two foreign settlements from Chinese attack to 16,000.[132] The French Concession had just 120 volunteers to call on so was entirely dependent on external imperial military support.[133]

The SVC erected a 16-mile cordon incorporating the Settlement and some of the external roads areas, although the fighting was unlikely to encroach on the Settlement itself, the military commanders having nothing to gain from engaging the foreign powers in warfare. The Zhabei authorities, with more cause for concern, asked the SMC to extend the cordon around the whole of the district, and Chinese business groups even asked for municipal protection of a much larger area encompassing most of the city west of the Huangpu, in return for support in extending the Settlement boundaries. Tempting though the offer was, no such undertaking could be given in writing, so the Council and consuls agreed against accepting it.[134] Given the widespread animosity towards the SMC prompted by the May Thirtieth Incident the following year, the Chinese request seems surprising, but the Council held out a promise of security, which was the primary concern for businesses, Chinese and foreign alike. This attitude contrasted with that expressed in the widely-read newspaper *Shenbao*, which argued that the maintenance of fortifications beyond the boundaries of the Settlement after the immediate threat had passed in November was an affront to Chinese sovereignty.[135] It was a view that would become commonplace the following summer.

In January 1925 the fighting resumed and came right into the western suburbs on the borders of the Settlement, briefly breaking the defence lines of the French Concession.[136] The SMC and other representatives of the foreign community such as the China Association called for foreign troops to defend the Settlement, but the British and American governments were more reluctant than they had been in earlier conflicts to antagonise the Chinese government to defend foreign interests. On the advice of military commanders who argued the Council's own forces were sufficient, London and Washington refused

---

[130] F2953/156/10 John Pratt, acting British consul-general, minute of 22 March 1927, cited in Clifford, *Spoilt Children of Empire*, 297, n. 8.
[131] HC Deb 10 February 1927 vol 202 cc279–80.
[132] 'How and why our fair city was "saved"', *China Weekly Review*, 31 December 1927, 115.
[133] Clifford, *Spoilt Children of Empire*, 81.
[134] Ibid., 89.
[135] *Shenbao*, 5 November 1924, 14.
[136] Clifford, *Spoilt Children of Empire*, 86.

the calls for help, leaving the Settlement more dependent than ever on the SMP and SVC for defence. They were fine on their own, the borders of the Settlement never being breached by the warlords' armies. Despite the preference for outside support, therefore, the SMC could defend the Settlement alone with its own forces.

Anti-imperialism

Global developments had a direct impact on events in Shanghai. On 4 May 1919, students gathered in Beijing to protest the terms of the Treaty of Versailles, which handed control of former German colonial possessions in Shandong, on the northeast Chinese coast, to Japan, instead of returning them to China. As China had joined the Allies in the First World War, its people had expected fairer treatment by their fellow victors. Protestors held the Beijing government primarily to blame, but the movement galvanised anti-imperial and particularly anti-Japanese feeling across the country. Over 30 Shanghai educational and business organisations together formed a Citizens' Association on 6 May, and the next day students, business people and workers gathered at the Public Recreation Ground to denounce the government's inadequate response to the terms of the treaty.[137] The recreation ground was the site of the racecourse at the heart of the International Settlement and the largest public space in the city. The Chinese press reported that 10,000 attended this rally, while the SMP estimated the crowd at 7,000; either way, it was an unprecedented gathering. The protest in Shanghai grew wider in its scope than elsewhere in the first serious anti-imperialist movement faced by the SMC.

During May, students in Shanghai published handbills spreading news of the Paris Peace Conference and encouraging a boycott of Japanese goods. Early disturbances to the peace reported by the SMP were minor, including holding up tramcars and 'the snatching and smashing of straw hats of Japanese manufacture'.[138] In response, the SMC published a stern notice in public places around the Settlement and in Chinese newspapers, warning that attempts 'to interfere with residents or merchants in pursuit of their business or to induce them to refrain from the exercise of their right to deal in any goods' would meet with arrest and prosecution. Business was paramount in Shanghai and the Council would use the police to ensure mere politics would not inhibit it.

The eight-day general strike from 5 June caused massive disruption to business, industry and transport, as 60,000 joined China's first 'triple stoppage' strike of students, business people and workers. Despite efforts by the

[137] S. A. Smith, *Like Cattle and Horses: Nationalism and Labor in Shanghai, 1895–1927* (London: Duke University Press, 2002), 93.
[138] Zhang (ed.), *Minutes of the SMC*, Vol. 20, 21 May 1919, 462.

Students' Union to keep the protest peaceful, dozens of arrests were made by the police forces of all three city authorities. The SVC was mobilised and the Council's chairman claimed that the presence of volunteers had 'a very salutary effect' on the protestors.[139] Major Trueman, the commandant of the Corps, refused, however, the chairman's request to station volunteers at the Waterworks, power stations and other key municipal facilities to prevent their workers from being intimidated into joining the strike.[140] Trueman found such guarding duties beneath the dignity of his force; the municipal police would have to contain the strike as best they could, while the volunteers remained on call in case of violence. Clashes between the SMP and May Fourth protesters were sometimes violent, and its heavy-handed approach backfired, prolonging the protests. The *North-China Herald* reported in August 1919 that shopkeepers identified the SMP's 'highhandedness' against students in June as a reason why they refused to pay their rates to the Council.[141] The Council used its police and, to a lesser extent, volunteers for the preservation of peace, attempting to contain the anti-imperial threat by the same means as colonial police and military forces around the world.

The May Fourth protests represented a novel source of disorder for the SMC, and it cooperated closely with other foreign and Chinese authorities in handling it. In a conversation with the SMC chairman, the British consul-general expressed fear that the situation could 'develop into a state of anarchy which would ultimately necessitate allied intervention'.[142] The chairman and secretary of the Council and the chairman of the Watch Committee discussed the Council's response with the British consul-general and the senior consul, agreeing a ban on public displays of signs, flags or unauthorised uniforms. Such bans were standard policing practice in colonial contexts. The consuls were thus involved in Council decisions, but it was the SMC that proposed the action to be taken and the SMP and SVC that enforced it. The French consul-general agreed that similar bans would be enforced in the French Concession and the Captain Superintendent of the SMP provided him with hundreds of copies of a notification of the ban: the SMC's influence extended to its French neighbour in times of crisis.[143] Meanwhile General Lu Yongxiang, who controlled Zhejiang at the time, informed the Captain Superintendent of the SMP that he would place the Chinese districts in and around Shanghai under martial law. As the most prominent colonial target, however, the International Settlement remained the focus of the protest movement, and the SMC directed the response.

[139] Zhang (ed.), *Minutes of the SMC*, Vol. 20, 8 June 1919, 476.
[140] Zhang (ed.), *Minutes of the SMC*, Vol. 20, 11 June 1919, 482.
[141] *NCH*, 13 August 1919, 389.
[142] Zhang (ed.), *Minutes of the SMC*, Vol. 20, 8 June 1919, 477.
[143] Zhang (ed.), *Minutes of the SMC*, Vol. 20, 11 June 1919, 481.

The SMC ordered the police to take particular care to prevent any anti-Japanese disturbances. It asked the Japanese consul-general to warn Japanese residents to stay indoors at night, with the assurance that 'everything possible would be done to protect Japanese property from damage'.[144] The SMC's apparent alliance with the Japanese authorities against Chinese protestors incensed many, ensuring the protest shifted in focus from its initial Japanese targets to opposing all foreign imperialism. Strike action persisted over the summer and the anti-Japanese boy-cott remained in place much longer. Small business-owners, realising that the most effective way to target the SMC was financial, refused to pay the General Municipal Rate when it increased in August. They demanded Chinese represen-tation on the Council, standing up for their rights as 'citizens' (国民 *guomin*) in the nationalist spirit of May Fourth. The SMC negotiated with the Chinese General Chamber of Commerce and agreed to a compromise of consulting a new Chinese Ratepayers' Association. Opposition to the SMC simmered down, but the legacy of May Fourth continued to be felt for many years.

The SMP's shooting of protestors on 30 May 1925 was a turning point in the development of Chinese nationalism and communism, but it was not in itself a surprising occurrence. Violent treatment of protestors by the SMP was not unusual, as witnessed in 1905 and 1919 in particular. The wider imperial context of racism combined with the imperative to retain control led to violent responses to nonviolent opposition, the most extreme example being the mas-sacre of nearly 400 demonstrators at Amritsar, India, in 1919. The Hong Kong police killed five workers during the Seamen's Strike of 1922, provoking a general strike that brought the colony to its knees and forced concessions from its government.[145] Meanwhile, nationalism and anti-imperialism were growing in China. Arthur Waldron argues that the uncertainty brought by the collapse of the Beijing government and the casualisation of violence created by the warlord conflicts of 1924–1925 enabled nationalism to become the dominant social force by 1925.[146] But the SMC ignored these changes and antagonised its opponents by drawing up plans yet again for a significant expansion to the Settlement.[147] It also proposed byelaws to limit the freedom of the press, to raise wharfage dues, to license and thus control stock exchanges, and to restrict the employment of child labour.[148] In a climate in which the SMC's right to govern the Settlement was beginning to be questioned, these were controver-sial proposals. Most significantly, the Council expected the SMP to maintain law and order by crushing the first signs of protest with force.

[144] SMA U1-1-86: Watch Committee, 5 June 1919.
[145] Carroll, *Concise History of Hong Kong*, 98–9.
[146] Waldron, *From War to Nationalism*, 5–10.
[147] Zhang (ed.), *Minutes of the SMC*, Vol. 23, 19 January 1925,
[148] Clifford, *Spoilt Children of Empire*, 101.

Anti-Japanese activities by Chinese nationalists and the bullish responses of the local Japanese community led to antagonism and violence on both sides. Workers striking at a Japanese mill outside the International Settlement in February 1925 attacked factory machinery and clashed with the Chinese city police.[149] Students supported the striking workers, strengthening the alliance between the two groups. A wage dispute in the same mill led to another strike in May, which spread to other Japanese-owned factories. When Japanese foremen shot at workers on 15 May, and one of the workers died two days later, students and workers united in protest. Students organised rallies for workers throughout the city, and the SMP responded by arresting six protestors on 23 and 24 May. As they would be tried at the Mixed Court on 30 May, large-scale protests were planned for that day in the centre of the Settlement. This was a deliberate strategy to gain maximum audiences for political speeches and to stand in direct defiance of the SMC's authority.[150]

Despite intense preparations by the students and the local Communist Party, the SMC took no special precautions, leaving the men of the SMP to deal with the protest as best they could.[151] On the morning of 30 May, 3,000 protestors flooded into the Settlement and demonstrated in small groups, waving banners and giving speeches.[152] Each time the SMP arrested those they thought were the ringleaders, more groups of protestors emerged, attracting crowds and denouncing the SMC. Hundreds converged on Louza station off Nanjing Road in the afternoon. In desperation, Inspector Everson, the British officer in charge of the station, gave an unheeded and largely unheard warning that the police would shoot, issued the order to his men, and fired the first shot himself.[153] It was the station that had been overrun by a similar crowd in 1905, and Everson was not going to let the same thing happen again. It was understood in the SMP (and the SVC) that men ordered to fire should 'shoot to kill'. This is exactly what the Chinese and Sikh constables under Everson did, killing four protestors instantly, while a further five died of their injuries. Other police shooting that day brought the total dead to 12, and dozens more were wounded.[154]

While protestors were being shot dead in the streets, Commissioner of Police McEuen was, by his own admission in the subsequent municipal inquiry, enjoying an afternoon at the Lawn Bowls Club, following tiffin at the racecourse and a break at the exclusive Shanghai Club.[155] He was about to proceed

---

[149] Jeffrey N. Wasserstrom, *Student Protests in Twentieth-century China: The View from Shanghai* (Stanford University Press, 1991), 98.

[150] Wasserstrom, *Student Protests*, 103.

[151] Rigby, *May 30 Movement*, 34.

[152] Smith, *Like Cattle and Horses*, 168.

[153] Bickers, *Empire Made Me*, 165.

[154] K. Suga, Summary Report, *China Year Book 1926–27*, 951.

[155] SMA U1-1–88: Watch Committee, 18 August 1925.

to his golf club when he heard news of the shooting. McEuen was heavily criticised by the Watch Committee's J. H. Teesdale, an American lawyer who was unable to agree with the Committee's exoneration of the SMP, finding the Commissioner to blame for being absent from the Settlement when trouble was expected without informing his deputy of his whereabouts. Had he been at the police headquarters, Teesdale argued, McEuen could have called on reserves from other stations to support Everson at Louza in controlling the crowd, obviating the need to shoot. Teesdale considered Everson's actions quite correct in the circumstances, preventing the protestors from overrunning the station and seizing the weapons within. Teesdale rejected the suggestion that McEuen could not have predicted the force of the protests, noting that if that were true the foreign community enjoyed no security whatsoever. He likened the situation to war, showing the fear that the unleashing of anti-imperial forces had brought to the fore:

I think the Commissioner of Police occupies the same position as the Commander of a Force during the time of War who would undoubtedly be court-martialled if by neglecting to station his outposts around his position in the evening, he discovered next morning that he was completely surrounded.[156]

By this interpretation, the SMC was at war with the Chinese community in the Settlement, the colonial power against the 'natives' in the unequal world of empire.

The day after the shooting, students and workers rallied in their thousands, and the Chinese General Chamber of Commerce, facing angry crowds demanding action against the municipal authorities, declared a strike to begin on 1 June. The triple stoppage of students, businesses and workers was coordinated and maintained by the General Labour Union that the invigorated Chinese Communist Party established on 31 May. Workers had participated in the student-led May Fourth Movement, but in 1925 they took over. Employees of municipal concerns joined the strike, including the power stations and waterworks, as well as the workers of the tram, bus and telephone companies, foreign-owned mills and foreign newspapers.[157] Shanghai, the commercial capital of East Asia, ground to a halt, and instead of the noise of transport and industry it was the sound of protest that filled the air. As many as 200,000 workers stopped work, spontaneously at first but later under threat from the General Labour Union. The movement came close to an armed uprising, the Federation of Street Unions proposing a military occupation of the Settlement, though this action was voted down. The SMC was under threat as never before.

The students and workers represented by the Federation of Street Unions had clear demands: the arrest of the perpetrators of the shooting and compensation

---

[156] SMA U1-1-88: Watch Committee, 15 December 1925.
[157] Bickers, *Empire Made Me*, 170.

for the surviving victims or the relatives of those killed, freedom of speech and association in the International Settlement, better treatment of workers, the end of the Mixed Court, and representation on the SMC.[158] They also listed some preliminary demands: the SMC should cancel its state of emergency, release the arrested protestors, and reopen schools and other institutions occupied by the SVC; and the foreign powers should withdraw their landing parties. The only demand that went beyond Shanghai was the abolition of extraterritoriality; otherwise the protestors' concerns were entirely local, confined specifically to the International Settlement. No reference was made to the French Concession, which had had no part in the events of 30 May and was unaffected by the protests (save a one-day sympathy strike). The SMC was seen not as part of a greater whole of colonialism in China, but as a local authority with which to negotiate in its own right. The demonstrations nonetheless spread beyond Shanghai as anti-imperialism became a national movement, with protests in Hankou, Tianjin and elsewhere, and particularly violent clashes in Guangzhou where 53 Chinese and one foreigner were killed on 23 June.[159] Richard Rigby claims the movement spread to almost every Chinese town and city.[160] But the focus of the movement remained very much on Shanghai's International Settlement.

The SMC's response was defensive. On 1 June, in the first of many special Council meetings called that summer, members unanimously agreed that the 'Police had no other alternative than resorting to firearms' and a greater loss of life would have resulted had they not fired on the protestors.[161] The Council declared a state of emergency, mobilising the SVC and calling on the consuls to make available 2,000 sailors and marines to guard municipal property and any municipal workers who wanted to resist the strike.[162] Their request was met in full: by 6 June, 22 foreign warships were in the harbour, over 1,300 men came ashore and over 800 more waited on their ships. Americans and Italians guarded the power station and waterworks, which were being operated by Russians during the strike; Japanese forces guarded Hongkou; and British sailors guarded the perimeters of the Settlement, interpreted to include extra-Settlement areas.[163] The mobilisation demonstrated the international imperial support for the SMC, as each treaty power had a vested and entwined interest in the outcome of the crisis.

Chinks showed in the SMC's armour, however. For the first time, it could not rely on its Chinese police: one third of them went on strike, and dozens

---

[158] S. A. Smith, *A Road is Made: Communism in Shanghai, 1920–1927* (Honolulu: University of Hawai'i Press, 2000), 91.
[159] Clifford, *Spoilt Children of Empire*, 119.
[160] Rigby, *May 30 Movement*, 63.
[161] Zhang (ed.), *Minutes of the SMC*, Vol. 23, 1 June 1925, 51–2.
[162] Zhang (ed.), *Minutes of the SMC*, Vol. 23, 2 June 1925, 63.
[163] Clifford, *Spoilt Children of Empire*, 108.

were dismissed. The other branches of the SMP and the SVC were used to full effect and given free rein with the municipal arsenal: fire hoses were used to disperse crowds and machine-gun posts were placed at street corners.[164] More protestors were injured and killed: at least 22 Chinese died in the May Thirtieth Movement in Shanghai alone. One member of the American naval forces was killed on 2 June, but foreigners were largely unhurt in the violence. All public gatherings, flags and banners were banned, and a curfew imposed, with offenders arrested. This reduced the rioting, but the Council's heavy-handed tactics confirmed its image as an aggressive colonial authority.

Despite the police violence, the strikes continued. The SMC eventually found an effective response, from 6 July stopping the power supply to the Chinese businesses and factories that were still operating. The Council had assumed initially that it could count on the support of the Chinese General Chamber of Commerce, quoting assurances from its acting chairman the day after the shooting 'that the Chamber was not in sympathy with the movement'.[165] The role of the General Labour Union and the Chinese Communist Party justified the Council's view that the trouble was stirred up by 'Bolsheviks', and it expected businessmen to be immune to such radical ideas. In fact the Chamber largely led the strike action over the summer, as nationalism and business interests coincided in the elimination of foreign competition. The SMC's power-cut meant Chinese-owned cotton mills and tobacco factories suddenly had to cease production, affecting 40,000 workers.[166] Mill-owners agreed to pay two dollars to their unemployed workers for two weeks, showing a rare solidarity between owners and their staff, but they could not afford the subsidy for long. As Chinese businesses were now suffering seriously, the Chamber was brought to the negotiating table. Yu Xiaqing, the president of the Chinese General Chamber of Commerce, led negotiations with the SMC. Divisions among the workers meant the strike could not last forever and in the end the protests died down and work resumed despite anger that the Chinese negotiators were not going far enough.

For the first time, significant concessions were made by the Council to Chinese nationalism. The Mixed Court would be abolished and there would be a form of Chinese representation on the SMC, but only from the elite business community. Rather than being arrested and tried, Everson and McEuen were retired with generous pensions of approximately half pay for life.[167] The SMC offered 75,000 dollars in compensation for victims and their families, but the cheque was returned by the Commissioner of Foreign Affairs as derisory.[168]

---

[164] Rigby, *May 30 Movement*, 41.
[165] Zhang (ed.), *Minutes of the SMC*, Vol. 23, 1 June 1925, 50.
[166] Smith, *Like Cattle and Horses*, 181.
[167] Zhang (ed.), *Minutes of the SMC*, Vol. 23, 18 December 1925, 195.
[168] Zhang (ed.), *Minutes of the SMC*, Vol. 23, 6 January 1926, 200.

These concessions prompted outrage among Shanghailanders and only went so far. No concessions to freedom of speech and association in the Settlement were made; rather, the SMC became more watchful for agitation and increased police surveillance activities. Workers saw no improvement in their working conditions. Their most far-reaching demand, the abolition of extraterritoriality, was rejected out of hand by both the SMC and the consular and diplomatic bodies that would have had to agree to it.

The SMC had the public support of the British diplomats in China and Stanley Baldwin's Conservative government at Westminster, though there was concern about the strength of the official Chinese reaction. The British Labour Party, however, condemned the SMP's use of firearms and recognised the justice of Chinese outrage. In Shanghai, the American consulate and diplomats urged restraint, and protestors brought before the American assessor at the Mixed Court were not punished but merely required to sign a bond to keep the peace.[169] Other consuls and diplomats were more openly critical of the SMC, frustrated by its provocation of Chinese nationalism. Some foreign ministers in Beijing considered whether they could disband the SMC entirely.[170] The Beijing government, still recognised internationally though it no longer controlled much of the country, protested at the police shooting and called on consular, diplomatic and foreign government representatives to bring to justice those responsible and effect changes in the governing of the International Settlement. A delegation sent by the Beijing government to investigate and seek a resolution failed to persuade the SMC to make further concessions. Meanwhile, the SMC flatly refused to follow the recommendations of the diplomatic body to compromise, demonstrating its autonomy from the foreign powers despite the military support it had relied upon to control the protests. Fessenden, the chairman of the Council, concluded his rebuff to the diplomats that, while it might take advice from them, the SMC was 'responsible only to the electorate of Shanghai'.[171]

The advice the SMC took was London's more modest suggestion that a judicial inquiry should be launched to investigate the circumstances of the May Thirtieth Incident. This was the recommendation of the influential British consul-general Sidney Barton, who was sympathetic to the Council and saw that the status quo served British business interests. Austen Chamberlain, British Foreign Secretary, was happy to be led by Barton if it appeased the pro-Shanghailander lobby in London, which had been writing letters to *The Times* defending the SMC's actions.[172] The diplomats nominated an international

---

[169] Clifford, *Spoilt Children of Empire*, 111.
[170] SMA U1-6-99: Secretary-General Fessenden to Edwin Howard, Editor of the *North-China Daily News*, 27 November 1935.
[171] Clifford, *Spoilt Children of Empire*, 121.
[172] Letters to the editor, *The Times*, 6 June 1925, 13; 8 June, 15; 9 June, 12; 12 June, 12; 15 June, 10; 18 June, 17.

panel of one Briton, one Japanese and one American to investigate 'the origins and character of the disturbances' of 30 May. The Beijing government was belatedly invited to nominate a member of the judicial committee but, assuming the process would be a whitewash, refused. The judicial commission interviewed McEuen, Everson and others involved, and published their findings in January 1926. The British and Japanese members, from Hong Kong and Hiroshima respectively, exonerated the SMC, as expected. But American Judge Finley Johnson of the Philippines echoed his compatriot on the Watch Committee, Teesdale, in finding that the failure to take precautions, particularly not sending in police reinforcements, led directly to the shooting.[173] He criticised the exclusion of Chinese from the management of the Settlement in their own city, finding ample justification in their calls for representation on the SMC and the rendition of the Mixed Court. This public, foreign support for Chinese demands contributed to the reluctant concessions of the SMC in its negotiations with the Chinese General Chamber of Commerce.

The May Thirtieth Movement marked a turning point in both Chinese and foreign, particularly British, perceptions of the SMC, which had implications for the future defence of the Settlement. After the Council refused to follow the instructions of the diplomats, damaging British and American relations with China, London and Washington were more cautious about defending Shanghailander interests. The Chinese population and authorities were now united in hostility to any action that hinted at expansionism, while communism had been given a huge boost. Though the scale of the killing was far smaller than the Indian massacre at Amritsar, the May Thirtieth Incident was comparable in its impact on the stability of the colonial presence. Thereafter, the SMC was on the defensive against an ascendant nationalism and 'Bolshevism'. Nationalist movements were sweeping across colonised parts of the world, from the successful overthrow of British rule in Ireland to the non-cooperation and mass civil disobedience campaigns in India.[174] In resisting Chinese nationalist demands, the SMC was behaving in the same way as colonial authorities throughout the British empire.

Communist and Nationalist Threats to the Settlement

Communist advances from the south in 1926 provided the first serious threat to the security of the Settlement after May Thirtieth, raising the spectre of a Communist takeover of China along the lines of Russia's Bolshevik revolution a decade earlier. The spread of Communism was feared worldwide, from

---

[173] *NCH*, 9 January 1926, 59.
[174] John Darwin, *The Empire Project: The Rise and Fall of the British World-System, 1830–1970* (Cambridge University Press, 2009), 388–91.

the Red Scare in the USA to Europe and European colonies. The SMC was at the forefront of the defence against communism in Shanghai, making it an unlikely ally of the Nationalist Party (Guomindang).

In 1926, however, the Guomindang was allied with the younger Chinese Communist Party in the First United Front, their shared goal of uniting China and ending the fractured rule of regional warlords temporarily superseding the two parties' differing ideologies. In July the Guomindang's new National Revolutionary Army (NRA) set off from Guangdong and headed north to defeat key warlord armies, capture important cities and establish a new national government. The NRA, which included Communists and others alongside the Guomindang forces, gained control of Hunan and moved on to capture Wuhan, a tri-city including Hankou, home to British, French and Japanese settlements. The NRA initially left these settlements alone, but revolutionary nationalism grew in the city and strikes broke out in British-owned factories in December. An anti-British rally attracted 100,000 demonstrators.[175] The British, the largest colonial presence locally and across China and the power behind the May Thirtieth Incident, were the primary target for anti-imperialist protest. Fearing for the safety of British residents and property, the consul-general requested naval landing parties to defend the Settlement, but they were quickly withdrawn following scuffles with protestors on 3 January. In post-May Thirtieth China, colonial authorities could not take the risk of dispersing crowds with force, and the British Settlement had to rely on Chinese troops to retain order. They agreed on condition of being given sole responsibility for policing the Settlement, effectively ending British control.[176]

The subsequent Chen-O'Malley Agreement ratified the transfer of power. 'Eugene' Chen Youren, representing the new Nationalist government at Wuhan, and British diplomat Owen O'Malley negotiated that a new municipal authority would run the former British settlement, with a Chinese director and six elected councillors, three Chinese and three British. The small British settlement at Jiujiang was also retroceded to China.[177] Meanwhile, Chiang had moved on to Jiangxi, the province to the south of Shanghai, and captured its capital, Nanchang. Shanghai was the next target, but the SMC, the wider British community in China and the British government in London were all determined that the International Settlement would not face the same fate as the British Settlement at Hankou.

To foreign observers the Guomindang – with its anti-imperialism and links to the Soviet Union – looked like a Bolshevik threat almost as serious as

---

[175] Clifford, *Spoilt Children of Empire*, 178.
[176] Edward S. K. Fung, *The Diplomacy of Imperial Retreat: Britain's South China Policy, 1924–1931* (Hong Kong: Oxford University Press, 1991), 113–14.
[177] Ibid., 128.

that posed by the Communist Party. The SMP redoubled surveillance efforts against suspected communists in Shanghai and shared intelligence with agencies throughout the British empire. Meanwhile, the SVC expanded recruitment and established the salaried Russian Unit.[178] The SMC's two defensive bodies were primed against a potential political attack. British troops were also on hand in Hong Kong to reinforce the Settlement's defences if necessary, but this time they would not land in Shanghai unless it was under direct threat. The decision to post troops to Hong Kong for the defence of Shanghai was in fact discussed by the cabinet of the British government and featured in the King's Speech opening parliament on 8 February, demonstrating the importance attached to Shanghai. The defence of the Settlement was not, however, the only consideration for the cabinet. Sir Miles Lampson, the British minister in Beijing, had suggested that the sending of troops could be used as a 'bargaining counter' with the Chinese authorities. If assurances were given that 'anti-British agitation', including the boycott of British goods in place since 1925, would cease, the British would refrain from sending Indian troops on from Hong Kong. Yet British representatives in Shanghai disagreed: the British consul-general and the naval Commander-in-Chief argued that one brigade and three battalions must be landed in Shanghai 'at all costs' to guarantee the port's security, claiming that 'any weakening relative to the landing of troops at Shanghai would be disastrous.' Chamberlain, anxious to limit the damage done to Sino-British relations by the SMC, pointed out that troops were sent to Shanghai as a precaution and to prevent the loss of life, so any attempt to use them to gain advantage vis-à-vis the Chinese authorities was 'a misapprehension of British policy'.[179]

Opinion in Shanghai was divided. The American and Japanese authorities were keen to maintain the neutrality of the Settlement by avoiding the deployment of foreign troops there, keeping defence of the Settlement in the hands of municipal forces. Yet the SMC wanted to ensure maximum British military protection. A Westminster cabinet meeting made explicit reference to the municipal position and to Council member Brigadier-General Macnaghten's professional military opinion that three brigades were necessary. After over three hours of discussion (and a one-and-a-half-hour break for lunch) the cabinet concluded that the decision of whether the Indian Mixed Brigade should be sent straight to Shanghai or landed in Hong Kong should be taken by those 'on the spot', meaning the consulate and military officers in Shanghai (not the SMC), so long as it was in keeping with British policy that troops were for the preservation of British life rather than any political purpose. As the naval commander-in-chief deemed it necessary to bring the Indian Mixed Brigade directly to Shanghai, the stronger

---

[178] SMA U1-1-88: Watch Committee, 29 October 1926.
[179] TNA, CAB 23/54: cabinet meeting, 7 February 1927.

defence measure was taken. These troops were to be confined to the Settlement 'except in case of grave emergency'.[180] The SMC was subordinate to the British consular and military authorities in these decisions, revealing its dependence on colonial assistance when the SVC and SMP were insufficient for the defence of the Settlement.

As Chiang Kai-shek's Northern Expedition neared Shanghai, the SMC prepared for it to besiege or attack the Settlement, but also for internal disorder. It was a general strike on 21 March 1927, encouraging fears of 'Bolshevism', that prompted the Council to declare a state of emergency, mobilise the SVC and SMP and call the naval forces to its defence.[181] The commander of the Shanghai Defence Force, Major-General Sir John Duncan, recalled later that he had been instructed not to command the international troops, 'but they practically all asked to come under me', with the exception of the Japanese troops.[182] The British and Americans recognised his senior military rank and the need for unified action, but the Japanese preserved the independence of their military protection of Shanghai's Japanese residents. Spanish, Italian, Portuguese and Dutch contingents also offered assistance, but were not needed.[183] The combined international force helped shelter the Settlement from the fighting between the NRA and the forces of Sun Chuanfang, the military governor of Fujian who had reclaimed authority over Shanghai in October 1925.[184] The Nationalists quickly seized the rest of the city except Zhabei, where fighting continued. This exposed to danger the northern area of the Settlement, where the consulates were, as there was no clearly demarcated boundary with Zhabei: Zhabei lay on one side of the street while the other side belonged to the Settlement.[185] This was the only area of the Settlement where fighting took place. On 22 March northern forces, cut off from their line of retreat by the Nationalists, charged at the Zhabei border defences. The British returned fire, killing 25 to 30 Chinese, and disarmed and interned hundreds more.[186] By the end of the day, Chiang Kai-shek's troops were victorious and the streets were silent.

It was a peace that would be shattered for anyone suspected of communist sympathies in the white terror that began in the early hours of 12 April. The

---

[180] TNA, CAB 23/54: telegraph to Sir Miles Lampson, 10 February 1927, appendix to cabinet meeting minutes, same date.

[181] Clifford, *Spoilt Children of Empire*, 217.

[182] John Duncan speaking at Chatham House, 22 February 1932. 'The Shanghai Crisis', *International Affairs*, Vol. 11, No. 2 (March 1932), 158.

[183] TNA FO 371/13206: 'General A. E. Wardrop, North China Command, Memorandum on the Defence of the International Settlements at Shanghai in the Absence of Regular Troops', 14 May 1928.

[184] Henriot, *Shanghai 1927–1937*, 18.

[185] Duncan in 'The Shanghai Crisis', 158.

[186] Clifford, *Spoilt Children of Empire*, 219; Duncan in 'The Shanghai Crisis', 159. Duncan claims the Shanghai Defence Force disarmed and interned 5,000 men.

bloody end of the First United Front saw communists purged comprehensively from the Guomindang.[187] But as the SMC shared opposition to communism and the violence did not affect the foreign community, it was silent on the outrages and even facilitated them. Fessenden agreed to allow Du Yuesheng's Green Gang forces, whose help Chiang Kai-shek had enlisted for the purge, to pass from the French Concession through the Settlement to Zhabei for a surprise attack on the communists.[188] The resulting violence was later euphemistically reported by the Commissioner of Police as the 'disarming' of the communists.[189] Such was the SMC's fear of communism that it assisted the feared Guomindang and the criminal underworld.

Although the Shanghai Defence Force was directed by the British Army, foreign residents attributed the safety of the Settlement to the Council, for its own defensive measures and for taking the decision to enlist the help of the foreign powers. The annual meeting of ratepayers the following month passed unanimously a resolution expressing 'heartfelt gratitude for the measures taken by the Municipal Council *in the first instance and afterwards* by the Foreign Powers for the protection of all residents of this Settlement'.[190] Gratified by the stress on the initial response taken by the SMC ahead of the foreign powers, Fessenden forwarded the resolution to the consular body. The Chinese response was more muted, *Shenbao* welcoming the lifting of the state of emergency (aptly *jieyanling* 戒嚴令, 'martial law', in Chinese) in the Settlement on 10 May 1927 and highlighting its negative impact on business.[191] The status quo ante was restored following the greatest peacetime mobilisation of foreign forces in China, acting together with the SMC's forces to defend the Settlement.

Japanese Imperialism

Sino-Japanese hostility proved the greatest test for the Council's ability to protect the Settlement, but ironically served to ensure its survival for a further decade. The British government was preparing in 1931 to sign a new treaty with China, renouncing extraterritoriality and setting a timetable for the retrocession of the concessions, but the treaty was shelved due to Japanese military incursions into China. Chinese nationalist resentment of foreign transgressions focussed on Japan and, following a massacre of Chinese living in Japanese-occupied Korea in the summer of 1931, found powerful expression

---

[187] C. Martin Wilbur, *The Nationalist Revolution in China, 1923–1928* (Cambridge University Press, 1984), 99–117.
[188] Martin, *Shanghai Green Gang*, 105–6.
[189] SMC, *Report for 1927*, 51.
[190] NARA RG 84/1686: Fessenden to consul-general, 20 April 1927, emphasis added.
[191] *Shenbao*, 11 May 1927, 9.

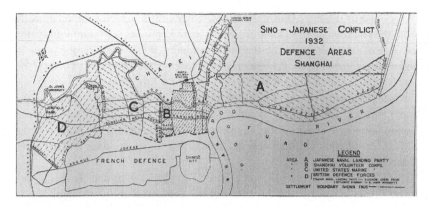

Map 3.2 Map of defence sectors, 1932.
Source: SMC, *Report for 1932*, 14, image courtesy of the *Virtual Cities Project*, Institut d'Asie Orientale, Lyon.

in an effective boycott of Japanese goods.[192] The existing antagonism only increased as Japan's ambitions crystallised in the occupation of Manchuria from September 1931. Tensions in Shanghai, the centre of the boycott movement, soared and, as the year drew to a close, conflict locally between Japan and China seemed inevitable.

The SMC chairman, Brigadier-General Macnaghten, convened a meeting of the Shanghai Defence Committee in December. The meeting brought together the commandant of the SVC, the Commissioner of Police, the commandant of the troops of the French Concession, the garrison commanders and staff officers of all the foreign forces present in the city, and Stirling Fessenden, secretary-general of the Council. They agreed to a defence scheme that, in the event of the SMC declaring a state of emergency, would divide the Settlement into sectors, each the responsibility of a different force (Map 3.2). According to the scheme, each force would protect the inhabitants of its sector regardless of nationality and confine its activities to that sector alone. The SMC was directing the entire combined foreign force from its chambers, and its role in deciding when and if to declare a state of emergency made it central to the defence of the Settlement.

Chiang Kai-shek's decision not to challenge the occupation of Manchuria in 1931 emboldened Japanese ambitions in China. Japan sent a naval force of 4,000 men to Shanghai – far smaller than the 17,000-strong naval landing force the British had sent in 1927. But when fighting broke out between Chinese

[192] Donald A. Jordan, *Chinese Boycotts Versus Japanese Bombs: The Failure of China's 'Revolutionary Diplomacy,' 1931–32* (Ann Arbor, MI: University of Michigan Press, 1991).

factory workers and Japanese monks on 18 January 1932, the Japanese naval commander demanded an apology, compensation and a crackdown on anti-Japanese demonstrations. The SMC, seeking to mollify Japan, closed down the Guomindang's offices in the Settlement. This time Chiang could not risk appearing weak in the face of Japanese aggression, so he moved troops from Nanjing nearer to Shanghai.

Tensions continued to rise. After a bomb exploded outside the Japanese consulate on the morning of 28 January 1932, the SMC declared a state of emergency to take effect from 4.00 pm that afternoon, on the recommendation of the Defence Committee.[193] Each force rushed to prepare to defend its sector. The Japanese sector included, on the insistence of Admiral Kōichi Shiozawa, not only Hongkou within the Settlement, but also part of Zhabei, where the Admiral claimed (hyperbolically) that 6,000 Japanese residents had pleaded for protection against 600,000 hostile Chinese troops.[194] There was indeed a large Japanese population in the area, but also many Chinese-owned factories, so it was an economic prize worth fighting for. But the Chinese military was not informed that the Japanese defence sector included this area: *Shenbao* reported the SMC's preparations for conflict earlier that day, but not the all-important extent of the Japanese defence plans.[195] The Japanese naval troops took their positions within the Settlement in time for the start of the state of emergency at 4.00 pm, but waited until nearly midnight to move into Zhabei. This advance beyond the limits of the Settlement was therefore taken by the Chinese 19th Route Army as an act of war and they opened fire, precipitating the outbreak of warfare.

The fighting was intense and bloody, especially on the Chinese side: 4,000 Chinese soldiers were killed and almost 8,000 wounded, while over 700 Japanese were killed and a further 1,800 wounded.[196] The war featured an early example of aerial bombing of civilians and at least 4,000 Chinese civilians were also killed. This was partly because of the Chinese forces' successful adaptation to the conditions of fighting in city streets; as traditional trench warfare proved ineffective, so fighters hid in buildings and among civilians. Rather than a rapid and easy Japanese victory, as many had expected, the 19th and Fifth Armies were able to withstand the onslaught and contain Japanese gains. But a high price was paid and atrocities abounded: Japanese bombs were dropped on a refugee camp and

[193] Donald A. Jordan, *China's Trial by Fire: The Shanghai War of 1932* (Ann Arbor, MI: University of Michigan Press, 2001), 32–3.

[194] Hallett Abend, *My Life in China, 1926–1941* (New York: Harcourt, Brace and Co., 1943), 187. Abend was a correspondent of the *New York Times*.

[195] *Shenbao*, 28 January 1932, 13–14.

[196] Christian Henriot, 'Beyond Glory: Civilians, Combatants and Society during the Battle of Shanghai', *War and Society*, Vol. 31, No. 2 (2012), 119; Jordan, *China's Trial by Fire*, 186–90.

the Commissioner of Public Health described 'deliberate shooting at [the] windows of [the] Mental Hospital'.[197]

The SMC, though it included two Japanese members, condemned the fighting inasmuch as it infringed on the Settlement. The French Concession was largely unaffected, leaving it able to assist in taking hospital patients from the Settlement. The Chinese press momentarily sided with the SMC's attempts to increase the area under its control, recognising that this would be at the expense of Japanese aggression.[198] *Shenbao* reported favourably on the Watch Committee's condemnation of Japanese aggression and highlighted the role of the SVC as the protector of the Settlement under the heading 'The important task of the Volunteer Corps' (*Wanguo shangtuan renhe zhongyao*, 萬國商團 任務重要).[199] Yet as the Council's powerlessness to curb Japanese militarism became clear, the newspaper criticised its neutral stance.[200]

The Council met daily during the crisis, bringing together the two Japanese and five Chinese members, and discussed how best to enable the usual business activities of the Settlement to continue despite the fighting. Chairman Brigadier-General Macnaghten and Vice-chairman G. W. Sheppard both urged Xu Xinliu as the representative of the Chinese banking community to try to keep the Chinese banks functioning. When Xu complained of Japanese sniping and looting of Chinese banks, Secretary-General Fessenden urged courage in the interests of business. He called on the Japanese councillors to 'impress on the Japanese military authorities the necessity of heeding the Council's representations in respect of the illegal arrest of reputable Chinese citizens'.[201] Fessenden's frustration that the Japanese authorities had ignored the SMC is palpable in the minutes of the meeting, accusing them of 'an entire lack of discretion', although he diplomatically expressed sympathy with 'the difficulties with which the Japanese have been confronted notably in respect of the activities of plain clothes Chinese gunmen'. Kimiji Fukushima, the Japanese banking representative on the Council, assured the meeting that armed Japanese civilians would no longer be able to 'get out of control'. Such promises had little effect.

The SMC also ensured the continuation of a supply of food and fuel to the Settlement, facilitated the evacuation of Chinese civilians from Hongkou, and helped people find missing relatives. Using Fukushima to communicate with the Japanese Naval Commander, the SMC protested against Japanese activity in defence sectors other than their own, successfully limiting the infringement

---

[197] SMA U1-16-10-216: J. H. Jordan, 'Diary of State of Emergency', 29 January 1932.
[198] *Shenbao*, 30 January 1932, 2; 31 January 1932, 2.
[199] *Shenbao*, 4 February 1932, 3; 13 February 1932, 2.
[200] *Shenbao*, 11 February 1932, 2; 12 February 1932, 2.
[201] Zhang (ed.), *Minutes of the SMC*, Vol. 25, 1 February 1932, 145–6. The banks reopened on 4 February following assurances that they would not be targeted.

of the Settlement's neutrality. Repeated efforts to stop Japanese aeroplanes fly-
ing over the Settlement were, however, unsuccessful, and bombs fell on the
municipality. Attempts to restore SMP control of policing in Hongkou were
similarly thwarted by the Japanese authorities, who were enforcing an informal
martial law, imprisoning or summarily executing suspected snipers without
trial: illegal activity in the absence of a formal declaration of war. The SMC
was able to effect some small changes for the benefit of the residents of the
Settlement, but no constraints that would harm the Japanese war effort.

Within 48 hours of the declaration of the state of emergency, 1,800 volunteers mobilised to defend the Settlement. Following the arrival of British and
American military reinforcements, the SMC proposed withdrawing the SVC
from the defence of their allocated sector to allow volunteers to return to their
normal employment. Vice-Chairman Sheppard explained to Brigadier Fleming,
the British officer commanding the combined international forces, that 'the
prolonged functioning of the Volunteer Corps has resulted in an almost complete sterilization of business as native employees are refusing to resume duty
owing to the lack of foreign supervision'.[202] Fleming was unmoved, however,
attending a Council meeting to emphasise that the SMC had placed the SVC
under his command and he believed the Corps remained a vital part of the
defences of the Settlement. The volunteers stayed at their posts.

Fessenden compared the position of the Settlement to that of Belgium at
the outbreak of the First World War: a neutral state that could not be blamed
for the actions of other powers. The Mayor of Greater Shanghai wrote to the
SMC criticising it for allowing Japan to use the Settlement as a base for military operations against the Chinese. Open letters to the same effect were subsequently published in the press, including calls to refuse to pay SMC rates as
the Council had failed to protect residents. Fessenden proposed replying that
'responsibility for the acts of any powers that may be construed as a violation of
[the Settlement's] neutrality rests with such powers and not with the Shanghai
Municipal Council'.[203] Fukushima argued that Japan was merely defending the
Settlement, at which Xu requested that the minutes record 'that he emphatic-
ally disagrees with the contention since this implies that the Settlement was
attacked by Chinese troops.' The exchange highlights the unusual situation
of having representatives of two nations effectively at war around the same
table, the SMC resembling a local parallel to the ineffectual League of Nations.
The peculiarity of the Council's position as an autonomous but not sovereign
authority was laid bare.

As the weeks of fighting continued, it was not clear how the conflict would
be resolved. Lampson, the British minister, suggested to Chiang Kai-shek

---

[202] Zhang (ed.), *Minutes of the SMC*, Vol. 25, 5 February 1932, 163.
[203] Zhang (ed.), *Minutes of the SMC*, Vol. 25, 6 February 1932, 168–9.

that a deal might be struck with Japan: China could agree to demilitarise the Wusong area just outside Shanghai in return for an end to the hostilities. Chiang rebuked Lampson for serving the cause of Japanese imperialism.[204] Meanwhile, Chinese appeals at the League of Nations for condemnation of Japanese aggression had a sympathetic hearing. But far from retreating, Japan sent 6,000 to 8,000 reinforcements at the end of February to shore up the growing front line: Emperor Hirohito wanted a swift end to the conflict, before the League could call for a truce. The Japanese authorities issued an ultimatum on 18 February that Chinese forces must withdraw to over 12 miles beyond the borders of the Settlement or face a renewed assault. In doing so, Japanese were using the Settlement as their own territorial base, despite its international and neutral status. The Chinese government rebuffed the ultimatum and the Japanese military embarked on a heavy combined infantry and naval offensive from 1 March, outflanking the Chinese forces and forcing their withdrawal to the line demanded in the ultimatum.[205] All this accomplished was a ceasefire and later (after negotiations lasting longer than the actual hostilities) a truce, agreed and signed in the British consulate building on the Bund on 5 May. The Sino-Japanese War that ended in 1945 began not in 1937 but in 1931 in Manchuria and 1932 in Shanghai.

The Council's own defence scheme and declaration of a state of emergency were the catalysts that led to an open exchange of fire on the night of 28 January. Without them, the Sino-Japanese hostilities would still have erupted, but the SMC's role was significant. It then stood by as fighting continued, sacrificing the northern and eastern districts of the Settlement and failing to safeguard Chinese life there as it protected only the core of the Settlement nearer to the Bund. Japan retained control of the northern and eastern districts for almost a year. And where the SMC had failed in annexing Zhabei, Japan succeeded. The SMC failed dramatically in its self-appointed role of maintaining the neutrality of this neighbouring district and in preventing the violation of the Settlement's borders. The SMC played no role in the mediation between China and Japan to negotiate the truce, which was undertaken by British, American, French and Italian diplomats. In the face of an aggressive nation-state, Japan, this transnational municipal body was powerless.

Following the war of 1932 the Council tried to contain Japanese ambitions in the Settlement to preserve peace and stability. Measured increases to the Japanese branch of the SMP and the promotion of its officers were permitted, though not the wholesale Japanese control of Hongkou which Japanese councillors desired. By 1937, the British and American councillors, staff and consuls-general were agreed that 'the 1932 Defence Scheme must die ... on

---

[204] Jordan, *China's Trial by Fire*, 161.
[205] Ibid., 184.

no account would Council Troops be partners with the Japanese in any scheme for the Defence of the Settlement'.[206] This tacit admission that the SMC had wrongly facilitated Japanese aggression in 1932 meant that in the coming war neutrality would be maintained by depending solely on the SVC and western forces. Japan, meanwhile, had been readying its military for war and exploiting its base in Manchuria to swell the number of Japanese troops in north China.

The Marco Polo Bridge (Lugouqiao) incident of 7 July 1937 finally provided the spark for total war. Japanese troops fired in the area of the bridge, just south-west of Beiping (as Beijing was known under the Nationalist Government). They claimed one of their men had gone missing and demanded access to the village of Wanping to search for him. When they were refused, fighting broke out. On 26 July Japan attacked Beiping and the city fell in just two days. The northern treaty port of Tianjin fell two days later.[207] Shanghai was next.

On the evening of 9 August, a Japanese officer and seaman attempted to force entry into the Chinese aerodrome at Hongqiao in western Shanghai, heedless of Chinese warnings. They and a Chinese sentry were killed in an exchange of fire. The incident broke the truce of 1932, providing Japan with the pre-text to dispatch warships and armed forces to Shanghai. They duly attacked the city on 13 August.[208] J. H. Jordan, Commissioner of Public Health, kept a vivid diary of events as they unfurled. Beginning with a few shots audible from the Dixwell Road Police Station at 9:35 am, heavy gunfire moved into the Settlement.[209] The following day brought the first aerial bombing, which caused the SMC administration building to reverberate for two minutes. The noise of anti-aircraft fire followed and late in the afternoon a shell burst over the administration building, shrapnel 'pattering down' on the roof and acrid fumes encircling the municipal staff as they responded to the crisis. Bombs fell on the Bund and in the French Concession, producing a death toll of over 1,200 in one day and shattering the carefully nurtured neutrality of the International Settlement.

The Public Works Department oversaw some of the digging of trenches by charity organisations to help dispose of the dead bodies that lay strewn in the streets, while the Public Health Department provided kerosene to the Japanese authorities to assist in the cremation of corpses in Hongkou.[210] The SMC continued to function, but staff could only enter the administration building

[206] SMA U1-6-130: Commissioner of Police F. W. Gerrard, 'Gist of Conversation with Mr Fessenden', 22 July 1937.
[207] Rana Mitter, *China's War with Japan, 1937–1945: The Struggle for Survival* (London: Allen Lane, 2013), 73–84.
[208] 'Chinese Government's Statement on the Responsibility for the War' (15 August 1937), *China Year Book* 1938, 357.
[209] SMA U1-16-10-217: J. H. Jordan, 'State of Emergency 1937: Diary of Events', 13 August 1937.
[210] Ibid., 17 August and 1 September 1927.

by showing identifying letters from their heads of department, which were checked by members of the SVC.[211] Shanghai fell in late October, after the loss of 300,000 Chinese lives.[212] Nanjing followed, and by December the Settlement was rendered an 'isolated island' (*gudao* 孤岛) in occupied China. Britain and its allies stood by as Japan seized most of eastern China, and the British and American councillors and employees of the SMC carried on as if nothing had changed while Japan occupied the rest of Shanghai. They were seemingly paralysed by the long-cherished neutrality of the Settlement, infringed though it was, and the international status of the Council with Japanese among the councillors.

From 1937 the SMC no longer ran the whole Settlement, as Hongkou and Yangshupu (Yangzepoo) came under solely Japanese control. The SMP no longer policed these districts and other municipal activities, such as health-care, were severely restricted.[213] Theoretically the neutrality of the rest of the Settlement was maintained, but the SMC served Japanese interests inasmuch as it suppressed Guomindang offices and censored political broadcasts, and the Commissioner of Police reported regularly to the Japanese authorities.[214] Chinese complained of Japanese soldiers seizing property and killing innocent Chinese within the Settlement and sought action by the SMC: 'The gentlemen of the Council are begged to teach them a lesson.'[215] Chinese residents also wrote to the SMC complaining of intrusive Japanese policing methods on extra-Settlement roads previously policed by the SMP, but met with little sympathy: the secretary-general explained that the Chinese authorities had refused to acknowledge SMC jurisdiction in the district so now the Japanese occupiers claimed it for themselves.[216]

War brought a new threat to the foreign settlements in the form of the refugees who flooded in from Japanese-occupied areas. The French Concession authorities tried to hold back the tide of refugees by closing the steel gates along its borders, but the attempt was futile.[217] The two foreign settlements were struggling by the end of the conflict in November to meet the needs of almost a million refugees, who were seen as conduits of disease and crime. Around a third of them were accommodated in camps, while most drew support from

[211] SMA U1-6–102: Deputy secretary to secretary-general, 19 August 1937.
[212] Wen-hsin Yeh, 'Prologue', in Wen-hsin Yeh (ed.), *Wartime Shanghai* (London: Routledge, 1998), 2.
[213] SMA U1-1–63: Joint Health and Finance Committee meeting, 31 March 1939.
[214] SMC U1-6–142: Secretary-general to Commissioner of Police Major F. W. Gerrard, 22 November 1937.
[215] SMA U1-6–142: Tseu Ying, Tsang Ping and Yao Ya-fong to secretary-general, 16 December 1937, and similar letters dated 14 and 26 December.
[216] SMA U1-6–142: Secretary-general to H. C. Lum, 15 December 1937.
[217] 'Four Months at War' (Shanghai: North-China Daily News, 1937), 127, cited in Diana Lary, *The Chinese People at War: Human Suffering and Social Transformation, 1937–1945* (Cambridge University Press, 2010), 27.

kin or native place ties, but thousands were without shelter on the streets.[218] The SMC and *Conseil municipal* supported native place associations in evacuating around 375,000 to their native villages. The SMP continued to serve the needs of the propertied classes of the city, assisting landlords in evacuating refugees.[219] Law and order took precedence over humanitarianism.

The SMP increased its intelligence work as Japanese forces and Wang Jingwei supporters sought to disrupt the SMC, including an alleged plot to assassinate all British, American and Chinese councillors in 1940.[220] The biggest problem for the SMP was trying to combat the criminality that saturated Shanghai's streets. Criminals based themselves in the 'badlands' west of the Settlement that had so long been semi-controlled by the Council under its policy of policing the outside roads.[221] Repeated municipal appeals to the Japanese authorities to control gambling and opium dens in the western district were fruitless since an opium monopoly and fees on gambling establishments constituted a significant source of revenue for the Japanese authorities.[222] With military power now firmly in Japanese rather than western hands, the SMC's position was fatally compromised.

The day after the attack on Pearl Harbor on 7 December 1941, the SMC agreed to a Japanese request to continue as normal. But on the same day Japanese armed forces were posted in the Settlement so the veneer of normality was thin.[223] The military authorities required Allied members of the SMC to resign in January, securing Japanese control of the Council. The SVC disbanded in September 1942, with a ceremonial hanging of the Corps Colours in the Council's Committee Room on 7 October.[224] The Japanese 'reorganised' the SMP, installing their countrymen in all senior positions. They also supplemented the regular police with a draconian 'Vigilance Corps' under a modified *baojia* (保甲) system developed in colonial Taiwan, which put civilian 'mutual responsibility' or surveillance units under direct police control.[225] The SMC annual report credited a sharp decline in crime in 1942 to these changes to policing in the Settlement.[226] The report listed 339 remaining 'foreign' members of the SMP at the end of the year, in addition to the 302 Japanese and larger

---

[218] Christian Henriot, 'Shanghai and the Experience of War: The Fate of Refugees', *European Journal of East Asian Studies*, Vol. 5, No. 2 (2006), 219

[219] Zhang (ed.), *Minutes of the SMC*, Vol. 27, 12 May 1938, 265.

[220] TNA FO 676/435: HM consul-general to Foreign Office, 20 April 1940, enclosing SMP report.

[221] Frederic Wakeman, Jr., *The Shanghai Badlands: Wartime Terrorism and Urban Crime, 1937–1941* (Cambridge University Press, 1996).

[222] SMA U1-6–143: 'Memorandum', February 1939.

[223] SMA U1-14–974: SMC, *Report for 1941*, 5.

[224] SMC, *Report for 1942*, 24.

[225] Wakeman, *Shanghai Badlands*, 135.

[226] SMC, *Report for 1942*, 35.

Chinese and Sikh branches. Most Allied nationals in Shanghai were interned from February or March 1943; the remnants of the Settlement's neutrality had crumbled. Yet it served Japanese interests to maintain Council activities and the existing boundaries of the Settlement, until abolishing both in August 1943. The Japanese staff even continued to use English for official Council business, so ingrained were the British ways of conducting municipal business.[227] The Japanese authorities apparently believed that the preservation of the outward appearances of transnational colonialism legitimised their presence.

Conclusion

The SMC defended its territory much like a state or colony. It maintained a militarised police force and a large transnational volunteer corps, including a paid Russian regiment, to defend life and property from Chinese threats. The Council also expected and usually received military support from Britain and, to a lesser extent, the USA when necessary, showing the limits of its autonomy and its position within imperial defensive networks. British military backing for the SMC reflected its status as a British-dominated expression of foreign colonialism in China. Links to Britain were tightened in times of turmoil, as the Settlement sacrificed some of its autonomy in return for naval protection, making it temporarily more like a colony. The bellicose attitude displayed repeatedly by the SMC and its expansionist tendencies in bringing areas well beyond the Settlement limits under its jurisdiction reflect the conviction of its members and those whom it represented that it had not only a right to exist but an imperative to expand. The Council's role of defending the residents of the Settlement often took the form of protecting its borders from the encroachment of Chinese authorities. It had in fact little legal entitlement to do so, given that the Settlement remained at all times Chinese territory.

Increasingly, however, defence was required against military threats, and the SMC deployed its police and volunteers effectively when their target was Chinese. It managed to preserve the neutrality of the Settlement in the face of successive and mounting military threats, even as it itself was far from neutral in its interference in Chinese politics. The SMC's impassivity to the appeals of Chinese nationalism sorely tested Sino-British relations as it represented a toxic mix of being both British-dominated yet beyond the control of British governmental authority. The SMC was, however, ineffective against Japanese aggression. Municipal actions were a significant factor in the growing Sino-Japanese tensions, which broke out into open warfare in 1932 and 1937, and

---

[227] Bickers, 'Settlers and Diplomats', 249.

the Council's declaration of a state of emergency was instrumental in accelerating tensions in 1932. As an aggressive, expansive city-state the Settlement's successes came in the nineteenth century, although it continued successfully to expand its influence on the growing network of extra-Settlement roads up to the 1930s. But as a militarised force the SMC strengthened in the twentieth century, only falling in the face of the might of Japan, and then only after Japan tightened control following the entry of the western Allies to the Pacific War. Throughout its existence, the SMC was able to exploit its independence from the control of any higher authority, pointing to its internationalism, but still rely on military support from Britain and other foreign powers when necessary. This was the strength of its transnational brand of colonialism.

4　Public Health and Hygiene

> Critics serve to defeat the very aims we have in view by weakening the morals of our own health workers and tax payers [in the International Settlement], and by causing the Chinese outside to deprecate the health organisation under foreign control ...

> During the past ten years I have travelled in fifteen of the eighteen provinces of China, and have visited every large port in Asia as far as Bombay ... It is always with a feeling of relief, pleasure and pride that I return to the International Settlement.[1]

Understanding disease and medicine are central to the study of colonial rule, as the prevention and treatment of disease formed a source of contact, conflict and sometimes eventual convergence between the coloniser and the colonised.[2] David Arnold shows that disease was a key element in the ideological and political framework of empire, as western confidence in science produced a growing sense of cultural superiority.[3] The quotation above of an American YMCA doctor exudes such confidence in the value of foreign public health work in Shanghai. Moreover, as Ruth Rogaski finds in her study of *Hygienic Modernity* in Tianjin, public health was central to contemporary notions of modernity for Chinese and foreigners alike.[4] This chapter therefore examines the development of public health provision in the International Settlement as a case study of how the Shanghai Municipal Council functioned in practice and how effective it was in governing the Settlement.

Examining the work of the SMC's Public Health Department (PHD) engages with all the themes of the book: the similarities to experience in formal British colonies, but also differences from them due to the unique form of colonialism

---

[1] SMA U1-16-9-198: Letter from W. W. Peter, Director of the Council on Health Education, to H. Holgate, President of the Rotary Club of Shanghai, 19 March 1925.
[2] David Arnold, 'Introduction', in David Arnold (ed.) *Imperial Medicine and Indigenous Societies* (Manchester University Press, 1988), 2.
[3] David Arnold, *Science, Technology and Medicine in Colonial India* (Cambridge University Press, 2000), 15–17.
[4] Rogaski, *Hygienic Modernity*.

in Shanghai; the transnational influences at work in Shanghai, notably the League of Nations Health Organisation and the Rockefeller Foundation, yet also the limits of transnationalism within the Settlement due to racial tensions between the western-dominated SMC and Chinese residents and authorities; and the challenges facing the SMC in the form of the financial limitations of a tight budget, the geographical limitations of the Settlement boundaries, and the legal limitations of the Land Regulations and Byelaws. Fundamentally, this chapter explains how colonialism in the form of the SMC shaped the city of Shanghai in terms of public health.

The SMC was charged by the Land Regulations with providing an environment and infrastructure conducive to business. This included, by implication and as Council activities developed, the implementation of a public health policy to provide a safer living and working environment for its residents – safer, that is, than the surrounding Chinese City; as was true in many colonial contexts, 'lines of hygiene were boundaries of rule'.[5] The SMC often appeared to prefer to see the Settlement as an isolated island, doing its best to ignore the other political authorities in the city and beyond. But as the demands of public health grew, this became impossible. The maxim that 'prevention is better than cure'[6] dictated that large-scale measures be taken to improve the health of the general population as the best defence against outbreaks of serious disease. Such measures would be less effective if confined to the 8.66 square miles of the Settlement, especially as these were exceptionally porous boundaries, through which the city's inhabitants crossed daily as they often lived, worked and enjoyed their leisure hours in parts of the city under different jurisdictions. Cooperation with the neighbouring authorities was therefore crucial and unavoidable, although the different sides viewed each other with suspicion and cooperation was far from smooth.

Political borders were not the only limits on the work of the PHD. The perennial problem of funding was particularly acute in laissez-faire Shanghai, where the SMC and ratepayers were largely allied in a desire to keep spending and thus taxation to a minimum. That minimum was often confined largely to the needs of the foreign population, especially prior to 1928 when the first Chinese Councillors were finally brought into the decision-making process. Public health provision in the early decades of the twentieth century was

---

[5] Alison Bashford, *Imperial Hygiene: A Critical History of Colonialism, Nationalism and Public Health* (Basingstoke: Palgrave, 2004), 1.

[6] This phrase was already in common currency in Victorian England, as evidenced by such publications as Sarah Ellis, *Prevention Better than Cure, or, The Moral Wants of the World We Live in* (London: Appleton, 1847); R. B. Richmond, *"Prevention Better than Cure": Practical Remarks on the Prevention of Cholera and Removal of other Troublesome States of the Bowels* (London: Nissen and Parker, 1849); unknown author, *What is Cholera? Or, Prevention Better than Cure, by a Bengal Doctor* (London: G. Purkess, 1860).

therefore driven by the concerns of the foreign residents, with disease prevention within the Chinese population motivated to an extent by the desire to protect foreigners from infection. Health officers with the best of intentions were forced to scale down their public health programmes in the face of budgetary constraints. They were also limited in what they could achieve by the peculiar legal basis of the SMC's authority, which rested on the Land Regulations and supplementary byelaws, the changing of which was no easy task. In addition, there was the suspicion of many Chinese towards western medical methods to overcome, and the corresponding lack of cultural understanding on the part of the Council's health personnel. Both were common features of colonial societies throughout the world. Nonetheless, pride in the scientific modernity of the Settlement's public health provision and international pressure resulted in increased public health expenditure year by year.

This chapter begins with an overview of the development of the SMC's public health provision from the late nineteenth century, before examining in depth how the health department functioned and the ways in which it sought to maximise its impact despite budgetary and legal limitations. This included everyday public health work as well as moments when the Council attempted far-reaching intervention in the daily lives of Chinese residents, such as during the plague epidemic of 1910. In this way, the reaction of Shanghainese to such measures is explored as indicative of the SMC's relationship with the population of the Settlement. The Council's claim to scientific modernity is examined in relation to medical research, including the international forums in which the PHD staff engaged. British imperial influence was dominant, but by the 1920s there were multiple transnational influences on the SMC.

Next, the chapter turns to the relationship between the SMC and its neighbours in the field of public health. Relations between the International and French Settlement authorities oscillated between cooperation and resentment. They had to reconcile differences of opinion on all areas of public health, including such contentious touch-points as the treatment of venereal diseases and the insane. The Chinese Municipal Government of Shanghai entered the arena of public health in 1927, and relations between it and the PHD were even more fraught. While health officers on both sides were keen to improve public health provision, there was little appetite for compromise on points of difference, and areas of public health policy were exploited for political gain. Despite frequent failure to cooperate with the authorities beyond the limits of the Settlement, however, the PHD was able to achieve marked improvements in certain areas of public health. Where joint efforts were made, progress was all the greater. Finally, the degree to which the department can be considered to have had a positive impact on the public health of the Settlement is assessed by analysing mortality rates. This chapter therefore sheds new light on the effects of transnational colonialism on the health of the International Settlement during a period of expanded municipal ambition in this vital field.

Laying the Groundwork: The Infrastructure of Public Health

Greater understanding of the causes of disease in the latter half of the nineteenth century produced growing demand for action on public health in Shanghai, as in urban centres in Europe, the USA and European colonies. The cholera epidemics that ravaged much of Europe from 1830 to 1847 led to a concerted international effort to tackle public health problems.[7] This in turn influenced European colonial societies as governments were soon held to be responsible for the provision of basic disease prevention measures. Similarly, the first large outbreaks of cholera in Shanghai in 1862–1863 (brought to China via ships from India) and 1883 prompted the Council to expand its role into this area, entailing an increase in its powers.[8] In 1870 the SMC's Watch Committee identified the need for a formal sanitary department to oversee medical work, markets and what was called the 'nuisance department', which sought to ensure the removal of ordure and waste, an issue that caused problems throughout the existence of the SMC. The Committee presented a memorandum on the subject to the Council which resulted in the appointment of Dr Edward Henderson as the first Medical Officer of Health (part time) in 1871.[9] The decades following Henderson's appointment saw the establishment of municipal markets and a municipal abattoir, which maintained a certain standard of hygiene, and the compulsory licensing of butchers and dairies.[10] A municipal laboratory was established in 1896 and became one of the major producers of vaccines in China as well as conducting numerous tests. These developments got under way in Shanghai before similar efforts were made elsewhere in China, including Hong Kong where a Sanitary Board was first established in 1883.[11]

The SMC's most significant nineteenth-century achievement was the establishment of a clean water supply, in keeping with concurrent developments in London, Paris and New York. The main supply of water in Shanghai had long been the polluted Huangpu River, which, like the Seine and the Thames, was

---

[7] Sunil Amrith, *Decolonizing International Health: India and South East Asia, 1930–65* (Cambridge University Press, 2006), 5.

[8] Rogaski, *Hygienic Modernity*, 95; Kerrie L. MacPherson, *A Wilderness of Marshes: The Origins of Public Health in Shanghai, 1843–1893* (Hong Kong: Oxford University Press), 30, 127; Ma Changlin et al., *Shanghai gonggong zujie*, 87–90.

[9] SMA U1-16-9-198: J. H. Jordan and C. Noel Davis, 'A Brief History of the Public Health Department', 1 August 1930. The Watch Committee continued to be responsible for the department until 1918, when a separate Health Committee was established.

[10] Jordan and Noel Davis, 'Brief History'.

[11] Carroll, *Concise History of Hong Kong*, 64.

teeming with waterborne diseases (though to a lesser extent than the rivers of the major European capitals). Many contemporaries blamed the SMC for having allowed land developments that filled in drains, and for replacing efficient Chinese drainage systems with sewers that bore waste directly into the waterways.[12] The Council finally entered into negotiations with the Shanghai Waterworks Company in 1880, having decided a private venture was preferable to public ownership as was common in British cities, and a state-of-the-art network of mains and hydrants was fully operational by 1883. Again, the SMC was ahead of other Asian cities: work only began on Delhi's waterworks in 1889,[13] while the Tientsin Waterworks Company opened operations in 1900. The latter was purchased by the British Municipal Council in 1922 and maintained as a public concern: Shanghai provided the model, but the authorities in Tianjin later deviated from it. The waterworks underpinned the public health of Shanghai, as in other cities, although, unlike the French *Conseil municipal*, the SMC did not pay for Chinese to have free access to water hydrants, so Chinese uptake of the comparatively expensive clean water supply was incomplete.[14] Care for the Settlement's poorer Chinese residents was not considered as important as ensuring the foreign community could access unpolluted water.[15]

The quality of the water was, however, subject to doubt: the Health Committee was informed in 1918 that the water was 'of fair quality' but 'could not be considered a really good water' as compared to that provided in cities such as Manchester, London or Calcutta.[16] The points of reference for Council activities were metropolitan Britain and that exemplar of the British empire, India. Although the supply of safe water undoubtedly underpinned the health of the residents of the Settlement, it was nevertheless considered inferior to that which the British and other foreign communities would have expected in the municipalities of their home countries or even in the formal British empire. In the constant comparisons foreigners made between Shanghai and 'Home', 'Home' represented an almost mythologised ideal, to which the SMC aspired but did not expect to attain.

---

[12] MacPherson, *Wilderness of Marshes*, 78–80.
[13] Gupta, *Delhi Between Two Empires*, 160.
[14] In 1932 the Health Committee considered a suggestion that free water should be supplied to the poor through water hydrants near 'beggar villages'. The members approved the idea in principle but recommended no action be taken, on the basis that 5 to 10 per cent of Chinese chose to use water from wells despite access to Waterworks water, and other factors were more significant than water supply in the prevention of cholera. SMA U1-1–124: Health Committee, 30 June 1932.
[15] Chinese were suspicious of piped water so slow uptake was not solely based on economic factors. Hanchao Lu, 'The Significance of the Insignificant: Reconstructing the Daily Life of the Common People in China', *China: An Interdisciplinary Journal*, Vol. 1, No. 1 (2003), 145–8.
[16] SMA U1-1–123: Health Committee, 17 June 1918.

Expectations of what could and should be provided in Shanghai were lower than in European cities of comparable size and prominence, or in Indian cities such as Calcutta, owing to assumptions about the nature of the Settlement. John Carroll identifies an attitude that remained prevalent in Hong Kong until much later in the twentieth century, that Chinese had come to the colony voluntarily and therefore 'neither expected nor deserved much from the colonial government'.[17] In the case of Shanghai, particularly prior to the 1920s, such an assumption went beyond Asians to encompass all poorer residents of Shanghai; the SMC did not consider itself duty-bound to provide welfare for anybody, Chinese or European, as all had come to the Settlement of their own volition to benefit from the commercial opportunities the city afforded. The SMC's role was simply to promote those opportunities. As late as 1939 the treasurer reiterated to the Finance Committee the Council's position of assuming no responsibility for poor relief.[18] The usual colonial reluctance to spend money recognised by Warwick Anderson – even as he describes the extensive public health work of the Americans in the Philippines – was far more pronounced in Shanghai, where no single colonial power accepted responsibility.[19] Sun Yat-sen's assertion that China, a 'hypocolony', was worse off than full colonies because it did not even benefit from a foreign power's responsibility for the suffering of its people appears to have been accurate.[20]

The secretary to the Council, in correspondence with the Health Officer in 1905, went so far as to correct a misapprehension that the SMC's motivation in its negotiations with the Waterworks Company was based on concern for the public health, saying 'The Waterworks Agreement, except in the one particular which I have referred to you, is *by no means a public health matter*; its details are purely financial, engineering and commercial.'[21] The 'one particular' in question was whether the agreement should include provision for a minimum standard for the bacterial purity of the water, which was set by the Health Officer, Arthur Stanley. The negotiations over this agreement, which revised the original terms for the Waterworks Company, betray the priorities of the Council and the way they restricted public health provision: the municipal finances came first in this city of commerce. Stanley could only grasp opportunities where he could to achieve public health benefits without placing too much of a burden on the public purse.

[17] John Carroll, 'A National Custom: Debating Female Servitude in Late Nineteenth-Century Hong Kong', *Modern Asian Studies*, Vol. 43, No. 6 (2009), 1492–3.

[18] SMA U1-1-63: Finance Committee, 5 July 1939.

[19] Warwick Anderson, *Colonial Pathologies: American Tropical Medicine, Race, and Hygiene in the Philippines* (Durham, NC: Duke University Press, 2006).

[20] Sun, *San Min Chu I*, 38–9.

[21] SMA U1-1-306: J. O. Bland to Arthur Stanley, 1 February 1905, emphasis added.

Although the Shanghai Waterworks was a private company, the SMC regulated prices for water as it did for other public utilities, keeping costs low for the benefit of both businesses and consumers. As was common practice in Britain, water bills were paid by landlords and no restriction was imposed on the consumption of water, again benefiting residents.[22] Xing Jianrong argues, however, that the Council always supported the waterworks and other utilities companies at the expense of residents,[23] and their interests were tied to the extent that the SMC was a major shareholder in such firms.[24] Indeed, the SMC pursued a long-term strategy to gain control of the Shanghai Waterworks Company. In 1916 it bought the entire new issue of shares in the company, and its holdings were sufficient to nominate two members to the company board.[25] Then in 1924 the SMC sought to buy out the company and run it as a municipal concern to resolve long-running disputes over its perceived neglect of consumer interests. When a price could not be agreed, the Council pressed for a revision of the terms of the company's agreement, which had last been settled in 1905, and emphasised the need 'to substitute the interests of the consumer for those of the shareholder as the chief incentive for the affairs of the Company being conducted on the most economical lines'.[26] In keeping with the Council's preoccupation with economy, this provision was listed third in a letter from the acting secretary to the manager of the company, beneath the priorities of aligning the company's and the Council's interests and ensuring adequate returns for shareholders. But it still demonstrates that the SMC was concerned about residents as well as returns, at a time when local and international pressure made the SMC pay more attention to the welfare of the Settlement's residents.

Assuming Greater Responsibility for Public Health

While in the earlier days of the Settlement the SMC confined its public health work to the provision of rudimentary infrastructure and the control of infectious diseases through the limited use of quarantine, from the turn of the century it took on an increasing role in providing health services. European colonisers were chauvinistic in their confidence that western medical practice

---

22 SMA U1-1-56: Finance Committee, 11 June 1903.
23 Xing, 'Shui, dian, mei', 100.
24 The SMC was able to negotiate favourable terms for the purchase of shares in the Waterworks Company, and by 1913 its holdings were worth £28,700. SMA U1-1-57: Finance Committee, 24 June 1913.
25 SMA U1-1-58: Finance Committee, 9 November 1916; U1-1-59: Finance Committee, 8 October 1920.
26 Memo attached to E. S. B. Rowe, acting secretary to Council, to F. B. Pitcairn, Engineer-in-Chief and Manager, Shanghai Waterworks Co., 3 April 1924, published in *Municipal Gazette*, 8 April 1924, 145–6.

was the sole route to improved public health and attempted to bring the habits of indigenous people closer to their own.[27] The SMC's staff implemented its public health policies with the intention of rendering the living environment more hygienic, with clear effects on the daily lives of residents.

These developments came during the tenure of the Council's first full-time Health Officer, Dr Arthur Stanley, from 1898 to 1922. With Stanley's arrival, the Health Department was established as a separate department in its own right. The SMC added to the existing private charitable hospitals by establishing municipal isolation hospitals for Chinese in 1900 and for foreigners in 1904. These provided for the treatment of infectious diseases under the direction of the Council. The SMC built more markets and extended municipal powers of inspection, though efforts to secure much greater powers through amendments to the byelaws failed in 1903 and in subsequent years. Municipal staff took measures to reduce the breeding grounds of flies and mosquitoes, focusing on raising public awareness of the issue due to the lack of powers to order the compulsory filling in of pools of stagnant water.[28] The link between mosquitoes and malaria had only been conclusively established by Ronald Ross in India in 1897 (earning him the Nobel Prize for Medicine in 1902).[29] Stanley was thus deploying the latest developments in medical science in attempting to limit the breeding grounds of the parasites. There was popular opposition to some of these measures, but Chinese letters to the SMC in later years complaining about unsanitary conditions in shops and demanding action by PHD health inspectors suggest a more favourable public reception of these efforts, at least among the literate.[30]

In 1912 branch health offices (BHOs) were established in 14 newly designated districts, to increase direct interaction between the Council's health personnel and Chinese residents. BHOs operated annual vaccination drives and promoted general hygienic practices through disseminating literature and holding public lectures. SMC campaigns promoting proper waste disposal and against spitting in the street, for example, were enacted mainly through the BHOs. These campaigns, as well as the success of vaccination drives, were reported in *Shenbao* and other newspapers, suggesting a degree of public

---

[27] David Arnold, *Colonizing the Body: State Medicine and Epidemic Disease in Nineteenth-Century India* (Berkeley, CA: University of California Press, 1993), 116–58.

[28] This echoed work done by Americans in Panama targeting mosquito breeding grounds in a crusade against yellow fever, following experiments by American doctors in Cuba that established the link between mosquitoes and the disease. Alexandra Minna Stern, 'Yellow Fever Crusade: US Colonialism, Tropical Medicine, and the International Politics of Mosquito Control, 1900–1920', in Alison Bashford (ed.), *Medicine at the Border: Disease, Globalization and Security, 1850 to the Present* (Basingstoke: Palgrave Macmillan, 2006), 41–59.

[29] Gordon Harrison, *Mosquitoes, Malaria, and Man: A History of the Hostilities since 1880* (London: John Murray, 1978), 73–7, 107–8.

[30] SMA U1-16-12-268. Complaints were received, however, from shopkeepers protesting at the regulations. U1-1-89: Watch Committee, 9 March 1928.

awareness among the consumers of print media.[31] The SMC was not the only body to promote public health education: the YMCA was particularly active in producing awareness-raising literature on hygiene issues for public consumption, and was taken as a model by the Chinese Government of Greater Shanghai in its campaigns from 1928.[32] In 1916 the YMCA cooperated with the Chinese Medical Missionary Association and the National Medical Association to form the Council on Health Education, which also disseminated informative literature. The SMC was one of a number of sources of public health information for residents of Shanghai, but was the most consistent source through the early decades of the twentieth century.

The branch health offices formed the face of the PHD to the public and in general people responded well, attending the regular health lectures and queuing at BHOs for free smallpox vaccinations in their thousands (58,213 were vaccinated by the SMC in 1929 alone, of whom over 56,000 were Chinese).[33] Not all these were residents of the Settlement: investigation in 1928 found that half the recipients of free vaccinations in a northern sub-district of the Settlement lived in Zhabei, north of the Settlement, where doctors were said to over-charge and use old and ineffective vaccines.[34] Large-scale vaccinations had a significant impact: by 1930 just 46 smallpox cases were admitted to the municipal Chinese Isolation Hospital, of whom 13 died. Many of those who survived were young adults who had been vaccinated and so contracted a less severe form of the disease.[35] Increasing the uptake of vaccinations had meant overcoming strong suspicion on the part of the majority of Chinese (as had also existed among Britons when vaccination was introduced).[36] There was a reported widespread preference for the traditional method of inoculation

---

[31] See, for example, '*Gongbuju weishengju zhangtie jingzhi suidi tutan, bingzhi tanyu*' ('The Public Health Department of the SMC is issuing handbills prohibiting casual spitting and promoting the use of spittoons'), *Shenbao*, 1 April 1924, 11; '*Gongbuju weishengju bugao qudi renyi qingdao laji*' ('The Public Health Department of the SMC has issued prohibition of the arbitrary dumping of waste'), *Shenbao*, 30 April 1924, 13; '*Zujie renkou siwang lü*' ('The Death Rate in the Settlement'), *Shenbao*, 14 January 1932, 15.

[32] Chieko Nakajima, 'Health and Hygiene in Mass Mobilization: Hygiene Campaigns in Shanghai, 1920–1945', *Twentieth-Century China*, Vol. 34, No. 1 (2004), 45–7.

[33] Jordan and Davis, 'A Brief History'.

[34] SMA U1-16-9-200: V. Ribbons, Inspector, 4th Northern Sub-district, 'Report on Investigation of Free Vaccines in Chapei', 11 December 1928. The rising rates of uptake of the free vaccines and falling number of cases have been carefully documented by Luo Suwen in *Jindai Shanghai: dushi shehui yu shenghuo* (*Modern Shanghai: Life and Society in a Great Metropolis*) (Beijing: Zhonghuo shuju, 2006), 38. There were concerns that not all the recipients of free vaccination were deserving: some were thought to find it easier to visit their local BHO rather than make an appointment to see a private doctor, even though they could afford to pay. SMA U1-1–126: Health Committee, 21 November 1938.

[35] SMA U1-16-9-199.

[36] Nadja Durbach, *Bodily Matters: The Anti-Vaccination Movement in England, 1853–1907* (Durham, NC: Duke University Press, 2005).

against smallpox, which involved nasal inhalation of skin cells from diseased pox, and had a mortality rate of up to 2 per cent (preferable to the 30 per cent mortality rate of smallpox) as well as rendering the inoculated individual infectious to others.[37] The SMC claimed that it was its own press and poster campaigns that had achieved the change in attitude. These and other campaigns by such organisations as the Council on Public Education were, however, simply a contributing factor in the broader picture of the acceptance of western medical practice in urban centres in China as part of the process of modernisation, as traced by Ruth Rogaski.[38] Whatever the role of SMC propaganda in promoting vaccination, the PHD was a pioneer in the provision of free vaccinations in Shanghai, years ahead of such provision being possible for the Chinese municipality. This suited the Council's self-perception as the sole provider of adequate modern public health measures, in contrast with the perceived lack of provision by the Chinese authorities. The high uptake of the free vaccinations, moreover, suggests that the BHOs were successful in implementing PHD goals in the local community. But SMC claims to be ahead of the rest of China in this area were somewhat exaggerated, Guangzhou and Tianjin, for example, both enjoying vaccination programmes at similar periods.[39]

The public health administration expanded under Dr C. Noel Davis, who succeeded Stanley as Commissioner of Public Health and held the post for the rest of the 1920s. Six divisions within the department – Administration, Laboratories, Hospitals, Food, Sanitation, and the School Medical Service – operated in 1930 from a combined budget of 848,040 taels, of a total municipal budget of 12.7 million for ordinary expenditure.[40] This compared with 5.4 million taels budgeted for the Shanghai Municipal Police and 3.8 million for the Public Works Department, the two biggest draws on the municipal budget. Health, the third largest area of spending, was not top of the municipal priorities. In this, as in so many other areas, the SMC was very much like colonial governments: Megan Vaughan demonstrates the extent to which British colonial authorities in Nyasaland, Africa, were uninterested in investing in public health, devoting just four pence per head to public health provision in 1921.[41]

[37] Alan D. T. Barrett and Lawrence R. Stanberry, *Vaccines for Biodefence and Emerging and Neglected Diseases* (London: Academic Press, 2009), 696.

[38] Rogaski, *Hygienic Modernity*, 225–53.

[39] Vaccination was introduced by American missionary doctors to Canton. Guangqiu Xu, *American Doctors in Canton: Modernization in China, 1835–1935* (New Brunswick, NJ: Transaction, 2011), 246. In Tianjin, free vaccination was offered in the late nineteenth century in a clinic established by a Chinese salt merchant with no foreign involvement. Rogaski, *Hygienic Modernity*, 71–2.

[40] SMC, *Report for 1930*, 426–7.

[41] Megan Vaughan, 'Health and hegemony: representation of disease and the creation of the colonial subject in Nyasaland', in Shula Marks and Dagmar Engels (eds.), *Contesting Colonial Hegemony: State and Society in Africa and India* (London: British Academic Press, 1994), 188–9.

The SMC's expenditure on public health compared unfavourably with rates of spending in Britain, as was pointed out in the Annual Report of the League of Nations Health Organisation: it recorded in 1929 that 1 shilling 9 ½ pence were spent per capita on public health in the International Settlement, compared with 6 shillings 9 pence in Liverpool and 7 shillings 3 pence in Glasgow.[42] Tellingly, the League counted only the foreign population of the Settlement in its calculations: the figure would be much lower if the Chinese population were also included. Financial constraints were ever-present for the PHD, although its budget increased significantly in later years as municipal expenditure rose, and also increased somewhat as a percentage of total municipal expenditure, from 7 per cent in 1910 to 10 per cent in 1930.[43]

Many decisions concerning public health were taken for economic reasons. In 1908 the Watch Committee recommended against publishing Stanley's report on the prevalence of plague among rats and the first confirmed human case in the Settlement because it would affect the trade of the port.[44] A glass roof was installed in a municipal market because it would increase the number of sellers working there and thus boost the department's revenues from licence fees.[45] When discussing whether or not to move the location of the foreign isolation hospital, S. J. Halse, a member of the Health Committee, urged that it be decided on the basis that it was 'a good business proposition', as the sites of the old isolation hospital and Victoria Nursing Home could be sold for considerable sums, rather than thinking of it being for the good of patients.[46] Stanley was praised for 'his very economical administration of the health department' and a report was submitted by his successor, Davis, on 'the increased earning power of the Health Department', in terms of licence fees and charges for laboratory and other services.[47]

Yet under Dr J. H. Jordan, Davis's successor as Commissioner of Public Health, there is evidence of a shift away from this preoccupation with economy, as spending by the department increased more and more in real terms and as a proportion of municipal expenditure. In disputes with the treasurer over the allocation of resources, Jordan sometimes prevailed, such as in 1936 when he insisted that the milk supplied to the SMC for consumption in its hospitals be Grade A tuberculin-tested milk, even though this would cost 4,310 dollars more than the standard Grade A quality. He argued that the Council must take

[42] SMA U1-16-9-198: table received from League of Nations prior to publication of its annual report. The League apparently shared the SMC's preference for comparing Shanghai with British cities.
[43] SMC, *Report for 1910*, 25a; *Report for 1930*, 426.
[44] SMA U1-1-82: Watch Committee, 21 December 1908.
[45] SMA U1-1-123: Health Committee, 4 August 1923.
[46] SMA U1-1-123: Health Committee, 14 June 1920.
[47] SMA U1-1-123: Health Committee, 12 August 1921 and 9 February 1922.

a lead in encouraging the members of the community to buy the safest milk on the market, which was available precisely because his department had pushed local dairies for its production.[48] This was the same year that the matter of tuberculin-tested milk was first raised in the House of Commons in London, when James de Rothschild enquired of the Under-Secretary of State for War whether the milk supplied to soldiers in the British Army was of this quality.[49] The SMC was keeping pace with developments in Britain. Despite such concessions, however, the commissioners of health constantly came up against the wall of limited finances.

Limited Powers

In addition to budgetary constraints, the PHD was restricted in its work by the legal limitations on the SMC's powers to enforce compliance with public health regulations. The Council's authority rested on the Land Regulations, which could only be revised with a vote of the ratepayers and the approval of the Chinese authorities in Shanghai (represented in the person of the Daotai or intendant) and Beijing.[50] The difficulty posed by this complex process of seeking approval from so many layers of authority, coupled with growing Chinese dissatisfaction with the foreign presence, meant it was never possible in the twentieth century to make any further changes to the regulations. Efforts therefore concentrated instead on adding or adapting byelaws which could give the SMC certain extensions to powers already conferred by the Land Regulations. Byelaws required only local approval, by the consular body and the ratepayers, though the latter were conservative by inclination and disengaged by nature: on several occasions they either rejected proposed new byelaws or simply failed to turn up in sufficient numbers for the meeting to reach the quorum of one third of qualified voters. The SMC lacked a full colonial government's capacity to effect change through legislation.

The prevention of infectious diseases was one area in which stronger measures than those provided for in the Land Regulations and existing byelaws were needed. An attempt to add new byelaws enforcing preventive measures failed in 1903 and again in 1906, due to the lack of a quorum at special ratepayers' meetings both years, but when plague threatened the Settlement strong action was taken. The first human case of plague was confirmed in 1908 and early the following year Stanley implemented preventive measures based on the latest aetiology: rats were trapped by PHD staff wherever possible; notices

---

[48] SMA U1-1-62: Finance Committee, 28 October 1936.

[49] HC Deb 10 March 1936, vol. 309 cc1053–4.

[50] Feetham, *Report*, I, 59. The Chinese magistrates of Shanghai's Mixed Court appeared to assume that the Daotai's proclamation upholding the authority of the Land Regulations in 1855 would apply to any such regulations.

were posted in Chinese promoting cat ownership; Chinese houses were lime-washed after notifying (but not seeking permission from) the owners; and the department offered a rat-proofing service for the homes of Chinese and foreigners at the owners' expense.[51] The way in which rats and their fleas acted as carriers of plague was only established in 1908, thanks in part to work by colonial doctors in India, so Stanley was again implementing the most up-to-date scientific methods in Shanghai.[52]

Chinese residents in the International Settlement complained about the forceful manner in which their houses were being disinfected and rendered rat-proof.[53] The Health Officer reiterated the need for tact and attributed the majority of complaints to the inability of one member of his staff to communicate with the householders directly in Chinese, therefore having to use a Chinese foreman as a translator and leaving room for misunderstanding. Study of the Shanghai dialect had been made compulsory in the department in 1906,[54] and had evidently yet to take full effect. The Watch Committee recorded that no proof had been found to support allegations of extortion, but the fact that such accusations were made demonstrates the deep unpopularity of the enforcers of measures for the prevention of plague. The Council was failing to take Chinese opposition to the plague prevention measures sufficiently seriously in its zeal to combat plague in accordance with the latest methods: typical behaviour in a colonial authority.

Plague often prompted a more intrusive and coercive approach to public health, from Bombay to the Philippines.[55] The coercive nature of colonial public health measures is familiar from the work of David Arnold and others, but Rogaski points out that all authorities in China, whether foreign or Chinese, adopted intrusive tactics in this field.[56] The SMC was no different. In 1910 fear enveloped Shanghai as plague spreading from Mongolia devastated much of China.[57] The Watch Committee was called to a special meeting in October to discuss what action to take after a Chinese victim of plague died in the northern district of the Settlement. The members emphasised that prevention measures must be taken with 'tact and discretion' towards Chinese, but laid out steps which anticipated the animosity to follow: police assistance was to be employed if Dr Moore, the acting Health Officer, found it necessary in enforcing preventive measures; segregation would be voluntary 'in the first place' but with the clear expectation that enforced quarantine could follow.[58] The committee

---

[51] Feetham, *Report*, 1, 59; Ma Changlin et al., *Shanghai gonggong zujie*, 91.
[52] Arnold, *Colonizing the Body*, 210.
[53] SMA U1-1-83: Watch Committee, 20 April 1909.
[54] Jordan and Davis, 'A Brief History'.
[55] Kidambi, *The Making of an Indian Metropolis*, 49–70; Anderson, *Colonial Pathologies*, 61.
[56] Arnold, *Colonizing the Body*; Rogaski, *Hygienic Modernity*.
[57] Carol Benedict, *Bubonic Plague in Nineteenth-century China* (Stanford University Press, 1996), 155–9.
[58] SMA U1-1-83: Watch Committee, 27 October 1910.

asserted that no action should be taken beyond Settlement limits 'for the present', again implying that such interference could occur later on. Indeed, it authorised a letter to the consular body requesting the senior consul to inform the Daotai of the Council's plague prevention measures and advising 'that the work of the Department be not impeded by the authorities in Chapei'.[59] The SMC did not see the Settlement's limits as the limits of its sphere of influence.

Opposition to the SMC's invasive methods was fierce. The Mixed Court Magistrate, Pao Yi, wrote to the British Ambassador advising that riots could follow if the Council's actions were not accompanied by greater caution and leniency.[60] Sure enough, the day after he wrote, street protests broke out. David Landale, chairman of the Council, replied via the senior consul that while he appreciated the need for tact in handling the situation, the experience of other cities warned 'that an exodus of residents and a consequent serious depression of trade is one of the certain effects of this devastating malady'. He went on:

The prosperity of this, the principal port of the Far East, is entirely dependent upon uninterrupted commerce. When its continuity is jeopardised by an imminent danger such as this, it becomes the imperative duty of the Council, and the community in its own interests, to leave no precaution untried in order to arrest it.[61]

Once more, the principal role of the SMC of creating an environment conducive to business is emphasised. The Council therefore proposed new byelaws for more extensive plague prevention measures, adapted and scaled back from those drawn up but not implemented in 1903. The new proposals met with objection from local guilds and others as too far-reaching in their powers.[62] The ratepayers agreed with these objections and passed a resolution tabled by a ratepayer to limit the application of the powers to combating plague alone rather than including other infectious diseases.[63] Landale therefore replied to the guilds that their request had been met and accepted their offer of cooperation, inviting them to nominate a committee to consult with the Council on its next step.[64] The SMC had better success cooperating with Chinese commercial elites than with the Daotai, who wrote criticising the new byelaws. He deprecated the introduction of measures hitherto unknown in China, including the reporting of cases of infectious diseases to the Health Officer (which

[59] Ibid.

[60] Pao Yi to British Ambassador, 10 November 1910, as published in *Municipal Gazette*, 18 November 1910.

[61] David Landale to Sir Pelham Warren, 16 November 1910, as published in *Municipal Gazette*, 18 November 1910.

[62] Representatives of Shanghai guilds and other bodies to the chairman of the Council, 13 November 1910, *Municipal Gazette*, 18 November 1910.

[63] *Municipal Gazette*, 18 November 1910.

[64] Landale to Chow Tsing-Piao, the members of the Shanghai Guilds and other signatories, 17 November 1910, *Municipal Gazette*, 18 November 1910.

Stanley and his fellow medical doctors regarded as crucial), the obligation to remove articles belonging to infected persons for fumigation, and setting a minimum space requirement in residences of 40 square feet per person.[65] The power to demolish the houses which were declared dangerous by the Health Officer owing to the presence of plague victims was naturally deeply resented by residents and came in for strong censure from the Daotai.

Similar strong measures against plague in the Cape Colony a few years earlier, stressing the need for physical changes in the living environment of non-whites to prevent disease, are used by Maynard Swanson to demonstrate the hardening of racial attitudes in pre-Apartheid South Africa.[66] That the SMC attempted similar tactics illustrates the racism that informed its policy decisions, and this is certainly the conclusion that Hu Cheng has drawn.[67] Yet later measures to prevent the spread of disease by the Nationalist government in Shanghai, particularly during the New Life Movement from 1934, were also highly intrusive. Vaccination drives involved teams of health workers stopping rickshaw pullers, demanding evidence of vaccination against cholera, and if none could be produced, forcing them to undergo vaccination.[68] The SMC's response to plague was draconian and based largely on racist ideas of 'unsanitary Chinese', but the Council was not unique in taking heavy-handed action in the name of public health, and for justifying such action by claiming superior understanding of public health needs to the ignorant masses. The colonial government in India was under international pressure, particularly from London, to try to prevent the spread of plague beyond India and therefore acted against it with unprecedented interventionism, until, as in Shanghai, popular protest forced the authorities to end the most coercive measures of house and body searches, compulsory segregation and hospitalisation, and the use of troops.[69] But the use of similarly draconian measures by Chinese authorities suggests fear of the poor was a greater factor than racism in Shanghai.

The Daotai, like the SMC, saw the protesting Shanghainese as ignorant, but used this to urge caution on the part of the Council for fear that they could be easily whipped up into a fury. He knew how to frame his criticism of the Council's proposals to best effect in light of the SMC's primary purpose of facilitating trade: he threatened that if the Council persisted in its plans, 'the

---

[65] Translation of letter from Daotai Liu Yen-Yi To to Sir Pelham Warren, 13 November 1910, in *Municipal Gazette*, 18 November 1910.

[66] Maynard W. Swanson, 'The Sanitation Syndrome: Bubonic Plague and Urban Native Policy in the Cape Colony, 1900–1909', *Journal of African History*, Vol. 18, No. 3 (1977), 387–410.

[67] Hu Cheng, '*Cong "bu weisheng" de huaren xingxiang: Zhong wai jian de butong shu – yi Shanghai gonggong weisheng wei zhongxin de guancha* (1860–1911)' ('The Image of the "Unsanitary Chinese": Differing Narratives of Foreigners and Chinese – Observations Based on Hygiene in Shanghai, 1860–1911'), *Jindai shi yanjiu suo jikan*, No. 56 (2007), 1–43.

[68] Nakajima, 'Health and Hygiene', 68.

[69] Arnold, *Colonizing the Body*, 203–6, 211–34.

Chinese will have to leave the Settlement with their businesses, with very serious effect on Chinese and foreign trade'.[70] But he differed from the Council on a fundamental principle by arguing that municipal byelaws could not be binding on Chinese citizens: a denial of the extraterritorial rights that underpinned the existence of the Settlement. In response, Landale wrote to the senior consul that Pao Yi appeared to misunderstand the basis of the SMC's legislative powers. The Daotai's objections were based on an assumption that the new plague measures would be simple municipal regulations such as those issued from time to time for police and other matters. In fact, byelaws when approved by the ratepayers and consular authorities would carry the full weight of the legal rights conferred by treaty with the foreign powers and would therefore be legally binding on all residents, foreign and Chinese.[71] The Daotai would have rejected this broad claim to jurisdiction, but the vagaries of the Settlement's legal status left it open to interpretation on both sides.

While the objections raised by the Daotai were rejected by the Council, the ratepayers responded to the petitions published by the Chinese guilds and associations of the Settlement, and the byelaws they passed were more limited in scope than Stanley and the Council had hoped. The emphasis therefore continued to be on education and persuasion, with, in the health commissioners' own words, only 'occasional acts of "benevolent despotism"'.[72] The PHD set up a plague barrier on the northern border of the Settlement, in keeping with efforts in Australia and elsewhere to contain infection within physical borders. In 1911 residents of Haining Road petitioned for the removal of this plague barrier, citing damage to their businesses. Stanley believed they had been inspired in their petition by the authorities in Zhabei and the Watch Committee decided to leave the barrier in place at least until the Chinese authorities admitted the SMC's right to police half the road.[73] The fact that Stanley thought the barrier should remain as an effective public health measure was of secondary importance to the assertion of the Council's political position.

When plague again threatened the Settlement in 1918, the byelaws were found to be insufficient as, due to the revision tabled at the ratepayers' meeting, they applied only to bubonic plague, whereas the threat was from pneumonic plague, and they provided only for the isolation of actual cases, not of contacts as was needed to prevent plague identified at Nanjing from reaching Shanghai.[74] The SMC's limited ability to legislate due to its ambiguous legal status was a long-term problem for the Public Health Department, but one which it circumvented by insisting on the powers the Council had established

[70] Daotai Liu to Sir Pelham Warren, 13 November 1910.
[71] Landale to Pelham Warren, 16 November 1910, in *Municipal Gazette*, 18 November 1910.
[72] Jordan and Davis, 'A Brief History'.
[73] SMA U1-1-83: Watch Committee, 16 October 1911.
[74] SMA U1-1-123: Health Committee, 20 March 1918.

and on its claim to a higher scientific rationale for its actions. It refused to be held back by the weakness inherent in its position, lacking the powers of a full colonial government.

Medical Research, the Municipal Laboratory and Scientific Modernity

Warwick Anderson describes the colonial medical laboratory as 'a delibidinized place of white coats, hand washing, strict hierarchy, correct training, isolation, inscription – in short, a place of semantic control and closure, organized around the avoidance of contamination', and thus 'the exemplary locus of colonial modernity'.[75] This overstates the case, but it was certainly true that science and modernity were important in the image and self-perception of the SMC and its departments, employees and rate-paying community. The late nineteenth and early twentieth centuries were the heyday of western scientific self-confidence, as medical science in particular made significant progress and great faith was placed in rationality. Developments such as the contributions of Louis Pasteur and Robert Koch to the new field of bacteriology from the 1860s to the 1880s ushered in a new age of 'curative confidence'.[76] In a colonial context, as such developments came from Europe, this confidence corresponded to European medical chauvinism.

Stanley described the municipal laboratory as 'the brain ... of the Public Health organism'.[77] In doing so, he was proudly proclaiming the modern, scientific nature of his department, which was part of a broader effort to raise its profile in the hope of gaining ratepayers' support for an increase in its staff and budget. In 1909, when he wrote these words for the Council's annual report, the PHD was working hard to prevent the spread of plague from rats to humans in the Settlement. The laboratory tested no fewer than 17,364 rats, of which 187 were found to be infected with plague.[78] These were spread throughout the Settlement, but were particularly concentrated in the northern area near the border with Zhabei. Stanley therefore attributed the blame to a lack of action by the Chinese authorities, a problem which could only be solved, he argued, by an extension of the Settlement.[79] Fear of plague was thus exploited in support of political aims and to bolster the scientific image of the PHD with a view to encouraging support for increased funds.

[75] Warwick Anderson, 'Excremental Colonialism: Public Health and the Poetics of Pollution', *Critical Inquiry*, Vol. 21, No. 3 (1995), 652.
[76] Arnold, 'Introduction', 12 and 12, n. 53. This development might be better described as characterised by 'diagnostic confidence' only.
[77] Arthur Stanley, 'Health Officer's Report', in SMC, *Report for 1909*, 107.
[78] Ibid., 123.
[79] Bickers, *Scramble for China*, 364–5.

The SMC and its ratepayers valued highly the laboratory work of the PHD. In 1917 Edward Little wrote to the Watch Committee to advocate a large expenditure on scientific research, as the mark of a world-class health department, to which Stanley responded by providing a detailed summary of the scientific work his department had performed in the preceding 16 years.[80] The committee agreed that such work was important, but replied to Little that no further budgetary allowance should be made for it before the end of the (First World) War and the completion of the new central offices, which would provide more accommodation for laboratories. The principle that a modern public health department required the latest in medical laboratories was not in question.

Laboratory work was used in the promotion of the health department, reassuring the public that their health was being protected with the best scientific techniques. The *Municipal Gazette* and *Shenbao* both reported the data provided in the SMC's annual report for 1920 concerning the increased number of rats captured and tested for plague, and emphasising the horrors of the disease to press home the important nature of the PHD's work.[81] The laboratory was thus an important element in the public relations of the Council and its PHD. It also provided some of the vast quantities of data that the PHD gathered about the health of the Settlement's residents, reflecting the colonial confidence that collating information would facilitate effective governance.

The department boasted both a pathological and a chemical laboratory, in which technicians examined water, milk and ice-cream for sale in the Settlement to check their safety for consumption, as well as testing to determine cases of infection, including the testing of rats for plague, dogs for rabies and human samples for the diagnosis of myriad diseases. Such samples were sent to them from private medical practitioners and hospitals in Shanghai as well as municipal institutions. This was far from unique to the Settlement at Shanghai: more than 7,000 faecal specimens were examined in Manila in 1909, rising to 126,000 in 1914 due to a cholera outbreak.[82] The SMC did not keep separate data on faecal specimens, but its laboratories performed between 18,000 and 20,000 examinations per year at this time (Shanghai suffered from no corresponding cholera outbreak), showing the municipal laboratories were at least keeping their own with Manila.[83] Where Council laboratories were more unusual in the scope of their activities was in the production of vaccines, particularly for smallpox and rabies, for use throughout China in smaller treaty

[80] SMA U1-1-86: Watch Committee, 8 October 1917.
[81] For example, *Municipal Gazette*, 19 March 1920, 84; *Shenbao*, 10 March 1921, 10.
[82] Anderson, 'Excremental Colonialism', 647.
[83] SMC, *Reports for 1909–14*.

ports and by missionaries inland, and even further afield in East Asia.[84] Such vaccines were also obtainable from elsewhere in China, such as the Peking Union Medical College in later years, but the SMC remained a significant provider throughout the existence of the laboratory.

Anderson's characterisation of the Philippines in the early twentieth century reflects an extreme case of the typical colonial drive to control the physical environment, although the extent to which this was possible in practice is open to question. Anderson links the colonial celebration of the ultimate sanitary environment of the laboratory to his broader thesis that colonial authorities in the Philippines were obsessed with trying to eradicate the pollution that was linked in the minds of the colonisers with the indigenous population, as was manifest in a preoccupation with the hygienic disposal of human waste. This was certainly evident in Shanghai, where in the annual report for 1909, Stanley describes in some detail the different ways in which house refuse was removed from the Settlement.[85] Such interest is hardly surprising, however, in a city where untreated refuse constituted a major source of infection, and this work remained important as the activities of the department increased dramatically over subsequent years. The modernity of the Settlement, claimed and celebrated by the Council and residents, required that basic sanitation was adequately managed.

The expansion of the research performed by the department sometimes led to criticism of its expense. Justice Feetham, during his investigations in Shanghai, put to Jordan the suggestion by the Chinese health minister Dr Heng Liu that the SMC was wasteful in its spending on laboratories.[86] Jordan bristled at the suggestion, arguing that his laboratories were more economical than comparable centres in the USA, where tests were performed by unqualified laboratory technicians, and the UK, where, as in Shanghai, doctors carried out such tests. He claimed that his department performed the most rigorous tests available and emphasised that their services were, with the exception of examinations for venereal disease, free of charge to those who had paid for them through rates (in the Settlement) or contributions (in the French Concession), and inexpensive to other users.[87] This defence was more than the natural desire for a (then acting) head of department to protect his budget: Jordan believed passionately in the importance of employing the latest scientific methods in public health,

[84] SMA U1-16–9: J. H. Jordan, 'Report' for R. Feetham, 5 May 1930.

[85] SMC, *Report for 1909*, 108. The preferred method was the collection of night soil for use as fertiliser.

[86] Dr J. Heng Liu held the post of Health Minister from 1929 to 1937, after training at Harvard Medical School and working in the Peking Union Medical College. Ka-Che Yip, 'Health and National Reconstruction: Rural Health in National China, 1928–1937', *Modern Asian Studies*, Vol. 26, No. 2 (1992), 399.

[87] SMA U1-16-9-198: Jordan to Feetham, 30 July 1930.

and laboratory work was key to this. His early work for the Council focused on laboratory research due to specialist training he had undertaken before arriving in Shanghai, and in 1925 he was appointed Chief Pathologist,[88] so the emphasis on the laboratories during his tenure as Commissioner of Public Health is unsurprising.

Jordan's interest in medical research was not unusual among colonial health officers: David Arnold, in his work on the Indian Medical Service, found that the opportunity to research tropical medicine was offered as 'bait' to potential recruits.[89] Men like Jordan (and Patrick Manson, the 'father' of the study of tropical medicine who began his career working as a medical officer to the Chinese Imperial Maritime Customs in Taiwan) were aware that they would have more chance of making their mark and progressing in their careers if they took such opportunities than if they stayed in the more comfortable medical practices of Britain.[90] The opportunities for research in Shanghai extended to experimentation with prisoners of the Ward Road Gaol, mainly in the form of adjustments to their diet to prevent tuberculosis, beriberi and scurvy,[91] but including the use of new drugs such as the treatment with sulphanilamide of trachoma in the eyes of prisoners.[92] This is an additional facet to the control over the bodies of the colonised which Arnold described taking place in India,[93] although such experimentation would have been equally permissible in gaols in Europe at the time. Inasmuch as these experiments (albeit without the consent of their subjects) resulted in policy changes to benefit the health of the prisoners, they indicate a shift from an earlier attitude to Chinese inmates that prioritised making their period of imprisonment as unpleasant as possible to avoid conditions inside gaol being preferable to life outside, with minimal consideration for their health needs.

Experimentation and research contributed to the PHD's reputation locally and overseas for scientific modernity. Increasingly, senior health officers of

---

[88] SMA U1-1-124: Health Committee, 30 October 1925.

[89] Arnold, *Science, Technology and Medicine*, 198. Douglas Haynes cautions, however, that the attraction of imperial service was rather that often no additional training or specialism was required. Douglas Haynes, *Imperial Medicine: Patrick Manson and the Conquest of Tropical Disease* (Philadelphia, PA: University of Pennsylvania Press, 2001), 155. On the experimental work of medical researchers in the British Empire, see Mark Harrison, *Medicine in an Age of Commerce and Empire: Britain and its Tropical Colonies* (Oxford University Press, 2010), 147–70.

[90] Haynes, *Imperial Medicine*, 15–18.

[91] In the years 1919–1921 investigations were made into the diet of Chinese prisoners and adjustments made which reduced the high incidence of tuberculosis from 69 to 42 per 1,000. Jordan and Davis, 'Brief History'. In 1938 Drs E. Vio and S. T. Hsiu of the Gaol Hospital found that an injection of Redoxon or the consumption of oranges and raw turnips prevented scurvy among inmates. SMA U1-16-10-229: 13 June 1938, S. T. Hsiu to W. R. Johnston, Superintendent of Hospitals.

[92] SMA U1-1-126: Health Committee, 17 March 1941.

[93] Arnold, *Colonizing the Body*.

the SMC published their research in leading medical journals. The results of the measures taken to reduce scurvy were published by Drs Vio and Hsiu in *Caduceus*, published by the University of Hong Kong, and they both published other research results. Dr W. R. Johnston, Superintendent of Hospitals, published an article in the prestigious *British Medical Journal* recounting 'A Unique Case of Foreign Bodies in the Intestinal Tract': a case of 16 fruit stones swallowed as a child suddenly causing health problems in a 24-year-old Chinese convict. Johnston also authored or co-authored several articles in the local *Journal of Clinical Medicine*, including one about a rare fatal case of Wallenberg's Syndrome in an Indian policeman and another on the results of a treatment for pulmonary tuberculosis. Jordan published his observations on the prognosis of rabies, and, with members of his staff, the results of the treatment of cerebrospinal fever by a new drug, in the leading journal *The Lancet*.[94] These publications served to demonstrate the world-class nature of work being carried out in Shanghai and the engagement of SMC employees, including senior Chinese staff like Hsiu, with medical research in the west. Jordan was even credited by *Time* magazine with correctly predicting the high rate of cholera in China in 1932,[95] demonstrating both the extent of his understanding of Chinese public health and the reach and international impact of his work. The scientific modernity of the municipal laboratory and staff brought the PHD onto the world stage, boosting its prestige locally and internationally and securing its position among a transnational medical elite.

A Transnational Department

The Public Health Department was a well-developed department by the international standards of the time. The Council's health officers (all of them British) enjoyed the best training available internationally in public health management, including courses for health inspectors at the Royal Sanitary Institute in Hong Kong and examinations in food safety in Britain and Australia.[96] The Commissioners of Public Health attended international conferences as SMC delegates, keeping abreast of the latest developments in disease prevention at events such as the International Rabies Conference. Jordan made use of periods of long leave to investigate how authorities in Europe and America tackled problems faced by his own department, such as a tour he made in 1930 inspecting waste incinerators.[97] His notes from a visit to Liverpool in 1937 show he was unimpressed by its abattoir, which he felt was dirty, dangerous

[94] SMA U1-16-10-229.
[95] *Time*, 10 October 1932.
[96] SMA U1-6-197: Commissioner of Public Health Y. Tashiro to secretary, 13 January 1943.
[97] SMA U1-1-124: Health Committee, 25 February 1930.

and 'disgracefully run'. Denmark fared no better, where he described dairies in Copenhagen ranging from, at best, equivalent only to a grade B dairy in Shanghai, and at worst 'slovenly in the extreme'.[98] Jordan was in no doubt that his department was one of the best in the world.

Dr Ludwik Rajchman, the Medical Director of the League of Nations Health Organisation (LNHO), suggested to Jordan that he should make more of these investigatory visits within China, but Jordan, disbelieving that he could learn from practice in China, replied tersely that the burden of his work and the limited leave that it was possible for him to take made frequent trips impossible.[99] There was no love lost between the two doctors: Rajchman was known for his leftwing political views and the western powers believed he was too sympathetic to China's plight as a victim of imperialism.[100] This did not endear him to the SMC.

China was a major focus of LNHO attention, as explored by Iris Borowy, and one of the few places in which 'technical' activity took place under its direction.[101] Recent decades have witnessed a revision of the previous dismal view of the League and its achievements, focusing on its Health Organisation.[102] The LNHO was a major proponent of international cooperation in the field of public health, and while in many regions the rhetoric was not accompanied by substantial internationally cooperative action, in China real operational cooperation was attempted. The SMC's health department embraced opportunities to play its part on the international stage, primarily by sharing statistical information with the Eastern Bureau of the Health Organisation, established in 1925 in Singapore after prompting from Japan.[103] The SMC gathered data on communicable diseases and the rate and causes of deaths to send in weekly reports to the Bureau by telegram, both from the Settlement and as provided by the French municipality.[104] Such engagement enabled the PHD to present

[98] SMA U1-16-10-215: Jordan, 'Diary Made During Commissioner's Leave' (n.d.).
[99] SMA U1-16-9-199: Jordan's notes on interview between himself and Rajchman, 19 January 1931.
[100] Jürgen Osterhammel, '"Technical Co-operation" Between the League of Nations and China', *Modern Asian Studies,* Vol. 13, No. 4 (1979), 664; Martin David Dubin, 'The League of Nations Health Organisation', in Paul Weindling (ed.), *International Health Organisations and Movements, 1918–1939* (Cambridge University Press, 1995), 62, 66–72.
[101] Iris Borowy, 'Thinking Big – League of Nations Efforts towards a Reformed National Health System in China', in Iris Borowy (ed.), *Uneasy Encounters: The Politics of Health and Medicine in China* (Oxford: Peter Lang, 2007), 205–28.
[102] Susan Pedersen, 'Back to the League of Nations', *American Historical Review,* Vol. 112. No. 4 (1997), 1091–117.
[103] Osterhammel, '"Technical Co-operation"', 663; Lenore Manderson, 'Wireless Wars in the Eastern Arena: Epidemiological Surveillance, Disease Prevention and the Work of the Eastern Bureau of the League of Nations Health Organisation, 1925–42', in Weindling (ed.), *International Health Organisations,* 109–33.
[104] SMA U1-1-124: Health Committee, 10 November 1926.

itself as the leading health authority in the region and a conduit to a transnational public health authority, adding a new facet to the transnationalism of the Settlement.

However, Jordan was intolerant of suggestions by the League that the Council did not serve the Chinese community sufficiently and failed to cooperate fully with the Chinese authorities. Justice Feetham put to Jordan the allegation made by Rajchman that the SMC made the wellbeing of the foreign community its first public health priority, to which Jordan responded at length, listing the ways in which his department served the Settlement's Chinese residents. This included the more than 1.5 million free vaccinations that had been administered by the department to date, the vast majority of which went to Chinese, as well as building hospitals for Chinese and providing local services: Jordan argued that 11 of the 14 BHOs and 10 of the 14 municipal markets were used exclusively by Chinese.[105] Feetham was apparently convinced by Jordan's arguments, inserting them almost verbatim into his final report.[106] Jordan failed, however, to address Rajchman's implication that the Council's motivation for attempting to improve the public health of Chinese in the Settlement was in large part for the benefit this brought to the foreign community by removing potential sources of infection. This was no doubt true, yet it is not an adequate explanation for all the work of the PHD: the Council's desire to maintain its international reputation was also a strong motivating factor, while medical practitioners simply did a professional job in serving the community. Successive attempts to increase provision for Chinese residents suggest that there was also a genuine desire to improve Chinese health for its own sake. Nonetheless, the SMC clearly only wanted to do so on its own terms and, like other colonial authorities, had a paternalistic conviction that it knew best how to provide for Chinese public health.

The SMC cooperated with the LNHO at a regional and international level, such as by contributing to the work of the Eastern Bureau, because it provided prominence on the international stage. But the Council rejected Health Organisation efforts at a local level when Rajchman or others questioned the superior understanding of local conditions that SMC staff assumed for themselves. The League focussed most of its work in China on improving health conditions in the poor rural majority of the country, so its impact on Shanghai was limited.

The other major western player in Chinese public health was the Rockefeller Foundation, which also maintained a largely rural focus, although it too received a degree of cooperation from the SMC. The Council was more receptive to the Rockefeller Foundation's capitalist ethos of improving the health of

[105] SMA U1-16-9-199: Jordan to Feetham, 15 January 1931.
[106] Feetham, *Report*, II, 50.

the working population for the general benefit to the economy. The Foundation began its public health work with a programme that aimed to eradicate hookworm in the American South to produce more productive workers, and as it expanded its operations overseas it continued to promote the goal of strong, healthy workers.[107] This emphasis on commercial justifications for public health provision sat much better with the Council's foreign businessmen than the League's perceived underlying anti-imperial ideology of promoting self-determinism.

The SMC's involvement with the Rockefeller Foundation exemplifies the kinds of transnational network that connected public health administrations around the world in the early twentieth century. The SMC's deputy secretary visited the headquarters of the Rockefeller Medical Foundation in New York in 1932 to study how their record-keeping methods could be applied to the health administration in the International Settlement.[108] The SMC was asked to provide the Rockefeller library in New York with copies of its annual reports, and in Shanghai it received a specialist from the Foundation during her global tour investigating child welfare.[109] Public health in Shanghai was both a local and a global matter.

Imperial Influence

Despite the transnational influences of the LNHO and the Rockefeller Foundation, the strongest outside influence on SMC public health policy undoubtedly came from Britain and the British empire. Prominent figures including Stanley, Davis and Jordan were all recruited directly from Britain to Shanghai, while health inspectors were trained in London and health officers attended conferences in Britain. In 1928 Davis represented the International Settlement at the Inaugural Congress of the Royal Institute of Public Health, held in Dublin, and was invited to give an address as a 'distinguished visitor'. He said, to the undoubtedly receptive ears at the congress:

An essential element in the development of this Department has been the example of, and the inspiration drawn from great Health Departments throughout the world, and the stimulus of great Congresses, such as this present one, from which new ideas and fresh encouragement radiate to the uttermost parts of the world.[110]

---

[107] E. Richard Brown, 'Public Health in Imperialism: Early Rockefeller Programs at Home and Abroad', *American Journal of Public Health*, Vol. 66, No. 9 (1976), 898–9. On the Rockefeller Foundation's work in China, see Yip, *Health and National Reconstruction*.

[108] SMA U1-16-12-257: Jordan to Geo. V. Allen, vice-consul in charge of the Passport Office, American consulate, 22 August 1932.

[109] SMA U1-16-12-257: Jordan to Dr J. C. Lawney, 27 September 1932.

[110] SMA U1-3–229: Personnel File for Dr C. Noel Davis. Text of address given by Davis at Congress of Royal Institute of Public Health, Dublin, 1 August 1928.

Davis and those he mixed with at the congress were very much alive to the potential of transnational interaction, though for these individuals the networks in which they participated were in practice overwhelmingly British and colonial in nature.

In addition to networks of individuals and organisations, Shanghai was linked to the formal organs of government in London. The SMC took instructions from the British War Office, or anticipated their desires, in their special treatment of the health of British military personnel stationed in the Settlement: in 1919 the PHD gave British armed forces in Shanghai free inoculations; concern for the health of British troops in Shanghai led to efforts by the PHD to improve the sanitary conditions of their barracks in 1927; and in 1931 the department waived the fee for laboratory examinations for the British Army.[111] The PHD followed the example set in Britain and its colonies, from the regulations for plague prevention to those governing the sale of poisons (which were based, in 1940, on those in operation in England).[112] Connections with different parts of the British empire were equally important, and here the SMC was influenced by practice elsewhere and acted as a source of influence for other administrations. Shanghai followed the precedent set in Hong Kong in plague prevention, as seen, yet also gave advice on public health literature to the International Settlement authorities at Gulangyu.[113] Health policy was decided in an environment of inter-colonial exchange.

Shanghai was also included in public health drives directed from the imperial metropole, such as the work of the Far Eastern Commission on Venereal Diseases, which was established under the auspices of the British Ministry of Health, the Colonial and Foreign Offices, and the Treasury.[114] The Commission targeted Hong Kong, Singapore and Shanghai as port cities in particular need of support in the empire-wide campaign against venereal diseases. Shanghai was the first port of call for the commission in December 1920.[115] The timing was excellent as the SMC was then under pressure to act on the recommendations contained in the report of the specially formed Vice Committee, which brought the extent of the public health problems caused by prostitution into the

---

[111] SMA U1-1-123: Health Committee, 31 January 1919; U1-1-124: Health Committee, 20 April 1927 and 3 February 1931. Similar benefits were not necessarily extended to other Allied armies.

[112] SMA U1-1-126: Health Committee, 30 June 1940.

[113] SMA U1-16-11-248: Jordan to C. H. Holleman, Medical Officer of Health, Gulangyu Municipal Council, 17 June 1940.

[114] Kerrie L. MacPherson, 'Health and Empire: Britain's National Campaign to Combat Venereal Disease in Shanghai, Hong Kong and Singapore', in Roger Davidson and Lesley A. Hall (eds.), *Sex, Sin and Suffering: Venereal Disease and European Society since 1870* (London: Routledge, 2001), 173.

[115] MacPherson, 'Health and Empire', 178.

glare of the public eye.[116] In a special joint meeting of the Health and Watch Committees, Dr Rupert Hallam, the Medical Commissioner, made detailed recommendations concerning the provision of a venereal disease clinic and free testing and treatment.[117] Despite the usual desire for economy, the SMC acted immediately to begin implementing his recommendations. The Council also consulted with Hallam in the selection of the new Assistant Health Officer with expertise in venereal diseases who was to be appointed in response to the commission's report.[118] The combination of local pressure from ratepayers and pressure from the imperial metropole forced the SMC into action.

Entente Cordiale? Relations with the French *Conseil Municipal*

Despite these leanings towards the British imperial world, the SMC had to function alongside its neighbouring French and Chinese administrations. Cooperation between the two foreign concessions was often uneasy, as in other treaty ports with multiple foreign concessions, notably Tianjin. Cooperation was particularly important in public health matters, but each council was reluctant to provide services, such as hospital treatment, that would benefit both foreign settlements without securing financial support from the other council. The result was often inactivity or delay. Representatives of the two councils sat together on the board of governors of the Country Hospital for foreigners, which was presented to the community by a private individual in 1926. But the SMC was responsible for guaranteeing any deficit in the hospital's accounts, and resented that the *Conseil municipal* did not share this burden.[119] In addition, the Council repeatedly complained that residents in the French Concession were treated in municipal hospitals in the Settlement without adequate compensation from the *Conseil municipal*. The SMC approached the French authorities seeking a greater contribution in view of the high numbers of Russian refugees who were resident in the French Concession but were being treated at the General Hospital at the expense of International Settlement ratepayers.[120] The French riposted that they made no charge for treating residents of the International Settlement in the Ste. Marie Hospital, and the matter was temporarily allowed to drop, only to be raised again in subsequent years.

The *Conseil municipal* paid a fee to the SMC to use some of its services, such as the municipal laboratory, rather than duplicate them. Meanwhile, the SMC also observed practices that proved effective in the French Concession

---

[116] Philippa Levine, *Prostitution, Race and Politics: Policing Venereal Disease in the British Empire* (New York: Routledge, 2003), 237–9.
[117] SMA U1-1-87: Watch Committee, joint meeting with Health Committee, 21 December 1920.
[118] SMA U1-1-123: Health Committee, 12 August 1921.
[119] SMA U1-1-60: Finance Committee, 25 January 1923.
[120] SMA U1-1-124: Health Committee, 30 October 1925.

and applied them to the Settlement, from methods of treating cattle plague,[121] to the tight control of the pork that could be sold, which would prove highly contentious with the Chinese authorities. The two foreign councils operated a scheme of reciprocal licensing and dual inspection of food vendors.[122] They also shared information on infectious diseases, including the weekly bulletins from the League of Nations Health Station, though Jordan grumbled that 'owing to the incompleteness of organisation of the Public Health Department of the French Administration the information proceeds mainly from one side'.[123] He bemoaned the French lack of a system for notification of infectious diseases as was in place in the Settlement, the lack of an isolation hospital or full-time medical officer, and what he held to be poor and incomplete French statistics (though data were simply gathered under different categories in the two administrations). Nevertheless, the French covered half the cost of the telegrams sent each week to Singapore on the local health situation, and it was the French Municipal Wireless Station that received and re-broadcast the reports on regional public health that came from the Bureau, including warnings of localities where, or individual ships on which, communicable diseases had broken out. The SMC and *Conseil municipal* therefore had a relationship of give and take, with each council anxious to ensure it was not giving more than the other.

This was an 'era of competitive imperialism', not least in the field of public health,[124] and the British and French were the staunchest of imperial rivals. On the whole, cooperation was more prevalent than competition between the two foreign concessions, but tensions remained. When Stanley complained that the French municipality lacked a direct counterpart to his position, and when Jordan criticised the record-keeping in the French Concession, they were setting their own administration above the French in practical and moral terms. Public Health had an aura of public service that gave it greater moral weight than most Council activities, so superiority in public health provision boosted the prestige of the SMC on a moral as well as an administrative level. However, entering the realm of morality brought its own difficulties.

Cooperation with the French was required in the most contentious areas of public health: venereal disease and the treatment of the insane. Health authorities have always struggled with how best to tackle the issue of prostitution and its accompanying diseases, and perhaps nowhere was this problem more pressing than in the infamous port city of early twentieth-century Shanghai, where fractured sovereignty limited the efficacy of attempted regulation. Christian Henriot

---

[121] SMA U1-1-82: Watch Committee, 8 July 1907.
[122] SMA U1-1-124: Health Committee, 5 November 1935.
[123] SMA U1-16-9-198.
[124] Arnold, *Imperial Medicine*, 14.

has shown how the two foreign municipalities, the Chinese and foreign residents, and the Chinese authorities, all had differing views on whether and how best to attempt to regulate and control prostitution.[125] Calls from the League of Nations for the three municipalities to cooperate in this area fell on deaf ears due to the different cultural perspectives from which they viewed the problem.

The different approaches favoured by the two foreign councils reflected the dominant forms of regulation that were established in Britain and France. France is considered the originator of the regulationist approach to prostitution which came to dominate practice in most of continental Europe and the European colonies. *Reglémentation* involved a system of licensed brothels which were regularly inspected for venereal disease, with prostitutes treated at a network of dispensaries as necessary or incarcerated in hospitals if deemed a threat to their clients' health. Britain developed a similar form of regulation domestically and in its colonies, registering known and tolerated prostitutes (though stopping short of formally endorsing them with a licence), inspecting them and isolating cases of diseases. Yet, British commitment to regulationism in the metropole was 'half-hearted', as the Contagious Diseases Acts of 1864 to 1886 were only in force for 20 years and only in certain military stations rather than across the country.[126] London's concern was primarily with the health of the armed forces, and it was in military and imperial contexts that regulationism was more widely accepted.

In Shanghai, the preferred route of the *Conseil municipal* was to try to generate revenue from what they saw as an inevitable trade. The SMC, on the other hand, sought to distance itself from the problem, favouring medical inspection only of Chinese prostitutes visited by foreign customers in an attempt to curb the rates of venereal disease among sailors and the Council's own staff, especially the police. This policy, emphasising the preservation of sexual health within the armed forces and as a secondary concern the preservation of a productive municipal workforce, reflected pressure from the British military for port cities to reduce the rates of infection among military men.[127] The Council was looking to colonial practice in Hong Kong as an example, where the regulationist approach was implemented more consistently.[128] Yet the SMC deviated from practice in Hong Kong and bowed to moral pressure from the ratepayers to attempt to eliminate prostitution. This was due in large part to the influence of the dominant Christian moral discourse in the United States in the 1910s and 1920s on missionaries and

---

[125] Christian Henriot, *Prostitution and Sexuality in Shanghai: a Social History, 1849–1949*, trans. by Noël Castelino (Cambridge University Press, 2001), 273–333.

[126] Philip Howell, *Geographies of Regulation: Policing Prostitution in Nineteenth-century Britain and the Empire* (Cambridge University Press, 2009), 3–4, 7–8, 14–15.

[127] Levine, *Prostitution, Race and Politics*, 145.

[128] Howell, *Geographies of Regulation*, 188–218.

other Christian groups in Shanghai. The Council abandoned regulationism only reluctantly and against the better judgement of its own medical personnel and other practitioners in the Settlement.[129] Chinese were less likely to see the issue in moral terms, emphasising instead practical concerns,[130] but this contrasted more with popular sentiment among the foreign communities than the pragmatism preferred by the councils. Significantly, foreign residents, councils and home governments were particularly concerned about the damage done to perceptions of white racial superiority by the presence of white prostitutes in Shanghai, as was true in colonial societies throughout the world.[131] The SMC deviated from the preferred British imperial model due to the pressure of the foreign ratepayers, despite local Chinese and French opposition, demonstrating the constituency it served.

Mental health was a no less contentious area of public health work (though for different reasons) and this was especially true in a colonial setting. The image of white racial superiority was compromised as much by the presence of insane foreigners as by white prostitutes. The SMC and other Chinese treaty ports shared with colonial India and Africa the practice of shipping long-term mental patients back to their country of origin where possible, both to relieve the municipality of the cost of their care and to avoid the local population witnessing such 'defective human material', in the words of Arthur Stanley.[132] Those without funds were repatriated at the cost of their consulate or national societies, as confirmed with the consular body in 1907 and 1912, and it fell to charitable institutions to fill in any gaps: this accorded with the well-established policy that the SMC should accept no responsibility for poor relief.[133] The strict colour bar applied as much for the insane as for the general population, and the Watch Committee ruled in 1907 that all 'Orientals' should be excluded from the mental ward, including Japanese.[134] The Council began to admit some liability in the case of the white 'mentally deficient who are Shanghai-born' in 1919.[135] The shift reflected the growing significance for the SMC of the Shanghailander mentality, whereby increasing numbers of Britons and Americans in particular identified Shanghai as a permanent home. It made no sense to 'repatriate' British or American citizens who had lived their whole lives in China.

---

[129] Levine, *Prostitution, Race and Politics*, 237.
[130] Henriot, *Prostitution and Sexuality*, 309–10.
[131] Eileen Scully, 'Prostitution as Privilege: The "American Girl" of Treaty-Port Shanghai, 1860–1937', *International History Review*, Vol. 20, No. 4 (1998), 855–6.
[132] SMA U1-1-123: Health Committee, 14 November 1918. For the treatment of the European insane in India, see Waltraud Ernst, *Mad Tales from the Raj: European Insane in British India, 1800–58* (London: Routledge, 2004).
[133] SMA U1-1-123: Health Committee, 14 November 1918.
[134] SMA U1-1-83: Watch Committee, 8 July 1907.
[135] SMA U1-1-123: Health Committee, 31 January and 7 June 1919.

The policy of refusing responsibility for incomers was increasingly difficult to enforce in Shanghai, however, as the stateless population grew with
successive waves of refugees, first Russians following the 1917 October
Revolution, and later Jews fleeing Nazi Europe. The SMC approached the
Chinese authorities in 1923 with a request that they assume financial responsibility for a Russian mental patient as China had accepted consular jurisdiction over stateless Russians,[136] but in general the Council paid for such
cases. The two foreign municipalities also provided increasingly generous
funding for institutions like the Shanghai Hospital for the Insane, which was
exempted from half of the general municipal rate as it assisted the SMC in
providing for the insane in the absence of a municipal mental hospital.[137]
This absence was felt increasingly, and when the Health Commission's work
was under discussion in 1930, Liu Hongsheng made the first minuted contribution by a Chinese member of the Health Committee, arguing that 'all
modern municipalities provide an asylum for the Insane and deprecating the
fact that Shanghai has no such institution'.[138] Although those present agreed
with Liu, it was not until 1935 that the SMC, in conjunction with the French
and Chinese municipal authorities, funded the construction of a new Mercy
Hospital for the insane outside the city, under the auspices of Catholic missionaries. The three authorities all contributed to its maintenance, though
suspicions that the others were not paying their share persisted.[139] The SMC
made increases in its contribution dependent on increases from the *Conseil
municipal* right up until the demise of the French Concession, making a
promised additional grant of 3,500 dollars to the hospital conditional on the
French providing 7,500 dollars on top of their existing (lower) contribution
in 1940.[140] The two municipalities influenced each other in other ways: in
January 1938 the SMC adopted the policy first implemented in the French
Concession a month earlier of funding refugee relief through an entertainment

---

[136] SMA U1-1-123: Health Committee, 27 December 1923.
[137] This was the recommendation of Xu Xinliu when asked by the chairman of the Finance
Committee, A. D. Bell, to comment on the worth of this hospital, based on Xu's personal
acquaintance with Dr Wu who managed the hospital. SMA U1-1-63: Finance Committee, 22
September 1933.
[138] SMA U1-1-124: Health Committee, 30 September 1939, emphasis added.
[139] At a joint meeting of the Health and Finance Committees in 1936, Dr Tongu claimed 'that
most mental cases occur among the Russians in the French Concession, and that the French
Authorities have therefore a greater financial responsibility for the undertaking than the
Council'. SMA U1-1-26: Finance Committee, 2 March 1936.
[140] SMA U1-1-63: Finance Committee, 25 May 1940. Later that year, the SMC's payment to
the hospital of $2 per patient (foreign or Chinese) per day was increased to $4 to reflect
the rampant inflation, again on the condition that the French municipality matched the rise.
SMA U1-1-63: Finance Committee, 12 October 1940. Council contributions to the National
Leprosarium, situated outside Shanghai, were also contingent on those made by the French
and Chinese municipal authorities. SMA U1-1-26: Finance Committee, joint meeting with
Health Committee, 2 March 1936.

levy on theatre tickets.[141] The stresses of war led to increased intervention by both colonial municipal authorities.

Cooperation between the different municipal authorities increased over time, as shown by the example of provision for mental health, but the foreign municipal authorities were most anxious to collaborate in times of emergency. In the face of the threat of an outbreak of pneumonic plague in Nanjing spreading to Shanghai in 1918,[142] the Acting French consul-general attended an emergency meeting of the Health Committee in his capacity as chairman of the *Conseil municipal* to discuss a joint strategy to prevent the disease reaching Shanghai. No Chinese were invited to the meeting, reflecting the consensus among the international authorities at the time that concerted action would come from the foreign community alone. When Sino-Japanese hostilities broke out in January 1932, Jordan turned to his French counterparts for assistance. The French provided hospital beds in the Ste. Marie Hospital for patients evacuated from the municipal Isolation Hospital, and the SMC provided them with extra staff and equipment to do so.[143] When presented with an emergency, the councils instinctively turned to each other for help, in recognition of their shared position as European colonial authorities on Chinese soil. In 1936, Dr Rabaute, the French Director of Public Hygiene, wrote to Jordan that in public health '*il n'y a pas de frontières*'.[144] This was a recognition of practical if not political realities.

A New Neighbour: The City Government of Greater Shanghai

Cooperation between the SMC and local Chinese authorities on public health, where attempted, was hindered by the often weak and transitory nature of those authorities and indeed by the lack of a health department in the Chinese City before 1926. Dr Ding Wenjiang (丁文江 'V. K. Ting') began in that year to set about establishing a new, 'modern' municipal infrastructure on behalf of Sun Chuanfang, the military governor who then controlled the region.[145] Ding's innovations included the establishment of the Shanghai Bureau of Public Health (*weisheng ju*) and he sought and was given information about the nature of the Council's PHD as he planned a similar structure.[146] Following the Guomindang's victory over Sun's forces in 1927, Chiang Kai-shek declared the city a Special Municipality and appointed Huang Fu (黃郛) as the first Mayor of Greater Shanghai. Ding was dismissed, but Huang continued the

[141] Chen, *Guilty of Indigence*, 143–4.
[142] SMA U1-1-123: Health Committee, 20 March 1918.
[143] SMA U1-16-9-216.
[144] SMA U1-16-12: Rabaute to Jordan, 3 August 1936.
[145] Henriot, *Shanghai 1927–1937*, 18.
[146] Jordan, 'Report'.

development of the Bureau of Public Health as part of the new municipal government. In July 1927 the municipal government announced the Greater Shanghai Plan, which was intended to raise the infrastructure of the municipality to match that of the foreign concessions – the latter taken as models for development.[147] Public health was also to be thus improved: the Guomindang derived its legitimacy in part from its concern for the welfare of the population, and public health provision was crucial to maintaining such legitimacy.[148] Similar ambitions for public health accompanied the establishment of Guomindang authority in Tianjin,[149] but Shanghai was the priority for the Nanjing government, a city in which it planned to showcase its success to the world. The SMC's Public Health Department was trying to keep up with the most modern trends in the field, so it was not a bad model for the Greater Shanghai government to take. This policy also fitted with the national government's plans concerning social medicine.[150] Cooperation with the SMC was therefore planned from the establishment of the Special Municipality.

The new Commissioner for Health of the Municipal Government of Shanghai, Dr Hu Hongji (胡鴻基 Hu Hou-ki), was introduced to Commissioner Davis of the SMC by Dr John Grant, the Rockefeller Foundation International Health Board's representative to China, in 1926. Davis invited Hu to visit the PHD to see how it ran its operations.[151] No doubt he was proud to show off his department in all its 'hygienic modernity'. But by this time Chinese elites were well-acquainted with western methods, as Rogaski shows.[152] Hu had had ample exposure to the most modern of western public health developments during his training at the Johns Hopkins School of Hygiene and Public Health from 1922, and in his subsequent post as Chief of the Division of Vital Statistics at the Health Demonstration Station at Beijing under John Grant.[153] Thus while Davis and Jordan looked down on their Chinese counterpart, Hu's experience

---

[147] Kerrie L. MacPherson, 'Designing China's Urban Future: The Greater Shanghai Plan, 1927–1937', *Planning Perspectives*, Vol. 5, No. 1 (1990), 39, 43.

[148] Nakajima, 'Health and Hygiene', 44; Yip, 'Health and National Reconstruction'; Zhang Daqing, *Zhongguo jindai jibing shehui shi (A Social History of Diseases in Modern China, 1912–1937)* (Jinan: Shandong jiaoyu chubanshe, 2006).

[149] Rogaski, *Hygienic Modernity*, 234.

[150] In 1933 the Chinese government welcomed Andrija Stampar of the LNHO to investigate rural public health in China. After three years he concluded that successful health work was impossible where basic living standards were intolerable, so the first task in China was to raise living standards. The Guomindang welcomed his recommendations, but action was slow. Andrija Stampar, 'Health and Social Conditions in China', *Quarterly Bulletin of the Health Organisation of the League of Nations*, 5 (1936), 1090–126, cited in Amrith, *Decolonizing International Health*, 26–7.

[151] Jordan, 'Report'.

[152] Rogaski, *Hygienic Modernity*, 234–5.

[153] Mary Brown Bullock, *An American Transplant: The Rockefeller Foundation and Peking Union Medical College* (Berkeley, CA: University of California Press, 1980), 147.

and qualifications were certainly at least as 'modern' and up-to-date as their own.[154]

Hu was in some ways a product of the transnational developments in public health.[155] The Rockefeller Foundation, which funded Hu's training at the Johns Hopkins School (he was the first Chinese recipient of a Rockefeller Foundation International Health Board fellowship) and supported the Health Station where he had worked, was perhaps the most significant organisation promoting public health on the international stage in the interwar period.[156] It was the time of a dramatic shift in the nature of public health across Asia, as improvements in basic sanitation and nutrition were championed and large gains made throughout the region. Representatives of the League of Nations worked hard to effect cooperation between the different authorities of Shanghai on health issues, but the relationship between the Chinese and Settlement administrations was plagued by mistrust.

Insignificant as it may seem, the issue of licensing and inspecting bakeries and dairies was the catalyst for a deterioration in the relationship between the two councils on health matters. In 1927 Hu Hongji suggested to Davis that, provided the licence conditions of both areas met the same standards, they should be mutually recognised, just as the French and International Settlement authorities recognised each other's licences. An SMC inspection in early 1928, however, found bakeries licensed by Hu to be unsanitary, so Davis decided to withhold reciprocity on licensing until standards improved. This marked the beginning of an antagonistic relationship between the two public health commissioners: Davis claimed that from then on Hu was hostile and 'carried on a persistent campaign of calumny and obstruction'.[157] Hu then proposed reciprocity on pork inspection, but the two councils refused to recognise the quality of the other's inspectorate. When the SMC introduced a system of inspecting pigs for Chinese consumption within the Settlement, all pigs in the Chinese City bearing the municipal stamp were confiscated.

Relations reached their low-point the following year over the disposal of human waste. The ever-increasing population of the Settlement meant previous solutions to the problem were no longer sufficient, and in 1929 the SMC agreed a contract to use a site in Greater Shanghai already in use by the Chinese and French authorities. In order to allow it to proceed, however, Hu demanded concessions from the Council on areas of contention from the reciprocal licensing of food outlets to the Shanghai Municipal Police arresting

---

[154] To compare their professional backgrounds, Jordan had qualified at Cambridge University in 1913, after which he served in the Army during the First World War and then worked in Middlesex Isolation Hospital.

[155] Amrith, *Decolonizing International Health*, 4–8, 25–7.

[156] Ibid., 25.

[157] Jordan, 'Report'.

students in uniform. Jordan declared that this was 'a deplorable instance of an attempt to sacrifice the public health and welfare to the attainment of political ends', but in the unequal world of the treaty ports it is unsurprising that the Chinese authorities should have seized opportunities to obtain concessions from the foreign authorities they were hoping to supersede. Jordan's objections were in fact based largely on Hu's perceived lack of respect for the SMC. He claimed Hu 'adopted a manner of studied insolence' during a meeting with the Commissioner of Public Works over the issue.[158] The Council and its employees were having trouble adjusting to a newly confident and ambitious Chinese authority. Deploring the 'refractory and short-sighted obstructiveness of the local authorities', Jordan recommended the SMC install incinerators to deal with the problem of waste disposal, which it duly did.[159] Cooperation between a colonial and a nationalist authority had, unsurprisingly, failed.

There were not always alternative options if cooperation was found to be difficult, and sometimes concessions had to be made. Diseases do not respect political borders, and the fight against cholera was one area in which the three municipalities in Shanghai made a concerted effort to cooperate, following the LNHO mission. The SMC, French *Conseil municipal* and Chinese municipal government all contributed funds and materials to annual anti-cholera campaigns from 1929, which aimed, for example, to inoculate 200,000 people in 1930.[160] The Public Health Bureau in the Chinese municipality had already developed a laboratory with a large capacity: the SMC planned to use 200,000 vaccines produced in its own laboratories and purchase further supplies from the Bureau. However, the minutes of the conference held in May 1930 to plan that year's campaign, led by Hu Hongji and attended by representatives of all three administrations and the League of Nations, reveal the deep tensions that existed between those involved.

The most serious area of disagreement was over the strength of the inoculation to be administered. The Chinese doctors were concerned that if too high a dose were given, patients would have such a severe reaction that people would be unwilling to undergo the inoculation. Fearing that they would be the only authority whose inoculation produced the severe reaction, the SMC agreed to a compromise dose much lower than that they thought advisable, but from comments made at the meeting Jordan suspected that Hu would proceed with the even lower dose he had planned. Perhaps uncomfortable in a meeting chaired by a Chinese, Jordan's personal dislike of Hu was apparent and he noted his disgust at the discussion in the margin of his copy of the minutes: 'the whole

---

[158] Jordan complained that Hu chose to speak only through a clerical assistant even though he spoke perfect English. Jordan, 'Report'.
[159] Jordan and Davis, 'Brief History'; SMA U1-1-124: Health Committee, 25 February 1930.
[160] Jordan, 'Report'.

thing is eye-wash'.[161] He also criticised Hu's inoculation of schoolchildren, who Jordan believed were at low risk of contracting cholera anyway: he evidently did not believe Hu was basing his work on a sound scientific basis.

Cooperation between the Council and the Chinese authorities was fraught with such differences of opinion right up to 1943, when the Japanese-controlled SMC met regularly with the local municipal governments of the two puppet regimes (Vichy France and Wang Jingwei's China) to iron out differences in regulating food and medicine standards.[162] Yet the effort was made, the annual cholera campaigns continued and the approach to the prevention of disease was one of partnership. The SMC contributed funds to other campaigns run by the Chinese municipal government to increase uptake of vaccinations and improve general hygiene standards, and city-wide campaigns were thought to achieve a greater impact than if they had been confined to the limits of the Settlement.

In other areas of public health management, the SMC was forced into a position of keeping up with the rapid improvements being effected in the neighbouring Chinese municipality. In December 1933, the Health Committee recommended that action be taken on school medical inspection. This had been suggested many times since Stanley first reported on the subject in 1920, but the Council ruled that 'the responsibility for attending to the health of School Children is properly a matter for parents' and therefore should not fall on the public purse.[163] As the culture of the SMC gradually changed and it took on greater responsibilities, such as the provision of education for Chinese due to the influence of Chinese members of Council, medical inspection in schools was still not approved due to calls for financial stringency. All that had altered in 1933 was that the Chinese municipal government had implemented a programme of school medical inspection, and the SMC could not appear to fall behind, as stated explicitly in the Health Committee minutes.[164]

The SMC employed a Dr Ward to investigate the need for school medical services. She reported in March 1934 that children in municipal schools were suffering from a high number of preventable eye and skin infections, and advocated the establishment of a school medical inspection service without delay. Work began in Chinese municipal primary schools in accordance with advice from Chinese members of the SMC Education Board, based on practice in the Greater Shanghai municipality. This episode reflects both a shift in dynamic as the Council followed the example set by the Chinese municipality, and the positive impact made by the Chinese councillors, who had prompted the decision. The achievements of the Greater Chinese municipal

[161] Jordan, 'Report'.
[162] SMA U1-6–192: Inter-municipal conference minutes, 20 July 1943.
[163] Zhang (ed.), *Minutes of the SMC*, Vol. 23, 2 July 1925.
[164] SMA U1-1–124: Health Committee, 7 December 1933.

authority in this and other areas of public health work contribute to the growing literature, by Julia Strauss and others, that rehabilitates the Nationalist government more broadly, redressing a long-held belief that it was doomed to fail from the outset.[165] The SMC had a powerful new neighbour in the Greater Shanghai municipal government, and in public health the two administrations learned to cooperate despite their mutual mistrust.

Assessing Success

Despite the improvements in the SMC's relations with its neighbours and all the increased activities of the Public Health Department, there is no evidence that it was successful in significantly reducing mortality rates in the Settlement among foreigners or Chinese. According to the PHD's own figures, mortality rates among the Chinese population varied from a peacetime high of 30.9 per thousand in 1902 (10,801 deaths were recorded that year, the first in which statistics on deaths in the Chinese population were kept) to a low of 10.3 per thousand in 1923 (when 8,436 deaths were recorded), with great fluctuations year to year. There is no discernable trend of a decline in mortality. Similarly, the mortality rate among foreigners, far fewer in total population, ranged from 11.2 per thousand in 1905 (129 deaths) to 20.7 in 1917 (410 deaths), with no general decline in mortality.[166]

Foreigners in Shanghai enjoyed lower mortality rates than their counterparts elsewhere in East Asia and overall mortality rates in the Settlement were comparable to those in Paris, except during cholera outbreaks.[167] But the failure of the PHD to make a positive impact on the rate of death over a period of such increased activity and investment requires explanation. The department operated in an environment with high levels of poverty, especially among the Chinese population, but also among some foreign groups, particularly Russian émigrés. Shanghai's population density was very high by both international and Chinese standards, with 115,000 per square mile by 1930: higher than other cities in China, Europe, the USA and Japan (and indeed higher than twenty-first century Shanghai, despite today's skyscrapers).[168] Overcrowding soared as refugees fleeing to the Settlement with limited resources posed new public health dangers and containing these was a growing struggle for the PHD.

[165] Julia C. Strauss, *Strong Institutions in Weak Polities: State Building in Republican China, 1927–1940* (Oxford: Clarendon Press, 1998); contributions to 'Special Issue: Reappraising Republican China', *China Quarterly*, No. 150 (1997), 255–458.

[166] SMC, *Reports for 1905–1937*.

[167] MacPherson, *Wilderness of Marshes*, 268; Christian Henriot, *Scythe and the City: A Social History of Death in Shanghai* (Stanford University Press, 2016), 16.

[168] Isabella Jackson, 'Habitability in the Treaty Ports: Shanghai and Tianjin', in Lincoln and Xu Tao (eds.), *The Habitable City in China*, 177.

Violence was a constant cause of death even in peacetime. That the mortality rate was kept relatively stable in the face of overcrowding and endemic violence can be seen as an achievement in itself, but even so the department was falling short of its aims for public health, born of faith in scientific progress.

The refugee problem became critical after the outbreak of war in 1937. The SMC, on behalf of Yu Xiaqing, obtained assurances from the Japanese consul-general that ships coming into Shanghai to take away refugees would not be attacked by the Japanese military if they flew both white and municipal flags.[169] But evacuation could not keep pace with those arriving: more than 150,000 refugees sought shelter in the foreign settlements of Shanghai in April 1938 alone, and the numbers were too great for charities to care for unaided. The initially impassive SMC reluctantly took action to support hospitals for refugees and refugee camps with basic hygiene facilities. To pay for the refugee relief, the SMC levied a voluntary entertainment tax on theatres, swimming pools and skating rinks, raising 275,000 dollars while addressing ongoing concerns for the municipal budget.[170] Mortality rose significantly in this period, but the PHD helped contain outbreaks of epidemic disease and a potential public health crisis was averted.

The most striking sign of the SMC's failure to address poverty as the underlying cause of mortality was the number of 'exposed corpses' that were cleared from the Settlement's streets on a daily basis.[171] These bodies of the destitute or of those whose families could not afford a burial were listed separately in municipal annual reports from 1930, when 5,783 such bodies were collected in the Settlement, representing 37.4 per cent of the total number of deaths.[172] This phenomenon increased through the decade until 20,796 corpses were collected in 1937, or 59 per cent of the total figure for deaths that year.[173] It was a mark of shame in a city with the wealth of Shanghai that such extreme poverty should be in such stark evidence, contrasting sharply with the modern image the Council sought to portray.

The SMC was constrained by its lack of reliable information on the causes of mortality in the Settlement: deaths were underreported and 80 per cent of those reported were attributed to 'old age'.[174] Chinese infant and maternal deaths went largely unregistered. Deaths from opium poisoning were not uncommon, but whether a case was due to chronic usage, accidental overdose or suicide was unclear. The department's approach to opium consumption was laissez-faire: Stanley considered it little more harmful than 'tea-drinking or

[169] SMA U1-6–142: Secretary to Yu Xiaqing, 21 August 1937.
[170] SMC, Report for 1938, 24.
[171] Henriot, Scythe and the City, 225–57.
[172] SMC, Report for 1930, 132.
[173] SMC, Report for 1937, 121.
[174] SMA U1-16–9: 'Deaths: Chinese', 27 January 1937.

tobacco-smoking' and attributed its popularity to the sedative effects being 'in keeping with the Chinese character'.[175] When the harms of opium addiction were better known, the Finance Committee blocked support for an opium addicts' hospital on the basis that addicts were criminals and facilities for their treatment existed in the Ward Road Gaol.[176] Similar moralising held back public health work on venereal diseases. Lack of information and failure to act on information available contributed to the limited achievements of the SMC in public health.

The SMC and its committees juggled the growing demand for public health services with the ever-present concern for economy. Yet over the decades there is clear evidence of increased public health provision and a greater sense of responsibility for the care of Chinese residents in the Settlement. Public health provision was never a priority for the laissez-faire Council, so the commissioners of public health did well to expand the work of their department to such an extent over the years. They also had to contend with the constraints on Council powers caused by the limited Land Regulations and the inability to alter them after 1899, coupled with the difficulty in securing ratepayer approval for changes to the byelaws, which prevented the SMC from taking the kind of action in the field of public health that was possible in other parts of the world. The PHD was able to circumvent this limitation by emphasising the work it could do within the existing legal structure of the Settlement. This meant a shift from attempting to force a change in the practices of Chinese residents, by enforcing draconian byelaws such as those introduced in 1910 to prevent the spread of plague, towards efforts through publicity and the community work of the BHOs to achieve improvements in public health. This coincided with the emergence of a concern among Chinese elites to embody 'hygienic modernity' and increased awareness globally of the role of public hygiene in preventing the spread of disease.

The Council also pursued its public health goals in the rarefied environment of the laboratory, conducting research that positioned the PHD at the forefront of international public health work. The SMC was subject to influences from around the world in an age in which newly emergent transnational bodies such as the LNHO and the Rockefeller Foundation were beginning to have a significant impact. The International Settlement was also positioned squarely in the 'British world',[177] through the professional circuits of its staff and its close links with public health training and measures in Britain and the British empire, including but not confined to Hong Kong and the China coast.

---

[175] SMA U1-16-10: Arthur Stanley, 'Chinese Hygiene', *China Medical Missionary Journal* (April 1903), 12 (by archived text page numbering).
[176] SMA U1-1-61: Finance Committee minutes, 30 December 1932.
[177] Carl Bridge and Kent Fedorowich (eds.), *The British World: Diaspora, Culture and Identity* (London: Frank Cass, 2003).

Locally, too, the SMC had to interact with different political actors, notably the French Concession authorities and the Chinese administration of Greater Shanghai, which it managed with varying degrees of success.

The PHD, therefore, reflects the realities of how the SMC functioned as a transnational colonial body in relation to local and international influences. The pride of the Council and many residents of the Settlement in its comparative modernity was due in no small part to its public health work. The fact that mortality rates in the Settlement remained effectively stagnant despite all the efforts of the PHD may appear to counter these claims but, given the increased population pressures in the Settlement, this in itself was an achievement. Yet despite the myriad activities of the PHD, poverty remained a barrier to significant improvements in public health, sorely compromising the efforts of the department to exemplify scientific modernity.

5 Industry, Welfare and Social Reform

It is no light task to try to prevent a city from blowing up![1]

Shanghai was the centre of light industry in China from the dawn of the twentieth century, particularly in the production of textiles, flour and tobacco. The largest sector was cotton manufacturing. The region had been a centre of cotton production and processing since the thirteenth century, but it was only with the relaxation of the laws restricting foreign industrial investment in 1895 that the industry took off, led by new mills with western technologies. The Treaty of Shimonoseki, which concluded the First Sino-Japanese War in April of that year, granted Japan and, therefore, through Most Favoured Nation clauses in other treaties, all the other treaty powers, the right for the first time to open factories and engage in industry in China.[2] Foreign investors in the larger treaty ports took advantage of the new privilege, initiating rapid industrial expansion. Chinese investors joined in, responding in part to the measures taken by the Qing government to boost industry following the disastrous First Sino-Japanese and Boxer Wars, such as the creation of a Ministry of Commerce in 1903 and the promulgation of a Company Law in 1904.[3] The concentration and growing number of foreign, modern Chinese and traditional Chinese banks in Shanghai ensured the city's position at the helm of this industrial revolution.

The heyday of the cotton industry came during the First World War due to the fall in overseas competition and the concurrent global rise in demand: this was what Marie-Claire Bergère dubs the 'golden age of the Chinese bourgeoisie'.[4] The number of cotton spindles and looms in operation in Shanghai

[1] MLMSS 770/1/2: E. M. Hinder to her mother, 5 May 1936.
[2] Immanuel C. Y. Hsu, 'Late Ch'ing Foreign Relations, 1866–1905', in John K. Fairbank and Kwang-Ching Liu (eds.), *The Cambridge History of China, Vol. 11, Late Ch'ing, 1800–1911, Part 2* (Cambridge University Press, 1980), 108.
[3] Albert Feuerwerker, 'Economic Trends in the Late Ch'ing Empire, 1870–1911', in Fairbank and Liu (eds.), *Cambridge History of China*, Vol. 11, Part 2, 33. For the industrialisation of Shanghai, see Marie-Claire Bergère, *Shanghai: China's Gateway to Modernity* (Stanford University Press, 2009), 59–63.
[4] Bergère, *Golden Age*, 64–83.

doubled between 1913 and 1920, from 484,192 spindles and 2,016 looms to 842,894 and 4,310 respectively.[5] The cotton mills that dominated the cityscape away from the grand façade of the Bund were the source of much of both the city's wealth and its inhabitants' suffering. Workers complained of being treated 'like cattle and horses', as analysed by S. A. Smith.[6] Shanghai thus earned a reputation for industrial exploitation alongside the other vices for which it was known.

The laissez-faire Shanghai Municipal Council was slow to respond to criticism of industrial conditions in the International Settlement. It took action only after sustained pressure from local and transnational institutions and welfare groups, predominantly directed or promoted by women, and from the Chinese government when it instigated industrial reforms.

Industry was a key component of nineteenth- and early twentieth-century notions of modernity. The mechanisation of traditional practices, the sociological impact of bringing workers together in the close confines of factory employment, and the cultural effect of the new consumption of manufactured goods – the growing significance of the 'things modern' that Frank Dikötter analyses – exemplified the modern industrial city.[7] Industry thus lay at the heart of Shanghai's status as the most modern city of East Asia. As the SMC claimed much of the credit for creating a modern municipality and the environment in which business flourished, it was staking its reputation on the nature of the industry in the International Settlement. When, therefore, criticism of industrial working conditions there began to trickle and later pour in from London and Geneva, not to mention Nanjing, the SMC reluctantly had to act to salvage its reputation by promoting industrial reforms.

This chapter demonstrates how the SMC's industrial, labour and welfare policies were influenced by local, national and transnational forces, as attention increasingly focused on humanitarian concerns in the interwar period. The SMC was the target of transnational campaigns in the same way as state governments were targeted elsewhere; although autonomous from metropolitan imperial control, it was subject to new trends that were beginning to shape government welfare policies independent of the borders of empires. The SMC was forced to change its policies and become more interventionist in governing local industry, showing how it changed over time to take on a greater role in public welfare, comparable to its increased spending on public health.

Municipal efforts to regulate industrial conditions were frustrated by the SMC's lack of legal authority to pass and enforce laws in the Settlement, so

---

[5] Ibid., 71.
[6] Smith, *Like Cattle and Horses*.
[7] Frank Dikötter, *Things Modern: Material Culture and Everyday Life in China* (London: Hurst, 2007).

they centred on the use of byelaws and other creative ways around the constraints of the Land Regulations. In this way, the SMC continued to pursue its policy of seeking to expand its powers and authority by whatever means it could. Politically active Chinese were sensible to this and opposed attempts by the Council to extend its powers into areas not specifically provided for in the Land Regulations, further complicating efforts to improve industrial conditions. This chapter therefore addresses the SMC's relationship with Chinese nationalism as it grew after the pivotal years 1925 to 1928. Despite serious tensions, the SMC worked increasingly closely with the Shanghai city government to improve labour conditions, following the Chinese lead in this area. This chapter thus contributes to the reassessment that has emerged in recent years of the Guomindang government's efforts to develop China, as legislative initiatives from Nanjing influenced municipal activities in the realm of industrial reform, perhaps more than in any other area of governance.[8]

An important new aspect of the SMC's nature becomes apparent over the following pages: its place within the development of a global women's movement in the interwar years. As Emily Honig has shown, the majority of Shanghai's exploited textile workers were female.[9] The suffering of women and particularly children in Shanghai's factories prompted women's groups to appeal to the Council for action. Global humanitarian movements were directed by women and the transnational SMC was increasingly connected to such networks, not least through its only female head of department, Eleanor Hinder, who led the Industrial Section.

The chapter addresses the Council's early limited regulation of industrial conditions in the first decades of the twentieth century, before turning to the first serious attempts to reform industry in the Settlement in the mid-1920s, in response to public pressure to control the use of child labour. The promulgation of the Factory Law by the Nanjing government in 1929 precipitated more wide-reaching reforms in the Settlement and the establishment of the Industrial Section, which expanded the reach of Council authority into the management practices of industrialists and the lives of workers. Finally, the activities of this section expanded greatly during the Second Sino-Japanese War as the conflict created greater need among the population and provided the opportunity for greater municipal control. The war expanded the governmental role of the SMC and its impact on the lives of the Settlement's inhabitants.

---

[8] For early examples of this development in the literature, see *China Quarterly*, No. 150, Special Issue: Reappraising Republican China (1997). See also Felix Boecking, 'Unmaking the Chinese Nationalist State: Administrative Reform among Fiscal Collapse, 1937–1945', *Modern Asian Studies*, Vol. 45, No. 2 (2011), 227–301, and other contributions to this special issue of the journal.

[9] Emily Honig, *Sisters and Strangers: Women in the Shanghai Cotton Mills, 1919–1949* (Stanford University Press, 1986).

Managing Industrial Conditions and Growing Expectations

Prior to the establishment of a specific section to address industrial conditions, the SMC paid scant attention to such matters. When they did arise, they fell under the purview of the Watch Committee, inasmuch as the public order of the Settlement was affected. The first reference in the minutes of the committee to industrial unrest came in June 1910 when the Captain Superintendent of Police reported that female workers at silk filatures in western Hongkou had created a public disturbance due to their employers withholding their pay as security for their work.[10] The chairman of the committee told the factory managers that if their employment practices were found to be behind public disturbances they would be prosecuted.[11] The SMC took action, therefore, not out of concern for workers' welfare but for the sake of public order, in keeping with its conviction that its primary function was to provide an environment conducive to business.

The general strike of June 1919 during the May Fourth Movement represented the first major industrial action in the city, but the protest was political rather than arising from poor working conditions. It nonetheless warned the Council of the power of strike action to damage public order and business interests, and to inconvenience the foreign community.[12] In 1922, the Hong Kong government's heavy-handed response to a strike by the Seamen's Union, including the killing of five strikers by the police, escalated the dispute to a general strike that almost paralysed Hong Kong.[13] Following this episode, the Deputy Commissioner of the SMP, Alan Hilton-Johnson, argued that the SMC should 'urge businesses to treat labour demands sympathetically, ... support conciliation, and ... avoid "bombastic utterances in official proclamations"'.[14] This was progressive rhetoric for its time in Shanghai (although the SMP would fail to learn the lesson from the Seamen's Strike when faced with its own crisis on 30 May 1925) but the stress was still on the preservation of public order rather than improving the lot of Shanghai's workers.

Discussions about building regulations were similarly pragmatic: they were revised in 1922 to encourage (though not insist on) the installation of water sprinkler systems in cotton mills where loose cotton constituted a serious fire hazard. The Chief Fire Officer and Commissioner of Public Works agreed on the benefits of the measures, in part for the safety of workers within the mills, but primarily for the prevention of fire which could spread to nearby

[10] This was common practice in Shanghai's factories and is related to the system of contract labour that Honig describes. Honig, *Sisters and Strangers*, 94–115.

[11] SMA U1-1-83: Watch Committee, 3 October 1910.

[12] Chen, *The May Fourth Movement*, 144–8.

[13] Steve Tsang, *A Modern History of Hong Kong* (London: I. B. Tauris, 2007), 88–9.

[14] Bickers, *Empire Made Me*, 168.

buildings.[15] The members of the Watch Committee were nonetheless reluctant to take any action, arguing that such precautions should be adopted due to incentives offered by insurance companies rather than regulations. They cited favourably the absence of such legislation in English cities, though noted that public places such as theatres in the United States were required to install sprinkler and drencher systems. Municipal responsibilities were seen in the light of practice globally, predominantly in what James Belich calls the Angloworld,[16] with a preference on the part of the Council for examples that supported minimal municipal action. But by the 1920s, outside expectations of the SMC's responsibilities were growing.

Following its participation in the First World War, China was included in post-war efforts to build a new global order, which extended to improved labour conditions to reduce the risk of conflict and revolution. Part XIII of the Treaty of Versailles established the International Labour Conference and its Office (ILO) at Geneva, under the auspices of the League of Nations.[17] All the founding member states of the League, including China, were automatically members of the ILO.[18] The ILO paid particular attention to China due to its size and the scale of its industrial problems. The Chinese government specifically was asked to adhere to the principle of protection of labour by factory legislation to regulate a maximum ten-hour day or 60-hour week for adults, with shorter hours for those under 15 years, and a weekly rest day.[19] These measures were enacted under the precarious presidency of Li Yuanhong in March 1923, with further stipulations that boys under 10 and girls under 12 were not to be employed, while older minors could engage only in light work and not at night. Employers were also to ensure that primary education and basic healthcare were provided for all – far-reaching goals by the standards of the day. Unfortunately, the regulations included no measures for enforcement and thus had no real impact, Beijing being too weak to impose its will on the nation. Similar laws passed by provincial governments, such as the ruling by the Governor of Jiangsu (to the north of Shanghai) that the working day should be no more than nine hours and that workers should be given Sunday as a day

[15] SMA U1-1-87: Watch Committee, 19 June 1922.

[16] James Belich, *Replenishing the Earth: The Settler Revolution and the Rise of the Angloworld, 1783–1939* (Oxford University Press, 2009).

[17] Introductions to the work of the ILO made an explicit link between improving labour conditions and the League of Nations' broader aims to promote world peace: 'people living under bad conditions, working far too long every day … will always probably be ready to make war'. Kathleen E. Innes, *The League of Nations and the World's Workers: An Introduction to the Work of the International Labour Organisation* (London: Hogarth Press, 1927), 9.

[18] International Labour Office, *The International Labour Organisation: The First Decade* (London: George Allen and Unwin, 1931), 36–7.

[19] Fang Fu-an, *Chinese Labour: An Economic and Statistical Survey of the Labour Conditions and Labour Movements in China* (Shanghai: Kelly and Walsh, 1931), 130–1.

of rest, were also not enforced.[20] Nevertheless, even prior to the stronger government established by Chiang Kai-shek in 1927, attempts were being made at better governance in the new republic.

The new international attention on labour conditions also influenced the Hong Kong government, which appointed a child labour commission in 1921 and, on its recommendations, promulgated an Industrial Employment of Children Ordinance in 1922. The ordinance banned the employment of young children in factories or dangerous trades: the first law of its kind in East Asia.[21] The English-language press in Shanghai reported these developments approvingly and letters to the editor of the *North-China Daily News* demanded similar action in Shanghai.[22] A Joint Committee of Women's Groups (later Organizations) met in November 1921 to determine how to end child labour in Shanghai.[23] The Joint Committee was led by the Young Women's Christian Association (YWCA) and included other American, British, German and Chinese women's groups based in the city.[24] Robin Porter emphasises the influence of Christian groups in the campaign, noting statements made by churches in Britain and the United States that more must be done to improve the conditions of labour around the world.[25] Yet the activists were united more by their gender than their religion: the international pressure now coming to bear on industrial Shanghai was led by women.

The Joint Committee of Women's Groups decided legislation was the best weapon against child labour and targeted the SMC as the most powerful authority in Shanghai. Agatha Harrison, representing the Joint Committee, visited the chairman of the SMC, H. G. Simms, to discuss the introduction of a municipal byelaw to regulate conditions in factories in the International Settlement.[26] Harrison had been appointed by the YWCA to investigate industrial conditions in China after holding the first British academic post in industrial welfare (at the London School of Economics). She persuaded Simms that the SMC should

---

[20] Chesneaux, *Chinese Labor Movement*, 228.

[21] Carroll, *Concise History of Hong Kong*, 108.

[22] *NCH*, 30 September 1922, 928.

[23] MLMSS 770/20/2: Joint Committee of Shanghai Women's Organizations, Bulletin No. 1: 'Toward the Regulation of Child Labour in Shanghai', compiled by E. M. Hinder (May 1927), 6.

[24] The YMCA was also calling for industrial reform in China in this period, though it was less involved in the high-profile campaign against child labour. See Robin Porter, *Industrial Reformers in Republican China* (Armonk, NY: Sharpe, 1994), 48–61. Peter Zarrow emphasises the importance of the YWCA, describing it as the sole autonomous organisation providing forums for female workers outside the Guomindang's control at this time. Peter Zarrow, *China in War and Revolution, 1895–1949* (London: Routledge, 2005), 261.

[25] Porter, *Industrial Reformers*, 98.

[26] Geoffrey Carnall, 'Harrison, Agatha Mary (1885–1954)', in H. C. G. Matthew and Brian Harrison (eds.) *Oxford Dictionary of National Biography* (Oxford University Press, 2004) www.oxforddnb.com/view/article/47749.

take action on child labour, despite him listing the obstacles to doing so. When the Council subsequently discussed what could be done, however, members concluded that results would only be achieved if Chinese and foreign factory and mill owners inside and outside the Settlement could be brought to unanimous agreement, which was highly unlikely. Further, councillors argued that the fault lay not with the owners for employing children but with the parents for sending them out to work. The practice could therefore be ended only 'by a process of gradual education and by improvement of the labourers' lot'.[27] This was tantamount to stating that nothing could be done at the municipal level: a refutation of the women's confidence in the SMC's powers.

The only action the Council recommended was to refer the question of child labour to the Employers' Federation. The Federation discussed child labour with the Cotton Mill Owners' Association and communicated with the Chinese General Chamber of Commerce, whereupon it learned of the Chinese government's plans to legislate against the employment of children. When the Federation reported this to the SMC, it was the first time the Council recognised that there were Chinese labour laws, having apparently only learned of them third hand, demonstrating the degree to which it felt able to ignore the weak Chinese government.[28] The Council intended to let the matter rest there, awaiting the results of the Chinese government's new laws, but the Joint Committee wrote an open letter to the chairman calling for the appointment of a commission to investigate child labour. Divided on the subject, the Council finally and reluctantly agreed and the commission was endorsed by the ratepayers at their annual meeting.[29] By raising the public profile of the issue of child labour, the activists had forced the SMC to consider taking interventionist action.

The SMC appointed an international range of female campaigners and male industrialists to the child labour commission. There were two Chinese women, Song Meiling, the Secretary of the Joint Committee, and Dr Mary Stone (Shi Meiyu 石美玉, the first Chinese woman to earn a medical degree from an American university), the American Mary Dingman, and Britons Elizabeth MacGillivray of the Christian Literature Society and Dame Adelaide Anderson, formerly the Chief Lady Inspector of Factories in Britain. Dingman and Anderson also advised Chinese officials on improving labour conditions.[30] Representatives of industry on the commission included Mu

---

[27] Zhang (ed.), *Minutes of the SMC*, Vol. 22, 15 November 1922, 211.

[28] Zhang (ed.), *Minutes of the SMC*, Vol. 22, 24 January 1923, 16.

[29] Zhang (ed.), *Minutes of the SMC*, Vol. 22, 28 March 1923, 316–17; *Municipal Gazette*, 16 April 1923.

[30] This was Song's first political role. Hannah Pakula, *The Last Empress: Madame Chiang Kai-Shek and the Birth of Modern China* (London: Orion, 2010), 71; Daniel H. Bays, *A New History of Christianity in China* (Chichester: Wiley, 2012), 115. Anderson made her visit to China in what was intended to be a short diversion on an extended trip to study labour conditions in Australia and India. She extended her stay in Shanghai on being invited to join the SMC's child

Ouchu, Director of the Chinese General Chamber of Commerce and a leading cotton manufacturer;[31] G. Okada, a Japanese industrialist; an American; and Britons including R. J. McNicol, Manager of Jardine, Matheson and Company. Jardine's had recently declared its intention to prohibit the employment of boys under 10 and girls under 12 in its mills, and the praise that this limited measure elicited indicates the prevalence of young children in industry. Through the commission, the SMC was exposed to a transnational range of views.

Simms informed the members of the commission at their first meeting that the Council believed the best route forward would be to follow the regulations recently promulgated by the Chinese government and to work out how best to implement them uniformly across Shanghai. Simms asserted that the French *Conseil municipal* would cooperate with whatever proposals the SMC put forward: the SMC was confident of its leading position in Shanghai.[32] The *North-China Herald* welcomed the appointment of the child labour commission as 'an illustration of how very far Shanghai has travelled', declaring that

the Municipal Council, which a comparatively little time ago was considered hardly more than a glorified ways and means organization, has set its hand to a great piece of social legislation in respect of which it may blaze a trail for all China to follow.[33]

The journalist was accurate in noting the vast expansion of the SMC's activities from being simply a 'ways and means organization' to attempting to legislate for social reform. Yet he neglected to note the chairman's recognition that it was Chinese legislation that was being taken as the model for the commission's recommendations. The foreign residents of the 'model Settlement' liked to enhance its self-perception as a beacon for enlightened governance in China, but in industrial legislation it was behind the Chinese government – though enforcement of the legislation was another matter.

While the commission investigated labour conditions in Shanghai, international interest grew. It was concern over the conditions of employment of children in factories that first brought an ILO delegation to Shanghai. Albert Thomas, the first director of the ILO, led the mission in 1924, helping to attract international attention to the issue of industrial conditions in China. Jean Chesneaux is dismissive of the impact of the ILO in China, describing the visit as 'a mission that had no mandate and no powers'.[34] He argues that the

labour commission. Her account of her visit was surprisingly positive about the SMC, due perhaps to the welcome she received in the Settlement. Adelaide Mary Anderson, *Humanity and Labour in China: An Industrial Visit and its Sequel (1923 to 1926)* (London: Student Christian Movement, 1928), 32, 125–62.

[31] A. R. Burt, J. B. Powell and Carl Crow (eds.), *Biographies of Prominent Chinese* (Shanghai: Biographical Publishing Company, 1925), 61.

[32] Report of meeting held 22 June 1923, *NCH*, 7 July 1923, 63.

[33] *NCH*, 14 July 1923.

[34] Chesneaux, *Chinese Labor Movement*, 385.

attitude of the ILO towards China suffered 'from the congenital defect of being meekly in line with the League of Nations attitude on colonial questions', a reference to the League's dominance by and support for colonial powers. He damned the ILO for its refusal to engage with the trade unions and communists who, he argued, represented the true nature of the labour movement in China. The ILO's impact on China was certainly limited, but the Chinese government chose to involve the Organisation in its industrial reform efforts and the ILO was far from insignificant in the British world to which the SMC belonged.

The ILO was not the only source of transnational pressure on the SMC. Harrison had appealed to the international committee of the YWCA to send their own delegation to look into child labour in China, so Mary Dingman, international industrial secretary of the YWCA, and her partner Evelyn Fox, both Americans, visited in 1923. After meeting the national committee of the YWCA, they travelled on to Australia where they met Eleanor Hinder, who they persuaded to return with them to see the factories of Hong Kong, Canton and Shanghai.[35] Harrison encouraged Hinder to move to Shanghai and work for the YWCA, investigating industrial working conditions and campaigning for reform. This was the critical mass of western women in Shanghai discussed by Sarah Paddle, a network whose members self-identified as 'world women' and worked together to support women in China.[36] Paddle's international feminists appear patronising ('maternalist' as Susan Pedersen characterises them), but Chinese women like Song Meiling and Mary Stone held leading positions in the child labour campaign in Shanghai and Karen Garner points out that Chinese women came to lead the YWCA in Shanghai.[37] Hinder later reported that the members of the SMC, representing as they did the business interests of the Settlement, were obstructive and unreceptive to what they saw as 'interference … from well-meaning social workers'.[38] The Council had long resisted outside interference, but was now the target of a new global force.

The child labour commission submitted its findings and recommendations to the Council in August 1924, to much fanfare in the *NCH*, which called the report 'easily one of the most significant documents published in

[35] MLMSS 770/13/8: draft of uncompleted autobiography of Eleanor Hinder, chapter 5, 2.

[36] Sarah Paddle, ' "For the China of the Future": Western Feminists, Colonisation and International Citizenship in China in the Inter-war Years', *Australian Feminist Studies*, Vol. 16, No. 36 (2001), 326.

[37] Susan Pedersen, 'The Maternalist Moment in British Colonial Policy: The Controversy over "Child Slavery" in Hong Kong 1917–1941', *Past and Present*, No. 171 (2001), 161–202; Karen Garner, 'Redefining Institutional Identity: The YWCA Challenge to Extraterritoriality in China, 1925–1930', in Anne-Marie Brady and Douglas Brown (eds.), *Foreigners and Foreign Institutions in Republican China* (London: Routledge, 2013), 72–92.

[38] MLMSS 770/19/8, A. Constance Duncan, 'Women in Pioneering Jobs', No. 1: Eleanor Hinder: Talk to be broadcast over 3.L.O. on 9 March 1938(?), based on interviews with and observation of Hinder in Shanghai.

this country'.[39] The report focused on the poor health of children in Shanghai compared to those in rural China, due to cramped conditions, long, arduous and dangerous working conditions, and extreme poverty. The authors found that conditions were worst in the silk filatures, where almost the entire work-force was female, with approximately one child for every two adult workers. Children worked the same hours and shifts as adult workers (typically twelve hours, including night shifts), for around half the wages. Employers neglected even basic fire precautions. Cotton factories were marginally better, while in tobacco factories shifts were limited to nine to ten hours of comparatively light work. Match factory workers had a day of rest each week, but faced numer-ous safety problems, including the continued use of poisonous phosphorous, banned by international agreement in many countries in 1906 and in Britain in 1908. Working conditions in general, not just for children, were thus badly in need of regulation and improvement.[40]

The report noted that legislative solutions would be difficult in view of the lack of central government in China, in line with the Council's own objections to municipal action on the question. Nevertheless, the commission recom-mended a minimum age, maximum working hours and other measures in line with those recommended by the ILO and legislated by the Chinese government in 1923.[41] It also looked to best practice within China and Asia, pointing to the safety procedures followed in a Chinese silk filature in Hangzhou and in com-mon use in Japan where the boiling room was kept separate from the cocoon reeling room, and cocoons were cooled before being peeled. Regional, national and international precedents were all influencing new standards in industrial regulation.

The report of the child labour commission was read widely in China and overseas, building pressure on the SMC to adopt its recommendations. The SMC resisted efforts by the consular body and Foreign Office in London to exert any control over it, and Shanghailanders blustered that those in Europe and North America had no idea what it was like 'in the East', but they were susceptible to attacks on the reputation of the International Settlement. The Manchester Chamber of Commerce wrote to the SMC calling on it to adopt the measures recommended by the commission.[42] Letters appeared in *The Times* prompting questions to be asked in Parliament; quoting the commis-sion's report, the Secretary for Foreign Affairs was asked by the Member of Parliament for Tynemouth 'whether he is aware that children under ten years

---

[39] *NCH*, 9 August 1924, 203.
[40] 'Report of the Child Labour Commission', *Municipal Gazette*, 19 July 1924.
[41] Ibid.
[42] The *NCH* reported this support for child labour legislation from Britain's industrial heartland as Manchester calling on Shanghai's foreigners to lead the way to industrial reform in China. *NCH*, 21 February 1925, 305.

old work in British-owned mills in Shanghai; what action His Majesty's Government have taken; what action they propose to take; and will Papers be laid?'[43] E. F. Mackay, a former vice-chairman of the SMC, defended British factory owners against the criticism appearing in the letters pages, but many in England were horrified by the description of child labour in British-owned factories in Shanghai.[44] The British government investigated conditions in British-owned factories in China and how they compared to other industrial concerns, appointing the Liberal MP Donald Maclean to report.[45] Maclean concluded that conditions in British factories were better than most, the main concern in Westminster being to avoid international embarrassment rather than seek an improvement in Chinese working conditions. International interest in the question was not confined to Britain. The *NCH* reported coverage of the controversy in Vancouver and the commission's report was even briefly taken up by an element within the union movement in Sydney as indicative of the exploitative nature of British imperialism to which Australian workers were also subjected.[46]

The cacophony of criticism locally and around the world contributed to the SMC's willingness to introduce a byelaw restricting child labour, based on the commission's report. In the weeks leading up to its submission to the ratepayers at a special meeting in 1925, the press was flooded with letters over the proposals, both in support of the legislation, many of which were written by women in the various organisations that were involved in the campaign, and in vocal criticism of it. Critics included the Chinese letter-writer Wang Mou, who warned that girls deprived of an honest living would find an alternative in brothels. He quoted the defence of the continuance of child labour given to the SMC by the Chinese Cotton Mill Owners' Association that attempts to eliminate it were unsuccessful 'owing to the pitiful requests of the parents of the children'.[47] But many employers signalled their support for legislation, including prominent British, American, Chinese and Japanese signatories of a letter to the *NCH*.[48] The tide of popular opinion was shifting in the direction of municipal intervention to improve labour conditions, as the perception of the role of a modern government expanded to encompass basic welfare legislation.

Yet, despite increased support for the proposed new byelaw, when it came to the special meeting to approve it, a quorum was not obtained. Only 399

---

[43] Mr West Russell, HC Deb 18 June 1925, vol. 185, 800.
[44] See, for example, a letter from philanthropist Charles Roden Buxton to *The Times*, 3 July 1925, 12.
[45] *NCH*, 4 July 1925, 508.
[46] *NCH*, 29 August 1925, 241; Sophie Loy-Wilson, '"Liberating" Asia: Strikes and Protest in Sydney and Shanghai, 1920–39', *History Workshop Journal*, Vol. 72, No. 1 (2011), 74–102.
[47] *NCH*, 4 April 1925, 31.
[48] *NCH*, 11 April 1925, 56.

ratepayers turned out for the meeting, representing between them 622 votes, significantly short of the one third of ratepayers' votes (which equated to 924 in 1925) required for the quorum. The *NCH* mourned this lost opportunity and the signal it sent to the world that Shanghai did not care, 'as if, perhaps, the attractions of a fine day and a game of golf were too much to be resisted, even for a matter of profound humanity and vital importance' – terms that presaged Arthur Ransome's damning description of the 'Shanghai Mind'.[49] This was strong criticism of Shanghailanders from the organ which was usually their staunchest ally. In fact, a higher proportion of British employers (50 per cent) turned out to the ratepayers' meeting than other national groups, perhaps reflecting their sensitivity to criticism in Britain.[50] Some blamed the Japanese community for staying away, partly it was thought because many of them could not follow business presented solely in English. The Council had dismissed a suggestion to provide a simultaneous translation because it would set a precedent: Anglo-American interests still dominated the SMC at this stage. But the *NCH* journalist pointed out that the Japanese ratepayers represented only 266 of the total and many of them were in fact present, so they could not be blamed for the failure to reach a quorum. Apathy, conservatism and a strong aversion to anything that might entail a cost to businesses on the part of the majority of voting ratepayers were the major blocks to socially progressive policies throughout the existence of the Settlement, coupled with the cumbersome procedures laid down by the Land Regulations. The need to call a ratepayers' meeting to approve new byelaws was less of a problem in the nineteenth century when there were fewer distractions for ratepayers, but by the 1920s Shanghai offered many more enticing ways to pass the time than sitting in the town hall. The SMC and many ratepayers were now willing to legislate for better industrial conditions, responding to national and international pressure, but could not secure the necessary byelaw change.

Political events then obstructed further efforts to unite Chinese and foreign groups in support of municipal action on child labour. The May Thirtieth Movement (itself one of the biggest labour movements in Chinese history, with a 119-day strike)[51] made it impossible for Chinese to support the SMC or any action it promoted. The second attempt to pass the byelaw at another special meeting came just three days after the infamous shooting of Chinese protesters by the SMP. Despite a higher turnout of 514 ratepayers, the number of votes represented at the meeting still fell short of the quorum by 177.[52] The child

[49] *NCH*, 18 April 1925, 88. Arthur Ransome published his articles, including 'The Shanghai Mind', written for the *Manchester Guardian* during his stay in China in 1926–1927, in *The Chinese Puzzle* (London: Unwin, 1927).

[50] Porter, *Industrial Reformers*, 111.

[51] Smith, *Like Cattle and Horses*, 185.

[52] Joint Committee, Bulletin No. 1, 20–3.

labour byelaw was being tabled with other municipal regulations that were unpopular with Chinese residents, including one that would restrict the freedom of the press. Even without this complication, nationalists held that regardless of the merits of the legislation, the SMC had no right to be legislating on Chinese soil. The SMC would have called off the meeting had a quorum looked likely, to avoid further antagonising Chinese public opinion, but with so many SVC members on military service, councillors were confident that insufficient ratepayers would attend.[53] Although Chinese ratepayers were still not eligible to vote in 1925, the support that had been obtained from Chinese firms and groups had been a strong element of the women's campaign. Eleanor Hinder later recalled that 'Foreign voters were not willing to force a measure providing purely for Chinese social welfare in the teeth of Chinese opposition.'[54] The Chinese women's organisations, backed by the YWCA, withdrew their support from the child labour byelaw and the SMC made no further attempts to regulate child labour through legislation, choosing to await further action by the Chinese government. The SMC was in no hurry to assume a greater governmental role and was taking its cue in part from international public opinion but primarily from China.

The Factory Law: Chinese Initiative and the SMC's Response

After letting industrial matters rest during the turbulent years of the May Thirtieth Movement and the entry of Nationalist and Communist troops into Shanghai in 1927, the SMC was prompted to return to the question of industrial reform by action from the new nationalist government of China. The Guomindang made it a priority to secure popular support and stability in the cities after its split from the Communist Party. One way to achieve this was to improve industrial conditions and thus appeal to the proletariat, the urban core of Communist support. Industrial reform also exemplified the Guomindang's programme of achieving a strong nation through scientific and technical modernity, to which rapid industrialisation was key.[55] When Chiang Kai-shek claimed control of China in 1927, factory regulation was high on the agenda in Nanjing. Among a raft of new laws drafted in the early years of the Nanjing government, the Factory Law, enacted in 1929, was one of the first.[56] It was

[53] Zhang (ed.), *Minutes of the SMC*, Vol. 23, 2 June 1925, 63–5.
[54] Hinder, *Life and Labour*, 6.
[55] William C. Kirby, 'Engineering China: Birth of the Developmental State, 1928–1937', in Wen-hsin Yeh (ed.), *Becoming Chinese: Passages to Modernity and Beyond* (Berkeley, CA: University of California Press, 2000), 137–9.
[56] New legislation included the constitution that was enshrined in the series of Organic Laws passed in the late 1920s and early 1930s, the civil code of 1929–31 that, *inter alia*, enfranchised women and gave them far greater rights, and the less liberal censorship law of 1930. Julia

officially promulgated on 1 August 1931 and on the same day, so as not to appear tardy in industrial reform – to local or international observers – the SMC issued a statement endorsing the principle of industrial regulation and indicating its intention to work towards safe working conditions.[57]

The Factory Law bore the hallmarks of ILO influence, stressing the role of factory inspection as stipulated by Article 427 of the Treaty of Versailles. Following the law's promulgation, inspectors appointed by the city government undertook initial surveys of conditions in factories throughout Shanghai in consultation with Dr Chen Da (陈达) of Tsinghua University in Beiping and Eleanor Hinder, who was by this point established as an authority on Chinese industrial welfare. In the Settlement these inspectors were sometimes accompanied by employees of the municipal fire department, but often they visited unaccompanied on the invitation of Chinese factory owners as the municipal government took the initiative to carry out inspections in the absence of an agreement on the issue with the SMC.[58] Their investigations demonstrated that most factories were so far from operating under the conditions required by the Factory Law that it would be impossible for all of its ambitions to be met at once. Certain aspects of the legislation were therefore given priority for immediate application, while longer would be allowed to work towards realising the full implications of the law. The city government's Bureau of Social Affairs declared 17 clauses of the law impracticable, but after consultation between Chen and Hinder, those measures that they considered the most desirable and achievable were published for the information of factory owners.[59] All credit for the recommendations was publically attributed to Chen, as foreign influence in the form of Hinder would have made them less palatable.[60]

The limited application of the law reflected current practice in Shanghai's factories: Article 15, for example, was among those earmarked for immediate implementation, as it called for a day of rest each week, which many employers were already allowing. Articles 41–43, specifying minimum safety provisions against fire and injury from machinery, the provision of good light and ventilation, adequate toilet facilities and training for the prevention of accidents were also to be enforced with immediate effect as they were considered among the most important measures that could be taken to improve

---

Strauss, 'The Evolution of Republican Government', *China Quarterly*, No. 150, Special Issue: Reappraising Republican China (1997), 343; *passim* for the Nanjing government's efforts at state-building. Suisheng Zhao argues that the Organic Laws were significant despite their limited application: Suisheng Zhao, *Power by Design: Constitution-Making in Nationalist China* (Honolulu: University of Hawai'i Press, 1996).

[57] Hinder, *Life and Labour*, 7.
[58] Report of Camille Pone.
[59] *Shenbao*, 12 November 1931.
[60] SMA U1-6–111: The secretaries of the Employers' Federation to the secretary of the SMC (Fessenden), 24 July 1931.

industrial conditions and safety. But measures such as Article 37, requiring factories to provide women with eight weeks of paid maternity leave, were suspended as placing an impossible burden on factory owners and because they were considered less important.[61] All parties – the ILO with its representatives in China, the Chinese government nationally and in Shanghai, the councils of the International Settlement and the French Concession (though as the latter had virtually no factories the French *Conseil municipal* had little input in the negotiations) and bodies such as the Employers' Federation representing factory owners – agreed that the legislation must be confined to achievable measures. The SMC had long cited the impossibility of enforcing the provisions of Chinese industrial laws as an excuse for its own inaction, but now there was an achievable set of objectives the Council had to demonstrate that it was genuine in its desire to seek industrial reform.

The Shanghai city government and the SMC now entered negotiations on the issue of factory inspection, which was to become a decade-long barrier to effective industrial legislation in Shanghai. The two municipal authorities held intractable opposing positions: the Chinese secretary-general insisting that city government inspectors must be allowed to inspect factories in the International Settlement as in the rest of the city to ensure equitable enforcement of the Factory Law; his SMC counterpart Stirling Fessenden equally adamant that this would be an infringement of the principle of extraterritoriality and thus a violation of the treaty rights of the foreign powers. Fessenden argued that factory inspections in the Settlement could only be undertaken by the SMC's own employees and could only enforce legislation agreed by the ratepayers.[62] At stake was the autonomy of the Settlement, which the British consular body in China was equally determined to defend: Sir Miles Lampson at the British sub-legation in Nanjing (the principal legation remained in Beiping even after the capital moved south) quoted the proverb cited by members of the Council, that 'one ship could not have two captains'.[63] This echoed the view of the British government as contained in a 1924 white paper on labour conditions in China.[64] But Westminster had also repeatedly made clear its condemnation of the SMC's tolerance of poor working conditions.[65] In seeking to maintain support in London, the SMC had to find a way for the measures of the Factory

---

[61] SMA U1-6-111: Chen Da and E. M. Hinder, 'Summary note on Inspection of Factories', 17 November 1931. Eight weeks was considered far longer than necessary for maternity leave.

[62] SMA U1-6-112: S. Fessenden to E. Cunningham, recalling the negotiations, 18 October 1933.

[63] SMA U1-6-112: Minutes of meeting between SMC and Waijiaobu officials, 12 October 1933, enclosed in letter from Miles Lampson, British sub-legation in Nanjing, to J. Davidson, Acting British consul-general in Shanghai, 13 October 1933.

[64] Foreign Office, *Papers Respecting Labour Conditions in China*, Cmd. 2442 (London: The Stationery Office, 1924).

[65] For an impassioned debate, see HC Deb 10 February 1927, Vol. 202, Cc. 310–426.

Law to be implemented in the Settlement without infringing the principles of extraterritoriality and the autonomy that was claimed in its name.

Taking the initiative and drawing on international resources, the Chinese Government invited the ILO to mediate between the two sides. The SMC was being treated like a state, engaging in inter-state negotiations. The ILO delegates, Adelaide Anderson and Camille Pone, focused on the practical matter of how to organise a factory inspection service to the satisfaction of both sides, to avoid being seen to have a political agenda.[66] After dragging its feet for so many years, the Council now listened to Anderson and Pone on the dangerous conditions prevailing in factories and investigated how it could address them. Its own Municipal Advocate, R. T. Bryan, advised that under the conditions of the Mixed Court Rendition Agreement of 1927, Chinese laws were applicable within the Settlement as long as they did not conflict with the Land Regulations, and would be enforced in the courts (primarily the Shanghai Provisional Court, which replaced the Mixed Court).[67]

Bryan advocated the enforcement of the Factory Law in the Settlement, citing a fire in the Sung Sing Cotton Mill in which six women died due to the fire doors being locked. Impeding fire exits was illegal under Article 24 of the Factory Law, so had it been followed the deaths would not have occurred. The Employers' Federation, though less enthusiastic about factory regulation, also agreed that premises should be inspected to enforce the basic provisions of the Factory Law, though it insisted that inspection should be kept strictly in the SMC's control. All advice to the Council thus concurred that the key provisions of the law should be implemented. The talks with the Chinese authorities progressed and an agreement appeared to have been reached whereby regulations identical to those aspects of the Factory Law that were being applied would be enforced within the Settlement by Chinese-trained inspectors reporting to the municipal councils. Satisfied that their work was done, Pone and Anderson returned to Europe.[68]

Yet this accord broke down almost as soon as the ILO delegation left, due to the Council's suspicions that the Chinese intention was to gain control of the Settlement: Council chairman Ernest Macnaghten warned the American consul-general, Edward Cunningham, that 'the local Chinese authorities persist in their ceaseless efforts to establish Chinese bureaucratic administration within the Settlement'.[69] The SMC's jealous guarding of its independence from Chinese authority made it hostile to efforts to enforce the Factory Law

[66] SMA U1-6-111: Report of Camille Pone, Head of Diplomatic Section, International Labour Organisation, Geneva, January 1932.

[67] SMA U1-6-111: R. T. Bryan to Stirling Fessenden, 24 October 1931.

[68] C. Pone, 'Towards the Establishment of a Factory Inspectorate in China', *International Labour Review*, Vol. 25, No. 5 (1932), 604.

[69] SMA U1-6-111: E. B. Macnaghten to Edward Cunningham, 14 May 1931.

in the Settlement. The Council also suspected that the ILO favoured its opponents. Chinese newspapers reported the activities and findings of the ILO in China, seizing on statements made by Albert Thomas that were critical of foreign administrations in Shanghai. *The Times* China Correspondent relayed Thomas's comments back to Britain as indicative of a stance at odds with the interests of the treaty powers, an accusation that was repeated in other media across Europe and which Thomas took pains to deny publicly.[70] The ILO, like the League of Nations Health Organisation, was seen by Shanghailanders as too left wing and supportive of Chinese objections to the foreign presence in China, in contrast to Chesneaux's objection that it was in hock to those same powers.

Instead of implementing the Chinese Factory Law, therefore, but not wanting another failed attempt to obtain new byelaws, the SMC confined its efforts in controlling industrial conditions to its existing powers, particularly regulations governing the licensing of buildings. These were tightened to improve basic health and safety standards in factories. Key to the enforcement of these regulations was factory inspection, as stipulated in Article 427 of the Treaty of Versailles. The same article stated that women should be involved in factory inspection to help safeguard female workers,[71] and as it happened, the Council's public commitment to industrial regulation prompted Eleanor Hinder to write offering her services to organise an inspectorate to make this happen.[72] Her experience at the YWCA and advising the Chinese government made her well-placed for the task and the Council, recognising that it would be unlikely to find another equally well-qualified candidate, accepted her offer, unwittingly adhering to the principle of involving women in factory inspection. The outbreak of Sino-Japanese hostilities in January 1932 postponed efforts by the SMC and the Chinese authorities to implement industrial reforms in Shanghai. It was not until a year later that Hinder was appointed Chief of the newly created Industrial Section of the SMC, initially based within the Secretariat. This Section gradually took over responsibility for factory inspection from the Fire Department, which already inspected premises for basic provisions against fire hazards.

In early 1933 the SMC drafted a byelaw to permit the licensing of industrial premises in the same way as it already licensed other concerns with a bearing on public health. This enabled it to appear to be taking action on the issue but retaining complete jurisdiction of control over factories in the Settlement. Hinder tried and failed to dissuade the Council from taking this unilateral

---

[70] See *The Times*, 22 February 1929, 10 for Thomas's denial of the article printed on 2 January and 26 April 1929, 12 for the China Correspondent's defence of his article.

[71] The Labour Party, *International Regulation of Women's Work: History of the Work for Women Accomplished by the International Labour Organisation* (London: Pelican Press, 1930).

[72] SMA U1-6–111: E. M. Hinder to Chairman, SMC, 13 December 1931.

action and alienating the Chinese authorities, who wanted Chinese laws to apply throughout the country. Unlike the efforts to change the byelaws in the 1920s, this time the SMC was able to secure a quorum at a special meeting of the ratepayers and the byelaw was passed and then ratified by the consular and diplomatic authorities, who adhered to the British position that extraterritorial privileges should be preserved, even at the expense of souring relations with the Chinese authorities.[73] Despite this victory, the SMC did not invoke its new right to license factory premises, fearing the Chinese reaction. In any case, any infringements of the new byelaw in factories under Chinese ownership would have had to be prosecuted in Chinese courts, which were unlikely to cooperate with the SMC's attempt to circumvent the national Factory Law. The Industrial Section therefore operated by means of persuasion and education without redress to legislation, Chinese or municipal.

Meanwhile, the City Government of Greater Shanghai pursued its own industrial policy outside the foreign settlements. Social affairs was one of the few areas fully devolved to the municipal level by the Nanjing government. Responsibility for industrial matters, including the implementation of the new Factory Law, fell to its Bureau of Social Affairs, which Christian Henriot stresses worked 'like an annex of the Guomindang'.[74] The Bureau understood that power comes with knowledge and set about as a first priority gathering data on the incidence of industrial disputes in the city, contributing to the state-building work of other branches of the new national government.[75] The ILO continued to support its work, as the Bureau's director acknowledged in regular surveys of strikes and lockouts in the city from 1930, alongside thanks to the Nanjing government, members of Chinese universities and a representative of the US Department of Labor.[76] The Guomindang government made good use of the ILO as a platform for raising its international profile as a progressive government, in opposition to and hindered by the colonial powers and specifically the persistence of extraterritoriality.[77] The ILO's China Branch, established in 1930, claimed that all the laws introduced by the Chinese Government concerning industrial conditions followed directly on ILO recommendations, from the banning of the use of white phosphorous in the manufacture of matches in 1925, reiterated in 1929, to the formation of Factory Safety and Health

---

[73] *Municipal Gazette*, 20 April 1933.

[74] Henriot, *Shanghai 1927–1937*, 40–1.

[75] Tong Lam, *A Passion for Facts: Social Surveys and the Construction of the Chinese Nation State, 1900–1949* (Berkeley, CA: University of California Press, 2011).

[76] Bureau of Social Affairs, City Government of Greater Shanghai, *Strikes and Lockouts, Greater Shanghai, 1929* (Shanghai: Bureau of Social Affairs, 1930), ii; Shanghai Bureau of Social Affairs, *Shanghai tebieshi laozi jiufen tongji 1930* (*Industrial disputes 1930*) (Shanghai: Bureau of Social Affairs, 1932), 2.

[77] See, for example, SMA U1-10-4: ILO China Branch, 'China and the International Labour Organisation' (n.d.).

Inspection Regulations in 1933.[78] Both the ILO and the Chinese Government thus emphasised the influence of the Organisation on Chinese legislation and practice in industrial regulation, which in turn shaped the response of the SMC.

The Bureau of Social Affairs' surveys of strikes in Greater Shanghai were the first of their kind in China. They reported that 111 industrial disputes occurred in 1929 – three lock-outs and 108 strikes – compared to 120 strikes in 1928, and the downward trend continued. The Bureau emphasised the progress being made as the labour agitation that followed the May Thirtieth Movement died away and the suppression of the Communist Party continued. Jürgen Osterhammel found that strikes were far less frequent during the Nanjing decade (1927–37) than in the mid-1920s as anti-imperialism declined as a popular force, and when industrial disputes arose they were 'motivated by economic despair rather than by a desire to strike back at imperialism'.[79] The Bureau's surveys indeed found that the most common factors in disputes were conditions of employment, including disputes over wages, hours or the treatment of workers. The gains recorded by the city government's Bureau of Social Affairs and by the SMC's Industrial Section were perhaps more attributable to the ebbing of labour politics than governmental initiatives, though addressing economic demands may have also alleviated political grievances.

The Bureau provided a mediation service in disputes, though mediators invariably sided with employers.[80] Foreign industrialists who were among the most vociferous defenders of the SMC's exclusive right to monitor industrial conditions within the Settlement used the mediation service.[81] They presumably found that it helped settle disputes in their favour and had no equivalent mediation service from the SMC until 1937: the city government was taking the initiative in this area where the SMC was slow to act. The Bureau's 1930 report noted that of the four complaints about workers being beaten, three emerged from foreign-owned factories, emphasising the problems posed by foreign imperialists employing Chinese workers on Chinese soil. However, the Bureau had problems of its own. The Labour Dispute Department, along with two other Bureau departments, was led by a senior Green Gang member by 1936, as the weakness of the Nationalist state led it to rely on criminals for policy enforcement.[82]

Guomindang ambitions for state-building included meeting the traditional governmental responsibility for the poor, as highlighted by Janet Chen.[83] This

---

[78] Ibid.
[79] Osterhammel, 'Imperialism in Transition', 279.
[80] Ibid., 277.
[81] Hinder, *Life and Labour*, 11.
[82] Elizabeth Perry, *Shanghai on Strike: the Politics of Chinese Labor* (Stanford University Press, 1993), 100.
[83] Chen, *Guilty of Indigence*, 91.

traditional role of the state was reinforced by Sun Yat-sen's principle that governments should provide for the 'people's livelihood'. The Bureau of Social Affairs therefore expanded its work beyond factory inspection to encompass collecting data on the cost of living, which varied greatly in the 1930s due largely to fluctuations in the global silver markets. Information showing inflation could be used by workers to support their claims for higher pay in response to higher prices, but similarly when China faced deflation due to the American silver purchase programme of 1933, employers could turn to the cost of living indices to justify keeping wages low. The data collected was useful not only to the Bureau itself, but also employers in Shanghai and other interested parties, including the SMC. Hinder compared the average annual income of the 305 families surveyed by the Bureau (416.51 dollars) with the average expenditure (454.38 dollars) to show that working families were typically unable to cover their basic needs without borrowing money or seeking supplementary income.[84] The sharing of data was the first area in which the Industrial Section benefited from its relationship with the Bureau.

The second round of negotiations over the implementation of the Factory Law stalled in 1933. The city government proposed a joint inspectorate for all industrial premises in Shanghai, which would report to all three municipal authorities. But the SMC rejected the notion that it should share jurisdiction in the Settlement and reiterated its position that separate inspectorates should enforce legislation similar to but distinct from the Factory Law in the Settlement. A stalemate ensued and international observers despaired at the inaction of both the Settlement and Chinese authorities.[85]

Nonetheless, Hinder's relationship with officials at the Bureau of Social Affairs was more constructive than that between their parent bodies. She met with Tian Heqing, Chief of the Inspection Branch of the Bureau of Social Affairs, in November 1933, when resolution to the issue of factory inspection still seemed achievable. They agreed that their first focus should be improving health and safety conditions rather than trying to eliminate child labour, citing the principle agreed with Camille Pone during his visit. Relations between the two could not be described as 'cordial', as Hinder later claimed, but they at least had a constructive working relationship.[86] Hinder became responsible for seeking

---

[84] Eleanor Hinder, *Social and Industrial Problems of Shanghai, with Special Reference to the Administrative and Regulatory Work of the Shanghai Municipal Council* (New York: Institute of Pacific Relations, 1942), 23.

[85] J. R., 'Shanghai Lagging in Factory Control', *Far Eastern Survey*, Vol. 4, No. 23 (20 November 1935), 186–7; Ma Changlin, '*Shanghai zujie nei gongchang jianchaquan de zhengduo – 20 shiji 30 niandai yichang kuangri tejiu de jiaoshe*' ('The Battle for Factory Inspection Rights within the Shanghai Foreign Concessions: The Prolonged Negotiations of the 1930s'), *Xueshu yuekan* (2003), 63–70.

[86] Hinder, *Life and Labour*, 10. Hinder's account of the relationship in 1933 shows their interactions could be testy: SMA U1-6-112: 'Hinder's Informal Conversation with Tian Ho Ching, Chief of Inspection Branch of the Bureau of Social Affairs', 11 January 1933.

solutions to the impasse on factory inspection and conveying the SMC's position to the Chinese authorities. Her existing relationship with Chen Da, with whom she had conducted a study on factory conditions to advise the Nanjing government prior to its enactment of the Factory Law, aided her relations with Chinese in the field. He introduced her, for example, to the new head of the China Branch of the ILO in 1934, Cheng Haifeng (程海峰), who was implementing some of the recommendations she and Chen Da had made.[87] Although the goodwill Hinder created with her counterparts did not solve the problem of factory inspection, it allowed her to expand the industrial work of the SMC without further worsening its relations with its neighbours, unlike other heads of SMC departments such as J. H. Jordan in Public Health. The Industrial Section also built bridges with Nanjing by participating in the National Factory Safety First Exhibition in the capital, sending exhibits and all staff members visiting during the spring vacation.[88]

Finally, an attempt to find a compromise succeeded in 1936. The SMC was under increasing international pressure as the Guomindang government had strengthened its position in the ILO, holding a seat on its Governing Body from 1934.[89] In this context, the Council relented to the enforcement of the Factory Law itself in the Settlement, rather than municipal byelaws, on condition that the Chinese government delegate authority for this to its own staff. This provision would remove the contentious element of inspectors under Chinese employ operating within the Settlement. This time, however, it was the consular body that blocked progress, holding fast to the principle that Chinese law could not be applied to factories owned by foreigners who enjoyed extraterritorial privileges.[90] For once, the SMC was not the most conservative foreign voice in Shanghai. The outbreak of the Sino-Japanese War the following year put paid to any further efforts to enforce the Factory Law in the Settlement, so the SMC and consular body were successful in preventing Chinese infringement of the autonomy of the Settlement.

---

[87] SMA U1-6–113: Hinder to Fessenden, 20 August 1934.
[88] SMA U1-14–966: SMC, *Report for 1936*, 31.
[89] The ILO passed a resolution tabled by delegates from China, Belgium, Japan and India declaring support of Chinese labour legislation being enforced equally in the foreign concessions and settlements in June 1937, so international pressure on the SMC was still mounting as the Sino-Japanese War legitimated shelving the issue. 'The Twenty-Third Session of the International Labour Conference', *International Labour Review*, Vol. 36, No. 3 (1937), 359–60. Marguerita Zanasi describes the way in which the Nationalists were 'able to manipulate the League's experts to their advantage' in her study of three League technical advisors in China. Marguerita Zanasi, 'Exporting Development: The League of Nations and Republican China', *Comparative Studies in Society and History*, Vol. 49, No. 1 (2007), 146. Zhang Li considers labour problems a key site of international cooperation in China. Zhang Li, *Guoji hezuo zai Zhongguo: guoji lianmeng jiaose de kaocha (International Cooperation in China: A Study of the Role of the League of Nations, 1919–1949)* (Taipei: Zhongchang yanjiuyuan jindai shi yanjiu suo, 1999), 267–99.
[90] SMA U1-14–966: SMC, *Report for 1936*, 25.

The Work of the Industrial Section: The Power of Persuasion

The SMC influenced the lives of the inhabitants of the International Settlement in many ways, but the efforts to improve industrial conditions in the 1930s marked a new degree of governmental intervention. Hinder was determined that the absence of municipal legislation governing industry would not prevent the improvement of working conditions in the Settlement. Just one month after she took up her post in January 1933, one of the worst industrial accidents of Republican Shanghai occurred in a rubber shoe factory. Petrol fumes caught alight causing an explosion that forced out the walls, bringing the roof crashing down and killing 81 women who were trapped on the upper floor. With no safety exits, the women had no escape from the fire. Tragic though the accident was, it gave the infant Industrial Section an opportunity to focus public attention on the dangerous conditions tolerated in the Settlement's factories. Hinder argued that all 26 remaining rubber shoe factories in the Settlement had similar risks and made it a priority to close the most dangerous premises and bring about significant improvements in others. SMC building inspectors ordered six rubber shoe factories to close, but just two complied. Another closed by order of the courts, five required considerable alterations to operate safely, and ten needed some alterations to meet minimum standards.[91] The factory inspectors put repeated pressure on the factories to improve, and achieved some success, but the absence of broader legislative powers hindered their work. In only one instance was the SMC able to bring a legal case against a factory considered highly dangerous, using its powers under existing byelaws against nuisances and hazardous or dangerous trades.

Existing municipal byelaws could be used where factories occupied new or converted buildings, which included many of the most dangerous premises. The majority of factories were in converted houses, so lacked proper ventilation, sufficient sanitary provision, or exits, among other basic safety features. The byelaws required plans to be submitted to the SMC for approval prior to the erection of new buildings or the conversion of existing buildings into dwellings, so it was possible to extend the existing rules to cover conversions of houses to industrial purposes.[92] Staff of the Public Works Department could then oversee the building or conversion to ensure compliance with the regulations. Yet enforcing compliance was not easy: in September 1933, following the rubber factory fire disaster, the 15 factories that were found by inspectors to need safety improvements were visited repeatedly by Rewi Alley, Chief of Factory Inspection, demanding to see plans for improvements, but in most

---

[91] SMA U1-6–116: E. M. Hinder to Fessenden, 8 July 1933.
[92] SMA U1-6–112: Harpur, Commissioner of Public Works, to Fessenden, secretary-general, SMC, 28 September 1933. The definition of a new building was based on the British Public Health Act of 1875, British precedent providing the blueprint as usual for municipal legislation.

cases none were forthcoming. In only one case did Alley report that he 'Found hazards greatly reduced by steps taken as required.'[93] The SMC's dependence on byelaw enforcement in the Chinese courts after 1927 weakened its authority.

Not only were the powers of the Industrial Section extremely limited when it began its work, but its staff was tiny; the SMC did not consider industrial conditions a priority. Hinder began with just three members of staff: a temporary assistant, Zhu Yubao, who had worked with Hinder at the YWCA, a Chinese clerk, and New Zealander Rewi Alley on loan from the Fire Department. The Industrial Section cooperated closely with other departments in the SMC. The fire, ambulance and police services relayed information on incidents they attended, and increasingly Hinder persuaded hospitals and factory managers to report other accidents. In 1935 the Public Works Department completed a 16-month survey of factories in the Settlement. It collected the information to help in planning sewerage and other works, noting the numbers working in factories and what chemicals they used and disposed of.[94] This was also valuable information for the Industrial Section, to which the three researchers were transferred on the completion of the survey to deploy their specialist knowledge of various industries in regular factory inspection. The data collected from these inspections identified risk factors such as faulty construction of boilers and other pressure vessels. The Industrial Section used this information to educate factory owners on the need to improve standards, and insurance companies used it to impose safety requirements on their industrial customers to minimise risk.[95]

Data collection was a key element of the Industrial Section's work, so the staff knew precisely what problems they were dealing with and were able to present an accurate picture of the realities in Shanghai's factories to the media, employers and local authorities. The emphasis on data collection reflected the SMC's governmental ambitions to control, despite its lack of legal powers. Much has been written about the propensity of colonial governments, from the British in India to the Japanese in Taiwan, to compile statistics on the territory under their control,[96] and the SMC was no different, but the statistical work of the Chinese city government demonstrates that this tendency is not unique to colonial governments. All the data obtained were carefully tabulated and recorded in the SMC's annual reports, providing a public declaration of the Council's capacity to understand and therefore, it intended, control the industry of the Settlement. The city government had been collecting data on industrial

[93] SMA U1-6–116: Table enclosed in Hinder to Fessenden, 25 September 1933.
[94] SMC, *Report for 1935*, 38.
[95] Porter, *Industrial Reformers*, 118.
[96] C. A. Bayly, *Empire and Information: Intelligence Gathering and Social Communication in India, 1780–1870* (Cambridge University Press, 1996); Bernard S. Cohn, *Colonialism and its Forms of Knowledge: The British in India* (Princeton University Press, 1996); Liao Ping-hui

incidents since 1929, and the SMC's Industrial Section collected similar data for the Settlement from the beginning of 1933: it was again following Chinese precedent.

The data informed the factory inspectors' priorities. One third of accidents involved workers aged under 20, contributing to the ongoing concern over the safety of young workers dating to the child labour commission.[97] Electrical accidents occurred more frequently during the wetter summer months, so the inspectors advised employers to ensure the working environment was kept dry. The SMC urged local manufacturers to adopt safer designs and materials such as Bakelite. Data analysis identified the four most dangerous types of machinery, the worst of which was transmission machinery such as belts, pulleys and gearing; Industrial Section staff therefore urged upon employers the need to provide proper guards and other safety measures with such machines. They also bought items of machinery and fitted guards to them to demonstrate to employers how such measures could be implemented, inviting owners and managers to see them after accidents in their factories which such guards might have prevented.[98] The employers generally accepted such invitations, indicating openness to the SMC's promotion of safety measures.

The work of the Industrial Section increased as employers and employees alike engaged with its services. In 1935 the Industrial Section received reports of 2,301 industrial accidents, a 29 per cent increase on the previous year. Hinder interpreted the rise as evidence of growing cooperation by employers, hospitals, police and ambulance services, volunteering the information at the Council's request. Industrial Section inspectors visited the premises on which accidents had occurred in 1,292 cases that year to advise how to prevent any repetition and Hinder reported that managers increasingly took the necessary preventive measures.[99] She found that employers were most likely to respond to such advice when it could be directly related to their recent experience of an accident. The Industrial Section even drove the managers of five tobacco factories that kept their exits obstructed to the site of a fire caused by such a hazard at another factory to see for themselves the possible consequences.

The Industrial Section printed thousands of leaflets with the main provisions of the Chinese Factory Law and SMC health and safety regulations and distributed them to factories, reading sections aloud to owners if they could not

and David Der-wei Wang, *Taiwan under Japanese Colonial Rule, 1895–1945: History, Culture, Memory* (New York: Columbia University Press, 2006), 42.

[97] Ding Yonghua and Lü Jiahang, '*Shilun 1920–1930 niandai Shanghai tonggong wenti*' ('On Child Labour in Shanghai 1920s–1930s'), *Shanghai daxue xuebao*, Vol. 15, No. 2 (2008), 91–8.

[98] SMC, *Report for 1935*, 44–5.

[99] SMC, *Report for 1935*, 38.

read, so they could not claim ignorance of their obligations.[100] Municipal staff also targeted workers directly by, for example, showing them illustrations of the value of wearing tighter fitting clothing to avoid garments from becoming caught in machinery and causing an accident. *Shenbao* reported on a municipal 'safety first' painting competition: another attempt to spread the message.[101] Through these efforts, Hinder claimed to have had a significant impact on practice in many establishments, but the Industrial Section had no recourse when managers were unreceptive and preventable accidents continued to occur in premises where factory inspectors had warned of dangerous conditions. There was no appetite for reducing working hours and it was difficult to ensure that safety standards, once achieved, were maintained. For example, extraction fans to clean the air or remove flammable fumes were costly to run, so were often simply turned off when inspectors were not present. With few staff and limited resources, the Section had to focus its efforts on particular industries (rubber and cotton) and on specific problems within them (such as fire safety). Improvements were effected in these areas in the absence of controversial legislation as the SMC found other ways to influence local employers.

Diplomacy was crucial if the Industrial Section's efforts were to be successful. On the rare occasions when the SMC was able to prosecute factory-owners for flouting building regulations, Hinder wrote personally to the secretary-general of the city government to explain the SMC's actions so he would not 'hear about this first in the press'.[102] Hinder took pains to stress that she was hoping to prevent a Japanese rubber shoe factory from opening with dangerous conditions to demonstrate that it was not only Chinese factories that were being targeted. The factory inspectors' first approach was, according to Hinder, 'to make friends' with the factory owners.[103] Chinese owners were often more receptive to advice than British employers, who knew that the Section staff lacked powers of enforcement. Inspectors then sought to persuade employers that taking steps to improve conditions for workers would be in their own interests. The SMC pursued a more diplomatic approach to relations with the Chinese authorities and industrialists in the 1930s, recognising that it could not achieve its goals by appearing imperious. The prominent Chinese businessmen on the Council also helped to smooth relations with local employers.

The transnational staff of factory inspectors was used to appeal to managers of different nationalities. Most of the staff were Chinese and Chinese inspectors could front the work in Chinese factories, while Japanese staff did the same in Japanese factories, and western staff inspected western-owned

[100] SMA U1-14–966: SMC, *Report for 1936*, 31.
[101] '*Anquan diyi yundong*' ('Safety First Movement'), *Shenbao*, 29 November 1939, 10.
[102] SMA U1-6–116: E. M. Hinder to O. K. Yui, 17 June 1933.
[103] Hinder, *Life and Labour*, 25–6.

factories, reducing the possibility for friction between different national groups. Hinder reported that 'Japanese employers were punctilious in install- ing safety devices suggested' and were generally willing to meet stand- ards obtaining in Japan, provided their factories were only inspected by Japanese.[104] Different tactics were tried: using foreign staff where Chinese had failed and vice versa; sending a woman when a man was not heeded – 'the eloquence of a Chinese woman, to which no mere Chinese man can stand up' apparently achieved results.[105] Hinder reported that a combination of appealing to the better nature of employers and the 'nuisance factor' of repeated visits by inspectors often achieved the desired improvements.[106] Where building regulations did not apply because premises were neither new nor being used for a new purpose, the SMC could only inspect a factory with the permission of the owners. The inspectors were surprisingly successful in persuading factory owners to allow them into their premises to observe the health and safety measures in place.

Gradually, the success of the Industrial Section enabled Hinder to persuade the SMC's staff committee, secretary-general and chairman to expand its remit and budget. It was sufficiently well-established in October 1940 to divorce from the Secretariat and become a separate Industrial Division with its own committee to formulate policy and oversee its operations. The Industrial and Social Affairs Committee was one of the few municipal committees, with the education and library committees, that included a woman: Mrs J. S. Barr, wife of John Barr of the London Missionary Society. As a separate division it expanded to over 50 staff, including a number of women, and while this was still dwarfed by the scores and hundreds of municipal employees in other departments, its impact on the lives of the Settlement's inhabitants and on the international stage was disproportionate to its size or status.

Transnational Influences

ILO influence was felt throughout the existence of the Industrial Section and Division. Hinder kept up a regular correspondence with Albert Thomas and his British successor as Director of the ILO, Harold Butler, reporting progress in industrial reform in Shanghai and China more broadly. They discussed exchanges of staff members between the SMC Industrial Section and the ILO, Hinder pondering which Chinese member of her staff could be spared, although it is not clear whether the plan was implemented.[107] Butler planned to

---

[104]   Ibid., 26.
[105]   Ibid.
[106]   Hinder, *Social and Industrial Problems*, 16.
[107]   SMA U1-10–4: E. M. Hinder to Harold Butler, Director, ILO, 3 October 1938.

visit Shanghai in 1937, but was prevented by the outbreak of the Sino-Japanese war.[108] Relations with the ILO were more important to the Industrial Section than formal imperial ties, though they operated within networks created in the British world.

Hinder's prime motivation for her ongoing contact with the ILO was political: in reporting on her attendance at the ILO's conference in Geneva in 1938, she stated that her main object was 'to counteract the impression generally given by Chinese delegates in their speeches that the Council was not assuming its full responsibilities in the matter of industrial regulation'. By making the work of the Industrial Section more widely known in Geneva she was 'establishing the fact that the Council was indeed aware of its responsibilities and fulfilling them to the best of its abilities'.[109] Through Hinder, the International Settlement was represented at the three-week conference alongside 50 states, although she was not a full delegate as membership, granting the right to speak in plenary meetings, was limited to sovereign states. Hinder's sex would have put her at a further disadvantage: of the 416 individuals who attended the ILO conference, just fifteen were women.[110] China sent 12 representatives, despite the ongoing Sino-Japanese War, showing the importance attached to the conference. Hinder commented that she was careful to remain on good terms with them: in the contested world of treaty-port China, every area of municipal activity was heavily politicised, and industrial regulation was no different.

Hinder was well aware of the need to give international observers a positive impression of the SMC to counteract increasing pressure for the retrocession of the International Settlement to Chinese control. Hinder later indicated that she was ambivalent about the Council's position, recognising the Chinese right to enjoy political control over its territory and population, to the extent that she wrote of her 'great satisfaction' on hearing that the British and American governments had signed a treaty in January 1943 renouncing extraterritoriality and the right of foreigners to administer the treaty ports.[111] Yet in the 1930s she believed that she could best effect change for the benefit of Shanghai's workers within the existing political apparatus of the Settlement, and she came to identify her goals with those of the SMC as she sought to reshape from within this organisation to which in the 1920s she had been openly hostile. Hinder therefore served municipal interests by presenting the SMC's industrial work in the best possible light at the ILO conference.

---

[108] SMA U1-10–4: E. M. Hinder, 'The I.L.O. Conference, Geneva, 1938', report submitted to Council, 22 September 1938.

[109] Ibid.

[110] 'The Twenty-Fourth Session of the International Labour Conference', *International Labour Review*, Vol. 38, No. 3 (1938), 302.

[111] MLMSS 770/13/8: Eleanor Hinder, Unpublished Autobiography, 28g.

Hinder used her visit to Geneva to meet with senior figures in the ILO who she hoped would influence the Chinese government in the interests of the Industrial Section. She met with Harold Butler and his successor, the American John Winant, as well as Camille Pone who had visited Shanghai in 1931. Hinder hoped that these men would help resolve the stalemate reached with the Chinese government over the implementation of the Chinese Factory Law. During her trip to Geneva Hinder also met with Edouard de Haller, the Director of the League of Nations' Mandates Section, which had responsibility for slavery. She met him in her capacity as Protector of Mui Tsai, a title she was given in addition to her position as head of the Industrial Section in 1937. The Council sought in making this appointment to demonstrate its responsiveness to pressure from the League Slavery Committee to curb the practice of poor Chinese parents selling daughters to wealthy families to become *mui tsai* or 'younger sisters' (*mei zai* 妹仔, but the Cantonese *mui tsai* was and remains the most common term).[112] This was another example of the League's impact on SMC policy, though Hinder used the powers the new title gave her to seek improvements in child welfare far more broadly than anticipated by either the Council or the League.

Following the ILO conference, Hinder extended her tour promoting the SMC internationally. She travelled from Geneva to London, where she met Sir George Maxwell, Vice-chairman of the Slavery Committee, Irene Ward, Conservative member of the House of Commons and a member of the League of Nations' Social Questions Committee, and Edith Picton-Turbervill, former Labour member, feminist and author of a League report on *mui tsai* in Hong Kong.[113] Hinder went on to Ottawa where she met Charlotte Whitton, another feminist humanitarian who was the founding director of the Canadian Council on Child Welfare, which by 1938 had become the Canadian National Welfare Council, and long-term Canadian representative to the League's Advisory Committee on Social Questions. The League of Nations linked these activists together, enabling Hinder to bring a transnational perspective to local problems. With these women, Hinder was mixing in elite global feminist humanitarian circles.[114]

Hinder's travels were not confined to Europe and North America. She also went to Japan in March 1936 where she visited the Tokyo mill of Dai Nippon,

---

[112] SMA U1-1–91: Watch Committee, 9 February and 29 April 1937; MLMSS 770/3/4: 'The Place of Administration in Child Care in Shanghai: Some Methods and Principles of Action', author unknown, n.d., n.p.

[113] Edith Picton-Turbervill, 'Minority Report' (1937), cited in David M. Pomfret, '"Child Slavery" in British and French Far Eastern Colonies 1880–1945', *Past and Present*, No. 201 (2008), 181, n. 13.

[114] Leila J. Rupp, 'Constructing Internationalism: The Case of Transnational Women's Organizations, 1888–1945', *American Historical Review*, Vol. 99, No. 5 (1994), 1571–600.

which also owned two mills in Shanghai. Conditions in the mill impressed her greatly: she reported that it operated just two shifts of eight and a half hours per day and that workers were allowed five days off per month. Safety standards were also much higher than those in Shanghai, Hinder noting particularly such features as guards and emergency stop buttons. Other factories in Japan were less impressive, such as the Takagi Ironworks factory with its lack of safety devices: Hinder reported it exhibited 'no difference from similar works in Shanghai'.[115] Yet even here Hinder was struck by the absence of child workers as education was compulsory in Japan (as the ILO advocated and had optimistically encouraged the SMC to enforce in 1925).[116] Hinder may have hoped to prove to foreign members of the Council that poor working conditions were not a necessary feature of Asian societies, as some had tried to argue in the 1920s. She may have also been targeting the increasingly influential Japanese members of the Council, attempting to persuade them of the importance of industrial reform by using examples from their homeland. Certainly western nations were not the sole point of reference or source of international influence in this field. Hinder maintained connections with Japan following her visit, sending Zhu Yubao to tour Japanese factories when she took leave in 1937 and welcoming Japanese visitors who in turn wished to inspect industrial concerns in the International Settlement.[117] It was largely through I. Ayusawa, the Director of the ILO in Japan, that these connections were forged and maintained, so the ILO's influence was apparent quite apart from its European heartland.

The China Branch of the ILO, based in Shanghai and headed by Cheng Haifeng, was an invaluable information resource for the Industrial Division.[118] Cheng travelled to Chongqing to renew his contacts with the Nationalist government in early 1941, as the ILO balanced relations with Japanese-occupied China and independent China.[119] Hinder gave him letters of recommendation to meet Chinese and foreign contacts, including Song Meiling who had served on the child labour commission nearly 20 years previously.[120] Hinder's praise for and familiarity with Cheng's work is indicative of a strong working relationship between them as well as the prominent role played by the ILO China Branch. The SMC no longer functioned in isolation, but reacted to the policies of the Chinese government and the transnational influences of the constituent bodies of the League of Nations.

[115] SMA U1-10–4: E. M. Hinder, 'My Visit to Japan, March 1936.'
[116] Zhang (ed.), *Minutes of the SMC*, Vol. 23, 8 April 1925, 27.
[117] SMA U1-10–4: E. M. Hinder to I. Ayusawa, 12 June 1937, and his reply 9 July 1937.
[118] SMA U1-10–4: E. M. Hinder to John Winant, McGill University, Montreal, 17 October 1940.
[119] SMA U1-10–4: John Winant to E. M. Hinder, 29 November 1940.
[120] SMA U1-10–4: E. M. Hinder to Madame Chiang Kai-shek, 20 March 1941.

War and Labour

The outbreak of the Sino-Japanese War in 1937 had a dramatic impact on the work of the Industrial Section, as it did on all areas of municipal activity. For most of the war the SMC continued to perform its functions, including in industrial and social work, with as close a semblance to normality as possible. The British in Shanghai were determined that if the Settlement must eventually be left, it should be left in good order, and Hinder subscribed to this rationale.[121] By this point the Industrial Section was established as a strong force on the industrial stage in Shanghai, despite the failure to secure much legal footing for its work or to resolve the issue of factory inspection. The war prevented much of the interaction that had hitherto existed between the SMC and international bodies such as the ILO, especially following the bombing of Pearl Harbor. Yet one result of the war and the abolition of the Chinese city government was the removal of a long source of frustration to some of the SMC's aims in industrial work. The Industrial Section could now expand its work without fear of offending the neighbouring authorities, as long as Japanese interests were not harmed.

Japanese bombing destroyed almost all industrial concerns outside the International Settlement in 1937, so workers flooded in looking for employment while industrialists set up makeshift workshops in any building that could be used for the purpose, however unsuitable.[122] The work of factory inspectors therefore increased dramatically, but their task was made harder than ever as conditions deteriorated and the swelled pool of labour weakened the bargaining position of workers. Unemployment grew due to both the closure of factories and the increased number of workers in the Settlement.[123] By the end of 1937, 95,777 refugees were living in 173 camps, unable to find work or afford housing at the dramatically inflated prices the increased demand produced.[124] Charities provided aid for them but the SMC could not ignore the scale of the humanitarian crisis in its midst. As a result, the Industrial Section expanded its work to encompass care for the urban population in general, rather than only industrial workers.

The new, expanded Industrial Division was divided into four sections: the Industrial Section continued the work of seeking safety and other improvements in working conditions; the Statistical Section compiled and published cost of living data and advised employers on giving allowances to their

---

[121] Bickers, 'Settlers and Diplomats', 233–5.
[122] Christian Henriot, 'Shanghai Industries under Japanese Occupation: Bombs, Boom, and Bust (1937–1945)', in Henriot and Yeh (eds.), *In the Shadow of the Rising Sun*, 20–5.
[123] MLMSS 770/13/8: Hinder, draft autobiography, 18g.
[124] SMA U1-16-10-224: Chief Health Inspector to Commissioner of Public Health, 31 August 1939.

employees based upon it; the Industrial Relations Section offered mediation in industrial disputes; and the Welfare Section addressed the living standards of workers and the unemployed, including issues of housing, nutrition and health, as well as taking responsibility for child protection. The enhanced functions of the Industrial Division increased the ways in which the impact of the SMC was apparent in the lives of the inhabitants of the Settlement.

As the war continued, rampant inflation, due largely to the declining value of the Chinese dollar, caused the cost of living to rise far ahead of wages, producing a new source of hardship for industrial workers. When Chinese officials fled inland and the Bureau of Social Affairs closed in 1938, Sun Zheng, its former head, moved into office space in the SMC Industrial Section.[125] He initially continued his work collecting data on industrial conditions using funds he raised himself, though he was restricted by the Japanese occupation to studying factories within the International Settlement alone, instead of the whole of Greater Shanghai.[126] Two years later Sun formally joined the staff of the expanded Industrial Division. Few would have foreseen that a senior figure within the Nationalist city government, who had made his opposition to the foreign administrations in Shanghai clear, would be able and willing to work for the SMC in the service of improving labour conditions.

At the same time, Rewi Alley, the Chief of Factory Inspection, resigned from the SMC to work for the wartime Nationalist Government in Chongqing, advising the government about labour regulations and helping to organise small-scale industrial co-operatives.[127] Alley's left-wing politics (he chose to remain in the new People's Republic following the Communist victory in 1949) put him at odds with the colonialism of the SMC, and once he could serve Chinese workers' interests better elsewhere, he did. The Guomindang government was willing to accept a former SMC employee in order to benefit from his knowledge and experience.

With Sun Zheng's expertise, the Industrial Division took over the compilation of statistics on the rising prices of basic commodities for the information of employers. The SMC, itself a large employer, was among the establishments that used these figures to calculate cost of living allowances in addition to salaried income for its employees. The rate of inflation is illustrated by the rises in the allowance for municipal staff in 1940: from 30 to 55 per cent of salary in May, rising to 60 then 85 per cent by October.[128] By the end of 1941, the SMC's High Cost of Living Allowance was set at 285 per cent of wages.[129] Many other

---

[125] Porter, *Industrial Reformers*, 123.
[126] SMA U1-10–4: Hinder to Butler, 3 October 1938.
[127] Ibid.
[128] SMA U1-1–63: Finance Committee, 24 May and 12 October 1940.
[129] SMA U1-14–974: SMC, *Report for 1941*, 3.

employers – Chinese, Japanese, British, American and others – used the data, and the cost of living indices were even forwarded to the USA for employers there to calculate fair allowances for their staff in Shanghai.[130] The SMC's measurement of the cost of living was thus of real benefit to many thousands of workers.

The Industrial Division also procured and distributed rice for the residents of the Settlement. Cut off from its rural hinterland, the city was running short of basic foodstuffs, as research for the cost of living indices made clear. The British consul-general wrote to the ambassador of 'the acute distress which is being felt alike by the tens of thousands of people in the middle and at the bottom of the wage scale, and by the thousands of people who roam the streets in an indigent condition', placing the blame squarely on Japanese disruption of supply routes.[131] The French *Conseil municipal* set maximum prices for daily necessities in the French Concession, but the SMC initially claimed that it did not have the legislative powers to do the same. Eventually, Hinder persuaded the Council to import rice from Indochina via Hong Kong to ensure supply at affordable levels. The profits from the sales were ring-fenced for the future purchase of 'military rice' – that is, rice bought from the Japanese military – when it was no longer possible for the SMC to source its own.[132] The SMC also fixed the price of flour and bread by Council proclamation, confiscating supplies sold above the set price, apparently finding that it did have such regulatory powers after all.[133] This picked up from work by the Chinese city government to combat sharp price rises in rice since 1929.[134] The SMC even banned the production of 'fancy breads, rolls, cakes and confectionary' in an unprecedented intrusion into Chinese consumption.[135] Rice procurement involved the SMC in unprecedented high risk investment (there was a strong chance of the cargo being lost in hostile waters) for the sake of public welfare, far removed from its laissez-faire approach to governance in earlier years.

[130] SMA U1-6-009-195: Industrial and Social Affairs Committee, 24 October 1941.
[131] FO 371/24700: Consul-General A. H. George to Sir Archibald Clark Kerr, H.M. Ambassador, Shanghai, 3 February 1940.
[132] SMA U1-1-63: Finance Committee, 23 March and 23 April 1942. Hinder's interest in nutrition went beyond the availability of rice to public health interventions: experiments she conducted in 1937 in collaboration with the Henry Lester Institute of Medical Research and in consultation with the Public Health Department with 75 boys in light-bulb factories demonstrated that beriberi could be eliminated if rice were simply de-husked shortly before cooking to preserve its vitamin B content. The outbreak of war prevented the SMC from attempting to convert the findings into widespread practice, but the experiment shows the breadth in which Hinder conceived her role and the appropriate activities of the SMC. MLMSS 770/3/4: E. M. Hinder, 'The Place of Administration in Child Care in Shanghai: Some Methods and Principles of Action', n.d., n.p
[133] SMA U1-14-974: SMC, *Report for 1941*, 5.
[134] Henriot, *Shanghai 1927–1937*, 214–15.
[135] SMA U1-14-974: SMC, *Report for 1941*, 5.

The expansion of the Industrial Division's work into technical education was another area in which the SMC took on new responsibilities far beyond its basic functions. The Division established a night school in 1941, using the laboratories of the Henry Lester Institute of Technical Education, with funding from the SMC Education Department. It offered training for mechanics and electricians to improve safety and, in order to increase the appeal of its graduates to employers, efficiency. Courses were wide-ranging, the three-year syllabus of technical training for skilled mechanics including mathematics, physics, English workshop terms, mechanical drawing and design, machine shop materials and practice, and machinery and electrical installation.[136] Admission to the courses required a primary education, which had the intended consequence of indirectly increasing the age at which young people would begin employment as machine shop workers: typically those enrolled were aged 16 to 21 and had between three and six years of education.[137] Teachers in the technical schools developed their own teaching materials in the absence of text books in Chinese.[138] The work of the technical education schools continued into 1943, when 519 students were enrolled in the various courses on offer, up from 404 the previous year.[139] The impact of the schools was thus growing until the abolition of the SMC.

In addition to the compilation of data on the cost of living, the Industrial Division also took over the mediation functions of the Bureau of Social Affairs. Widespread strikes broke out in 1939 and 1940 as workers bore the brunt of the worsening economic situation.[140] The Industrial Division laid greater emphasis on prioritising the workers' interests than the Bureau had done. If approached by the management rather than the workers for mediation in the first instance, the Division would wait for several days trying to persuade the workers to seek its services as well before stepping in.[141] In its sympathetic approach, the Division differed from the SMP which, much like the Bureau of Social Affairs, prioritised the maintenance of public order over workers' welfare. Hinder claimed that as the reputation of the Division grew, its advice on matters such as wages and factory rules was increasingly sought before disputes escalated into strikes. This suggests that the Industrial Relations Section was successful in its work.[142] Over 100 disputes were referred to the SMC for mediation in

---

[136] SMA U1-1-1200: Hinder to N. W. B. Clarke, Director of the Engineering Society of China in Shanghai, 30 December 1940.
[137] Hinder, 'The Place of Administration in Child Care', n.p.; SMA U1-1-1299, trade apprentice application forms.
[138] MLMSS 770/3/18, vii.
[139] MLMSS 770/3/18 (ix): Social Welfare Department Reports for 1943, 173.
[140] Hinder, *Life and Labour*, 14.
[141] Hinder, *Life and Labour*, 75.
[142] MLMSS 770/3/4: E. M. Hinder, 'The Organisation and Functions of the Industrial and Social Division', n.d.

1940, compared to just seven in 1938, and municipal mediation averted strikes in 56 cases.[143] The SMC was now perceived as a source of support by workers who had once taken to the streets to protest against it.

Child protection, the original focus of demands for a greater welfare role for the SMC, also expanded during the Sino-Japanese War. From an unpromising beginning, when the SMC appointed Hinder Protector of Mui Tsai in reluctant acquiescence to international pressure, she established a Child Protection Service with a much broader remit. As in the resolution of industrial disputes, child protection required cooperation with the SMP. One area in which they worked together was in attempting to reduce the exploitation of young children by beggars to gain sympathy and donations, which increased greatly with the presence of so many refugees from 1937. The police agreed that, although they could not refer such cases to the courts, they could act in a purely 'administrative' function by detaining infants exploited in this way and entrusting them to the care of the Shanghai Refugee Babies' Nursery, a charity supported in part by a municipal grant-in-aid.[144] The SMC thus addressed child protection with its existing powers and at minimal cost to the municipal purse. The Council was, however, also increasingly willing to fund child protection work, appointing its first full-time social worker in 1937. Hinder recommended in 1940 that the SMC increase its grants-in-aid to charities that took in abandoned children found by the SMP. Despite opposition from the treasurer, anxious as ever to curtail expenditure, Hinder's requests were granted.[145] The following year, when the grants-in-aid were again under review, the treasurer cited the old principle that the SMC accepted no responsibility for poor relief. But the chairman, secretary and members of the finance committee all supported Hinder and approved her recommendations for increased grants-in-aid: the Council acknowledged that it had now accepted responsibility for limited welfare provision.[146]

When the Allied members of the SMC resigned in January 1942, many Allied national employees stayed in their posts. Hinder was among them, convinced that she was helping Chinese in the Settlement, particularly in the distribution of staple foods. She also persuaded the Japanese authorities to contribute towards the cost of third-class travel to unemployed workers returning to their native place to reduce overpopulation, an opportunity that she estimated many thousands seized.[147] By the summer of 1942, however, there were growing

---

[143] Porter, *Industrial Reformers*, 124.

[144] SMA U1-1-92: Watch Committee, 4 July 1939.

[145] SMA U1-1-63: Finance Committee, 7 March 1940.

[146] SMA U1-1-63: Finance Committee, 10 April 1941.

[147] MLMSS 770/13/14: E. M. Hinder, 'Shanghai 1942, Philadelphia 1944, Sydney 1945', address to The Australia Institute of International Affairs, Melbourne, 18 April 1945.

opportunities for skilled workers in factories in Japan that were no longer able to source their employment needs locally due to the war. The Industrial Section established an employment exchange to help unite employers requiring staff with those seeking work.[148] The Japanese leadership of the SMC had repeatedly asked Hinder to help in this, but she refused on the basis that she should not be required to do anything that directly supported the Japanese war effort, which aiding Japanese industry to obtain labour certainly constituted. The mounting pressure contributed to her decision to quit Shanghai.

T. Fukuda was promoted from Deputy head of the division to succeed Hinder and continued to ensure the Japanese-controlled SMC maintained its work on industrial welfare in its last days. The Council even committed funds to a proposed hospital for industrial workers, although the SMC was disbanded before the plan was realised.[149] As late as 14 July 1943 the Staff Sub-committee promoted Fukada due to the increased scope of his work and considered whether his division should become a junior department, apparently unaware that the decision to disband the SMC had already been taken.[150] One of the SMC's last acts was to send funds to local charities: the re-organised Japanese authorities directed in August that officials should send cheques to charities with a note (in English) that 'although the cheques are in the name of the First District Administration, they are sent by decision of the former Shanghai Municipal Council'.[151] Over the course of a decade, industrial welfare had become a core function of the SMC.

Conclusion

Pressure on the SMC to address poor working conditions in the International Settlement built from the campaigns against child labour in the early 1920s, led by groups of foreign and Chinese women. The SMC came to adopt a much stronger stance on industrial reform in the 1930s in response to outside pressure from the ILO and other international organisations, and from the action that was being taken by the Guomindang government at Nanjing and in Greater Shanghai. The SMC was independent of formal imperial oversight, but it was subject to the growing transnational forces of the interwar world, notably the ILO and feminist reformers who operated throughout the English-speaking world. The Industrial Section was thus more outward-facing than other departments in the SMC. It was also more diverse itself, with a more international

---

[148] SMA U1-6-009-195: Industrial and Social Affairs Committee, 1 September 1942.
[149] SMA U1-6-009-195: Industrial and Social Affairs Committee, 25 June 1943. This was the committee's last meeting.
[150] SMA U1-6-197: Staff Sub-committee minutes, 14 July 1943.
[151] SMA U1-4-261: K. Takagi, 16 August 1943.

range of employees. Australian, New Zealander, Japanese and Chinese employees appealed to factory owners and managers of different nationalities, as the absence of municipal legislation meant the Industrial Section depended on achieving change through persuasion. Transnational colonialism was manifest in both the influences on the SMC's Industrial Section and the backgrounds and networks of its staff.

The Council's priorities changed over time, from taking no responsibility for industrial conditions to undertaking extensive work to alleviate working and living conditions in the International Settlement. Hinder was successful in cooperating with other municipal departments, especially the Fire and Public Works Departments in factory inspection and the SMP in child protection. Cooperation with the Chinese authorities was more difficult, but in the late 1930s significant progress was being made. Although industrial conditions in the Settlement remained poor, real progress was made and many thousands of lives were directly affected by the SMC's actions. Its wartime work, including measuring the rising cost of living and providing funds for the unemployed to travel to their native place, affected the largest number of people.

The clashes between the SMC and the Chinese authorities over factory inspection reflect the fact that both were attempting to engage in state-building activities in the same urban space, each seeking to claim greater capacity to control industry, and thus, symbolically, modernity, in the contested city of Shanghai. The dramatic expansion of the role of the Industrial Section from 1938 in the absence of the constraining force of the Chinese city government further demonstrates the state-building tendencies of the SMC. It was both increasing its responsibility for the welfare of the population and increasing its governmental functions, behaving more like the national governments of European states than the laissez-faire authority of nineteenth-century Shanghai.

Epilogue: Dismantling and Remembering Transnational Colonialism

On 20 May 1943, Britain and the USA both formally ratified their treaties for the Relinquishment of Extraterritorial Rights in China. For the Foreign Office, this date marked the end of the existence of the Shanghai Municipal Council and its International Settlement, because the Land Regulations from which the Council derived its authority 'rested solely and firmly upon' extraterritoriality and 'with the total abolition of that extra-territorial system in regard to all of the Powers concerned, the whole foundation upon which the international instrument [of the Land Regulations] was built has been swept entirely away'.[1] Both treaties explicitly stated that the British or American government relinquished all rights in the settlements and that each government 'considers that the International Settlements at Shanghai and Amoy should revert to the administration and control of the Government of the Republic of China'.[2] Thus the legal status of the International Settlement derived ultimately from foreign imperial governments and they could sign away its existence, even though they had not controlled the SMC. The treaties state merely that these settlements and other concessions 'should' revert to the Chinese government because in reality they were under Japanese control, but the western Allies were assuring China that they recognised its claim to complete sovereignty. Winston Churchill had stated in parliament in 1940 that the relinquishment of extraterritoriality and British concessions in China would be agreed only after the end of the war, but when Japan seized control of the Settlement the process was expedited and both treaties were signed on 11 January 1943.[3] The Japanese-controlled SMC

---

[1] TNA FO371/46192: Sir Allan G. Mossop, 'Memorandum on payments in respect of superannuation due to British employees of the former Shanghai Municipal Council', 17 September 1945.

[2] 'Great Britain and Northern Ireland and India and China: Treaty for the Relinquishment of Extra-territorial Rights in China and the Regulation of Related Matters', Article IV, League of Nations, *Treaty Series: Treaties and International Engagements Registered with the Secretariat of the League of Nations*, Vol. 205 (1944–1946), 71; 'Treaty between the United States of America and the Republic of China for the Relinquishment of Extraterritorial Rights in China and the Regulation of Related Matters', Article III, in *United States Statutes at Large*, Vol. 57, Part I: *Public Laws* (1943), 769.

[3] HC Deb 18 July 1940, vol. 363 cc399–401. The Anglo-Chinese treaty was signed in Chongqing on 11 January 1943 by T. V. Soong, Chinese Minister for Foreign Affairs, Sir Horace James

continued to function until August, making much of its internationality, but for the British and Americans who had established the SMC together in 1854, it could not really exist without them.

In October 1945, the members of the pre-Japanese takeover Council met informally with the British and American consuls-general to discuss how the Relinquishment treaties were to be implemented locally. The former councillors planned to make representations to the Chinese government, with the assistance of the consuls-general, regarding the assets and liabilities of the SMC, particularly pensions owed to former employees. The American consul-general reported to Washington that the 'Council considers itself still in being'.[4] In fact, the services of these representatives of the old order were not required, but the assumption that the Council was still the municipal authority with a right to deal with the Chinese government shows the same bullish self-confidence of the pre-war Shanghailanders. For them, Shanghai without foreign governance was unimaginable.

During the war, interned Allied nationals had been similarly unaware, or in denial about the fact, that the status quo ante would not be resumed after the war.[5] So many British former SMC staff wrote to the Foreign Office about being reemployed in the Council that a civil servant produced a pro forma letter in July 1945 assuring them that their names would be passed on to the Chinese city authorities, but ending with a gentle warning: 'We would, however, advise you not to count on any prospect of re-employment.'[6] The Chinese government in theory took on the rights, responsibilities, assets and liabilities of the SMC under the Relinquishment treaties, but foreign employees would be unwelcome in the new municipal government and they would receive no compensation for lost earnings, nor would the Chinese government take on the payment of their pensions. Former SMC employees lost their old homes if they had lived in municipal barracks or houses, so they continued to stay in camps after the end of the war in the absence of anywhere else to go or jobs to do. One former member of the SMP, Bernard Francis Warman, wrote in desperation to the former British Ambassador to China, now in Moscow, that 'here in Shanghai we are in the anomalous position of having won the war whilst

Seymour, British ambassador to China, and Hugh Edward Richardson on behalf of India: the whole British empire was represented. The Sino-American treaty was signed the same day in Washington, DC, by Cordell Hull, American Secretary of State, and Wei Tao-ming, Chinese ambassador to the USA. Britain and the USA thus acted in concert, though 7,700 miles apart, to end the colonial enterprise in China in which they had jointly shared.

[4] Ralph E. Goodwin et al. (eds.), *Foreign Relations of the United States, 1945. The Far East: China, Vol. 7* (Washington, DC: United States Government Printing Office, 1969), document 1027: Consul-General Josselyn to the Secretary of State, Shanghai, 27 October 1945.

[5] Most SMC employees were interned together in Ash Camp and Yu Yuen Road Camp. Greg Leck, *Captives of Empire: The Japanese Internment of Allied Civilians in China and Hong Kong, 1941–1945* (Philadelphia, PA: Shandy Press, 2006), 428 ff., 512 ff.

[6] TNA FO371/46192, 23 July 1945.

losing everything else' and claimed former SMC employees were 'walking around this town like so many beggars'.[7] While Warman admitted that men like him had capital to draw on, he was reluctant to do so, convinced that he had done his bit for the war effort, following British government instructions to stay in Shanghai, and was owed a position – with a good salary. Warman and his colleagues were accustomed to occupying an inflated position in society in the International Settlement and were not ready to accept the change in their circumstances. The end of the SMC was a shock to the Shanghailanders and especially to the Council's former foreign employees.

The British government was adamant that it was under no obligation to these former employees of 'an international body', but agreed reluctantly to make ex gratia payments 'on moral and humanitarian grounds' to those members of the staff who were British by direct connection to the UK.[8] The Foreign Office appointed J. W. Morcher, the former treasurer of the SMC, to process the claims (without payment). Initially, the Foreign Office expected that the Chinese government would soon agree to take on the pension obligations it inherited from the SMC, but the increasingly forlorn hopes for this outcome were given up entirely when the Chinese Communist Party came to power in 1949. The British government therefore agreed to pay limited pensions to British nationals, allocating £70,000 per annum for the purpose on top of lump sum payments in 1950 totalling £1.5 million.[9] But this did not cover the claimants' full entitlements under the SMC's generous terms of service, and the government did not link the pension payments to inflation or otherwise treat SMC pensioners the same as British state or colonial pensioners: the payments were to be considered ex gratia rather than an obligation. The treatment of SMC employees was based on the precedent of payments to Britons who had been employed by the Siamese government following official British encouragement: the British government was classing the SMC with a foreign government that had contributed to British interests overseas.[10]

Former employees of the SMC continued to lobby for the payment of their full entitlements. The China Association, established in 1889 by British merchants in London with links to China, had taken up the cause immediately in 1945, writing to the Foreign Office to seek payments for former SMC employees. It even sent a representative to meet returning Shanghai internees off the ship in Southampton with the news that they would receive some government

---

[7] TNA FO 371/53540: Bernard Francis Warman, 984 Bubbling Well Road, Shanghai, to Sir A. Clerk Kerr, HBM Ambassador to the USSR, Moscow, 15 November 1945.

[8] FO 371/110365: Mr Oates, Treasury, to Ambassador Vincens Steensen-Leth, Danish Embassy, London, 30 March 1954.

[9] Bickers, *Empire Made Me*, 323.

[10] HC Deb 8 July 1943, vol. 390 cc2285–6W.

support while they awaited payments from the Chinese government.[11] The China Association did not accept the British government's denial of responsibility for those who had worked for the SMC, and in 1964, after SMC pensioners were excluded from an increase in payments to British state and colonial pensioners, H. J. Collar, the secretary of the Association, argued his case to the Minister of State for Foreign Affairs. Setting out the history of the SMC and its 'vital ... protection of the vast British investment in China', he claimed that the Council should be considered to have served British interests sufficiently closely for its former employees to enjoy the same benefits as those who worked for colonial governments. He argued that:

[The SMC's] British officials have always regarded themselves in a sense as part of the system by which extra-territorial rights in China were maintained and rendered workable. They submit that their services were not merely municipal and local, but that they formed an essential part of British influence in the Far East.[12]

While the SMC had positioned itself as international throughout its existence, its former British employees now hoped that their municipal work could be counted as British in order to secure better pensions for themselves. It did not work: C. M. MacLehose (a future Governor of Hong Kong) wrote a 'curt' reply offering sympathy but no room for negotiation. The British government position was clear that the SMC had been not British but international.

The claims of British former SMC employees were only finally settled in 1987 under the Foreign Compensation (People's Republic of China) Order, which made over £20 million available to compensate all Britons who were owed money by the Chinese government that the latter would never pay. A similar arrangement was made for debts of the USSR. Advertisements in newspapers encouraged applications for the compensation, and as late as 1990 the British Secretary of State confirmed that 24 living former employees of the SMC had lodged claims for compensation for pay or pensions that they now hoped to recoup from the British government.[13] The government's lump sum payments to the claimants did not include compensation for the 50 years of lost interest because the fixed amount available could not cover all possible unpaid debts of the Chinese government to British nationals. As in the 1940s, the government did not accept responsibility for SMC debts but was rather compensating for a failure of the Chinese government to honour debts to British nationals.

The British government accepted no responsibility for non-British nationals who had worked for the SMC, including subjects of British colonies. In the

---

[11] FO 371/46192, 23 October 1945.

[12] FO 371/175961: H. J. Collar, China Association, to Peter Thomas MP, Foreign Office, 22 January 1964.

[13] 'Chinese compensation', *Glasgow Herald*, 29 February 1988, 7; HC Deb, 15 January 1990, vol. 165 cc53–4W.

1940s it recommended that the governments of the Dominions should grant ex gratia payments to Canadian or Australian former SMC employees, but they were unwilling to do so. The suggestion that the Indian government should be asked to take on the same responsibility was superseded by Indian independence.[14] The Chinese government did, however, make a single payment to Chinese former employees of the SMC in 1947. Other nationals, including a Dane and a Czechoslovakian who each sought to claim their pensions from various authorities, received nothing.[15] Working for a transnational colonial institution proved costly for its staff.

Both Britain and the USA were anxious that the Chinese government should accept its debt liabilities as well as the assets that it gained by taking over the International Settlement, and acted together to try to obtain payment of the substantial debts owed to their nationals. The American government asserted its right to help determine the fate of municipal assets alongside Britain in strong terms:

the American Government has a substantial interest, both political and financial, in the Settlement, which it has sponsored and protected by diplomatic representations, and even armed force, almost from its inception.[16]

The American authorities were in no doubt that the SMC had not been a solely British entity. The SMC had ceased to exist at a time when it owed over £515,000 to the Hongkong and Shanghai Bank in loans, overdrafts and interest, a further £10,500 to its London agents Pook's and Company, and almost 700 US dollars to its New York agents Balfour Guthrie and Company, in addition to significant local debts in Shanghai. Anticipating that the Chinese government might delay paying these debts, the American consul-general had sought to obtain payment of the amounts owed to American concerns, including the Shanghai Power Company, prior to the end of the war.[17] When this failed, the American State Department's Division of Chinese Affairs advocated the American and British governments jointly pushing for the appointment of a judicial commission of foreign consuls to oversee the fulfilment of the Relinquishment treaties in Shanghai. The Division based the proposed commission on the Board of Judicial Inquiry that reported on the May Thirtieth Incident of 1925: it was not only the former SMC councillors and staff who failed to grasp that political power in Shanghai had shifted out of their hands.

[14] FO 371/46192: 1 December 1945; FO 371/ 69562.
[15] FO 371/110365.
[16] Ralph R. Goodwin et al. (eds.), *Foreign Relations of the United States, 1945. The Far East: China*, Vol. 7, document 1029: Memorandum Prepared in the Division of Chinese Affairs, Washington, DC, 29 November 1945.
[17] E. Ralph Perkins et al. (eds.), *Foreign Relations of the United States: Diplomatic Papers, 1944, China*, Vol. 6 (Washington, DC: United States Government Printing Office, 1967), document 874: The Secretary of State to the Ambassador in China (Gauss), Washington, DC, 11 September 1944.

Instead of a foreign consular judicial commission, the transfer of the SMC's role and assets was administered by the fully Chinese Commission for the Liquidation of Official Assets, Obligations and Liabilities of the Former International Settlement at Shanghai, with one British and one American former member of the SMC present only in the capacity of advisors.[18] Efforts by the American and British advisors to the liquidation commission to retain certain municipal assets, such as the Victoria Nurses Home, in foreign hands failed: the Shanghai Municipal Government inherited all assets of the SMC. Meanwhile, attempts to secure Chinese government payment of SMC debts were not even entertained. Neither the British nor the American authorities had apparently anticipated that the Chinese government would simply refuse to accept the financial obligations incurred by the former SMC. When it became apparent that China would not pay, the Hongkong and Shanghai Bank sought redress for its municipal loan from the British government, on the basis that it was the British government that had dissolved the SMC. But the Foreign Office denied liability and instead sought to assuage the bank's demands by reassuring it that Foreign Office staff were doing everything they could to secure payment by the Chinese government, despite no expectation of success: 'The urgent thing', according to an internal memorandum of July 1949, was 'to satisfy the Bank by making further pro forma representations before the present Chinese Govt. disappears.'[19] The bank, despite holding the British government responsible for transferring municipal property to China that was effectively mortgaged to the bank, was forced to abandon its claim. The SMC's anomalous international status meant that no national government was willing to accept its debts.

Within Shanghai, the city government took on most governmental roles previously played by the SMC, but in the midst of a growing inflation crisis funds were scarce, and in any case the new authorities had no intention of picking up the SMC's special provisions for foreign residents. The British community therefore tried to meet some of its needs itself: the British Chamber of Commerce and British Residents' Association established a British Community Interests (BCI) group in 1946 to cater for the 4,000 Britons who remained in Shanghai. The members of this diminished community were continuing with their business ventures and standard of living much as they had before the Japanese occupation, despite the change in municipal administration. The BCI concentrated on providing British boys' and girls' schools and contributing to the costs of the Country Hospital (which was

---

[18] Goodwin et al. (eds.), *Foreign Relations of the United States, 1946, The Far East: China*, Vol. 10, document 1082: The Counselor of Embassy in China (Smyth) to the Secretary of State, Chongqing, 3 April 1946.

[19] TNA FO 371/75809: 'Memorandum of claims by the Hongkong and Shanghai Bank against the Shanghai Municipal Council', 15 July 1949.

privately managed so was not included in the handover of municipal assets), so British children could be educated by British teachers and British patients could be treated by British medical staff.[20] The former SMC General Hospital, now under Chinese control, was no longer considered fit for foreign patients, while new housing was deemed necessary to attract good teachers and nurses as the Chinese authorities had possession of the former municipal properties. The diverse foreign community in Shanghai thus splintered in the absence of a unifying international municipality, and each national constituency sought to serve its own interests. British Community Interests organisations were set up in Tianjin and Qingdao to similarly attempt to ensure local British education and healthcare, but they would not be permitted for long. Colonialism in China would not be resurrected.

Some former foreign employees of the SMC found work locally for a few years, but all had to move on within a decade of the end of the SMC and most left China soon after discovering that their old posts would not be open to them. Many sought new careers in the British empire or Anglophone world. The 15 or so Americans returned to the USA, the Canadians to Canada, Australians to Australia, and New Zealanders to New Zealand, while Britons went to the UK or found work in Britain's colonies and Dominions, particularly Hong Kong (in the police force), Singapore (both short-term roles in the War Crimes Commission and longer-term positions in the Naval Base Police Force), and Canada and Australia. Others found their way to Australian New Guinea, to the former Italian North African colonies (100 applied to go to Libya, which was briefly under British control, and the 40 'best' were selected), and even to Germany.[21] The transnationalism of the SMC continued after its demise as its staff scattered around the world.

The 50 former members of the SMP who were employed in Europe policed the British zone of defeated Germany, and later the Bizone (jointly controlled by Britain and the USA from 1 January 1947). Though very different from Shanghai, the often reluctant and mutually suspicious international sharing of authority in the Allied Control Council that oversaw the different occupation zones, and in the Bizone, would have been somewhat familiar to former Shanghailanders. Occupied post-war Berlin and Vienna were managed by two of the few international urban authorities that can be compared to the SMC.[22] The Inter-Allied Governing Authority or

---

[20] 'British Community in Shanghai', from Our Special Correspondent in Shanghai, *The Times*, 13 April 1948, 3.

[21] TNA FO 371/53588: Re-employment of Shanghai Municipal Council employees; Bickers, *Empire Made Me*, 322–3. On the communist expulsion of foreigners in the early 1950s, see Beverley Hooper, *China Stands Up: Ending the Western Presence, 1948–1950* (Sydney: Allen and Unwin, 1986).

[22] The other notable example is the International Zone of Tangier, which was subject to the joint authority of the consuls of Britain, France and Spain, with the later addition of Italy, the

Kommandatura was responsible for the administration of Berlin as a whole, above the authority of the commanders of each sector, although by late 1947 cooperation had broken down.[23] The *Innere Stadt* in central Vienna was an international zone, surrounded by four separate zones each under the authority of a different Allied power but also subject to the joint authority of a quadripartite *Kommandatura*.[24] Legal authority for these bodies rested on defeat of the Nazis and the subsequent right of occupation for the victorious Allies, but in practice both cities were soon governed day-to-day by Germans or Austrians. While the International Settlement in Shanghai had no such strong legal foundation as the military occupation of a defeated enemy territory, its very legal ambiguity helped the SMC to gain for itself greater control and autonomy over the decades.

Like the foreign staff of the SMC, the foreign councillors and senior officials also moved around internationally after the demise of the SMC, continuing to enjoy high status in influential roles. Former SMC chairman William J. Keswick served as a Brigadier in North Africa, France, Belgium and the Netherlands. He then undertook further war work in Singapore and Washington, DC, before becoming London director of the secret Special Operations Executive and helping plan the Normandy Landings from the War Cabinet Office.[25] After the war, Keswick returned to Jardine, Matheson and Company in London as company director and later chairman, and was also governor of the Hudson's Bay Company and a director of the Bank of England and British Petroleum.[26] Two other British former chairmen of the Council, Harry Edward Arnhold and John Hellyer Liddell, both moved to the USA, to New York and California respectively. Liddell earned a CBE, as did long-serving Secretary-General Godfrey Phillips. Godfrey Phillips's honour was awarded for negotiating the exchange of British and Japanese prisoners of war on behalf of the British government in 1942, after which he worked in the Special Operations Executive (on Keswick's

---

USA, Belgium, the Netherlands and Portugal, and administered by an international Legislative Assembly. Just as the territory of the International Settlement at Shanghai remained Chinese, the International Zone of Tangier remained technically Moroccan, but all Moroccan claims to administer the zone were handed over in perpetuity to international control in the 1923 Statute of the International Zone of Tangiers. The zone was returned to Moroccan control in 1956. On this and other examples of international territorial administration in the last century, see Carsten Stahn, *The Law and Practice of International Territorial Administration: Versailles to Iraq and Beyond* (Cambridge University Press, 2008), 57–8 and *passim*.

[23] J. L. Simpson, 'Berlin: Allied Rights and Responsibilities in the Divided City', *International and Comparative Law Quarterly*, Vol. 6, No. 1 (1957), 84–5.

[24] I. L. G., 'The Allied Commission for Austria: A Preliminary Account of its Organization and Work', *The World Today*, Vol. 1, No. 5 (1945), 208–9.

[25] Wasserstein, *Secret War*, 195.

[26] Jeremy Brown, 'Keswick, Sir William Johnston (1903–1990)', rev. *Oxford Dictionary of National Biography* (Oxford University Press, 2004), online edition, www.oxforddnb.com/view/article/40119.

invitation) for the remainder of the war,[27] and then became a solicitor and partner in the legal firm Linklaters and Paines. At the end of the war he lobbied on behalf of former employees of the SMC seeking pension payments, meeting with his MP and writing to both the Foreign Office in London and State Department in Washington: he did not confine his advocacy to the British members of the SMC.[28] He held many influential positions, including director of *The Times*, which published a glowing obituary when he died in London in 1965.[29] Australian Eleanor Hinder, former Chief of the Industrial Section of the SMC, worked for the British Foreign Office in the International Labour Organisation in Canada during the war and then took up a position in the United Nations Economic Commission for Asia and the Far East, earning an OBE for her work in 1950 before retiring to her home city of Sydney.[30] For these high-flyers, it was not difficult to move on from life in Shanghai, although Godfrey Phillips's obituary claims that the rest of his successful career was 'something of an anti-climax' after he left the SMC.

Chinese former municipal employees and council members had more mixed careers after leaving the SMC. Yu Xiaqing, the most politically prominent of the Chinese councillors, resisted Japanese pressure to become mayor in occupied Shanghai, and moved to Hong Kong and then Chongqing in 1941, where he died in 1945. His coffin was sent to Shanghai where he was buried with full honours.[31] Hsi Yulin, who had served on the Council for seven years, proceeded on a six-month study of municipal administration in American cities in February 1943 on the instructions of Chiang Kai-shek and T. V. Soong (Song Ziwen, Minister of Foreign Affairs), in preparation for drawing up a new Municipal Charter for Shanghai.[32] At this stage the Relinquishment treaties had been signed but not yet ratified, yet the Chinese government was already working on its plans for post-war, post-colonial Shanghai. Hsi's experience of municipal governance in the SMC prepared him well for the work. Yuan Lüdeng, the longest serving Chinese councillor, from 1928 to 1941, was less in favour with the Guomindang government. He was convicted in 1946 as a Chinese traitor (汉奸, *hanjian*) for serving the Japanese war effort and

---

[27] Wasserstein, *Secret War*, 196–7.

[28] FO 371/53540.

[29] 'Mr. Godfrey Phillips', *The Times*, 25 October 1965, 14.

[30] Meredith Foley and Heather Radi, 'Hinder, Eleanor Mary (1893–1963)', *Australian Dictionary of Biography*, Vol. 9 (Melbourne University Press, 1983), online edition, http://adb.anu.edu.au/biography/hinder-eleanor-mary-6678/text11515.

[31] Parks M. Coble, *China's War Reporters: The Legacy of Resistance Against Japan* (Cambridge, MA: Harvard University Press, 2015), 97, 221, n. 51.

[32] G. Bernard Noble and E. R. Perkins (eds.), *Foreign Relations of the United States: Diplomatic Papers, 1943, China* (Washington, DC: United States Government Printing Office, 1957), document 662: Memorandum of Conversation, by Mr. Edwin F. Stanton of the Division of Far Eastern Affairs, Washington, DC, 1 March 1943.

sentenced to life imprisonment.[33] He Dekui, the deputy secretary of the SMC, was accused in July 1946 of treason for working under the Japanese occupation forces, but an investigation cleared him of wrongdoing and he became Deputy Major of the Greater Shanghai City Government.[34] He travelled to Guangzhou in late 1947 on the invitation of T. V. Soong, newly appointed Guomindang Governor of Guangdong province,[35] and then on to Hong Kong, where he remained until his return to Shanghai in 1974. Prominent employees of the Nationalist Government went to Taiwan or Hong Kong, and the small number of Chinese who had been promoted to senior roles in the SMC would have belonged to this group. Many former Chinese police constables found work policing the city for its Chinese authorities, and after their campaign for the pensions owed to them by the SMC, the city government gave them limited compensation.[36] Other Chinese employed by the SMC for mundane work would have similarly been able to find work locally, many of them in the municipal government. After the Communist seizure of Shanghai in May 1949, stability was the priority, and those who had once worked for the SMC at junior levels had little to fear by association. Those who had collaborated with the imperialists at higher levels, however, and especially those who worked with the Japanese, would have been vulnerable, but Yuan Lüdeng died in 1954 and other prominent Chinese councillors also died or otherwise escaped persecution in the political campaigns that would come under Mao Zedong.

Mao declared that 'we [Chinese communists] are different in nature from imperialism, and the very sight of it makes us sick'.[37] The vestiges of imperialism in Shanghai, the site of China's greatest 'national humiliation' in terms of the numbers subject to foreign authority and the duration of that foreign authority, had to be swept away or reclaimed. The Shanghai Municipal Government occupied both the former SMC administration building, which it still uses to this day, and the iconic Hongkong and Shanghai Banking Corporation building on the Bund (although the latter has been leased by the Shanghai Pudong Development Bank since 1995). It thus laying claim to the headquarters of both political and economic power in the city.

A flurry of historical writing for popular consumption emerged in the 1950s, in response to the Marxist need to identify the historical explanations for what had to be portrayed as the inevitable rise of socialism in China. It included

[33] Fang Zhanjiang, '*Dahanjian Yuan Lüdeng shoushenji*' ('Remembering the Trial of Great Chinese Traitor Yuan Lüdeng'), *Wenshi tiandi*, January 2010.

[34] Chen, *Guilty of Indigence*, 199, 273, n. 115.

[35] Goodwin et al. (eds.), *Foreign Relations of the United States, 1947. The Far East: China*, Vol. 7, document 243: The Ambassador in China (Stuart) to the Secretary of State, Nanking, 2 October 1947.

[36] Bickers, *Empire Made Me*, 324.

[37] Mao Zedong, 'US Imperialism is a Paper Tiger', 14 July 1956, in Mao Zedong, *Selected Works of Mao Tse-tung*, Vol. 5 (Beijing: Foreign Languages Press, 1977), 311.

accounts of the evils of foreign imperialism in Shanghai as the counterpoint to
the glories of the New China brought by the communist revolution.[38] The acceptable line for the writing of history, as for all other aspects of public life, was
taken from Mao, who claimed that 'the history of imperialist aggression upon
China ... constitutes precisely the history of modern China'.[39] Imperialism was
seen as central to the development of the Chinese nation, and the International
Settlement was central to imperialism in China. Historical writing in the press
and in books was full of the transgressions of foreign imperialists, but short
on detail. Foreign oppression of Chinese in Shanghai was symbolised by the
legendary sign at the entrance to the public gardens reading 'Dogs and Chinese
not admitted', a myth that was first developed in a 1951 guidebook and which
was repeated in every subsequent guidebook, textbook and popular history of
the city.[40] The Chinese Communist Party erected a plaque emphasising the
contrast between the sentiments expressed in the alleged sign and the opening to all of the old public gardens as the new Huangpu Park. At the same
time, the immorality of foreign administration was stressed in the campaign
to eradicate prostitution, which was promoted as the purification of the city
from the corruption brought and tolerated by Shanghai's foreign authorities.[41]
Condemnation of foreign imperialism was unambiguous.

In the Reform Era, however, the emphasis of the dominant historical narrative shifted from revolution to first modernisation in the 1980s and then Chinese
nationalist identity and heritage in the 1990s.[42] All three elements remained,
however, apparent in representations of the colonial past. The International
Settlement was and is portrayed as the source of Shanghai's status as a special
city within China, particularly by the city government. It is also used to suggest
a pedigree for Shanghai's reputation as a cosmopolitan city, a meeting place
for different cultures, which underpins Shanghai's claim to being a global city
– with the appeal to international investment that this entails.

In 1990 Zhang Zhongli (张仲礼) wrote about Shanghai's history to address
the concerns of the day, before the post-1992 boom, when Shanghai was lagging
behind other centres of economic growth. The contrast he draws is a surprising
reassessment of the city's colonial past: in the 1930s Shanghai was soaring to

---

[38] Albert Feuerwerker, 'Preface', in Albert Feuerwerker (ed.), *History in Communist China*
(Cambridge, MA: MIT Press, 1968), v.

[39] Mao Zedong, 'On New Democracy', in *Selected Works of Mao Tse-tung*, Vol. 3 (Beijing: Foreign
Languages Press, 1967), 123.

[40] Bickers and Wasserstrom, '"Dogs and Chinese Not Admitted"', 452.

[41] Christian Henriot, '"La Fermature": The Abolition of Prostitution in Shanghai, 1949–58',
China Quarterly, No. 142 (1995), 467–86.

[42] Vivienne Shue, 'Global Imaginings, the State's Quest for Hegemony, and the Pursuit of
Phantom Freedom in China: From Heshang to Falun Gong', in Catarina Kinnvall and Kristina
Jönsson (eds.), *Globalization and Democratization in Asia: The Construction of Identity*
(London: Routledge, 2002), 211.

new heights whereas in the 1980s it sank to new lows ('30年代, 使人就呼: 大上海在腾飞; 80年代, 有人慨叹: 大上海在沉沦'; '30 niandai, shiren jiuhu: da Shanghai zai tengfei; 80 niandai, youren kaitan: da Shanghai zai chenlun').[43] Popular histories are explicit about their aim to indulge or stimulate the 'nostalgia' of the older generation and educate the younger in both the humiliation and modernisation brought by the foreign concessions.[44] Museums are as likely to present dioramas of humiliating court scenes and brothels, showing the inequality and immorality of colonial Shanghai, as they are to list the modern innovations introduced to China first in Shanghai, including gas, electricity, tap water and telecommunications, all of which were overseen by the SMC.[45]

Some popular histories even link the growing presence of foreign expatriates in the city to former colonial settlers. Chen Danyan (陈丹燕), a celebrated Shanghai author, quotes a Shanghainese who told her that 'he likes them no better now, with their expatriate salaries, than when they were making their fortunes by exploiting Chinese labour in the Republican era'.[46] Chen muses that:

Each time I came to the Bund, I always imagined I smelled opium and the scent of the sea in the air. In the warm breeze I often thought of the words by Shi Zhecun: "Take back the Concessions and regain our spirit."[47]

The legacy of the SMC and the International Settlement is thus both a celebration and a warning in China today. The city was subject to a uniquely transnational form of colonial authority in the SMC that brought diverse international influences but enabled the International Settlement to maintain its autonomy, keeping it apart from the structures and controls of formal empire. The relinquishment of extraterritorial rights by the foreign powers in 1943 made this form of colonialism impossible. The Japanese occupying forces abolished the council the same year when the function it had long served of providing a cloak of internationality for colonial ambitions was no longer deemed important. The staff and councillors scattered around the world, continuing their transnational lives elsewhere. But the marks the SMC left on the city remain, both in the physical layout and infrastructure of the former International Settlement and, more importantly, on the perception of Shanghai locally, nationally and internationally as a global city, set apart from the rest of China by its connections to the wider world.

[43] Zhang Zhongli, *Jindai Shanghai chengshi yanjiu (Research on Modern Urban Shanghai)* (Shanghai: Shanghai Renmin Chubanshe, 1990), 1.

[44] *Zhongguode zujie (The Foreign Concessions in China)* (Shanghai: Shanghai guji chubanshe, 2004), 9, 12.

[45] Shanghai Municipal History Museum, Orient Pearl Tower, Shanghai, which opened at its present site in 2001; Shanghai Municipal Archives exhibition, opened 2001.

[46] Chen Danyan, *Shanghai: China's Bridge to the Future* (Shanghai: Shanghai Literature and Art Publishing House, in English and Chinese, 1995), 19.

[47] Ibid., 23.

Bibliography

ARCHIVES AND ABBREVIATIONS

Mitchell and Dixson Libraries Manuscripts Collection, State Library of New South Wales, Sydney: Eleanor M. Hinder papers: MLMSS 770: I. Personal correspondence, 1923–1963 and II. Professional files, ca. 1919–1963, primarily E. Shanghai (China) Municipal Council, 1933–1954.

The National Archives, Kew (TNA): Foreign Office records (FO); Colonial Office records (CO); Treasury records (T).

Shanghai Municipal Archives (SMA): U 1–3, SMC Secretariat files, 1920–1932; U 1–4, SMC Secretariat files, 1932–1943; U 1–10, Industrial and Social Division files; U 1–14, Public Works Department records; U 1–16, Public Health Department records.

US National Archives and Records Administration (US NARA): Consular Records.

PRIMARY SOURCES

Abend, Hallett, *My Life in China, 1926–1941* (New York: Harcourt, Brace and Co., 1943).

Alley, Rewi, *Travels in China, 1966–71* (Beijing: New World Press, 1973).

Anderson, Adelaide Mary, *Humanity and Labour in China: An Industrial Visit and its Sequel (1923 to 1926)* (London: Student Christian Movement, 1928).

The Battle of 'Muddy Flat,' 1854: being an historical sketch of that famous occurrence, written specially for the jubilee commemoration thereof at Shanghai, April 1904 (Shanghai: North-China Herald, 1904).

British Municipal Council, Tientsin, *Report for the Year* (Tianjin: Tientsin Press Ltd, 1937, 1939).

Burt, A. R., J. B. Powell and Carl Crow (eds.), *Biographies of Prominent Chinese* (Shanghai: Biographical Publishing Company, 1925).

Bureau of Social Affairs, City Government of Greater Shanghai, *Shanghai tebieshi laozi jiufen tongji 1930 (Industrial Disputes 1930)* (Shanghai: Bureau of Social Affairs, 1932).

Strikes and Lockouts, Greater Shanghai, 1929 (Shanghai: Bureau of Social Affairs, 1930).

The China Press (Shanghai, 1937).

China Weekly Review (Shanghai, 1926–1934).

China Year Book 1926–1927, 1938 (Tianjin and Shanghai).

The Colonial Office List (London: Harrison, 1910–40)

Davis, C. Noel, *A History of the Shanghai Paper Hunt Club, 1863–1930* (Shanghai: Kelly and Walsh, 1930).

Digby, George, *Down Wind* (London: Collins, 1939).

Edinburgh Gazette (Edinburgh, 1925).

Ellis, Sarah, *Prevention Better than Cure, or, The Moral Wants of the World We Live in* (London: Appleton, 1847).

Fang Fu-an, *Chinese Labour: An Economic and Statistical Survey of the Labour Conditions and Labour Movements in China* (Shanghai: Kelly and Walsh, 1931).

Fang Teng, 'Yu Xiaqing lun' ('On Yu Xiaqing'), *Zazhi yuekan*, Vol. 12 (1943).

Fang Zhanjiang, '*Dahanjian Yuan Lüdeng shoushenji*' ('Remembering the Trial of Great Chinese Traitor Yuan Lüdeng'), *Wenshi tiandi*, January 2010.

Feetham, Richard, *Report of the Hon. Mr. Justice Feetham, C.M.G. to the Shanghai Municipal Council*, 3 vols. (Shanghai: North-China Daily News and Herald, 1931).

Finer, Herman, *English Local Government* (London: Methuen, 1950; first published 1933).

Foreign Office, *Papers Respecting Labour Conditions in China*, Cmd. 2442 (London: The Stationery Office, 1924).

G., I. L., 'The Allied Commission for Austria: A Preliminary Account of its Organization and Work', *The World Today*, Vol. 1, No. 5 (1945), 204–13.

Glasgow Herald (Glasgow, 1988).

Goodwin, Ralph E., Herbert A. Fine, John G. Reid and Francis C. Prescott (eds.), *Foreign Relations of the United States, 1945. The Far East: China, Vol. 7* (Washington, DC: United States Government Printing Office, 1969).

Goodwin, Ralph R., Herbert A. Fine, Francis C. Prescott and Velma H. Cassidy (eds.), *Foreign Relations of the United States, 1946, The Far East: China, Vol. 10* (Washington, DC: United States Government Printing Office, 1972).

'Great Britain and Northern Ireland and India and China: Treaty for the Relinquishment of Extra-territorial Rights in China and the Regulation of Related Matters', Article IV, League of Nations, *Treaty Series: Treaties and International Engagements Registered with the Secretariat of the League of Nations*, Vol. 205 (1944–1946), 69–107.

Hansard British Parliamentary Debates (HC Deb).

Hinder, Eleanor M., *Life and Labour in Shanghai: A Decade of Labour and Social Administration in the International Settlement* (New York: Institute of Pacific Relations, 1944).

Social and Industrial Problems of Shanghai, with Special Reference to the Administrative and Regulatory Work of the Shanghai Municipal Council (New York: Institute of Pacific Relations, 1942).

Hsü Shuhsi, *Japan and Shanghai*, No. 4, Political and Economic Studies (Shanghai: Kelly and Walsh, 1928).

Hudson, Manley O., 'International Problems at Shanghai', *Foreign Affairs* (October 1927).

'The Rendition of the International Mixed Court at Shanghai', *American Journal of International Law*, Vol. 21, No. 3 (1927), 451–71.

Innes, Kathleen E., *The League of Nations and the World's Workers: An Introduction to the Work of the International Labour Organisation* (London: Hogarth Press, 1927).

International Labour Office, *The International Labour Organisation: The First Decade* (London: George Allen and Unwin, 1931).

Johnstone Jr., William Crane, *The Shanghai Problem* (Stanford University Press, 1937).

Jones, F. C., *Shanghai and Tientsin, with Special Reference to Foreign Institutions* (London: Oxford University Press, 1940).

J. R., 'Shanghai Lagging in Factory Control', *Far Eastern Survey*, Vol. 4, No. 23 (20 November 1935), 186–7.

Kotenev, A. M., *Shanghai: Its Mixed Court and Council* (Shanghai: North-China Daily News and Herald, 1925).

Shanghai: Its Municipality and the Chinese (Shanghai: North-China Daily News and Herald, 1927).

Kounin, I. I. (comp.), *Eighty Five Years of the Shanghai Volunteer Corps* (Shanghai: Cosmopolitan Press, 1938).

The Labour Party, *International Regulation of Women's Work: History of the Work for Women Accomplished by the International Labour Organisation* (London: Pelican Press, 1930).

Leavens, Dickson H., 'The Silver Clause in China', *American Economic Review*, Vol. 26, No. 4 (1936), 650–9.

Lo Hui-min (ed.), *The Correspondence of G. E. Morrison*, Vol. 1, 1895–1912 (Cambridge University Press, 1976).

The London Gazette (London, 1929).

Mao Zedong, *Selected Works of Mao Tse-tung*, Vols. 3 and 5 (Beijing: Foreign Languages Press, 1965, 1977).

Maugham, W. Somerset, *The Painted Veil* (London: Vintage, 2007; first published 1925).

Municipal Gazette, Being the Official Organ of the Council for the Foreign Settlement of Shanghai (Shanghai, 1900–1940).

Nellist, George F. (ed.), *Men of Shanghai and North China: A Standard Biographical Reference Work* (Shanghai: Oriental Press, 1933).

Noble, G. Bernard and E. R. Perkins (eds.), *Foreign Relations of the United States: Diplomatic Papers, 1943, China* (Washington, DC: United States Government Printing Office, 1957).

The North-China Daily News (NCDN) (Shanghai, 1900–1941).

The North-China Herald, Supreme Court and Consular Gazette (NCH) (Shanghai: North-China Daily News and Herald).

Perkins, E. Ralph, S. Everett Gleason and John G. Reid (eds.), *Foreign Relations of the United States: Diplomatic Papers, 1944, China*, Vol. 6 (Washington, DC: United States Government Printing Office, 1967).

Peters, E. W., *Shanghai Policeman*, ed. Hugh Barnes (London: Rich and Cowan, 1937).

Pone, C., 'Towards the Establishment of a Factory Inspectorate in China', *International Labour Review*, Vol. 25, No. 5 (1932), 591–604.

Pott, Francis Lister Hawks, *A Short History of Shanghai, Being an Account of the Growth and Development of the International Settlement* (Shanghai: Kelly and Walsh, 1928).

Ransome, Arthur, 'The Shanghai Mind' in Arthur Ransome (ed.), *The Chinese Puzzle* (London: Unwin, 1927), 29–32.

The Rattle (Shanghai, 1901).

Richmond, R. B., *'Prevention Better than Cure': Practical Remarks on the Prevention of Cholera and Removal of other Troublesome States of the Bowels* (London: Nissen and Parker, 1849).

Robert, Donald (ed.), *The Municipal Year Book of the United Kingdom for 1908* (London: Municipal Journal, 1908).

Royal Tank Corps Journal (1927).

'The Shanghai Crisis', *International Affairs*, Vol. 11, No. 2 (March 1932), 153–79.

Shanghai Mercury (Shanghai, 1927).

Shanghai Municipal Council, *Reports for the Year* (Shanghai: Kelly and Walsh, 1899–1942).

Shanghai Times (Shanghai, 1930).

Shenbao 申報 (Shanghai, 1918–1942).

Shishi Xinbao 時事新報 (Shanghai, 1930).

Sowerby, R. R., *Sowerby of China: Arthur de Carle Sowerby* (Kendal: Titus Wilson and Son, 1956).

Sun Yat-sen, *San Min Chu I: The Three Principles of the People*, ed. L. T. Chen, trans. Frank W. Price (Shanghai: Institute for Pacific Relations, 1927).

Time (New York).

The Times (London).

'The Twenty-Third Session of the International Labour Conference', *International Labour Review*, Vol. 36, No. 3 (1937), 359–60.

'The Twenty-Fourth Session of the International Labour Conference', *International Labour Review*, Vol. 38, No. 3 (1938), 301–75.

'Treaty between the United States of America and the Republic of China for the Relinquishment of Extraterritorial Rights in China and the Regulation of Related Matters', Article III, in *United States Statutes at Large*, Vol. 57, Part I: *Public Laws* (1943), 767–99.

Weale, Putman (Bertram Lenox Simpson), *Why China Sees Red* (New York, 1925).

What Is Cholera? Or, Prevention Better than Cure, by a Bengal Doctor (n.a.) (London: G. Purkess, 1860).

Who's Who in China (Shanghai: China Weekly Review, 1931).

Winsley, T. M., *A History of the Singapore Volunteer Corps, 1854–1937: Being also an Historical Outline of Volunteering in Malaya* (Singapore: Government Printing Office, 1938).

Wright, Arnold and H. A. Cartwright (eds.), *Twentieth Century Impressions of Hong Kong, Shanghai and Other Treaty Ports of China: Their History, People, Commerce, Industries, and Resources* (London: Lloyd's Greater Britain Publishing Co., 1908).

Zhang Qian (ed.), *The Minutes of Shanghai Municipal Council* (Shanghai: Shanghai guji chubanshe, 2002).

SECONDARY WORKS

Adshead, S. A. M., *The Modernization of the Chinese Salt Administration, 1900–1920* (Cambridge, MA: Harvard University Press, 1970).

Airaksinen, Tiina Helena, *Love Your Country on Nanjing Road: The British and the May Fourth Movement in Shanghai* (Helsinki: Renvall Institute, University of Helsinki, 2005).

Amrith, Sunil, *Decolonizing International Health: India and South East Asia, 1930–65* (Cambridge University Press, 2006).

Anderson, Warwick, *Colonial Pathologies: American Tropical Medicine, Race, and Hygiene in the Philippines* (Durham, NC: Duke University Press, 2006).

'Excremental Colonialism: Public Health and the Poetics of Pollution', *Critical Inquiry*, Vol. 21, No. 3 (Spring 1995), 640–69.

Arnold, David (ed.), *Colonizing the Body: State Medicine and Epidemic Disease in Nineteenth-century India* (Berkeley, CA: University of California Press, 1993).

'Introduction', in David Arnold (ed.), *Imperial Medicine and Indigenous Societies* (Manchester University Press, 1988).

Science, Technology and Medicine in Colonial India (Cambridge University Press, 2000).

Axton, Matilda F., Rogers P. Churchill, N. O. Sappington et al. (eds.), *Foreign Relations of the United States, 1938: The Far East, Vol. IV* (Washington, DC: United States Government Printing Office, 1969).

Aydin, Cemil, *The Politics of Anti-Westernism in Asia: Visions of World Order in Pan-Islamic and Pan-Asian Thought* (New York: Columbia University Press, 2007).

Barrett, Alan D. T. and Lawrence R. Stanberry, *Vaccines for Biodefence and Emerging and Neglected Diseases* (London: Academic Press, 2009).

Bashford, Alison, *Imperial Hygiene: A Critical History of Colonialism, Nationalism and Public Health* (London: Palgrave, 2004).

Bayly, C. A., *Empire and Information: Intelligence Gathering and Social Communication in India, 1780–1870* (Cambridge University Press, 1996).

Bays, Daniel H., *A New History of Christianity in China* (Chichester: Wiley, 2012).

Beal, Edwin George, *The Origin of Likin, 1853–1864* (Cambridge, MA: Harvard University Press, 1958).

Belich, James, *Replenishing the Earth: The Settler Revolution and the Rise of the Angloworld, 1783–1939* (Oxford University Press, 2009).

Benedict, Carol, *Bubonic Plague in Nineteenth-century China* (Stanford University Press, 1996).

Bergère, Marie-Claire, *The Golden Age of the Chinese Bourgeoisie 1911–1937*, trans. Janet Lloyd (Cambridge University Press, 1989; first published as *L'Age d'or de la bourgeoisie chinoise*, Flammarion, 1986).

Shanghai: China's Gateway to Modernity, trans. Janet Lloyd (Stanford University Press, 2009; first published as *Histoire de Shanghai*, Fayard, 2002).

Betta, Chiara, 'The Land System of the Shanghai International Settlement: The Rise and Fall of the Hardoon Family, 1874–1956', in Robert Bickers and Isabella Jackson (eds.), *Treaty Ports in Modern China: Law, Land and Power* (London: Routledge, 2016), 61–77.

'Marginal Westerners in Shanghai: The Baghdadi Jewish Community, 1845–1931', in Robert Bickers and Christian Henriot (eds.), *New Frontiers: Imperialism's New Communities in East Asia, 1842–1953* (Manchester University Press, 2000), 38–54.

Bhattacharya, Sabyasachi, *The Financial Foundations of the British Raj: Ideas and Interests in the Reconstruction of Indian Public Finance 1858–1872* (Hyderabad: Orient Longman, 2005).

Bickers, Robert, 'Bland, John Otway Percy (1863–1945)', in *Oxford Dictionary of National Biography* (Oxford University Press, 2004), www.oxforddnb.com/view/article/31920.

Britain in China: Community, Culture and Colonialism 1900–1949 (Manchester University Press, 1999).

'Changing Shanghai's "Mind": Publicity, Reform and the British in Shanghai, 1928–1931', lecture to the China Society, 20 March 1991.

'Death of a Young Shanghailander: The Thorburn Case and the Defence of the British Communities in China in 1931', *Modern Asian Studies*, Vol. 30, No. 2 (1995), 271–300.

Empire Made Me: An Englishman Adrift in Shanghai (London: Allen Lane, 2003).

Getting Stuck in for Shanghai: Putting the Kibosh on the Kaiser from the Bund (Melbourne: Penguin, 2014).

'"The Greatest Cultural Asset East of Suez": The History and Politics of the Shanghai Municipal Orchestra and Public Band, 1881–1946', in Chi-hsiung Chang (chief ed.), *Ershi shiji de Zhongguo yu shijie* (*China and the World in the Twentieth Century*) (Nankang: Academia Sinica, 2001), 835–75.

'Incubator City: Shanghai and the Crises of Empires', *Journal of Urban History*, Vol. 38, No. 5 (2013), 862–78.

The Scramble for China: Foreign Devils in the Qing Empire (London: Allen Lane, 2011).

'Settlers and Diplomats: The End of British Hegemony in the International Settlement, 1937–1945', in Christian Henriot and Wen-hsin Yeh (eds.), *In the Shadow of the Rising Sun: Shanghai under Japanese Occupation, 1937–45* (Cambridge University Press, 2004), 229–56.

'Shanghailanders and Others: British Communities in China, 1843–1957' in Robert Bickers (ed.), *Settlers and Expatriates: Britons Over the Seas* (Oxford University Press, 2010), 269–301.

'Shanghailanders: The Formation and Identity of the British Settler Community in Shanghai, 1843–1937', *Past and Present*, No. 159 (1998), 161–211.

Bickers, Robert and Jonathan Howlett (eds.), *Britain and China, 1840–1970: Empire, Finance and War* (London: Routledge, 2015).

Bickers, Robert and Isabella Jackson (eds.), *Treaty Ports in Modern China: Law, Land and Power* (London: Routledge, 2016).

Bickers, Robert and Jeffrey N. Wasserstrom, 'Shanghai's "Dogs and Chinese Not Admitted" Sign: Legend, History and Contemporary Symbol', *China Quarterly*, No. 142 (June 1995), 423–43.

Boecking, Felix, 'Unmaking the Chinese Nationalist State: Administrative Reform among Fiscal Collapse, 1937–1945', *Modern Asian Studies*, Vol. 45, No. 2 (2011), 227–301.

Bonney, Richard (ed.), *The Rise of the Fiscal State in Europe, c.1200–1815* (Oxford University Press, 1999).

Borowy, Iris, 'Thinking Big – League of Nations Efforts towards a Reformed National Health System in China', in Iris Borowy (ed.), *Uneasy Encounters: The Politics of Health and Medicine in China* (Oxford: Peter Lang, 2007), 205–28.

Brady, Anne-Marie, *Friend of China: The Myth of Rewi Alley* (London: Routledge, 2003).

Brailey, Nigel, 'The Scramble for Concessions in 1880s Siam', *Modern Asian Studies*, Vol. 33, No. 3 (1999), 513–49.

Bramsen, Christopher Bo, *Open Doors: Vilhelm Meyer and the Establishment of General Electric in China* (Richmond: Curzon Press, 2001).

Bridge, Carl and Kent Fedorowich (eds.), *The British World: Diaspora, Culture and Identity* (London: Frank Kass, 2003).

Brown, E. Richard, 'Public Health in Imperialism: Early Rockefeller Programs at Home and Abroad', *American Journal of Public Health*, Vol. 66, No. 9 (1976), 897–903.

Brown, Jeremy, 'Keswick, Sir William Johnston (1903–1990)', rev. *Oxford Dictionary of National Biography* (Oxford University Press, 2004), online edition, www. oxforddnb.com/view/article/40119.

Bullock, Mary Brown, *An American Transplant: The Rockefeller Foundation and Peking Union Medical College* (Berkeley, CA: University of California Press, 1980).

Cain, Peter and A. G. Hopkins, *British Imperialism, 1688–2000* (Harlow: Pearson, 2002).

Callahan, William A., 'National Insecurities: Humiliation, Salvation, and Chinese Nationalism', *Alternatives: Global, Local, Political*, Vol. 29, No. 2 (2004), 199–218.

Carnall, Geoffrey, 'Harrison, Agatha Mary (1885–1954)', in H. C. G. Matthew and Brian Harrison (eds.), *Oxford Dictionary of National Biography: From the Earliest Times to the Year 2000* (Oxford University Press, 2004), www.oxforddnb.com/index/101047749/Agatha-Harrison.

Carroll, John M., *A Concise History of Hong Kong* (Lanham, MD: Rowman and Littlefield, 2007).

'A National Custom: Debating Female Servitude in Late Nineteenth-century Hong Kong', *Modern Asian Studies*, Vol. 43, No. 6 (2009), 1463–93.

Cassel, Pär Kristoffer, *Grounds of Judgment: Extraterritoriality and Imperial Power in Nineteenth-century China and Japan* (Oxford University Press, 2012).

Chan, Ming K., 'The Legacy of the British Administration of Hong Kong: A View from Hong Kong', *China Quarterly*, No. 151 (1997), 567–82.

Chandler, J. A., *Explaining Local Government: Local Government in Britain since 1800* (Manchester University Press, 2007).

Chen Danyan, *Shanghai: China's Bridge to the Future* (Shanghai: Shanghai Literature and Art Publishing House, in English and Chinese, 1995).

Chen, Janet Y., *Guilty of Indigence: the Urban Poor in China, 1900–1953* (Princeton University Press, 2012).

Chesneaux, Jean, *The Chinese Labor Movement, 1919–1927*, trans. H. M. Wright (Stanford University Press, 1968; first published in French in 1962 as *Le mouvement ouvrier chinois de 1919 à 1927*).

Chu Xiaoqi, '*Yuan Shuxun yu danao huishen gongtang an*' ('Yuan Shuxun, the Dao tai of Shanghai, and the 1905 Case of Madam Li Huang'), *Shilin* (2006), 6, 31–9.

Clifford, Nicholas R., 'A Revolution is not a Tea Party: The "Shanghai Mind(s)" Reconsidered', *Pacific Historical Review*, Vol. 59, No. 4 (1990), 501–26.

Spoilt Children of Empire: Westerners in Shanghai and the Chinese Revolution of the 1920s (Hanover, NH: Middlebury College Press, 1991).

Coble, Parks M., *China's War Reporters: The Legacy of Resistance Against Japan* (Cambridge, MA: Harvard University Press, 2015).

Cohen, Paul A., *Discovering History in China: American Historical Writing on the Recent Chinese Past* (New York: Columbia University Press, 1984).

Cohn, Bernard S., *Colonialism and its Forms of Knowledge: The British in India* (Princeton University Press, 1996).

Constantine, Stephen, *The Making of British Colonial Development Policy 1914–1940* (London: Frank Cass, 1984).

Cornet, Christine 'The Bumpy End of the French Concession and French Influence in Shanghai, 1937–1946', in Christian Henriot and Yeh Wen-hsin (eds.), *In the*

Shadow of the Rising Sun: Shanghai under Japanese Occupation, 1937–45 (Cambridge University Press, 2004), 257–76.

Darwin, John, *The Empire Project: The Rise and Fall of the British World-System, 1830–1970* (Cambridge University Press, 2009).

'Imperialism and the Victorians: The Dynamics of Territorial Expansion', *English Historical Review*, Vol. 112, No. 447 (June 1997), 614–42.

Daunton, Martin, *Just Taxes: The Politics of Taxation in Britain, 1914–1979* (Cambridge University Press, 2007).

Trusting Leviathan: The Politics of Taxation in Britain, 1799–1914 (Cambridge University Press, 2001).

Dikötter, Frank, *Crime, Punishment and the Prison in Modern China* (London: Hurst, 2002).

Things Modern: Material Culture and Everyday Life in China (London: Hurst, 2007).

Dilley, Andrew, *Finance, Politics, and Imperialism: Australia, Canada, and the City of London, c.1896–1914* (Basingstoke: Palgrave Macmillan, 2012).

Ding Richu and Du Xuncheng, '*Yu Xiaqing jianlun*' ('On Yu Xiaqing'), *Lishi yanjiu*, No. 3 (1981), 145–66.

Ding Yonghua and Lü Jiahang, '*Shilun 1920–1930 niandai shanghai tonggong wenti*' ('On Child Labour in Shanghai 1920s–1930s'), *Shanghai daxue xuebao*, Vol. 15, No. 2 (2008), 91–8.

Duara, Prasenjit, *Rescuing History from the Nation: Questioning Narratives of Modern China* (Chicago, IL: University of Chicago Press, 1995).

Dubin, Martin David, 'The League of Nations Health Organisation', in Paul Weindling (ed.), *International Health Organisations and Movements, 1918–1939* (Cambridge University Press, 1995), 66–72.

Durbach, Nadja, *Bodily Matters: The Anti-Vaccination Movement in England, 1853–1907* (Durham, NC: Duke University Press, 2005).

Endacott, G. B., *Government and People in Hong Kong, 1841–1962: A Constitutional History* (Hong Kong University Press, 1964).

Englehart, Neil A., 'Liberal Leviathan or Imperial Outpost? J. S. Furnivall on Colonial Rule in Burma', *Modern Asian Studies*, Vol. 45, No. 4 (June 2011), 759–90.

Ennals, Peter, *Opening a Window to the West: the Foreign Concession at Kobe, Japan, 1868–1899* (Toronto: University of Toronto Press, 2014).

Ernst, Waltraud, *Mad Tales from the Raj: European Insane in British India, 1800–58* (London: Routledge, 2004).

Ewen, Shane, 'Transnational Municipalism in a Europe of Second Cities', in Pierre-Yves Saunier and Shane Ewen (eds.), *Another Global City: Historical Explorations into the Transnational Municipal Moment, 1850–2000* (Basingstoke: Palgrave, 2008), 101–17.

Fairbank, John King, *Trade and Diplomacy on the China Coast: the Opening of the Treaty Ports, 1842–1854* (Stanford University Press, 1969).

Fan, Connie and April Ma, 'A Brief Look at the Rotary Club of Shanghai from 1919 to 1949' (Rotary Club of Shanghai, 2006), www.rotaryshanghai.org/index.php?id=6andlang=en.

Farnsworth, Robert M., *From Vagabond to Journalist: Edgar Snow in Asia, 1928–1941* (Columbia, MO: University of Missouri Press, 1996).

Farrer, James and Andrew Field, *Shanghai Nightscapes: A Nocturnal Biography of a Global City* (Chicago, IL: University of Chicago Press, 2015).

Feng Xiaocai, *"Zuo" "you" zhijian: beifa qianhou Yu Xiaqing yu Zhonggong de hezuo yu fenbie'* ('Between the "Left" and "Right": Cooperation and Division between Yu Xiaqing and the Chinese Communist Party around the Time of the Northern Expedition'), *Jindaishi yanjiu* (May 2010), 31–48.

Ferguson, Niall and Moritz Schularick, 'The Empire Effect: The Determinants of Country Risk in the First Age of Globalization, 1880–1913', *Journal of Economic History*, Vol. 66, No. 2 (2006), 283–312.

Feuerwerker, Albert, 'Economic Trends in the Late Ch'ing Empire, 1870–1911', in John K. Fairbank and Kwang-Ching Liu (eds.), *The Cambridge History of China*, Vol. 11, *Late Ch'ing, 1800–1911*, Part 2 (Cambridge University Press, 1980), 1–69.

'The Foreign Presence in China', in John King Fairbank (ed.), *Cambridge History of China*, Vol. 12, Republican China, 1912–1949, Part I (Cambridge University Press, 1983), 128–207.

(ed.), *History in Communist China* (Cambridge, MA: MIT Press, 1968).

Fogel, Joshua A., '"Shanghai-Japan": The Japanese Residents' Association of Shanghai', *Journal of Asian Studies*, Vol. 59, No. 4 (2000), 927–50.

Foley, Meredith and Heather Radi, 'Hinder, Eleanor Mary (1893–1963)', *Australian Dictionary of Biography*, Vol. 9 (Melbourne University Press, 1983), online edition, http://adb.anu.edu.au/biography/hinder-eleanor-mary-6678/text11515.

Foucault, Michel, *Discipline and Punish: the Birth of the Prison* (London: Allen Lane, 1977).

Fox, Josephine, 'Common Sense in Shanghai: The Shanghai General Chamber of Commerce and Political Legitimacy in Republican China', *History Workshop Journal*, No. 50 (2000), 22–44.

Frankema, Ewout, 'Colonial Taxation and Government Spending in British Africa, 1880–1940: Maximizing Revenue or Minimizing Effort?', *Explorations in Economic History*, Vol. 48, No. 1 (2011), 136–49.

Fung, Edmund, *The Diplomacy of Imperial Retreat: Britain's South China Policy, 1924–1931* (Hong Kong: Oxford University Press, 1991).

Gallagher, John and Ronald Robinson, 'The Imperialism of Free Trade', *Economic History Review*, New Series, Vol. 6, No. 1 (1953), 1–15.

Garner, Karen, 'Redefining Institutional Identity: The YWCA Challenge to Extraterritoriality in China, 1925–1930', in Anne-Marie Brady and Douglas Brown (eds.), *Foreigners and Foreign Institutions in Republican China* (London: Routledge, 2013), 72–92.

Garrett, Shirley S., 'The Chambers of Commerce and the YMCA', in Mark Elvin and G. William Skinner (eds.), *The Chinese City Between Two Worlds* (Stanford University Press, 1974), 213–38.

Gerth, Karl, *China Made: Consumer Culture and the Creation of the Nation* (Cambridge, MA: Harvard University Press, 2003).

Goodman, Bryna, 'Being Public: The Politics of Representation in 1918 Shanghai', *Harvard Journal of Asiatic Studies*, Vol. 60, No. 1 (2000), 45–88.

'Democratic Calisthenics: The Culture of Urban Associations in the New Republic' in Merle Goldman and Elizabeth Perry (eds.), *Changing Meanings of Citizenship in Modern China* (Cambridge, MA: Harvard University Press, 2002), 80–90.

'The Locality as Microcosm of the Nation? Native Place Networks and Early Urban Nationalism in China', *Modern China*, Vol. 21, No. 4 (1995), 387–419.

Native Place, City and Nation: Regional Networks and Identity in Shanghai, 1853–1937 (Berkeley, CA: University of Californai Press, 1995).

'The Politics of Representation in 1918 Shanghai', *Harvard Journal of Asiatic Studies*, Vol. 60, No. 1 (2000), 45–88.

Goodman, Bryna and David Goodman (eds.), *Twentieth Century Colonialism and China: Localities, the Everyday, and the World* (London: Routledge, 2012).

Gu Xiaoshui, '1926 nian Shanghai gonggong zujie huishen gongxie shouhui jiaoshe shuping' ('Commentary on the Negotiations for the Rendition of the Shanghai International Settlement Mixed Court in 1926'), *Lishi dang'an* (February 2007), 97–109.

Gupta, Narayani, *Delhi Between Two Empires 1802–1931: Society, Government and Urban Growth* (Delhi: Oxford University Press, 1981).

Harrison, Brian, 'Women in a Men's House: the Women MPs, 1919–1945', *Historical Journal*, Vol. 29, No. 3 (1986), 623–54.

Harrison, Gordon, *Mosquitoes, Malaria, and Man: A History of the Hostilities since 1880* (London: John Murray, 1978).

Harrison, Mark, *Medicine in an Age of Commerce and Empire: Britain and its Tropical Colonies* (Oxford University Press, 2010).

Havinden, Michael and David Meredith, *Colonialism and Development: Britain and its Tropical Colonies, 1850–1960* (London: Routledge, 1993).

Haynes, Douglas, *Imperial Medicine: Patrick Manson and the Conquest of Tropical Disease* (Philadelphia, PA: University of Pennsylvania Press, 2001).

Henriot, Christian, 'August 1937: War and the Death *en masse* of Civilians', in Lü Fangshang (ed.), *War in History and Memory* (Taipei: Academia Historica, 2015), 76–87.

'Beyond Glory: Civilians, Combatants and Society During the Battle of Shanghai', *War and Society*, Vol. 31, No. 2 (2012), 106–35.

'"La Fermature": The Abolition of Prostitution in Shanghai, 1949–58', *China Quarterly*, No. 142 (1995), 467–86.

'"Little Japan" in Shanghai: An Insulated Community, 1875–1945', in Robert Bickers and Christian Henriot (eds.), *New Frontiers: Imperialism's New Communities in East Asia, 1842–1953* (Manchester University Press, 2000), 146–69.

Prostitution and Sexuality in Shanghai: a Social History, 1849–1949, trans. Noël Castelino (Cambridge University Press, 2001), 273–333.

Scythe and the City: A Social History of Death in Shanghai (Stanford University Press, 2016).

Shanghai 1927–1937: Municipal Power, Locality and Modernisation (Berkeley, CA: University of California Press, 1993).

'Shanghai and the Experience of War: The Fate of Refugees', *European Journal of East Asian Studies*, Vol. 5, No. 2 (2006), 215–45.

'Shanghai Industries under Japanese Occupation: Bombs, Boom, and Bust (1937–1945)', in Christian Henriot and Wen-hsin Yeh (eds.), *In the Shadow of the Rising Sun: Shanghai under Japanese Occupation, 1937–45* (Cambridge University Press, 2004), 17–45.

'Slums, Squats, or Hutments? Constructing and Deconstructing an In-Between Space in Modern Shanghai (1926–65)', *Frontiers of History in China*, Vol. 7, No. 4 (2012), 499–528.

Henriot, Christian and Wen-hsin Yeh (eds.), *In the Shadow of the Rising Sun: Shanghai under Japanese Occupation, 1937–45* (Cambridge University Press, 2004).

Hershatter, Gail, *Dangerous Pleasures: Prostitution and Modernity in Twentieth-century Shanghai* (Berkeley, CA: University of California Press, 1997).

Honig, Emily, *Sisters and Strangers: Women in the Shanghai Cotton Mills, 1919–1949* (Stanford University Press, 1986).

Hooper, Beverley, *China Stands Up: Ending the Western Presence, 1948–1950* (Sydney: Allen and Unwin, 1986).

Howell, Philip, *Geographies of Regulation: Policing Prostitution in Nineteenth-century Britain and the Empire* (Cambridge University Press, 2009).

Hoyle, Mark S. W., *Mixed Courts of Egypt* (London: Graham and Trotman, 1991).

Hsu, Immanuel C. Y., 'Late Ch'ing Foreign Relations, 1866–1905', in John K. Fairbank and Kwang-Ching Liu (eds.), *The Cambridge History of China*, Vol. 11, *Late Ch'ing, 1800–1911*, Part 2 (Cambridge University Press, 1980), 70–141.

Hu Cheng, *'Cong "bu weisheng" de huaren xingxiang: Zhong wai jian de butong shu – yi Shanghai gonggong weisheng wei zhongxin de guancha (1860–1911)'* ('The Image of the "Unsanitary Chinese": Differing Narratives of Foreigners and Chinese – Observations Based on Hygiene in Shanghai, 1860–1911'), *Jindai shi yanjiu suo jikan*, No. 56 (2007), 1–43.

'Venereal Disease Prevention, Moral Welfare and Civilized Image: The Shanghai Moral Welfare Committee and the Anti-Prostitution Campaign in the Shanghai International Settlement, 1918–24', *Frontiers of History in China*, Vol. 6, No. 2 (2011), 243–63.

Jackson, Isabella, 'Chinese Colonial History in Comparative Perspective', *Journal of Colonialism and Colonial History*, Vol. 15, No. 3 (2014), doi: 10.1353/cch.2014.0042.

'Habitability in the Treaty Ports: Shanghai and Tianjin', in Toby Lincoln and Xu Tao (eds.), *The Habitable City in China: Urban History in the 20th Century* (New York: Palgrave Macmillan, 2017), 161–91.

'The Raj on Nanjing Road: Sikh Policemen in Treaty-Port Shanghai', *Modern Asian Studies*, Vol. 46, No. 6 (2012), 1672–1704.

'The Shanghai Scottish: Volunteers with Scottish, Imperial and Local Identities, 1914–41', in T. M. Devine and Angela McCarthy (eds.), *The Scottish Experience in Asia, c. 1700 to the Present* (London: Palgrave Macmillan, 2017), 235–57.

Jordan, Donald A., *China's Trial by Fire: The Shanghai War of 1932* (Ann Arbor, MI: University of Michigan Press, 2001).

Chinese Boycotts Versus Japanese Bombs: The Failure of China's 'Revolutionary Diplomacy,' 1931–32 (Ann Arbor, MI: University of Michigan Press, 1991).

Kidambi, Prashant, *The Making of an Indian Metropolis: Colonial Governance and Public Culture in Bombay, 1890–1920* (Aldershot, Hampshire: Ashgate, 2007).

Kirby, William C., 'The Internationalization of China: Foreign Relations at Home and Abroad in the Republican Era', *China Quarterly*, No. 150, Special Issue: Reappraising Republic China (June 1997), 433–58.

King, Frank H. H., *Money and Monetary Policy in China, 1845–1895* (Cambridge, MA: Harvard University Press, 1965).

King, Frank H. H., Catherine E. King and David J. S. King, *The History of the Hongkong and Shanghai Banking Corporation* (Cambridge University Press, 1987).

Kirby, William C., 'Engineering China: Birth of the Developmental State, 1928–1937', in Wen-hsin Yeh (ed.), *Becoming Chinese: Passages to Modernity and Beyond* (Berkeley, CA: University of California Press, 2000), 141–52.

Ladds, Catherine, *Empire Careers: Working for the Chinese Customs Service, 1854–1949* (Manchester University Press, 2013).

'"Youthful, Likely Men, Able to Read, Write and Count": Joining the Foreign Staff of the Chinese Customs Service, 1854–1927', *Journal of Imperial and Commonwealth History*, Vol. 36, No. 2 (2008), 227–42.

Laidlaw, Zoë, *Colonial Connections, 1815–1845: Patronage, the Information Revolution and Colonial Government* (Manchester University Press, 2005).

Lam, Tong, *A Passion for Facts: Social Surveys and the Construction of the Chinese Nation State, 1900–1949* (Berkeley, CA: University of California Press, 2011).

Lambert, David and Alan Lester (eds.), *Colonial Lives across the British Empire: Imperial Careering in the Long Nineteenth Century* (Cambridge University Press, 2006).

Lary, Diana, *The Chinese People at War: Human Suffering and Social Transformation, 1937–1945* (Cambridge University Press, 2010).

Leck, Greg, *Captives of Empire: The Japanese Internment of Allied Civilians in China, 1941–1945* (Philadelphia, PA: Shandy Press, 2006).

Lee, Leo Ou-fan, *Shanghai Modern: The Flowering of a New Urban Culture in China, 1930–1945* (Cambridge MA: Harvard University Press, 1999).

Lester, Alan, *Imperial Networks: Creating Identities in Nineteenth-century South Africa and Britain* (London: Routledge, 2001).

Levine, Philippa, *Prostitution, Race and Politics: Policing Venereal Disease in the British Empire* (New York: Routledge, 2003).

Liao Ping-hui and David Der-wei Wang, *Taiwan under Japanese Colonial Rule, 1895–1945: History, Culture, Memory* (New York: Columbia University Press, 2006).

Littlewood, Michael, *Taxation without Representation: The History of Hong Kong's Troublingly Successful Tax System* (Hong Kong University Press, 2010).

Liu Shuyong, 'Hong Kong: A Survey of its Political and Economic Development over the Past 150 Years', *China Quarterly*, No. 151 (1997), 583–92.

Louis, Wm. Roger, *British Strategy in the Far East, 1919–1939* (Oxford: Clarendon Press, 1971).

Loy-Wilson, Sophie, '"Liberating" Asia: Strikes and Protest in Sydney and Shanghai, 1920–39', *History Workshop Journal*, Vol. 72, No. 1 (2011), 74–102.

Lu, Hanchao, *Beyond the Neon Lights: Everyday Shanghai in the Early Twentieth Century* (Berkeley, CA: University of California Press, 1999).

'The Significance of the Insignificant: Reconstructing the Daily Life of the Common People in China', *China: An Interdisciplinary Journal*, Vol. 1, No. 1 (Spring 2003), 144–59.

Lu, Tracey Lie Dan, *Museums in China: Power, Politics and Identities* (London: Routledge, 2014).

Luo Suwen, *Jindai Shanghai: dushi shehui yu shenghuo (Modern Shanghai: Life and Society in a Great Metropolis)* (Beijing: Zhonghuo shuju, 2006).

Ma Changlin, '*Shanghai zujie nei gongchang jianchaquan de zhengduo – 20 shiji 30 niandai yichang kuangri tejiu de jiaoshe*' ('The Battle for Factory Inspection Rights within the Shanghai Foreign Concessions: The Prolonged Negotiations of the 1930s'), *Xueshu yuekan* (2003), 63–70.

Ma Changlin et al. (eds.) *Shanghai gonggong zujie chengshi guanli yanjiu (Research on the Urban Management of the Shanghai International Settlement)* (Shanghai: Zhongxi shuju, 2011).

MacPherson, Kerrie L., 'Designing China's Urban Future: The Greater Shanghai Plan, 1927–1937', *Planning Perspectives*, Vol. 5, No. 1 (1990), 39–62.

'Health and Empire: Britain's National Campaign to Combat Venereal Diseases in Shanghai, Hong Kong and Singapore', in R. Davidson and L. A. Hall (eds.), *Sex, Sin and Suffering: Venereal Disease and European Society since 1870* (London: Routledge, 2001), 173–90.

A Wilderness of Marshes: The Origins of Public Health in Shanghai, 1843–1893 (Hong Kong: Oxford University Press, 1987).

Magee, Gary B. and Andrew S. Thompson, *Empire and Globalisation: Networks of People, Goods and Capital in the British World, c. 1850–1914* (Cambridge University Press, 2010).

Manderson, Lenore, 'Wireless Wars in the Eastern Arena: Epidemiological Surveillance, Disease Prevention and the Work of the Eastern Bureau of the League of Nations Health Organisation, 1925–42', in Paul Weindling (ed.), *International Health Organisations and Movements, 1918–1939* (Cambridge University Press, 1995), 109–33.

Martin, Brian G., *The Shanghai Green Gang: Politics and Organized Crime, 1927–1937* (Berkeley, CA: University of California Press, 1996).

Meng Yue, *Shanghai and the Edges of Empires* (Minneapolis, MN: University of Minnesota Press, 2006).

Meyer, Maisie J., 'The Sephardic Jewish Community of Shanghai 1845–1939 and the Question of Identity' (Unpublished PhD Thesis, London School of Economics and Political Science, 1994).

Mitter, Rana, *China's War with Japan, 1937–1945: The Struggle for Survival* (London: Allen Lane, 2013).

Muldoon, Andrew, *Empire, Politics, and the Creation of the 1935 India Act: The Last Act of the Raj* (Farnham: Ashgate, 2009).

Nakajima, Chieko, 'Health and Hygiene in Mass Mobilization: Hygiene Campaigns in Shanghai, 1920–1945', *Twentieth-Century China*, Vol. 34, No. 1 (2004), 42–72.

Osterhammel, Jürgen, 'Britain and China, 1842–1914', in Andrew Porter (ed.), *The Oxford History of the British Empire, Vol. 3: The Nineteenth Century* (Oxford University Press, 1999), 146–69.

'Imperialism in Transition: British Business and the Chinese Authorities, 1931–37', *China Quarterly*, No. 98 (June 1984), 260–86.

'Semi-colonialism and Informal Empire in Twentieth-Century China: Towards a Framework of Analysis', in Wolfgang J. Mommsen and Jürgen Osterhammel (eds.), *Imperialism and After: Continuities and Discontinuities* (London: Allen and Unwin, 1986), 290–314.

'"Technical Co-operation" Between the League of Nations and China', *Modern Asian Studies*, Vol. 13, No. 4 (1979), 661–80.

Paddle, Sarah, '"For the China of the Future": Western Feminists, Colonisation and International Citizenship in China in the Inter-war Years', *Australian Feminist Studies*, Vol. 16, No. 36 (2001), 325–41.

Pakula, Hannah, *The Last Empress: Madame Chiang Kai-Shek and the Birth of Modern China* (London: Orion, 2010).

Peattie, Mark R., 'Japanese Treaty Port Settlements in China, 1895–1937', in Peter Duus, Ramon H. Myers and Mark R. Peattie (eds.), *The Japanese Informal Empire in China, 1895–1937* (Princeton University Press, 1989), 166–209.

Pedersen, Susan, 'Back to the League of Nations', *American Historical Review*, Vol. 112, No. 4 (1997), 1091–117.

 The Guardians: The League of Nations and the Crisis of Empire (Oxford University Press, 2015).

 'The Maternalist Moment in British Colonial Policy: The Controversy over "Child Slavery" in Hong Kong 1917–1941', *Past and Present*, No. 171 (2001), 161–202.

Perry, Elizabeth J., *Shanghai on Strike: The Politics of Chinese Labor* (Stanford University Press, 1993).

Petersson, Niels, 'Gentlemanly and Not-so-Gentlemanly Imperialism in China before the First World War', in Shigeru Akita (ed.), *Gentlemanly Capitalism, Imperialism and Global History* (Basingstoke: Palgrave Macmillan, 2002), 103–22.

Pomfret, David M., '"Child Slavery" in British and French Far Eastern Colonies 1880–1945', *Past and Present*, No. 201 (2008), 174–213.

Porter, Robin, *Industrial Reformers in Republican China* (Armonk, NY: Sharpe, 1994).

Pye, Lucian, 'How China's Nationalism was Shanghaied', *Australian Journal of Chinese Affairs*, No. 29 (1993), 107–33.

Ray, Rajat Kanta, 'Asian Capital in the Age of European Domination: The Rise of the Bazaar, 1800–1914', *Modern Asian Studies*, Vol. 29, No. 3 (1995), 449–554.

Remer, C. F., *Foreign Investments in China* (New York: Howard Fertig, 1968).

Richards, F., *Expatriate Adventures* (Bloomington, IN: Trafford, 2012).

Rigby, Richard W., *The May 30 Movement: Events and Themes* (Folkestone: Dawson, 1980).

Ristaino, Marcia, *Port of Last Resort: The Diaspora Communities of Shanghai* (Stanford University Press, 2002).

Robb, Peter, *Empire, Identity, and India: Liberalism, Modernity, and the Nation* (New Delhi: Oxford University Press, 2007).

Robinson, Ronald, 'Non-European Foundations of European Imperialism: Sketch for a Theory of Collaboration', in Roger Owen and Bob Sutcliffe (eds.), *Studies in the Theory of Imperialism* (London: Longman, 1972), 117–40.

Rogaski, Ruth, *Hygienic Modernity: Meanings of Health and Disease in Treaty-Port China* (Berkeley, CA: University of California Press, 2004).

Rupp, Leila J., 'Constructing Internationalism: The Case of Transnational Women's Organizations, 1888–1945', *American Historical Review*, Vol. 99, No. 5 (1994), 1571–600.

Sand, Jordan, 'Subaltern Imperialists: The New Historiography of the Japanese Empire', *Past and Present*, No. 225 (2014), 273–88.

Sassen, Saskia, *The Global City: London, New York, Tokyo* (Princeton University Press, 1991).

Saunier, Pierre-Yves and Shane Ewen (eds.), *Another Global City: Historical Explorations into the Transnational Municipal Moment, 1850–2000* (Basingstoke: Palgrave, 2008).

Scully, Eileen P., *Bargaining with the State from Afar: American Citizenship in Treaty Port China, 1844–1942* (New York: Columbia University Press, 2001).

 'Prostitution as Privilege: The "American Girl" of Treaty-Port Shanghai, 1860–1937', *International History Review*, Vol. 20, No. 4 (1998), 855–83.

Shiroyama, Tomoko, *China During the Great Depression: Market, State, and the World Economy, 1929–1937* (Cambridge, MA: Harvard University Press, 2008).

Shue, Vivienne, 'Global Imaginings, the State's Quest for Hegemony, and the Pursuit of Phantom Freedom in China: From Heshang to Falun Gong', in Catarina Kinnvall and Kristina Jönsson (eds.), *Globalization and Democratization in Asia: The Construction of Identity* (London: Routledge, 2002), 210–29.

Skinner, G. W. (ed.), *The City in Late Imperial China* (Stanford University Press, 1977).

Simpson, J. L., 'Berlin: Allied Rights and Responsibilities in the Divided City', *International and Comparative Law Quarterly*, Vol. 6, No. 1 (1957), 83–102.

Smith, Richard J., *Mercenaries and Mandarins: the Ever-Victorious Army in Nineteenth Century China* (Millwood, NY: KTO Press, 1978).

Smith, S. A., *Like Cattle and Horses: Nationalism and Labor in Shanghai, 1895–1927* (London: Duke University Press, 2002).

A Road is Made: Communism in Shanghai, 1920–1927 (Honolulu: University of Hawai'i Press, 2000).

Stahn, Carsten, *The Law and Practice of International Territorial Administration: Versailles to Iraq and Beyond* (Cambridge University Press, 2008).

Stephens, Thomas B., *Order and Discipline in China: the Shanghai Mixed Court 1911–27* (Seattle, WA: University of Washington Press, 2002).

Stern, Alexandra Minna, 'Yellow Fever Crusade: US Colonialism, Tropical Medicine, and the International Politics of Mosquito Control, 1900–1920', in Alison Bashord (ed.), *Medicine at the Border: Disease, Globalization and Security, 1850 to the Present* (Basingstoke: Palgrave Macmillan, 2006), 41–59.

Stokes, Eric, *The Peasant and the Raj: Studies in Agrarian Society and Peasant Rebellion in Colonial India* (Cambridge University Press, 1980).

Strauss, Julia C., 'The Evolution of Republican Government', *China Quarterly*, No. 150, Special Issue: Reappraising Republican China (1997), 329–51.

Strong Institutions in Weak Polities: State Building in Republican China, 1927–1940 (Oxford: Clarendon Press, 1998).

Swanson, Maynard W., 'The Sanitation Syndrome: Bubonic Plague and Urban Native Policy in the Cape Colony, 1900–1909', *Journal of African History*, Vol. 18, No. 3 (1977), 387–410.

Thomas, W. A., *Western Capitalism in China: A History of the Shanghai Stock Exchange* (Aldershot, Hampshire: Ashgate, 2001).

Thompson, Leroy, *The World's First SWAT Team: W. E. Fairbairn and the Shanghai Municipal Police Reserve Unit* (Barnsley: Frontline Books, 2012).

Tomlinson, B. R., *The Economy of Modern India, 1860–1970* (Cambridge University Press, 1993).

The Political Economy of the Raj, 1914–1947: The Economics of Decolonization in India (London: Macmillan, 1979).

Tsang, Steve, *A Modern History of Hong Kong* (London: I. B. Tauris, 2007).

Turnbull, C. M., *A History of Modern Singapore, 1819–2005* (Singapore University Press, 2009).

Uyehara, Cecil, 'The Uyehara Story: The Tale of Two People: Shigeru Uyehara and Vera Eugenie Foxwell Uyehara' (unpublished manuscript lent to me by the author, dated 2009).

Van de Ven, Hans, *Breaking with the Past: The Maritime Customs Service and the Global Origins of Modernity in China* (New York: Columbia University Press, 2014).

Vaughan, Megan, 'Health and Hegemony: Representation of Disease and the Creation of the Colonial Subject in Nyasaland', in Shula Marks and Dagmar Engels (eds.), *Contesting Colonial Hegemony: State and Society in Africa and India* (London: British Academic Press, 1994), 173–201.

Veracini, Lorenzo, *Settler Colonialism: A Theoretical Overview* (Basingstoke: Palgrave, 2010).

Volz, Yong Zhang, 'Transplanting Modernity: Cross-Cultural Networks and the Rise of Modern Journalism in China, 1890s–1930s' (Unpublished PhD dissertation, University of Minnesota, 2006).

Wakeman Jr., Frederic, *Policing Shanghai 1927–1937* (Berkeley, CA: University of California Press, 1995).

   The Shanghai Badlands: Wartime Terrorism and Urban Crime, 1937–41 (Cambridge University Press 1996).

Waldron, Arthur, *From War to Nationalism: China's Turning Point, 1924–1925* (Cambridge University Press, 1995).

Wang Limin, *Zhongguo de zujie yu fazhi xiandaihua – yi Shanghai, Tianjin he Hankou wei li* ('China's Concessions and the Modernisation of the Legal System – using the examples of the concessions at Shanghai, Tianjin and Hankou'), *Zhongguo faxue* (2008), 167–77.

Wang Min, *Zhong-Ying guanxi biandong beijing xia "Feitang baogao" de chu-long ji geqian* ('In the Background of the Change in Sino-British Relations, the Publication and Running Aground of the "Feetham Report"'), *Lishi yanjiu*, No. 6 (2012), 83–96.

Wang Zheng, *Women in the Chinese Enlightenment: Oral and Textual Histories* (Berkeley: University of California Press, 1999).

Wasserstein, Bernard, *Secret War in Shanghai* (New York: Houghton, 1998).

Wasserstrom, Jeffrey, 'Cosmopolitan Connections and Transnational Networks', in Nara Dillon and Jean C. Oi (eds.), *At the Crossroads of Empires: Middlemen, Social Networks, and State-building in Republican Shanghai* (Stanford University Press, 2008), 206–23.

   Global Shanghai, 1850–2010: A History in Fragments (New York: Routledge, 2009).

   'Questioning the Modernity of the Model Settlement: Citizenship and Exclusion in Old Shanghai', in Merle Goldman and Elizabeth Perry (eds.), *Changing Meanings of Citizenship in Modern China* (Cambridge, MA: Harvard University Press, 2002), 110–32.

   Student Protests in Twentieth-century China: The View from Shanghai (Stanford University Press, 1991).

   'The Second Coming of Global Shanghai', *World Policy Journal*, Vol. 20, No. 2 (2003), 51–60.

Wilbur, C. Martin, *The Nationalist Revolution in China, 1923–1928* (Cambridge University Press, 1984).

Wright, Tim, 'Shanghai Imperialists versus Rickshaw Racketeers: The Defeat of the 1934 Rickshaw Reforms', *Modern China*, Vol. 17, No. 1 (1991), 76–111.

Wu Jian Zhong and John Harris, '"An Absolute Necessity": The Evolution of the Public Library of the Shanghai Municipal Council, 1849–1943', *Journal of Librarianship and Information Science*, Vol. 25, No. 1 (1993), 7–14.

Xing Jianrong, '*Shui dian mei: jindai Shanghai gongyong shiye yanjiang ji huayang butong xintai*' ('Water, Electricity, Gas: The different mentalities of Chinese and westerners regarding Public Utilities in Modern Shanghai'), *Zhongguo jindaishi* (April 2004), 95–103.

Xu, Guangqiu, *American Doctors in Canton: Modernization in China, 1835–1935* (New Brunswick, NJ: Transaction, 2011).

Xu Tao, 'The Chinese Corpsmen in the Shanghai Volunteer Corps', in Toby Lincoln and Xu Tao (eds.), *The Habitable City in China: Urban History in the Twentieth Century* (New York: Palgrave Macmillan, 2017), 23–41.

Yeh, Wen-hsin (ed.), *Wartime Shanghai* (London: Routledge, 1998).

Yip, Ka-Che, 'Health and National Reconstruction: Rural Health in Nationalist China, 1928–1937', *Modern Asian Studies*, Vol. 26, No. 2 (1992), 395–415.

Young, Arthur N., *China's Nation-Building Effort, 1927–1937* (Stanford University Press, 1971).

Young, John Parke, 'The Shanghai Tael', *American Economic Review*, Vol. 21, No. 4 (1931), 682–4.

Zanasi, Marguerita, 'Exporting Development: The League of Nations and Republican China', *Comparative Studies in Society and History*, Vol. 49, No. 1 (2007), 143–69.

Zarrow, Peter, *China in War and Revolution, 1895–1949* (London: Routledge, 2005).

Zhang Daqing, *Zhongguo jindai jibing shehui shi* (*A Social History of Diseases in Modern China, 1912–1937*) (Jinan: Shandong jiaoyu chubanshe, 2006).

Zhang Li, *Guoji hezuo zai Zhongguo: guoji lianmeng jiaose de kaocha* (*International Cooperation in China; A Study of the Role of the League of Nations, 1919–1949*) (Taipei: Zhongchang yanjiuyuan jindai shi yanjiu suo, 1999).

Zhang Zhongli, *Jindai Shanghai chengshi yanjiu* (*Research on Modern Urban Shanghai*) (Shanghai: Shanghai Renmin Chubanshe, 1990).

Zhang Zhongli and Pan Yunxiang, 'The Influence of Shanghai's Modernization on the Economy of the Yangzi Valley', in Frederic Wakeman, Jr. and Wang Xi (eds.), *China's Quest for Modernization: A Historical Perspective* (Berkeley, CA: University of California Press, 1997), 279–99.

Zhao, Suisheng, *Power by Design: Constitution-making in Nationalist China* (Honolulu: University of Hawai'i Press, 1996).

Zhongguode zujie (*The Foreign Concessions in China*) (n. a.) (Shanghai: Shanghai guji chubanshe, 2004).

Zhuang Zhiling, '*Shanghai gonggong zujie zhong de "duoguo budui" – wanguo shang-tuan*' ('The "Multinational Militia" of the Shanghai International Settlement – the Shanghai Volunteer Corps'), *Dang'an yu shi xue* (April 1997), 72–4.

Index

Made in the USA
Coppell, TX
28 August 2020

35434942R10164